Bahar Başer is Associate Professor at the Centre for Trust, Peace and Social Relations. She is also an associate research fellow at the Security Institute for Governance and Leadership in Africa (SIGLA), Stellenbosch University, South Africa and a visiting fellow at Tampere Peace Research Institute (TAPRI), Tampere University, Finland. She is the author of "Diasporas and Homeland Conflicts: A Comparative Perspective (2015) and she has numerous articles on ethnic and migration studies with a specific focus on Middle Eastern diasporas. She has a PhD from the European University Institute, Florence, Italy.

Ahmet Erdi Öztürk is Associate Professor and Marie Sklodowska-Curie Fellow at the Centre for Trust, Peace and Social Relations at Coventry University and GIGA. He is also faculty member at School of Social Science at London Metropolitan University, UK and associate researcher (Chercheur Associé) at Institut Français d'Études Anatoliennes and Non-Residence Scholar at ELIAMEP's Turkey Programme. He gained an MA from the Political Science Department, Hacettepe University and an MRes from the Political Science Department, Barcelona Autonoma University. Öztürk has recently published in *Southeast European and Black Sea Studies* (2016), the *Yearbook of Muslims in Europe* (2016), as well in academic and online journals, books and newspapers, including *Birgün, The Conversation, Hürriyet Daily News, Open Democracy, T24 and Diken.*

"A few years ago, Turkey seemed to be that rare phenomenon in the 'Muslim world': a Muslim-majority country moving decisively away from authoritarianism towards democracy. Turkey was rare, as the conventional wisdom in Western political science was that (certain kinds of) Christianity were conducive to democratization while Islam was not. But how quickly and apparently decisively things change. Turkey remains, officially, a democracy – indeed, the ruling AKP party and especially the national president, Recep Tayyip Erdoğan, are electorally popular, despite being in power for a decade-and-a-half. But things are not as rosy as this observation might superficially suggest. As Başer and Öztürk's book makes plain, today's path towards authoritarianism in Turkey fits well with the ideological mindset of the government and the national president. This volume is a fine collection of informed, critical and up to date reflections on Turkey's current political journey. It should be read by all with an interest in Turkey's politics, in order to find out how Turkey got to where it is today and the nature of the political journey the country is on."

Jeffrey Haynes Professor of Politics and Director of the Centre for the Study of Religion, Conflict and Cooperation at London Metropolitan University

"Sound and solid political history is mostly written ex post facto, especially when the aim is to unpack what Hannah Arendt called 'novel forms of government' in her critical depiction of the emergence and nature of totalitarian regimes. Nevertheless, this book contains a coherent set of early and rigorous essays by a new generation of social scientists who are considering emerging categories for comprehending the nature of the new authoritarian regime that has been taking shape in Turkey during the past decade. None of the analyses in this book surrender to easy answers and popular new concepts. An unrelenting and refreshing skepticism is their common trait. They portray some of the critical turning points that have shaped the contours of the new authoritarianism in Turkey that is streaked with a fascistic 'desire.' The authors also shed light on the seeds of different forms of opposition and resistance in the existing state of the 'new normal.'"

Ayşe Kadıoğlu, Professor of Political Science, Sabancı University, Istanbul

Editors: **Bahar Baser** and **Ahmet Erdi Öztürk**

AUTHORITARIAN POLITICS IN TURKEY

Elections, Resistance and the AKP

I.B. TAURIS

LONDON • NEW YORK • OXFORD • NEW DELHI • SYDNEY

I.B. TAURIS
Bloomsbury Publishing Plc
50 Bedford Square, London, WC1B 3DP, UK
1385 Broadway, New York, NY 10018, USA
29 Earlsfort Terrace, Dublin 2, Ireland

BLOOMSBURY, I.B. TAURIS and the I.B. Tauris logo are
trademarks of Bloomsbury Publishing Plc

First published in Great Britain 2017
This paperback edition published in 2021

Library of Modern Turkey 29

ISBN: HB: 978-1-7845-3800-2
PB: 978-0-7556-4352-3
ePDF: 978-0-7867-2227-0
eBook: 978-1-7867-3227-9

Typeset by OKS Prepress Services, Chennai, India

To find out more about our authors and books visit
www.bloomsbury.com and sign up for our newsletters.

To my beloved grandmother Hikmet Başer – BB
&
To my devoted parents Nükhet and Kemal Öztürk – AEÖ

CONTENTS

LIST OF ILLUSTRATIONS

Figures

Tables

LIST OF CONTRIBUTORS

Samim Akgönül is a professor at Strasbourg University and a researcher at the French National Centre for Scientific Research. He also teaches political science at Syracuse University. He studies the evolution of the minority concept as well as religious minorities in Europe, especially non-Muslim minorities in Turkey, Muslim minorities in the Balkans, and new minorities in Western Europe. He is the co-editor of both the *Yearbook of Muslims in Europe* and the *Journal of Muslims in Europe*. His most recent monograph is *The Minority Concept in the Turkish Context: Practices and Perceptions in Turkey, Greece and France* (2015).

Karabekir Akkoyunlu is an assistant professor at the Centre for Southeast European Studies, University of Graz. He completed his PhD at the London School of Economics, where his research focused on the transformation of hybrid regimes in Turkey and Iran. He studied Persian at Isfahan University and taught courses on Middle East politics and theories of democratization at the LSE. In 2011–12, he co-directed a research project on Southeast European Studies at Oxford (SEESOX) on Turkey's Western relations in the context of the Arab uprisings. He blogs on Turkish politics and foreign affairs on the *Huffington Post* and has contributed to forums such as *Open Democracy, Al-Monitor, Birikim, Hürriyet Daily News, The Hindu* and *CNN International*. Akkoyunlu holds a BA in history from Brown University and an MPhil from the University of Cambridge. His MPhil dissertation on military reform and democratization in Turkey and Indonesia was published as an Adelphi paper by the International Institute for Strategic Studies in 2007.

Kıvanç Atak works on social movements, protests, policing and public order. His research draws on interdisciplinary perspectives to the political sociology of the state and employs a mix-method approach to empirical analysis. Atak holds a PhD from the European University Institute, Florence.

He has contributed to internationally peer-reviewed journals and edited volumes.

Onur Bakıner is Assistant Professor of Political Science at Seattle University. His research and teaching interests include transitional justice, human rights and judicial politics, particularly in Latin America and the Middle East. He is the author of *Truth Commissions: Memory, Power and Legitimacy* (2016). His articles on transitional justice, social memory and judicial politics have been published in the *Journal of Law and Courts*, the *International Journal of Transitional Justice*, *Memory Studies*, and *Nationalities Papers*.

Bahar Başer is a research fellow at the Centre for Peace, Trust and Social Relations at Coventry University. She is also an associate research fellow at the Security Institute for Governance and Leadership in Africa (SIGLA) at Stellenbosch University in South Africa. She completed her PhD in social and political sciences at the European University Institute in Florence, Italy. Bahar's research interests include ethno-national conflicts and political violence, conflict resolution, third-party mediation, migration and diaspora studies. Bahar is the author of *Diasporas and Homeland Conflicts* (2015) and has various publications in peer-reviewed academic journals such as *Terrorism and Political Violence*, *Studies in Conflict and Terrorism*, *Ethnopolitics* and *Middle Eastern Journal of Culture and Communication*.

Anna Maria Beylunioğlu completed her PhD in social and political sciences at the European University Institute in Florence, Italy. She is a member of the Arab-speaking *Rum* Orthodox minority community in Turkey. After receiving her BA degree in political science, she completed a master's degree thesis entitled "A comparative study of religion–state relations in Greece and Turkey: The identity cards controversy" at Istanbul Bilgi University in 2009. She concentrated on religion–state relations, freedom of religion, and religious minorities during her PhD studies and coordinated the Religion and Politics working group at the EUI between 2012 and 2013. She is currently finalizing her PhD thesis entitled "Freedom of religion in Turkey between secular and Islamic values: The situation of Christians."

Emrah Çelik received his PhD from Keele University in the United Kingdom in 2015. His PhD research was on the negotiation of Muslim identities, expressions, and practices in the modern secular world, focusing specifically on Turkish university students. He received his master's degree in Islamic studies at the University of Birmingham in 2009 with a focus on the renewal in classical and modern Islamic thought. Dr Çelik worked as an editor for Kilden, a Danish publishing company, between 2003 and 2008. He had a regular column in the Turkish daily *Taraf* between 2013 and 2015, where he contributed articles on contemporary developments in Islamic thought, Islamism, secularism, modernity, religious movements, reformism, and Turkish studies. He is also a member of the British Sociological Association (BSA).

Cuma Çiçek is an associate fellow in the Centre for International Studies (CERI) of Paris Institutes of Political Studies (*Institut d'Etudes Politiques de Paris – Sciences Po*). He worked in the Political Science and International Relations Department of Mardin Artuklu University from 2014–17. He had his PhD degree in Political Science (Political Sociology and Public Action) from Sciences Po in 2014. His recent publications are *The Kurds of Turkey: National, Religious and Economic Identities* (London, I.B.Tauris, 2017) and "Kurdish Identity and Political Islam Under the AKP Rule", *Research and Policy on Turkey* (2016). His research interests cover conflict resolution and peace-building, collective action and collective identities, sociology of election, state reform/change (regionalization, decentralization, Europeanization), and the Kurdish issue.

Abdülkadir Civan graduated from the Chemistry Department, Koç University in 1999. He obtained his doctorate in economics from Clemson University in 2004. His research concentrates on health economics but his work covers a range of different facets of microeconomics, including agricultural economics, energy economics, intellectual property rights, and economics and politics. Dr Civan has published in the following prestigious national and international journals: *İktisat, İşletme ve Finans, Health Economics, Public Choice,* and *Economic Analysis and Policy*. He offers microeconomics, macroeconomics and public economics courses at undergraduate level and he teaches microeconomics and health economics courses at postgraduate level.

Bezen Balamir Coşkun completed her PhD in the Department of Politics, History, and International Relations, Loughborough University and her master's degree in the Department of Development and International Studies, Aalborg University, Denmark. She specializes in security studies, with a particular interest in issues such as foreign policy and security, identity and security, human security, and forced migration and security. Her publications include: "Neighborhood narratives from 'zero problems' to 'precious loneliness': Turkey's re-securitized Middle East policy after the Arab Spring," in *Regional Insecurity After the Arab Uprising*, ed. Elizabeth Iskander Monier (2015); "An Evaluation of the EU's Migration Policies after Arab Spring," *Moment Journal*, 2/1 (2015); and (with Selin Akyüz) "Gendered (In)securities: Refugee Camps in Southeastern Turkey," *Journal of Conflict Transformation and Security*, 4/1-2 (Winter 2014).

Mustafa Demir holds a PhD in politics from the School of Politics and International Relations, (SPIRE), Keele University. His research interests are current developments in the Middle East, Turkey's foreign and security policies, perceptions of ethnic and religious minorities in the Middle East and world politics. His doctoral thesis examined Turkey's relations with the Kurdistan Region of Iraq (2003–13).

Salih Doğan is a researcher on international relations and political science with particular interest in security studies, Eurasia and South Asia. His main fields of interest are Afghanistan, Pakistan, Central Asian countries, the Taliban, Al-Qaeda, international security and terrorism. He also has a keen interest in Turkish politics, Turkish foreign policy, the Kurdish issue, and the PKK. Doğan is a PhD candidate within the School of Politics and International Relations (SPIRE), Keele University.

Taptuk Emre Erkoç holds a PhD in Economics from Keele University. Having completed his bachelor's degree in the Department of Economics, Fatih University, he began his doctoral studies at Keele University in 2010. During his PhD research, he was a visiting student at the London School of Economics and Political Science. He worked as a graduate teaching assistant at Keele University and a visiting research fellow at Queen Mary, University of London. Currently, he is working on the political-economic dimensions of government policies and regulations in Turkey. His research interests cover applied microeconomics, education economics, efficiency analysis, and political economy. His research papers appear in international peer-reviewed journals on economics, management sciences and politics and he is a referee for a number of journals on applied microeconomics, operational research, and political economy. He is also a member of the Royal Economic Society.

İştar Gözaydın is a professor of law and politics. Gözaydın completed her Master of Comparative Jurisprudence at the School of Law, New York University in 1987 and her PhD at Istanbul University in 1992. Gözaydın is a founder and current member of the executive committee of the Helsinki Citizens Assembly, a human rights organization in Turkey. She is also a research fellow at the Turkey Institute, a London-based centre of research, analysis, and discussion on Turkey. Professor Gözaydın was a research fellow at Birkbeck College, University of London, in 2009.

Dağhan Irak is a PhD candidate and a lecturer at the University of Strasbourg. After receiving his BA degree in journalism and internet publishing at Galatasaray University in Istanbul, he completed his MA research on the sociopolitical history of football in Turkey at Boğaziçi University. Before working as a senior researcher in a Dubai-based international social media agency, he worked for more than ten years as a sports journalist and a media critic in national and international media outlets. Since 2013, he has been working on a doctoral research project on football fans' political use of Twitter in Turkey. Dağhan Irak teaches on the subjects of social network analysis, data journalism, and the sociology of sport. His most recent publications are *"Istanbul United? Le Supportérisme comme lutte culturelle et résistance au pouvoir politique en Turquie* [Istanbul United? Football fandom as a means of cultural battle and resistance in Turkey], in *Aux Frontières du football et du politiques* (2016) and "A Close-Knit Bunch: Political Concentration in Turkey's Anadolu Agency through Twitter Interactions," in *Turkish Studies* 17/2 (2016). He has published two books in Turkish, *Türkiye ve Sosyal Medya* [Turkey and Social Media] (co-authored with Onur Yazıcıoğlu, 2012) and *Hükmen Yenik: Türkiye'de ve İngiltere'de Futbolun Sosyopolitiği* [Lost by Default: The Sociopolitics of Football in Turkey and England] (2013).

Ahmet Erdi Öztürk is a research assistant in the Faculty of Law, Social Science and History at the University of Strasbourg, where he has also been based for his doctoral research. He has held a research fellowship at the Centre for Southeast European Studies at the University of Graz. He gained an MA from the Political Science Department, Hacettepe University and an MRes from the Political Science Department, Barcelona Autonoma University. Öztürk has recently published in *Southeast European and Black Sea Studies* (2016) the *Yearbook of Muslims in Europe* (2016) as well in academic and online journals, books and newspapers, including *Birgun*, *The Conversation*, *Hurriyet Daily News*, *Open Democracy*, *T24* and *Diken*. He is the Turkey correspondent for EUREL (Sociological and Legal Data on Religions in Europe) and has been a regular guest on television programmes such as *France 24* to discuss Turkish politics.

Efe Kerem Sözeri is an independent researcher. After receiving his BA from Boğaziçi University, he undertook an MSc in social research at VU Amsterdam, writing a master's thesis in urban studies titled "The sense of belonging and the strategies of dwelling among Turkish-Dutch public housing residents in Amsterdam-East." He is now writing a dissertation on the effect of migration on political preferences entitled "Political Baggage and Ideological Remittance." Besides academic research, he writes about freedom of speech and censorship in Turkey for various outlets including *Daily Dot* and *Global Voices*. He is also an editor at the independent news portal *Jiyan*, which is currently censored in Turkey.

"Power is never so overwhelming that there's no room for resistance."

Henry Giroux

CHAPTER 1

IN LIEU OF AN INTRODUCTION: IS IT CURTAINS FOR TURKISH DEMOCRACY?

Bahar Başer and Ahmet Erdi Öztürk

Introduction

In recent years, scholars of Turkish studies have started to address political developments in Turkey from a more nuanced perspective. Since early 2002, when the reign of the Justice and Development Party (*Adalet ve Kalkınma Partisi*, AKP) began, the main focus in academia was usually on (1) how the AKP would bring its Islamic and conservative agenda into the Turkish political arena; (2) how compatible Islam is with democracy; (3) the AKP's clash with the military over its influence on politics; and (4) its movement towards acknowledging minorities and their rights in Turkey.[1] In terms of foreign policy analysis, the emphasis was on understanding the Turkish desire to become a dominant but cooperative power in the Middle East, as well as in Africa, the Balkans, and the Caucasus.[2] These discussions gave rise to another field of research that is becoming increasingly popular: Turkey and authoritarianism. As Yeşilada very well summarizes, the positive environment of the early 2000s has been replaced by "a grim picture of illiberal political developments that are characterized by President Recep Tayyip Erdoğan's power grabs, loss of judicial independence, and electoral manipulations to achieve the desired election outcome that favoured Erdoğan and the Justice and Development Party."[3] The AKP and its charismatic and influential leader, Recep Tayyip Erdoğan, have transformed Turkey into an ambiguous presidential system where the president has increasing control over each and every aspect of judiciary and legislative, which is perceived as both perturbing and polarizing.[4] The final objective appears to be a full 'executive presidency' in which all power is concentrated in the hands of the president. Authors such as Esen and Gümüşçü define the current situation as *competitive authoritarianism* by arguing that Turkey no longer satisfies even the minimal requirements of democracy.[5] Irak uses the term "autocratic Islamists"[6] when referring to the ruling party and its leader, while Özbudun prefers to explain matters by using the term "majoritarian drift".[7] Almost every scholar has a different way of interpreting the authoritarian shift in Turkey. However, one thing is clear: the current situation shows no movement towards further democratization.

The AKP was founded in 2001 and is based on conservative and Islamic principles. The party came to power in 2002 after what Jeffrey Haynes describes as "eighty years of aggressive secularization,"[8] which suppressed Islam in the political arena. The AKP rose as a new actor full of promises for reform. It quickly became the main and dominant political party on the Turkish political scene. It won landslide victories in elections[9] until the elections of June 2015, which showed "an erosion of popular support for the AKP."[10] Despite this, the party was able to reconsolidate its power following a snap election in November 2015. This election received much criticism from international and domestic observers who "pointed to irregularities in the campaign, including media bias and self-censorship, misuse of state resources to support Erdoğan's election bid, lack of transparency in campaign finances, and voter fraud."[11]

The victory of the AKP in the November 2015 snap election failed to bring political stability. President Erdoğan expected 100 per cent compliance and loyalty from Prime Minister Davutoğlu but following several disagreements, the former pushed the latter to resign and brought in a new prime minister, Binali Yıldırım,[12] whose loyalty to Erdoğan is unquestioned.[13] While this would have been considered highly irregular in many other countries, in the Turkish context it is widely seen as the "new normal".[14]

In an article published immediately following the resignation of Davutoğlu, Alon Ben-Meir wrote that "this is not a travesty for Turkey, it is a tragedy," and posited that "with the departure of Davutoğlu, Turkey has become a *de facto* dictatorship, and there is now no one to stand in Erdoğan's way."[15] After a couple of weeks, *Foreign Policy* published an article (with a particularly harsh tone) by John Hannah entitled "How do you solve a problem like Erdoğan?" It read:

> Houston, we have a problem. A serious problem. Slowly, but inexorably, Turkey is headed off a cliff. The signposts ahead are bleak indeed. Despotism. Terrorism. Civil war. Just over the horizon, scenarios like failed state and forced partition are coming into view. The day may be approaching when U.S. policymakers, much as they'd prefer not to, will finally be forced to grapple with the question: What do you do with a NATO ally gone seriously bad?[16]

These are just a few examples of how the international press has covered the current political situation in Turkey. Many other media outlets such as the

BBC,[17] the *New York Times*,[18] the *Guardian*,[19] and the *Financial Times*[20] have also noted that recent developments in Turkey are disquieting. These outlets have all recognized that Turkey is gradually drifting into authoritarianism. Once praised by Western governments and media outlets for its reforms and neo-liberal economic policies, the AKP and President Erdoğan now regularly make headlines for their oppression of opposition groups in Turkey.

In addition to this, as mentioned the AKP and President Erdoğan have not shied away from openly stating their ultimate objective of changing Turkey's regime into a full-blown presidential system. Indeed, today Turkey has a *de facto* presidential system pending constitutional change. Almost every aspect of social, political and economic life in Turkey is already directly regulated by Erdoğan and his orders. He has a huge impact on legislative and executive mechanisms. Patrimonialism is becoming more and more embedded in Turkish politics. Based on this, we can argue that the international media was just pointing out the obvious (perhaps saying too little, too late), and on top of that using a patronising tone which irritated even Erdoğan's Turkish critics.

The leaders of the party have used a quasi-democratic system to advance an agenda that was anti-democratic and authoritarian in many respects. During the last decade, dozens of activists, academics, politicians, journalists, and others have been detained simply for disagreeing with government policies, or for opposing Erdoğan's discourses on political, economic, and social matters. What is particularly interesting about this is that these people have been criminalized using the discourse of counter-terrorism, which has been both disproportionate and ill-tailored.[21] Whilst there has been a historical precedent for stigmatizing and labelling pro-Kurdish actors as "terrorists", today anyone in opposition to the government is labelled a "terrorist". The term is stretched such that its reference point is no longer the law, the Turkish constitution, or international norms and regulations but merely Erdoğan's own diktat. Everybody is under his gaze and the struggle between those in power and those in opposition is no longer solely confined to the political arena but also to courtrooms. Turkey has become an example of how democratically-elected governments take undemocratic paths to cling to power and how counter-terrorism policies go hand in hand with authoritarianism on the route to one-man rule.

When the AKP came to power, its foreign policies were also widely praised for advancing Turkey's status a rising power with capabilities of soft and hard power. It is worth noting, however, that Davutoğlu's aspiration to have "zero problems with neighbours" turned out to be a complete disaster and Turkey now has problems with almost all of its neighbours. Turkey's problematic Syria policy and its power struggle over the international approaches to Rojava destabilized domestic and international dynamics in the Middle East. The collapse of the peace process between the the Kurdistan Workers' Party

(*Partiya Karkerên Kurdistan*, PKK) and the Turkish state also led to the resumption of political violence. Turkey has lost prestige internationally and is now constantly criticized for its domestic and foreign policies. Despite these developments, neither the AKP nor President Erdoğan have relinquished their grip on the Turkish political arena. Half of the country still votes for this party and each domestic or international "failure" is packaged and sold to voters as an act of "glory". Amid these multifaceted problems, Turkey is day by day heading to a place that is far from democracy, human rights, and freedom of speech. Authors such as Tezcür argue that although President Erdoğan has established his personal dominance over every facet of Turkish politics his rule still lacks the institutional basis for absolute power. Turkey has a history of political pluralism and the AKP still needs other political parties to cooperate with it to change the constitution. Therefore, hurdles remain in Erdoğan's quest for untrammelled power.[22] However, the recent coup attempt and the state of emergency that followed hold the very real prospect that these hurdles will be swept away.

The idea for this edited book thus arose because of academic curiosity and interest in understanding the ongoing process of political, economic and social transition in Turkey. It aims to re-energize the debate on elections, democracy and authoritarianism by focusing on recent political developments. It engages in particular with the issue of how elections (legislative, presidential, or referenda) are instrumentalized to create the facade of a democratic regime, while shifting to increasingly autocratic measures. This is not, therefore, a compilation of chapters that merely focus on contemporary Turkish politics, the AKP's Islamic policies (and their compatibility with democracy), or the Gezi protests in general.[23] We wish to add to such work by focusing on the complexity and the alternative ways of exercising democracy in Turkey by concentrating predominantly on elections and alternative resistance mechanisms beyond the ballot box. As Jason Brownlee has stated "in the last quarter of the twentieth century, democratically elected governments replaced authoritarian regimes at an astounding rate."[24] Within academia, there is an increasing interest in electoral authoritarianism,[25] authoritarian regimes, and democratization,[26] and there is a growing literature on competitive authoritarianism.[27] Our aim is to scrutinize this experience and unpack the meaning of such seemingly certain terms as "democracy", "elections", and "authoritarianism" in Turkey. By doing this, we will draw attention to the blurred nature of these concepts and how they can be manipulated. Perhaps more importantly, the chapters in this book will show how people who are oppressed by autocratic regimes find ways to flourish through resistance mechanisms to bring back democracy at different levels.

Levitsky and Way[28] have, in the past, defined Turkey as a restricted or semi-competitive democracy. Whilst this is beginning to change, this change is by no means for the better. This edited volume will enable us to better understand how a democratically elected political party, which takes its power from elections, manages to implement increasingly autocratic measures. What is the reason for the retreat from democracy? What creates this vacuum? Why do people opt for authoritarian leaders? And how do others resist this democratic reversal?

Notes on the Rise and Triumph of the AKP: Moving Towards an Authoritarian Path

When we talk about recent democratic reversal in Turkey, we should still emphasize that Turkey was never a fully functioning democracy. Because of the Kemalist legacy, minority groups were still oppressed, the military's influence on politics was visible and the state adopted a security-oriented military solution to address the Kurdish question in south-eastern Turkey.[29] Political Islam was supressed under the secular regime and many groups felt underrepresented in the pre-AKP era. It is for this reason that when the AKP came to power, despite its dedication to Islamic principles, domestic actors and Western countries openly embraced it.[30] The AKP's efforts to limit the power of the military in Turkey, and constant remarks about its dedication to Turkey's membership to the European Union were much appreciated by the international community. The so-called "Kurdish Opening" under the Copenhagen criteria and reforms that originated from the wish for EU membership were praised by external actors.[31] Turkey even initiated a peace process with the PKK, which was a great milestone in Turkish political history. In the early years of the AKP, a liberal transformation was launched in Turkey's legal and political structures. The AKP acted in accordance with European Union criteria regarding the principles of liberty, freedom of religion, and democratization in areas including educational reform, the open market economy, and military guardianship.

By using this transformation, the AKP created a huge coalition that embraced different groups, such as liberals, prominent scholars, columnists, key members of the financial sector, Muslim and non-Muslim groups, ethnic minorities, and civil society organizations. During these early years, Erdoğan played a prominent role in the establishment of these normative and practical coalitions. In this way, the discourse of democratization both enabled Erdoğan to put down his rivals and gain support from the aforementioned groups. By doing so, the AKP assured its position as the dominant political force. However, as Whiting and Kaya observe "[r]eining the military and judiciary has allowed the AKP to assert its power free of checks and balances. The result is an intermeshing of the state and the party."[32] A new period of transition occurred following the 2007 elections and this was marked by increasing human rights abuses, the oppression of minorities, and attacks on the freedom of the press and freedom of speech in general.[33]

Another milestone for Turkey, the AKP, and Erdoğan was the 2010 referendum on constitutional changes. On 12 September 2010 (the thirtieth anniversary, it must be noted, of the 1980 coup), approximately 77 per cent of Turkey's electorate participated in a national referendum for a series of constitutional amendments proposed by the AKP. These included a package of 30 amendments to Turkey's current 1982 constitution, promulgated by a military junta during the last coup-led government. Of the participating voters, 57.88 per cent were in favour of 30 amendments to significant portions of the constitution, which among other things affected the composition and membership of, and appointment to, the highest judicial bodies in the country. The main outcomes of this referendum are that, after 2010, military officers who commit crimes against the state (such as preparing coup plans) can be tried in civilian courts, problems between the state and citizens can be resolved by way of an ombudsman without having to go to court, and parliament can choose some of the members of the Turkish Constitutional Court.[34] Although, at first glance, most of these constitutional changes seem compatible with contemporary understandings of democracy, they were endorsed as a tool on the path to an authoritarian shift. After 2010, Erdoğan's parliamentary monopoly combined with his extensive public support has meant that he has been able to instrumentalize reforms with arbitrary treatments.

The AKP has based its power and actions on being elected by the majority and has constantly underlined that whatever it does must be legitimate because it has been democratically elected. The regime started drifting towards one-man rule despite being a democratically elected party – a tyranny of the majority. Opposition groups were suppressed and political groups were pushed out of the political scene. NGOs and young people in particular could no longer find a platform to express their demands. These oppressive dynamics brought about the Gezi protests of 2013,[35] which became a momentous anti-government movement[36] and challenged the government's credibility. The answer of the AKP government to the demonstrations and public dissent was even more oppression, which in the end led to deep unrest within Turkish society. As Andrew Garner, the Turkey expert of Amnesty International, has asserted: "The attempt to smash the Gezi Park protest movement involved a string of human rights violations on a huge scale. They include the wholesale denial of the right to peaceful assembly and violations of the rights to life, liberty and the freedom from torture and ill-treatment."[37] This was one of the turning points in Turkish history which unleashed the autocratic intentions and clearly revealed the democratic backlash in Turkey.

The clashes between the Gülen movement[38] and the AKP also deserve mention.[39] The Gülen movement is a network organised under the ideas of the Islamic preacher Fethullah Gülen, who is the indisputable moral and ideological vanguard of the movement. The Gülen movement originated in

Turkey and is a voluntary, civil-society organization inspired by the Islamic faith. It is active in almost 160 countries across the globe. Even though the Gülen movement has a civic face with its dialogue, education, philanthropy and media, it also has a political face dedicated to the service of power that has been aiming to reach the determinant positions in state mechanisms. The Gülen movement strongly supported the AKP and its policies until 2011. Through the AKP government, members of the Gülen movement had managed to obtain top positions in the state bureaucracy. After 2011, however, their differing perspectives and interests have transformed into social and political tension. Without a doubt, one of the most significant events in Turkey in 2014 was the corruption, bribery, and money-laundering investigations (17–25 December 2013) that implicated President Erdoğan's son Bilal as well as cabinet ministers, businessmen with close links to the AKP government, and executives of the Turkish banking system. At the time, many recordings were leaked of phone conversations considered to be evidence of corruption. Although there is no legal evidence, many in AKP circles and several media outlets pointed to police officers loyal to the Gülen movement as the source of the leaks and the corruption investigation. At the same time, it is fair to argue the common understanding among public and other political groups in Turkey that, indeed, the Gülen movement was behind the leak. Many interpreted these events as a power struggle over domination of the state between the Gülen movement and those AKP supporters who had distanced themselves from the movement.

Within days, police officers leading multiple investigations (some of which had begun two years earlier) were reassigned and new prosecutors were allocated to the investigations. This was followed by a government decree removing more than 600 detectives and police officers from their positions, including the chiefs of the units dealing with corruption and organized crime. The original prosecutors who led the investigations were eventually reassigned, demoted and, finally, dismissed. While the four cabinet ministers implicated in the investigations resigned from their ministerial positions, the newly-assigned prosecutors who took over the investigations withdrew all charges and the cases have since been closed. After the grand money-laundering investigation, Erdoğan and the AKP government intensified their purge against the Gülen movement and its affiliated institutions. The Gülen movement was classified as a "terrorist group and parallel state" by the government and based on this classification the AKP government began to directly appoint trustees to the private universities, high schools, businesses, and media outlets of the movement, such as the daily newspaper *Zaman*.[40]

On 20 January 2012, the Turkish parliament passed an act containing new rules and procedures by which Turkey's next head of state would be elected. The head of state was to be elected by popular vote for the first time in Turkey's history with elections to be held on 10 August 2014. Despite Erdoğan's triumph in the first round, he did not moderate his harsh and divisive discourse. He won the presidential election, and as head of state was required to stay "above" the political fray and represent the country as a whole in a non-partisan fashion. Instead, he continued to focus on supporting the AKP. Serious questions were raised about the extravagance of the presidential budget, particularly the expenditure on the construction of a new presidential palace and the purchase of a presidential plane. As for Turkey's unicameral system of parliamentary democracy, Erdoğan's self-professed political goal has been to convert it into a 'Turkish-style' presidential system. Erdoğan has been advocating for a presidential system for several years in the context of complaints about the "separation of powers". Checks and balances on the executive branch of government have been framed as a hindrance and an annoying inconvenience rather than as a necessity of democracy. He speaks of needing to "sprint" and "lunge" forward in a way that cannot be achieved in the current system, given the restraints placed on the executive by the legislature and judiciary. These are not only unconstitutional, but also incompatible with commonly-accepted democratic norms.

In the context of this fraught political and social atmosphere, the AKP experienced a major setback for a short period in 2015. The AKP lost its parliamentary majority in the legislative elections of June 2015. The elections did not pave the way for the presidential system[41] that the AKP and the president had sought, tarnishing the image of invincibility that the party and its leader had worked hard to cultivate.[42] Moreover, during the negotiations to form a new coalition government, Erdoğan indirectly intervened by making public speeches hinting that his preferred option to settle the issue was a rapid return to the polls. Although the other political parties, except for the Republican People's Party (*Cumhuriyet Halk Partisi*, CHP), had no intention of establishing a coalition government with the AKP, Erdoğan's own intervention was arguably one of the most significant reasons why a coalition government was never established. Additionally, in this process the ideals of stability and defending the status quo played a prominent role and were used extensively by Erdoğan and the AKP. Suicide attacks had taken place in Suruç and Ankara and economic indicators had slipped following the June elections. Social and political fear was thus instrumentalized as a propaganda tool which eventually led to victory for the AKP in the snap elections of November 2015.[43]

Since the most recent elections, the country has been going through turbulent times. There have been alleged attacks by ISIS and the low-intensity civil war with the PKK has caused the deaths of military personnel, PKK fighters, and a considerable number of civilians treated as casualties of war. The peace process has collapsed with these recent developments, although many ask whether it was really going anywhere in the first place. A state of emergency has been declared in certain parts of Turkey and this has led to gross human rights violations as there have been extensive civilian casualties. When the curfews in various Kurdish cities were lifted, the devastation of many towns and villages was exposed for all to see.[44] Many townships have been destroyed and many people have been compelled to migrate from their hometowns. This is surely not a good sign and the hope of returning to peace talks is rapidly fizzling out. There have also been numerous attacks against the offices of the pro-Kurdish People's Democratic Party (*Halkların Demokratik Partisi*, HDP).[45] Inter-communal violence has occurred not only at the mass level but also at the individual level.

The HDP remains one of the few actors left with the capability challenge the AKP's hegemony. It is a left-leaning, pro-minority rights party predominantly supported by the Kurds. It managed to pass the 10-per cent threshold in the June and November elections and this curbed the AKP's ability to claim the absolute majority needed to change the constitution. As Balta suggests: "Maybe one of the most important reasons behind the HDP's success is the fact that many Kurds who had previously voted for the AKP retracted their support."[46] She also argues that the AKP aimed to coopt Kurdish voters with the peace process but instead drove them away by opening the space for the Kurdish movement in the political arena and strengthening the HDP by enlarging its voter base.[47] That is why the ruling elite's reaction to the triumph of the HDP was very harsh. By using vague counter-terrorism discourse, the parliament stripped the immunity of Kurdish MPs and accused them of supporting the PKK and creating terrorist propaganda. Once again, the manoeuvring space for Kurdish politics was limited after many years of peace discussions. The HDP is highly affected by the authoritarian shift but nevertheless retains mass support and manages to rally popular resistance.

There is no doubt that polarization has always been problematic for Turkish society and the cleavage between the secularists and religious conservatives has historically been the most salient dividing line.[48] Right wing vs. left wing, Kurd vs. Turk, Alevi vs. Sunni and secular vs. religious divisions have also been present since the early republican era. Besides these, the June 2015 elections has given way to a new type of polarization – those "with" the AKP and those "against" it.[49] Although this polarization and the contentious political and social atmosphere seems to be poisonous, it nonetheless remains one of the key points that underlie Erdoğan's political power and hegemony. In other words, Erdoğan and his political party have been aware that political crises provide a useful opening to mobilize even more power and control. As Giorgio Agamben emphasizes in his *State of Exception*,[50] exceptional conditions and situations provide an opportunity for political figures to become exceptional leaders by ignoring constitutions, the law, and democratic principles. Likewise, Erdoğan has been keen on making political and social issues out of nothing and blowing ordinary issues out of all proportion to both consolidate his support base and instrumentalize the state apparatus.[51] He has been using this ruling methodology to set and change the main agenda of Turkey when he and his political establishment get into a scrape.

After its success in the November 2015 elections, the AKP bills itself aggressively as the only party that can save Turkey from the chaos it has been drifting towards for a long time. This electoral victory also meant that "the trend towards the establishment of a competitive authoritarian regime under the personalist rule of Erdoğan"[52] gained immediate force. As Brownlee argues:

> not all authoritarian regimes permit such elections, but most do, and the practice became increasingly common in the 1980s and 1990s. Results in these limited elections, manipulated as they are to the advantage of incumbents, act as a barometer of a regime's control over the political arena and the opposition's capacity to contest that dominance.[53]

Sometimes elections only help the dominant structure to size-up the opposition. The fantasy of fair elections might cause many in the opposition to see a mirage of democratic elections and show their true colours, an act for which they pay dearly. Both the June and November elections served this purpose in a way. They clearly indicated who deserved to be punished for standing in the way of Erdoğan's absolute rule.

Where is Turkey Going? Staring into the Abyss

Esen and Gümüşçü's account describes the situation in a nutshell by highlighting the rise of political violence against the opposition and the limitations of freedom of speech and media:

> The AKP's desire to hang on to power despite its electoral defeat accompanied a dramatic rise in political violence and extra-parliamentary opposition, which, in turn increased government pressure on dissent, including censorship in the media and implicit endorsement of violent attacks against the opposition by AKP supporters.[54]

In terms of human security, the Freedom House report *Turkey 2016* reveals worrying results. It starts by stating that:

> Turkey received a downward trend arrow due to renewed violence between the government and Kurdish militants, terrorist attacks by the Islamic State group, and intense harassment of opposition members and media outlets by the government and its supporters ahead of November parliamentary elections.[55]

By acknowledging that the snap elections of November 2015 were conducted during a politically volatile environment, it comments on the situation of human rights in Turkey as follows:

> A continued crackdown on the media added to the pressure on the electoral environment. Throughout the year, dozens of journalists were arrested and prosecuted for insulting the president and other government officials or for allegedly supporting terrorist organizations. Numerous websites were also blocked. A week before the November elections, the government seized the assets of a major conglomerate, including two daily newspapers, *Millet* and *Bugün*, and two television channels that had been critical of the ruling party.[56]

The report also clearly shows the oppression and limitations on media freedom, academia, and associational and organizational rights. More than 2,000 legal cases were opened with the allegations of "insulting the President" against people who criticized Erdoğan on social media and elsewhere.[57]

So how does the international community react to this? The EU was once Turkey's main source of criticism but those were the days when Turkey was sincere in its desire to become a member. Today, even though the government continues to claim that the desire is still there, Turkey is further and further away from fulfilling the Copenhagen criteria. Whatever discussion there is between EU officials and the Turkish state is little more than lip service and anyone who understands how the EU functions and what membership entails will immediately recognize that Turkey has a long and almost impossible way to go. In the last couple of years and especially with the collapse of the peace process,[58] opposition groups (as they have done in the past) have turned to the EU for help. These cries, however, have fallen on deaf ears among EU politicians and member states, with only a few dozen exceptions. The EU's hesitant criticisms were not coincidental. And even if the EU were to make harsher criticisms, Turkey would not take them into consideration as the EU has also lost its leverage on Turkey. Because of Erdoğan's speeches and the AKP's policies, there is growing anti-European, and more specifically anti-German and anti-US, sentiment within Turkish society.[59] Loyalist mass media has also contributed to such sentiment, as they are the mouthpiece of the government and the president.

The EU-Turkey deal on the refugee crisis also made newspaper headlines. This is another explanatory factor that shows that the EU is no longer in a position to insist on human rights reform in Turkey while it desperately needs to find a solution to the crisis.[60] Kerem Öktem has rightly asked "[w]ho will think of the EU as a global actor with normative power, now that it finds itself in the role of rubber stamping and in fact facilitating Turkey's slide into the abyss?"[61] There have been times when the EU has had so much leverage on Turkish politics that each year's progress report would be anxiously awaited and discussed extensively on every single TV channel. Those were the days when the EU actually thought Turkey might manage to further democratize. Although perhaps not enough to become a member of the EU, it was thought that Turkey would democratize enough to be considered a democratic country on the outskirts of the EU. Today, we have a different deal. We are witnessing a bargain with human lives – a bargain that will not be remembered with dignity in the years to come. On this, Öktem makes the following contribution:

> It [Turkey] is now a country that is not able to ensure the right to physical integrity of its citizens, let alone of refugees. It goes without saying that the promised visa liberalization for Turkish citizens is a charade. To be realised, it [the EU-Turkish refugee deal] needs Turkish compliance on basic fundamental rights, which are not forthcoming. There will be no long-term visa-free travel for Turks in any case, since it is not possible legally, but also because there are a sufficient number of EU member state governments to ensure that visa liberalization does not happen. Once the visa deal falters, the Turkish President Erdoğan can only benefit politically by accusing the EU of double standards. And for very good reasons indeed.[62]

At the same time, more recent developments have accelerated Turkey's authoritarian shift more than anything else in the previous decade-and-a-half.

The Coup Attempt and the Rise of Authoritarianism under Exceptional Conditions

The 15 July 2016 coup attempt in Turkey was undoubtedly one of the signal events in the country's modern history. According to testimonies and popular news, a medium-sized group of flag officers of Turkey's army attempted an overthrow of Erdoğan and the AKP government.[63] Turkey, of course, has suffered long periods of military tutelage and a variety of different types of military intervention in politics. This particular coup attempt, however, was distinctive. Although the first couple of hours of the coup attempt saw the momentum apparently with the putschists and brought about perturbation among Turkey's citizens, the government managed to counter the putsch with the support of mostly pro-AKP citizens who took to the streets to defend elected political structures after President Erdoğan's FaceTime call.

Quashing the overthrow is, of course, perceived as an important accomplishment but it must still be noted that 265 people lost their lives (a further 2,797 were wounded), which is an absolute tragedy.[64] Had the coup succeeded, it would almost certainly have resulted in a deep retrenchment of the gains made in Turkish political democracy, something that would be incredibly difficult to recover from. From the outset, the finger of blame for the putsch was laid squarely at the Gülen movement by both President Erdoğan and other prominent political figures. The precise source and planning of the coup attempt remains as yet something of a mystery but, in any event, it was obvious that there was no public support for such an attempt and the opposition leaders also constantly underlined that it would have been a tragedy. The way that the international media interpreted the complex developments in Turkey as well can be defined as a tragedy. Indeed, some media outlets were quick to 'welcome' the coup attempt or praised it without even noticing that it was still-born. It showed that the international media was almost expecting a coup to happen in Turkey and more importantly that they actually believed that this is what citizens of Turkey would desire or at least secretly feel content with.

However, it turned out to be the opposite. By the call of the AKP and Erdoğan, as well as various opposition leaders, many people took to the streets to celebrate the failure of the coup attempt and celebrate the assured might and power of the president. They called these "democracy meetings" or even "democracy watch" where they organized demonstrations of power in the name of the AKP and Erdoğan and the "citizens of the new Turkey" that did not let the coup plotters succeed. The HDP was completely left out of these meetings, even though it repeatedly underlined that the coup would have been a disaster for the Kurds and the rest of the country. Thus, no place was given to them in this picture of the post-putsch 'New Turkey'. Once the dust had settled, Western leaders and the international media were somewhat more circumspect, praising Turkey's firm democracy and how this coup strengthened democratization efforts in Turkey. In between these two extremes lies the reality, which the West either cannot or does not wish to understand.

Five days after the coup attempt, the AKP government declared a state of emergency for three months and President Erdoğan announced it to the public as a positive step and as an opportunity to clean out pro-Gülenist people from the public sector.[65] Although, on paper, the state of emergency seems to be related to the putsch, it is fair to argue that President Erdoğan has been using his emergency powers to overhaul most of the opposition groups and potential social and political targets. The need to protect the Turkish nation and state in these exceptional circumstances gives a patina of legitimation to these moves. On the one hand, according to figures released by the Turkish media, the putsch involved 1.5 per cent of the armed forces or 8,651 officers.[66] On the other hand, in the first two weeks of the state of emergency, 15 universities and hundreds of civil society associations, media centres and companies were shut down. Additionally, thousands of teachers in their probation period were let go, thousands of passports were annulled and hundreds of people – including journalists, scholars, judges, bureaucrats, and state officials – were suspended under investigation and/or arrested, including many Alevis, leftists, and Kemalists who did not have any relations with the Gülen movement. The government made these moves on the grounds that the accused had aided and abetted the coup attempt. Under these conditions, with this lurch towards authoritarianism under a state of exception, it is fair to say that this state of emergency has opened a new chapter in the ongoing discussions about the meaning of democracy in Turkey.

At this point we may ask how many critical junctures one country can experience in a decade. Turkey, it would seem, is constantly facing a new fork in the road. And, indeed, the 15 July putsch has opened yet another new door to the unknown, or as some would say to an undesirable but predictable end. After 15 July, "New Turkey" has finally found its "founding myth," As Akyol stated in an article in *Al Monitor*:

> In this new founding myth, Erdoğan replaces Atatürk, and the July 15 failed coup replaces the War of Liberation. One major difference is that Islamic symbols are much more prominent this time, reflecting the values of Erdoğan and the majority that supports him. While the Old Turkey always suffered from being a regime based on the secular minority, the New Turkey relies on the conservative majority.[67]

Turkey is part of a global trend when it comes to democratic retrenchment. As Schedler argues, many political regimes all around the world "have established institutional facades of democracy, including regular multiparty elections for the chief executive, in order to conceal (and reproduce) harsh realities of authoritarian governance."[68] However, the situation in Turkey cannot be defined as "durable authoritarianism"[69] just yet. Elections are still being held – despite the probable election fraud and unfair competition – and the media is censored and journalists are being jailed, but still there are enclaves of freedom and openness where people can make their voice heard against all odds. At the beginning of the chapter, we asked whether it was curtains for Turkish democracy. After describing the political context and giving background information, we still believe that it is not yet over. Neither a coup nor Western intervention are cures for Turkey's debilitating problems. Lessons learnt from the past clearly show that a true democracy will not rise after such practices. One might hope that his democratic retrenchment is actually paving the way for grassroots democratic movements and contingent alliances among various groups with diverging interests. Turkey is going through a painful period of transition which will potentially give birth to popular resistance movements that might be the bottom up force needed to push Turkey and its policy makers towards further democratization.

Contributions in the Volume

This book offers a dozen chapters of original reflection and research on the current political situation in Turkey today. We asked the authors to analyse various issues in their own areas of expertise and to comment on authoritarian drift in Turkey. Beyond this, we have not provided any toolbox of concepts or theoretical frameworks to be adopted, as we believe that in this period of transition many scholars have differing views that might sometimes overlap and yet remain distinct. Our aim was to show how each author interprets the course of events differently but at the same time may meet at certain common junctures. This book is an attempt to analyse the "rite of passage" that Turkey has been experiencing by exploring path-dependencies, the legacy of the Kemalist regime, and the future scenarios that the current situation is promising.

The chapter by Onur Bakıner sets the scene for the subsequent discussions in the book by focusing on the roots of authoritarian drift in Turkey. Drawing from various reports from Freedom House, Amnesty International and Human Rights Watch, among others, he argues that the seeds of what has now eventuated were sown in the mid-2000s. He argues that there is nothing surprising about the democratic retrenchment we are facing right now. After his solid and sound analysis, the following chapter by Karabekir Akkoyunlu focuses on the shift of tutelary democracy to competitive authoritarianism in Turkey. It complements the previous chapter by Bakıner and provides an excellent background on the political developments that paved the way for the *de facto* presidential system of today.

In Chapter 4, Abdülkadir Civan and Taptuk Emre Erkoç discuss the political economy of elections. They focus on the Turkish example by considering the utilization of public expenditure in the election campaign. They also examine the strategies of incumbent parties in Turkey (including the AKP) during election periods in relation to three specific pillars: the level of public expenditure in health and education, local government spending and regional development policies and, finally, governmental support given to the agricultural sector. Bezen Balamir Coşkun, Salih Doğan and Mustafa Demir in Chapter 5, on the other hand, focus on the foreign policy aspects of the AKP and Erdoğan. They argue that Turkish foreign policy has been instrumentalized to legitimize domestic-level hegemonic projects. Their contention is that during the AKP era, Turkey's foreign policy issues and foreign relations have been framed by the AKP ruling elite to strengthen their hegemony in Turkish politics and society.

In Chapter 6, Emrah Çelik discusses the relationships between the AKP and faith-based groups. He paints a picture of the heterogeneity of political Islamic groups in Turkey and the complexity of their power struggles. It is an essential chapter to understand how the AKP has thrived among them and consolidated its power despite being challenged from below. In Chapter 7, Samim Akgönül focuses on the transnational policies of the AKP by paying specific attention to external voting and transnational election campaigns. His analysis shows how complex diaspora identity is and how the ruling party has instrumentalized it for political purposes. He chooses the Turkish community in France as a case study but also comments on the general voting patterns of the Euro-Turks.

In Chapter 8, Anna Maria Beylunioğlu shares her analysis with us on a much-understudied topic: non-Muslim communities' attitudes towards the AKP in Turkey. Her chapter is important when it comes to showing the impact of Kemalist policy legacies on minority behaviour and the path-dependency that it engenders when it comes to voting patterns. Cuma Çiçek's chapter presents a rigorous analysis of Kurdish citizens' voting patterns. He compares changes in voting behaviour in the period 1991–9 to the period 1999–2014 and offers up digital maps revealing the differences. His analysis sheds light on the rise of the HDP in the Turkish political scene and demonstrates that the HDP did not merely increase its societal support in the period of the last elections but, rather, that it has gradually expanded and deepened its hegemony in Turkey over the last decade.

In Chapter 10, Kıvanç Atak discusses the recent trajectory of the political regime in Turkey by specifically considering the question of freedom of assembly. He suggests that authoritarian *practices* at the expense of the freedom of assembly have not waned but have been perpetuated in the AKP period. In his analysis, he places the current situation in a broader theoretical framework. In Chapter 11, Efe Kerem Sözeri focuses on the pressures put on, and the censorship of, academia and the media by focusing on the high-profile case of the 'Academics for Peace' petition that caused uproar within AKP circles. He provides a carefully prepared data set on the death of the free press and information in Turkey by showing some of the worrisome consequences of the recent transformations under the AKP. In Chapter 12, Dağhan Irak provides insights into the role of social media in popular resistance by focusing especially on the Gezi protests. His chapter sheds light on the authoritarian shift in Turkey through analysing its reflection on social and digital media in Turkey. The book ends with an epilogue from the prominent professor İştar Gözaydın, who summarizes the course of events so far with a trajectory for the future of Turkey.

Notes

1. See, for example: William Hale and Ergun Özbudun, *Islamism, Democracy and Liberalism in Turkey: The Case of the AKP* (Abingdon, New York: Routledge, 2010), pp. 54–97.

2. See, for example: Meliha B. Altunışık and Lenore G. Martin "Making Sense of Turkish Foreign Policy in the Middle East under AKP", *Turkish Studies*, 12/4 (2011), pp. 569–87.
3. Birol A. Yeşilada, "The Future of Erdoğan and the AKP", *Turkish Studies*, 17/1 (2016), p. 19.
4. See also: Matthew Whiting and Zeynep Kaya, "Floating or sinking? The state of democracy in Turkey and the rise of the HDP", *openDemocracy* (25 February 2016), https://www.opendemocracy.net/westminster/zeynep-n-kaya-matthew-whiting/floating-or-sinking-state-of-democracy-in-turkey-and-rise-of-hdp, accessed 1 November 2016.
5. Berk Esen and Sebnem Gumuscu, "Rising competitive authoritarianism in Turkey", *Third World Quarterly*, 37/9 (2016), pp. 1581–1606, at 1581–2.
6. Dağhan Irak, "A Close-Knit Bunch: Political Concentration in Turkey's Anadolu Agency through Twitter Interactions," *Turkish Studies*, 17/2 (2016), pp. 336–60, at 336–7.
7. Ergun Özbudun, "AKP at the Crossroads: Erdoğan's Majoritarian Drift", *South European Society and Politics*, 19/2 (2014), pp. 155–67.
8. Jeffrey Haynes, "Politics and Islam in Turkey: From Ataturk to the AKP", in Jeffrey Haynes and Anja Hennig (eds), *Religious Actors in the Public Sphere: Means, Objectives and Effects* (Oxon: Routledge, 2013), p. 192.
9. 34.63 per cent in 2002, 46.58 per cent in 2007, 49.53 per cent in 2011, 40.87 per cent in June 2015 and 49.50 per cent in November 2015.
10. Sabri Sayarı, "Back to a Predominant Party System: The November 2015 Snap Election in Turkey", *South European Society and Politics*, 21/2 (2016), pp. 263–80.
11. For more information on the limitations of freedom of media and speech see: Freedom House, *Freedom in the World 2016, Turkey Country Report*, https://freedomhouse.org/report/freedom-world/2016/turkey, accessed 25 June 2016.
12. Yıldırım previously served almost continuously as the minister of transport, maritime and communication from 2002 to 2013 and again between 2015 and 2016. Between 2014 and 2015, he served as a senior advisor to President Erdoğan.
13. John Hannah, "How do you solve a problem like Erdoğan?", *Foreign Policy* (15 June 2016), http://foreignpolicy.com/2016/06/15/how-do-you-solve-a-problem-like-erdogan/, accessed 25 June 2016.
14. Ahmet Erdi Öztürk, "In the Home Stretch of Erdoğan's Presidential System who is the Real Enemy?" *Research Turkey* (16 May 2016), http://researchturkey.org/in-the-home-stretch-of-erdogans-presidential-system-who-is-the-real-enemy/, accessed 1 November 2016.
15. Alon Ben-Mair, "How Turkey Became a De Facto Dictatorship", *Middle East Eye* (12 May 2016), http://www.yourmiddleeast.com/opinion/how-turkey-became-a-de-facto-dictatorship_40817, accessed 1 November 2016.
16. Hannah, "How do you solve a problem like Erdoğan?"
17. "Recep Tayyip Erdoğan: Turkey's dominant president", BBC News (21 July 2016), http://www.bbc.co.uk/news/world-europe-13746679, accessed 1 November 2016.
18. Alison Smale and James Kantermay, "President Erdoğan's Authoritarian Tilt Threatens Visa Deal With Europe", *New York Times* (6 May 2016), http://www.nytimes.com/2016/05/07/world/europe/erdogan-turkey-visas-europe.html, accessed 1 November 2016.

19. "Growing autocracy threatens a crucial country", the *Guardian* (1 June 2015), https://www.theguardian.com/commentisfree/2015/may/31/guardian-view-turkey-recep-tayyip-erdogan, accessed 1 November 2016.
20. "Turkey's Erdoğan lurches toward authoritarianism", *Financial Times* (6 May 2014), http://www.ft.com/cms/s/0/e89e8d74-cfc1-11e3-a2b7-00144feabdc0.html#axzz4CUszVU6x, accessed 1 November 2016.
21. Lizzie Dearden, "President Erdoğan says freedom and democracy have 'no value' in Turkey amid arrests and military crackdown," the *Independent* (18 March 2016), http://www.independent.co.uk/news/world/europe/president-erdogan-says-freedom-and-democracy-have-no-value-in-turkey-amid-arrests-and-military-a6938266.html, accessed 1 November 2016.
22. Güneş Murat Tezcür, "Historical and Contemporary Trends in the Turkish Political System", in, Zeynep N. Kaya (ed.), *The AKP and the Turkish Foreign Policy in the Middle East*, LSE Middle East Centre Collected Papers, Volume 5 (April 2016), p. 11.
23. For more information on the Gezi protests see: Mehmet Barış Kuymulu. "Reclaiming the right to the city: Reflections on the urban uprisings in Turkey", *City*, 17/3 (2013), pp. 274–8; Özbudun, "AKP at the Crossroads"; Yeşilada, "The Future of Erdoğan".
24. Jason Brownlee, *Authoritarianism in an Age of Democratization* (New York: Cambridge University Press, 2007), p. 2.
25. Andreas Schedler (ed.), *Electoral Authoritarianism: The Dynamics of Unfree Competition* (Boulder, CO: Lynne Rienner, 2009).
26. See, for example: Rex Brynen, Pete W. Moore, Bassel F. Salloukh and Marie-Joelle Zahar (eds) *Beyond the Arab Spring: Authoritarianism and Democratization in the Arab World* (Boulder, CO: Lynne Rienner, 2012).
27. Steven Levitsky and Lucan A. Way, *Competitive Authoritarianism: Hybrid Regimes after the Cold War* (Cambridge: Cambridge University Press, 2010).
28. Ibid., p. 14.
29. For an excellent critical account of contemporary Turkish politics see: Kerem Öktem, *Angry Nation: Turkey since 1989* (New York: Zed Books, 2011).
30. For an excellent account of the impact of President Erdoğan see: Yeşilada "The Future of Erdoğan".
31. Ahmet Erdi Öztürk, "The Presidential Election in Turkey: History and Future Expectations", *Contemporary Southeastern Europe* 1/2 (2014), pp. 110–18; Irak, "A Close-Knit Bunch".
32. See also: Whiting and Kaya, "Floating or Sinking?"
33. See: Human Rights Watch reporting on torture and ill-treatment of the police in Turkey after 2007: Human Rights Watch, *World Report 2009, Turkey*, https://www.hrw.org/world-report/2009/country-chapters/turkey, accessed 1 November 2016.
34. Ergun Özbudun, "Turkey's Constitutional Reform and 2010 Constitutional Referendum", *IEMed Mediterranean Yearbook 2011* (Barcelona: European Institute of the Mediterranean, 2011), http://www.iemed.org/observatori-en/arees-danalisi/arxius-adjunts/anuari/med.2011/Ozbudun_en.pdf, accessed 1 November 2016.
35. See: Human Rights Watch, *World Report 2015, Turkey*, https://www.hrw.org/world-report/2015/country-chapters/turkey, accessed 1 November 2016.
36. Sayari, "Predominant Party System".

37. Amnesty International, "Turkey accused of gross human rights violations in Gezi Park protests" (2 October 2013), https://www.amnesty.org/en/latest/news/2013/10/turkey-accused-gross-human-rights-violations-gezi-park-protests/, accessed 1 November 2016.
38. The Gülen movement, Gülen community, Voluntary movement, the Cemaat, and the Hizmet movement are among different names given to this group in various settings. Furthermore, since the 17–25 December 2013 corruption cases, the AKP government have referred to the group as FETÖ (Fethullah Gülenist Terror Organization).
39. For more information see: Özbudun, "AKP at the Crossroads"; Öztürk, "Presidential Election in Turkey".
40. For more information see: Ahmet Erdi Öztürk "Takeover of opposition newspaper is a death warrant for speech in Turkey", *The Conversation* (8 March 2016), https://theconversation.com/takeover-of-opposition-newspaper-is-a-death-warrant-for-free-speech-in-turkey-55902, accessed 1 November 2016.
41. Baha Güngör, "Turkey's Erdoğan aims to expand presidential power", *Deutsche Welle* (28 August 2014), http://www.dw.com/en/turkeys-erdogan-aims-to-expand-presidential-power/a-17885582, accessed 1 November 2016.
42. Sayari, "Predominant Party System".
43. Bahar Başer and Ahmet Erdi Öztürk, "Turkey election: Erdoğan and the AKP get majority back amid climate of violence and fear", *The Conversation* (1 November 2015), https://theconversation.com/turkey-election-erdogan-and-the-akp-get-majority-back-amid-climate-of-violence-and-fear-49963, accessed 1 November 2016.
44. Kiran Nazish, "Cizre in ruins as Turkey lifts curfew on Kurdish towns", *Al Jazeera* (13 March 2016), http://www.aljazeera.com/news/2016/03/cizre-ruins-turkey-lifts-curfew-kurdish-towns-160312113030597.html, accessed 1 November 2016.
45. "İl il, Kürtlere ve HDP binalarına yönelik saldırılar", *Evrensel* (9 September 2015), http://www.evrensel.net/haber/260224/il-il-kurtlere-ve hdp binalarina-yoneli k-saldirilar, accessed 1 November 2016.
46. Evren Balta, "The Pendulum of Democracy: The AKP Government and Turkey's Kurdish Conflict", in Kaya, *Turkish Foreign Policy*, p. 22.
47. Balta "Pendulum of Democracy", p. 22.
48. Özbudun, "AKP at the Crossroads", p. 155.
49. "Growing autocracy threatens a crucial country"
50. Giorgio Agamben, *State of Exception* (tr. Kevin Attell) (Chicago: University of Chicago Press, 2003), pp: 36–7.
51. Ahmet Erdi Öztürk, "Turkey's Diyanet under AKP rule: From protector to imposer of state ideology?", *Southeast European and Black Sea Studies*, 16/4 (2016), pp. 619–35.
52. Sayari, "Predominant Party System".
53. Brownlee, *Authoritarianism*, p. 3.
54. Esen and Gumuscu, "Rising Competitive Authoritarianism", p. 1.
55. Freedom House, *Turkey 2016*.
56. Ibid.
57. "Nearly 2,000 legal cases opened for insulting Turkey's Erdoğan", Reuters (2 March 2016), http://www.reuters.com/article/us-turkey-erdogan-lawsuit-idUSKCN0W42ES, accessed 1 November 2016.

58. For further information on the collapse of the peace process see: Balta, "Pendulum of Democracy", pp. 19–24.
59. For more information on Turkish perceptions of foreign countries see: GMF, *Turkey Perceptions Survey 2015* (Washington, DC: The German Marshall Fund of the United States, 2015), http://www.gmfus.org/sites/default/files/TP%20Key%20Findings%20Report%20English%20Final_0.pdf, pp. 5–11, accessed 1 November 2016.
60. For more information on the EU-Turkey deal see: Elizabeth Collett, "The Paradox of the EU-Turkey Refugee Deal", Migration Policy Institute (March 2016), http://www.migrationpolicy.org/news/paradox-eu-turkey-refugee-deal, accessed 1 November 2016.
61. Kerem Öktem, "Zombie politics: Europe, Turkey and the disposable human", *openDemocracy* (19 March 2016), https://www.opendemocracy.net/kerem-oktem/zombie-politics-europe-turkey-and-disposable-human, accessed 1 November 016.
62. Öktem, "Zombie politics".
63. For detailed information about the issue see: Sam Adams, "Turkey coup 2016 explained: What happened and what is a military coup?", *Mirror* (18 July 2016), http://www.mirror.co.uk/news/world-news/what-happened-turkey-attempted-coup-8432395, accessed 1 November 2016.
64. For detailed information about the issue see: Will Worley and Harry Cockburn, "Prime Minister says 265 people killed in attempted military coup, including at least 100 'plotters'", *Independent* (16 July 2016), http://www.independent.co.uk/news/world/europe/turkey-coup-dead-erdogan-military-chief-ankara-istanbul-death-toll-plotters-how-many-killed-wounded-a7140376.html, accessed 1 November 2016.
65. For detailed information about the state of emergecy declaration see: Gareth Jones and Asli Kandemir, "Turkey's Erdoğan announces three-month state of emergency," Reuters (20 July 2016), http://www.reuters.com/article/us-turkey-security-erdogan-emergency-idUSKCN1002TU, accessed 1 November 2016.
66. For detailed information see: Laura Pitel, "Erdoğan uses state of emergency to overhaul Turkey's military", *Financial Times* (2 August 2016), https://www.ft.com/content/a60fd9f0-587b-11e6-8d05-4eaa66292c32, accessed 1 November 2016.
67. Mustafa Akyol, "'New Turkey' finds founding myth in failed coup", *Al-Monitor* (22 September 2016), http://www.al-monitor.com/pulse/originals/2016/09/turkey-july-15-coup-attempt-founding-myth.html, accessed 1 November 2016.
68. Andreas Schedler, "The Logic of Electoral Authoritarianism," in Schedler, *Electoral Authoritarianism*, p. 1.
69. Brownlee, *Authoritarianism*, p. 4.

CHAPTER 2

HOW DID WE GET HERE? TURKEY'S SLOW SHIFT TO AUTHORITARIANISM

Onur Bakıner

Introduction

Turkey's authoritarian drift under successive Justice and Development Party (*Adalet ve Kalkınma Partisi*, AKP) governments has astonished many observers who, only a few years back, portrayed the country as a model democracy for the greater Middle East region.[1] Police brutality against protesters in Istanbul and other cities in the summer of 2013, the government's lawless crackdown upon the Gülen movement, its erstwhile ally,[2] the increasing concentration of pro-government media outlets, arrests of dissenting journalists, the failure to prosecute corruption allegations and, finally, the end of the peace process with the Kurdistan Workers' Party (*Partiya Karkerên Kurdistan*, PKK) that has resulted in a rising death toll and fundamental rights violations, have all come together to shatter the country's reputation as a democratizing regime.

Why does a government enjoying widespread popular support and facing weak rivals seek to eliminate checks and balances and violate fundamental rights? How are we to explain an authoritarian shift under a party that has long been considered an agent of democratization and liberalization by many domestic and international observers? This chapter explains the sources of the authoritarian shift by emphasizing the multiplicity of interests and values within the governing elite and the contextual factors that structure the political opportunities they face. Unlike most descriptions of Turkey under the leadership of the AKP and President Recep Tayyip Erdoğan, I show that the liberal reform agenda was not suddenly abandoned some time after 2011. It had already been stagnating in 2006–7, and signs of an authoritarian turn were present even then. The dramatic shift towards authoritarianism after 2011 may be unpredictable in its speed, but not necessarily its direction.

I argue that a political movement may endorse limited constitutional government, the rule of law, and respect for fundamental liberties on principled grounds or as a strategic move to muster domestic and international support, eliminate rivals and consolidate administrative control over a divided society. These ideational and strategic factors also explain why political alliances that promote liberal-democratic reform in some periods of time or for some issue areas may fail to maintain momentum in the face of illiberal shifts under changing opportunity structures.[3] Transformations in the international environment, changing governing coalitions, and the elimination of democratic and undemocratic rivals may all signal the weakening and even disappearance of the reformist impulse.

The AKP came to power in 2002 with a claim to transform Turkish politics in an irreversibly liberal and democratic direction. It brought together a vast alliance of reformed Islamists, centre-right politicians and voters, and a considerable section of the country's Western-minded liberal elite who saw in the AKP an opportunity to end the tutelary role of the military and high courts in Turkish politics. The last group had few votes to contribute, but their ongoing political support was necessary for the AKP's electoral success, as they built bridges between the party, international observers, and the country's Westernized economic and cultural elite. This coalition proved invaluable to the AKP when the European Union accession process was a popular platform, and when the high courts and the military held an actively hostile attitude toward the government, especially between 2005 and 2009.[4] Once those conditions no longer held, because of the AKP's agency as well as a host of exogenous factors, the party leadership began to question the benefits of liberal reformism. Thus, as a catch-all party with a considerable nationalist and conservative voter base, the AKP has used a mixed strategy of liberal reformism and illiberal policies for much of its existence, and has abandoned the limited reform agenda altogether under shifting strategic conditions.

The chapter is organized as follows. The first section provides an overview of the literature on hybrid regimes that mix liberal and illiberal (and democratic and authoritarian) ideas and practices. This section also specifies the chapter's theoretical contribution. The second section offers a descriptive picture of basic civil and political rights in Turkey for the period 2003–15. The data are derived from Freedom House, Amnesty International, and Human Rights Watch reports, as well as the Worldwide Governance Indicators. It shows that the authoritarian shift began as early as 2006–7 and not around 2011–13, as is often claimed. The following section explains the sources of this authoritarian shift through a stylized history of the AKP period. The conclusion summarizes the main claims and the broader implications of this case study, and suggests avenues for future research on authoritarian politics in Turkey and elsewhere.

Understanding Liberal-Democratic Reform and Authoritarian Turns: A Theoretical Framework

Observers have long noted the hybrid character of various regimes that have democratized since the early 1990s.[5] In contexts as diverse as Russia, Rwanda, Venezuela, and Egypt, regime elites have not eliminated nominally-democratic institutions altogether, but they do not allow fully competitive elections either. Campaign financing practices, media control, cleverly crafted electoral rules, and some degree of repression ensure that regime-backed candidates keep winning most, if not all, elections.[6] In explaining why these regimes do not turn fully authoritarian, some point to the reputational costs associated with abandoning democracy, while others claim that democracy (understood as rule by majority) has been at odds with constitutional liberalism (understood as the protection of citizens' fundamental rights, and especially those of minority groups) in all but a few historical contexts.[7]

The reverse question – that is, why it is that authoritarian regimes use nominally democratic institutions in the first place – provides further insights into the formation of hybrid regimes. Reviewing the literature on democratic institutions under authoritarian regimes, Brancati finds that such institutions can help regimes eliminate potential threats by signaling the regime's strength to opposition, acquiring information about societal discontent, providing channels to distribute patronage, demonstrating credible commitment to domestic investors, and monitoring high-level and low-level officials in the governing coalition.[8]

This chapter takes its inspiration from the vast literature on so-called authoritarian, competitive authoritarian, or illiberal democratic regimes, and especially the strategic accounts of democratization and liberal reform summarized in Brancati.[9] It is important to refine this literature with three observations. First, principled ideas matter. Politicians, civil society activists, and intellectuals may have strategic reasons to support democratization and liberalization reforms, as described above, but it is also possible that they hold limited democratic government under a system of constitutional guarantees in esteem for its own sake. Second, all kinds of regimes are coalitions that consist of a multiplicity of individual and organizational actors with varying levels of normative commitment to liberal-democratic principles, with different strategic interests in mind and varying levels of political power. As a result, changing opportunity structures and shifting alliances may result in full democratization, simultaneous reformist and authoritarian policies, or a shift to full authoritarianism. Finally, electoral survival need not be the only motivation for a regime's use of democratic institutions or authoritarian measures. Sometimes governments that face no serious electoral opposition may still resort to authoritarian measures to limit political competition.

In addition, electoral survival can be a means to another political end, such as the implementation of desired policies.

What are the motivations that lead a governing coalition, in part or in whole, to undertake liberal reform or switch to authoritarian policies? I believe that several ideational and strategic factors motivate political actors, ranging from the intrinsic value attached to limited government to the instrumental benefits that politicians can derive from liberal reform. In what follows, I offer a hypothesized list of motivations that may prompt liberal reform, as well as the likely motivations to oppose such reform.

The normative value of liberal democracy

A government may undertake liberal reforms simply because its leadership and some of the key constituencies believe in the virtues of limited constitutional government. I expect the effect of this ideational factor to be strong if committed politicians, intellectuals, and constituencies are in a dominant position within the governing coalition. While it would be wrong to assume that the only motivation for liberalization is genuine commitment to political liberalism, it is also misleading to rule out this important ideational factor.[10]

I use the term "liberal" throughout the chapter to refer to individuals and groups who self-designate in that way. However, one caveat is in order: outside of the Anglo-Saxon world, political liberalism has rarely, if ever, had a powerful independent presence as a philosophical outlook or political practice. Social democrats, socialists, religious conservatives, and other political movements have endorsed politically liberal causes alongside other political agendas. In Turkey, the self-designation "liberal" was virtually absent before the 1980s, in great part because the concept was often associated with the defence of laissez-faire capitalism rather than politically liberal causes. Thus, support for liberal causes is not limited to self-designated liberals.

Ideational factors may militate against liberal-democratic causes as well. Politicians, intellectuals and constituencies often mobilize against the idea of limited constitutional government in which all citizens enjoy a set of rights and liberties equally. The limited appeal of liberal democracy is not confined to openly illiberal movements. In fact, liberal reform coalitions are likely to be uneasy alliances of groups with varying levels of commitment to liberal causes. Supporting the expansion of some civil and political rights for some constituencies may or may not spill over to overarching support for the expansion of rights for all. Therefore, the normative appeal of liberal-democratic reform should be considered one ideational factor among many.

The administrative value of liberalism

The value of liberal reform is sometimes understood in terms of "good governance"[11] – that is to say, enhanced administrative capacity. It has long been suggested that accountable institutions, fair and efficient dispute resolution procedures, and non-violent mechanisms for the alternation of power are necessary conditions for economic development and social peace. Thus, politicians and policy advisors may support liberal reform to enhance output legitimacy.

However, the causal connection between liberal democracy and good governance is by no means uncontested.[12] While rule-of-law institutions are often praised for their contribution to "economic, social and political development",[13] others highlight the fact that authoritarian regimes also seek, and occasionally achieve, desirable economic and political outcomes – the sustainability of these outcomes is another relevant question, of course. Thus, the perceived benefits from rule-of-law institutions do not necessarily push governments to abandon repressive and unaccountable policies.

Mobilizing support for a reform agenda

Liberal reforms are likely to draw support from liberal intellectuals, as well as the international community comprising other governments,[14] international organizations, civil society groups and foreign media.[15] Although none of these actors constitute an important voter base, their endorsement may determine the prospects of a political party by signaling its commitment to internationally valid standards of good governance. Such endorsement is crucial for political parties and movements suspected of authoritarian, radical or extremist tendencies. Furthermore, the promise of freedom and equal political representation is likely to increase the support base for a government in a society divided along religious, ethnic, cultural and ideological lines. Commitment to liberal reform may enhance the cohesion of a broad governing coalition by appealing to diverse social sectors.

However, voters and party activists do not always appreciate the extension of rights to minorities and disadvantaged groups or limits on government power. A government that is perceived to be "too liberal" might lose support from constituencies who advocate the preservation of class, ethnolinguistic, religious and gender hierarchies. Likewise, support by liberal intellectuals and foreign governments may strain a government's relationship with its conservative and nationalist base.

Elimination of illiberal rivals

A government that respects fundamental rights and limits the exercise of political power is likely to eliminate the privileges and immunities of those actors who rely on repressive and arbitrary procedures to maintain their power. A government that has undemocratic and/or illiberal rivals (such as a politicized military, a powerful bureaucratic apparatus or a coup coalition) would benefit from liberal reform which, if successful, would undermine those rivals' legitimacy and political clout. However, liberal reform is not the only means for eliminating rivals. A government can also resort to repression, either as the only way of eliminating opponents or alongside liberal reforms.

Liberal reform may eliminate some rivals, but the expansion of fundamental civil and political rights facilitates organized opposition to the government. Even if a government wants to reap the above-mentioned benefits of liberal reform, it should take into consideration the fact that political openness invites vocal and organized rivals to join the political competition. In other words, a government's expected benefits from liberal reform should be considered in conjunction with its expected cost arising from increasing political contestation.

As the preceding discussion suggests, individual and organizational actors have a variety of normative, administrative, and tactical motivations to promote liberal and democratic reform, but they also consider the expected costs of such reform, such as increasing political competition and the loss of core supporters. Moreover, reformism is not the only way in which a political movement can achieve its stated ends. Sometimes the support of domestic and international observers can be ensured through illiberal promises (such as fighting international communism or promoting economic, but not political, liberalization). Moreover, economic and administrative policy goals may be achieved through authoritarian policies. Furthermore, governments may eliminate their rivals through repression and arbitrary rule rather than through liberal reform. In other words, the striving for limited constitutional government that respects fundamental rights is one among many formulations of politics for politicians, civil society groups, intellectuals, and ordinary citizens – not to mention the possibility that individuals and groups may support liberal-democratic measures in some issue areas while rejecting them in others.

What explains shifts in a government's overall direction? Considering the discussion above, it can be inferred that a government is likely to back liberal-democratic reformism when its components exhibit a strong normative commitment to liberal democracy, or when the opportunity structure in the political system favours the strategic implementation of reformist policies, or both. By contrast, a government that relies on constituencies without a strong commitment to liberal democracy and that can achieve political goals (like the consolidation of power and policy implementation) in the absence of a reform agenda is likely to abandon reformism. Needless to say, most governments find themselves somewhere in between; thus, liberal and illiberal policies may be implemented simultaneously.

Policy direction is likely to change abruptly only if a government receives clear signals that justify a democratic or authoritarian shift. Elections and major political crises provide just those signals because it gives a government a good sense of the size and composition of its supporters, as well as the relative power of its opponents. As we will see in the case of Turkey, the 2007 general election, the slowdown in the EU-accession process, and the AKP's victories against its illiberal allies in the military and the judiciary between 2007 and 2009 all served as clear signals to the government that its support base was broad enough to sideline liberals, that its undemocratic rivals were increasingly weakened and, consequently, that it could do away with the reform agenda without facing serious repercussions.

The State of Democracy and Human Rights in Turkey (2003–15)

What is the state of democracy and basic rights in contemporary Turkey? An outline of the trends between 2003 and 2015 is necessary, not only to document the nature of the current regime but also to develop and assess theories that explain when and why policy shifts occur. In order to offer a comprehensive picture of the state of democracy and human rights in Turkey, I use four sources: (1) the quantitative "freedom of the press" and "freedom in the world" measures compiled by the Freedom House (FH), available for 2003–15; (2) the qualitative human rights reporting of Amnesty International (AI), available for 2007–15; (3) the qualitative human rights reporting of Human Rights Watch (HRW), available for 2004–14[16] and; (4) the Worldwide Governance Indicators, funded by the World Bank (WB), that track the rule-of-law situation over the years. Following the Freedom House categorization, I identify the relevant issue areas as *political rights* that enable free and fair democratic competition,[17] *civil rights* that enable citizens' meaningful participation in social and political processes,[18] and *press freedom*. In addition, two core components of civil liberties – namely *freedom of expression/speech* and *freedom of assembly* – are analysed in further detail, using the FH scores as well as the AI and HRW reports. A separate line of analysis is the government's treatment of the Kurdish issue, which raises a mixture of political, civil, and cultural rights concerns. I pay special attention to AI and HRW reports for statements that describe disagreements between the government and the civilian and military bureaucracies to account for the possibility that some of the authoritarian shifts took place against the AKP government's wishes. Finally, the WB indicators present a broad picture of the rule-of-law improvements and decline over time.

All sources agree that Turkey underwent a quick, if uneven, human rights reform process between 2003 and 2005, followed by stagnation and decline. While the country has maintained basic democratic institutions and processes throughout, it has remained a middle-ranking country in terms of democracy and human rights. In other words, at no point have we witnessed a "democracy-and-human-rights revolution". Certainly, the eradication of systematic and heavy torture (but not necessarily ill treatment), and the elimination of military/judicial tutelage stand out as considerable achievements under the AKP rule. Beyond these two issue areas, however, quantitative measures reveal that the situation of human rights in the mid 2010s is not better than it was in the early 2000s and, indeed, it may well be worse.

Human rights reports by AI and HRW have consistently documented the following human rights violations: the criminalization of dissenting opinions; arbitrary limits on the freedom of assembly; prosecutions against political opposition based on vague anti-terrorism laws and in violation of fair trial standards; ill treatment of protesters; and vulnerable persons by the police and the massive incarceration of journalists. Figure 2.1 shows that political rights (i.e., basic political institutions) have remained more or less stagnant during the period of AKP government, while overall civil rights – and press freedom in particular – have worsened steadily since 2006. Moreover, the rate of decline has become steeper since 2011.

Figure 2.2 presents a timeline that pays special attention to the twists and turns of Turkey's democracy and human rights situation between 2003 and 2015. Six major trends are observed:

(1) Considerable improvements in the elimination of torture and respect for political rights, civil liberties and press freedom took place between 2003 and 2005. There is sufficient data to suggest that, at least in the area of press freedom, the improvements go back to 2000; that is to say, before the AKP came to power.

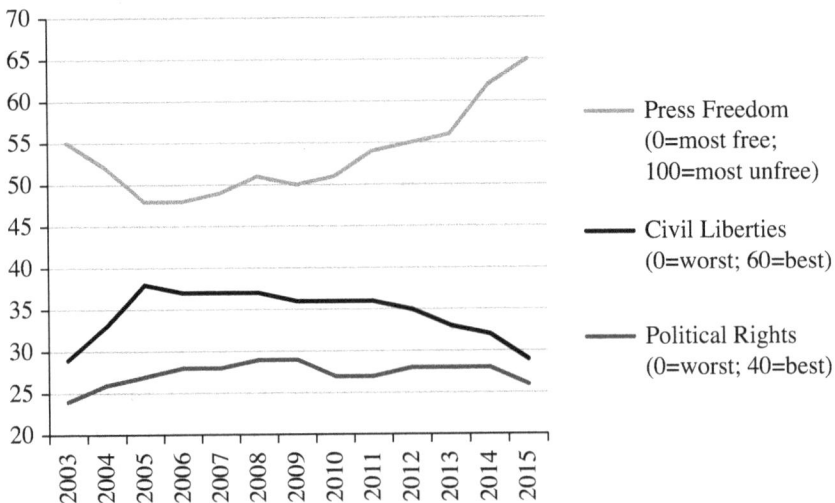

Figure 2.1 Freedom in the world – aggregate scores for Turkey (2003–15).

(2) While the improvements in electoral democracy were maintained after 2005, no further improvements were observed.

(3) The period 2006–9 witnessed an upsurge of police violence against political protest, while the scores concerning the freedom of expression were stagnant.

(4) Starting from 2009, the freedom of expression score began to decline steadily, in part because of the prosecution of journalists and the overall erosion of press freedom. The deterioration in freedom of assembly continued and intensified after 2013.

(5) The 2004 legislation that enabled broadcasting in Kurdish and the 2009 Kurdish initiative have generated optimism but both processes ended in disappointment, as the implementation of the broadcasting legislation was slow and uneven and the Kurdish initiative did not bear results. To the contrary, many Kurdish activists, politicians and journalists faced prosecution between 2010 and 2013.

(6) Human rights reports indicate that at least part of the downturn between 2007 and 2010 can be attributed to civilian and military forces that operated outside the government's control. However, the deterioration continued, and in some issue areas intensified, after the anti-government forces in the military and the high courts lost their grip on power. In fact, all indices related to the rule of law, press freedom, and civil liberties show signs of decline sometime between 2010 and 2012, and no improvement afterwards.

This summary of trends reveals that the deterioration of basic rights in Turkey did not occur in an abrupt shift around 2011 or 2013; the downward trend has been in place at least since 2006–7, but it has become more pronounced recently. Erdoğan's increasingly personalist style of rule, liberal intellectuals' growing disenchantment with the government around 2011–13, and the fallout with the Gülen community in late 2013 may have contributed to this steep decline, but they are definitely *not* its underlying causes. Likewise, the recalcitrance of the anti-AKP forces in the civilian and military bureaucracy is not the primary or only source of this decline because the quantitative measures kept declining even after the downfall of military and judicial tutelage after 2009, and qualitative reports document many violations (at the AKP government's discretion) before, during, and after this period.

Explaining the Authoritarian Shift under the AKP Government

Limited reformism (2002–7)

The AKP ended a decade of unstable coalition governments in Turkey by winning the 2002 general election in a landslide.[19] The party achieved this unprecedented success by creating a broad-based movement supported by

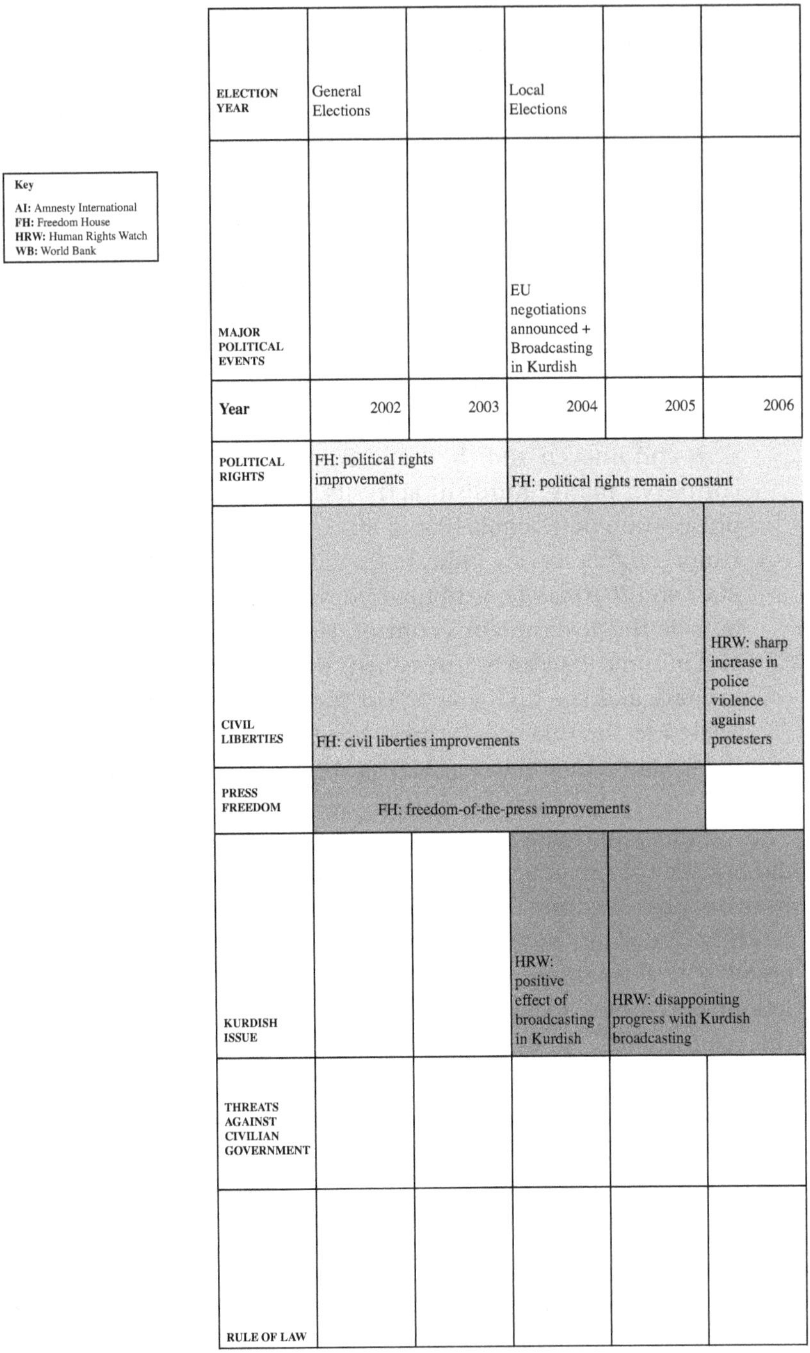

Key

AI: Amnesty International
FH: Freedom House
HRW: Human Rights Watch
WB: World Bank

	2002	2003	2004	2005	2006
ELECTION YEAR	General Elections		Local Elections		
MAJOR POLITICAL EVENTS			EU negotiations announced + Broadcasting in Kurdish		
Year	2002	2003	2004	2005	2006
POLITICAL RIGHTS	FH: political rights improvements	FH: political rights remain constant			
CIVIL LIBERTIES	FH: civil liberties improvements				HRW: sharp increase in police violence against protesters
PRESS FREEDOM	FH: freedom-of-the-press improvements				
KURDISH ISSUE			HRW: positive effect of broadcasting in Kurdish	HRW: disappointing progress with Kurdish broadcasting	
THREATS AGAINST CIVILIAN GOVERNMENT					
RULE OF LAW					

Figure 2.2 Timeline for democracy and human rights in Turkey (2002–15).

2007	2008	2009	2010	2011	2012	2013	2014	2015
General Elections		Local Elections		General Elections			Local Elections + Presidential Elections	General Elections
Military-civilian tension: April 7 memorandum	AKP ban trial + Ergenekon indictment	Kurdish initiative	Balyoz trial begins; Constitutional amendments	Military-civilian tension: Chief of Staff resigns	Balyoz verdict	Peace process announced + Gezi protests + Ergenekon verdict + fallout with the Gülen movement	Ergenekon and Balyoz verdicts overturned	Peace process fails
HRW: human rights reforms "retrograde"; HRW: increasing police violence against protesters		FH: first year of decline in "freedom of expression and belief"		FH: steady decline in "freedom of expression and belief"			FH: first year of decline in "associational and organizational rights"	
		prosecution of journalists	FH: freedom of the press declines; AI: peak in reports of prosecution of journalists					
			HRW and AI: KCK arrests and failure to continue the Kurdish initiative					
AI and HRW: mention of military and other anti-AKP forces				AI and HRW: mention of trials of anti-AKP forces				
WB: rule-of-law improvements				WB: rule-of-law decline				

the moderate wing of the Islamist political tradition, as well as "Turkey's pragmatic middle class, business community, and liberal intellectuals."[20] It was particularly successful in voicing the political aspirations of the emerging provincial bourgeoisie, while ensuring that it would not harm the interests of the country's established business community.

The government's endorsement of the EU-accession process and promises of deepening the country's democratization efforts won the support of self-designated liberal intellectuals. Thus, the AKP cemented "an odd coalition including Islamists and liberal democrats"[21] in its early years. However, the AKP government also faced stiff opposition from the secular-nationalist bureaucracy, which included the military high command and high courts. It was in this context that the alliance between the moderate Islamists and liberal intellectuals proved valuable to the party. Liberals, domestic and foreign, defended the government's bid to join the EU, especially its rapid incorporation of accession-oriented legislation.[22] Popular support for the government and its bold stance against the military/judicial establishment were perceived to have created a window of opportunity for liberalizing change. When things came to a head between the bureaucratic-military "old guard" and the government in April 2007, especially after the commander-in-chief of the armed forces sent a memorandum to threaten the civilian order before the presidential election in the parliament,[23] liberals overwhelmingly supported the government. The increasingly illiberal discourse of the secular nationalists leading the main opposition Republican People's Party (Cumhuriyet Halk Partisi, CHP) only served to consolidate the pro-government liberal reform coalition.[24]

Furthermore, the AKP leadership voiced interest in resolving the Kurdish issue through cultural recognition. The "Kurdish openings" in 2004 and 2009 reflected the government's position that promotion of the Kurdish language and culture as part of a broader project of eschewing the secular nation state's assimilationist policies would bring peace and stability to the Kurdish region. In fact, it was claimed by pro-government sectors that replacing secularist nationalism with a multicultural model of citizenship that endorses the majority's Sunni Muslim character without denying the minorities their fundamental rights would overcome the long-standing divide between the citizens and the state in Turkey.[25] In a way, a mixture of ideational, administrative, and strategic logics was at play during the AKP's much-hailed liberal phase.

However, the AKP government's apparent reformist phase was not devoid of setbacks. Broadcasting in Kurdish began in 2004, but it was only limited to several hours on the state-run television channel. While the state established a channel dedicated to the Kurdish language in 2009, restrictions on private broadcasting have limited the impact of this initiative. Meanwhile, many elected officials were removed from their posts and prosecuted for using Kurdish at official functions in 2007.[26]

The failure of cultural recognition was not an isolated rights-related concern in the period 2006–7. Human rights reports were expressing alarm at increasing violence against all kinds of protesters in Turkey as early as 2006. Although less frequent than the post-2011 period, government officials were using inflammatory language against ethnic and religious minorities. In a high-profile case, continuous verbal harassment and lawsuits against intellectuals who characterized the mass killing of Armenians as genocide resulted in the assassination of journalist Hrant Dink on 19 January 2007. Dink was under prosecution for "insulting Turkishness" at the time of his death. Evidence suggests that local police and gendarme chiefs knew about the murder plot. Many of those officials, including the police chief of Istanbul where the crime took place, have received promotions since then.[27]

Turkey–EU relations have been rocky even in the best of times. Mutual gestures of friendship around 2004, when the EU finally began to open accession negotiations, came to an end around 2006–7. The cooling of relations owed in part to Turkey's failure to legislate and implement accession-oriented norms. The EU Commission's 2006 Progress Report contains a powerful critique of Turkey's failure to live up to standards on democratic governance and human rights.[28] However, the slow pace of reform is not the only reason for the setback. The election of Angela Merkel in 2005 and Nicolas Sarkozy in 2007 to chief executive positions in Germany and France, respectively, turned the tide against Turkey's membership. Discourses around Turkey's failed democratization were complemented by culturally-essentialist notions of European identity, which led Turkey's citizens and governing elites to believe that EU accession was a lost cause.[29] Thus, the enthusiasm for accession reforms died down.[30]

The AKP's gradual abandonment of liberal reform (2007–11)

2007 was a consequential year in the government's struggle with unelected bureaucracies and for its future direction. First, the tension between the military/judicial establishment and the AKP government reached a climax when the Turkish Constitutional Court (CCT) invalidated the parliament's election of Abdullah Gül as president on procedural grounds. The stalemate was resolved when the voters gave the party a clear mandate in the July 2007 general election. With 47 per cent of the vote, and more than 60 per cent of the seats in Parliament, the AKP government set out to further weaken the hold of military/judicial tutelage on Turkish politics. The new parliament elected Gül as president, but the conflict between the AKP and the high courts did not end there and the party narrowly escaped a ban by the CCT in 2008. The ruling declared the party to be a focus of anti-secular activities but fell short of a party ban, as the pro-ban judges failed to secure the necessary qualified majority.[31]

Once that ordeal was over, the government and sympathetic prosecutors started a counter-offensive. A series of prosecutions was initiated as part of an ambitious campaign to prosecute the civilians and military officers who were allegedly plotting to overthrow the government. It is worth mentioning that the Gülen movement, then the government's ally, played a key role in carrying these processes forward. In the eyes of government supporters, the *Ergenekon* (named after a legendary valley in Turkic mythology) and *Balyoz* (Sledge-hammer) trials signalled the end of military tutelage, as scores of retired and active-duty military officers faced trial before civilian courts. The coup trials constituted an important challenge for the cohesion of the liberal-conservative coalition. Although many liberals believed in the overall culpability of the coup plotters, the irregularities in the hearings and in the evidence-gathering processes could have led to disagreements among those sensitive to human rights norms. The long arrest periods, inconsistencies in the evidence collected by the state prosecutors and the selectivity with which alleged coup plotters were brought to court raised doubts around the courts' respect for the rule of law in a process that was supposed to introduce the country to "genuine" rule of law.[32] Nonetheless, the coalition survived, as most members of the domestic liberal intelligentsia supported the prosecutions in the utilitarian hope that some past perpetrators would be punished, even if fair trial standards were violated along the way.

The next standoff concerned a set of constitutional amendments that proposed a number of rights-related improvements, including individual applications before the CCT, aimed at breaking the hold of high-court judges on judicial administration.[33] The proposed selection mechanism would increase the number of high-court judges and judicial administrators, open some seats on the Supreme Board of Judges and Prosecutors to intra-judicial elections and include more members coming from outside of the legal profession on the bench of the Constitutional Court. While the government and its liberal allies defended the amendments as the boldest step in the country's march towards "advanced democracy", others saw in the amendments a thinly-veiled effort to pack courts with pro-government judges and prosecutors. The Kurdish political movement, pointing at the absence of proposals to improve the civil and cultural rights of Kurds, decided to boycott the referendum organized to ratify the amendments.[34] The amendments were approved with 58 per cent of the popular vote on 12 September 2010.

However, the AKP's ongoing electoral success and its astonishing capacity to eliminate rivals, which many liberals hailed as the harbinger of liberal-democratic consolidation, ironically signalled the end of liberal reform. The government needed liberal support when it was insecure about voters' perception of the party, and when attacks from the military and the judiciary required a broad-based coalition held together by liberal-democratic rhetoric.

Once the voters acknowledged the AKP as the only viable centre-right party in the 2007 general election, the electoral gains from liberal posturing vanished. Furthermore, the elimination of the judicial and military threats after 2010 made it unnecessary to maintain an alliance with domestic and international observers who had been defending the government against undemocratic attacks. Paradoxically, political liberalism could be an inspiration for government rhetoric and practice only when the enemies of political liberalism were powerful.

The post-referendum period validated the fears of the AKP's opponents. The intra-judicial election to select ten new members for the Supreme Board of Judges and Prosecutors resulted in the victory of pro-government candidates, while liberal judges who had supported the government during the referendum process were entirely sidelined. Since then, various AKP leaders have admitted that the reconfiguration of the judiciary was meant to enable the then-allied Gülen movement to dominate high courts and judicial administration.[35] The AKP government, like the others before it, has consistently chosen to take undemocratic bureaucratic institutions under its control rather than abolish them. The military coup in 1980 had produced largely unaccountable institutions, like the Supreme Board of Judges and Prosecutors and the Board of Higher Education, which were tasked with disciplining the judiciary and the universities, respectively. The undemocratic and hierarchical nature of these institutions has been widely criticized across the political spectrum, including by AKP leaders and ideologues. However, rather than abolish them or reform them in any meaningful way, the AKP's strategy in dealing with these institutions has been to staff them with sympathizers. What distinguishes the AKP from earlier political movements is that its long-term electoral success has enabled it to consolidate its grip on bureaucratic administration by appointing pro-government persons to institutions of higher education, the judicial system, and supervisory bodies for extended periods of time.

Likewise, the coup plot trials were marked by serious due-process violations and, in at least one case, the forging of key evidence.[36] As a result of these violations, what might have been hailed as a bold attempt at punishing the enemies of civilian government appeared more like a witch-hunt. What is more, the prosecution was associated with pro-Gülen prosecutors and police chiefs to such an extent that after the fallout between the government and the Gülen movement in late 2013, the AKP leadership withdrew its support from the prosecutions completely.

The end of the liberal reform alliance (2011–13)

The setbacks in terms of democracy and human rights between 2007 and 2011 were alarming, but the dominant academic and journalistic narratives of the time portrayed this period as a tug-of-war between the military/

judicial establishment and the government's allies.[37] Therefore, the government's authoritarian tendencies received scant attention, and even when they did domestic and international observers characterized these problems as a holdover from military/judicial tutelage. The decline became more apparent after 2011 in part because the AKP government became increasingly aggressive and lawless in its quest to eliminate perceived enemies, and in part because liberals became active dissidents after the liberal-conservative coalition split between 2011 and 2013.

The ouster of the liberals from the governing coalition was a slow process, partly because the AKP government still relied on the coexistence of liberal rhetoric with increasingly more authoritarian forms of governance. After securing 49.8 per cent of the national vote in the 2011 general election, then Prime Minister Erdoğan vowed to embrace the entire nation regardless of their ethnic and religious background, and endorsed the drafting of a new constitution that would eliminate the authoritarian provisions of the 1982 document. Yet the post-election period saw the unabated imprisonment of journalists on charges of terrorism and coup plotting, as well as ongoing police brutality against all kinds of demonstrators. When military jets killed 35 unarmed Kurdish civilians (presumably mistaking them for PKK rebels) in December 2011 in the border town of Uludere/Roboski, the government did nothing to establish the facts and punish those responsible. In addition, the EU reform process, which had already slowed down considerably after 2006, came to a complete halt. Meanwhile, debates around the new constitution centred on promoting presidentialism (or in precise terms, promoting Erdoğan's future presidency), moving further away from the pursuit of a democracy-and-human-rights agenda through constitutionalism.

As constitutional reform, EU accession, and the overall strengthening of rights protections ended in bitter disappointment, the peaceful resolution of the Kurdish issue remained the only issue area in which liberals could hope to collaborate with the government. The announcement of peace talks between the government and the PKK rebels in late 2012 presented the last opportunity for such cooperation. The government appointed 63 individuals as "wise people" (akil insanlar) from among liberal and Islamist intellectuals and celebrities, tasked with explaining the importance of the peace process before public audiences, identifying sources of discontent with the peace talks, and drafting a final report with recommendations. The setup of this ad hoc panel reflected the power disparity between the government and the country's intelligentsia. The recommendations of the wise people were not binding on the government; in fact, there was no guarantee that the government would even receive those recommendations formally. In the end, there is no indication that the government made use of the panel's recommendations. The entire exercise seemed to serve merely as a publicity stunt.

What ended liberal collaboration with the government altogether was the police response to the Gezi protests. The peaceful demonstrations that started after the government decided to demolish one of the remaining green spaces in downtown Istanbul ended with 11 dead, hundreds arrested and thousands injured. If the liberal-conservative coalition was limited to the peace process before the protests, it came to a total end afterwards. Notable exceptions notwithstanding, self-designated liberals have distanced themselves from the government,[38] and some of them have faced repercussions in terms of dismissals from jobs in the private media sector and criminal arrests.

Turkey's transformation into a competitive authoritarian regime (2013–present)

Since 2013, liberal democracy in Turkey has been in free-fall.[39] After the August 2014 presidential election, from which Erdoğan emerged victorious, he has made a concerted effort to transform the regime into a presidential system.[40] In the absence of a constitutional mandate or a qualified parliamentary majority to pass a constitutional amendment, Erdoğan and his close circle have declared *de facto* presidentialism. His wish to rule over the cabinet and the prime minister, verbal attacks on government officials and independent bureaucrats (like the governor of the Central Bank) who disagree with him and open endorsement of the "unification of powers" as opposed to their separation, have created a lawless situation in which the constitutional system of checks and balances no longer operates.

The confusion arising from institutional paralysis has been one of the contributing factors, if not the main cause, of the end of the peace process with the PKK. Erdoğan turned down a preliminary deal reached between government representatives and the leadership of the Peoples' Democratic Party (*Halkların Demokrasi Partisi*, HDP) in March 2015, possibly because the agreement did not include any provisions to support his presidency. The government did not make any further attempts to revive the peace process after Erdoğan's clear rejection. As the HDP, a party born out of the Kurdish political movement, crossed the national election threshold of 10 per cent and effectively denied the AKP a parliamentary majority in the June 2015 election, Erdoğan and the AKP leadership began to threaten the Kurdish political movement with war. A month later, violence between the Turkish security personnel and the PKK restarted and quickly escalated to a level of destruction not seen since the early 1990s. The increasing number of civilian deaths, the destruction of entire neighbourhoods, and the *de facto* suspension of basic constitutional rights signal a serious human rights crisis.

While the relative popularity of Erdoğan and the AKP cannot be denied, elections are far from free and fair. The consecutive general elections of June 2015 and November 2015 took place under conditions of outright violence against the HDP, whose success would have meant a declining share of parliamentary seats for the AKP. HDP activists suffered more than one hundred violent attacks by lynch mobs, including an arson attack that burned down the party's headquarters on 10 September 2016. Between June and October 2015, suicide bombers with alleged connections to ISIS attacked three HDP rallies and pro-peace events, killing 4 in Diyarbakır, 33 in the border town of Suruç, and 109 in Ankara.

Outright violence against the opposition has been accompanied by restrictions on the free media. News reporting on public television channels gives nearly exclusive coverage in favour of Erdoğan and the AKP while private media, either owned by pro-government businesspeople or intimidated into acquiescence, shy away from defying government propaganda or appearing to support the opposition. Mobs led by an AKP member of the parliament attacked the mainstream *Hürriyet* newspaper in September 2015. *Hürriyet* columnist Ahmet Hakan was punched in front of his house a month later. Two journalists from the daily *Cumhuriyet* who covered the government's alleged connections to ISIS supply routes are facing jail; one of the journalists, Can Dündar, survived an assassination attack in front of the courthouse in May 2016.

Ironically, the erosion of democracy under the AKP government has taken its toll on the party as well. Leading members, including Abdullah Gül, a former president of the republic, and founding member Bülent Arınç, were replaced by Erdoğan loyalists. The exclusion of the old-timers did not bring much peace inside the party, however. Ahmet Davutoğlu, who became party chairman and prime minister in an uncompetitive party congress in August 2014, had to resign his post in May 2016 when Erdoğan no longer wanted to work with him. As of the time of writing, there is no clear indication that the AKP can withstand pressures from Erdoğan's circle to serve its function as a governing party with autonomous intra-party norms and institutions. It seems that the transformation of politics into a wholesale power grab with no regard for institutional checks and balances devours the regime's allies at an increasing speed.

Explaining the authoritarian shift

What explains the increasingly authoritarian policies of a government praised for liberalization reforms? The motivations of key actors in the governing coalition and their responses to changing opportunity structures explain the liberal and illiberal shifts. The AKP government was a coalition of self-designated liberals, who were negligible in numbers but a powerful presence in the media and academia, and conservatives (who identify themselves alternatively as conservative democrats, moderate Islamists or nationalist conservatives). Their ideational and strategic interests converged because they faced a common enemy: the military and judicial institutions that justified their infringements upon democratic politics with the defence of the secular republic and assimilationist Turkish nationalism. Liberal-democratic rhetoric provided the AKP government with domestic legitimacy and international support at a time when it faced uncertainty about the reception of its claim to be Turkey's centre-right party. In turn, the AKP government provided its supporters, liberal and conservative alike, with access to political power.

Two trends have changed the political opportunity structure in recent years. First, the mutual fallout between the policy elites of the EU and Turkey since 2006–7 has eliminated external pressure for reform. Second, the elimination of illiberal rivals (the establishment that controlled the military and judicial institutions) was nearly complete as of 2010, which reduced the incentive to push for further liberalization. Once the government stopped needing international validation nor faced a domestic threat, liberal reform became largely unnecessary, except to win over the part of the Kurdish vote that was not fully committed to the Kurdish political movement. Minority-appeasing measures were increasingly abandoned in favour of conservative and nationalist rhetoric, while the self-designated liberals were excluded from the governing coalition. Especially since the 2011 general election, in which the AKP leaders received a clear signal that they could secure a parliamentary majority without emphasizing liberal-democratic or centrist credentials, the governing coalition has been appealing to a mixture of religious conservatism, Turkish nationalism and varying levels of endorsement for Kurdish identity claims, ranging from limited recognition between 2011 and 2015 to denial since then.

Conclusion

The main premise of this chapter is that ideational and strategic factors can serve to foster both liberal-democratic reform and authoritarian tendencies. In the case of Turkey, the AKP has managed to entrench itself as the only nationwide party capable of attracting voters across class, ethnic, and geographic lines. Part of the party's success is due to its capacity for using liberal-democratic rhetoric and introducing piecemeal liberal reform, but the AKP's leaders have also realized the limits of liberalism as an all-encompassing ideology. A big part of the party's voter base are conservative Sunni-Muslim Turks. While this constituency may agree with certain aspects of the liberal reform agenda, there is no reason to suggest that they would support reform, especially when such reform is perceived to benefit ethnic and religious minorities. Indeed, the party's vote share has not suffered significantly because of its recent authoritarian turn, except among its Kurdish constituencies in the June 2015 election. Encouraged by this fact, the AKP leadership has increasingly portrayed democracy not as a system of checks and balances, but rather as a majoritarian process in which the winner takes all.

In strategic terms, the AKP leadership had good reasons to push for democracy and human rights at a time when EU accession was popular with voters, the party was not secure about whether the voters perceived it as a centrist movement and it faced an existential threat from the high courts and the military – two institutions known to have interfered with civilian, democratic politics before. As the EU prospects dwindled and the AKP established itself firmly as the country's ruling party, the need to appeal to domestic and international audiences as a reformist party vanished – the party's interest in attracting the Kurdish voters can be considered a partial exception to that. Ironically, the elimination of illiberal rivals made it unnecessary for the AKP to seek alliances with liberal intellectuals. Thus, the party gradually abandoned its reform agenda between 2007 and 2011, and has turned authoritarian at an increasing pace since then.

The stylized political history of Turkey presented in this chapter hopes to contribute to debates on authoritarian politics. The authoritarian turn is not simply a consequence of Erdoğan's power grab, even if his recent push for presidentialism has thrown this ambition into sharp relief. Many of the institutional setbacks and rights violations took place before Erdoğan and his close circle had accumulated their present level of political power, and many individuals and groups who later protested this power grab were responsible for the authoritarian turn. Furthermore, the simultaneous liberal and illiberal shifts described in this chapter rule out cultural essentialism. Neither the fact that the population is predominantly Muslim nor the AKP's roots in political Islam explain the recent transformations, given the abundance of within-case variation as well as the large number of non-Muslim countries undergoing similar authoritarian transformations around the world.

Yet, the rejection of cultural essentialism does not mean that religious identity is irrelevant to the construction of conservative majoritarianism. The appeal to majoritarian identity claims has led Erdoğan and other AKP leaders to imagine and propogate a vision of Turkey in which devout Sunni Muslim identity is the primary form of belonging, and in which ethnic minorities (especially Kurds) are expected to integrate into the societal mainstream through this primary identity. While secularist Turkish national-ism is rejected, reimagining Turkish identity as the perfect synthesis of Islam and Turkishness has become the official identity project under the AKP government. This particular construction of conservative nationalism, rather than religion or religiosity *per se*, is partly responsible for the erosion of safeguards for political, ethnic and religious minorities.

Several theoretical implications follow from Turkey's recent political history. First, governments, even single-party ones, are coalitions in which a variety of ideational and strategic preferences and capabilities coexist. Self-designated liberals have at times managed to insert themselves as key policy players thanks to their influence in the media and academia in Turkey, even in the absence of broad electoral support. Yet, their political activism comes at a cost: political liberalism inspires policy only under a limited set of conditions. Second, governing coalitions are not democratic or undemocratic, liberal or illiberal, by default; political dynamics inside and around those coalitions shape their strategic choices. Third, political movements (in Turkey and elsewhere) often implement liberal reform and illiberal policies *simultaneously*. What appears to be a contradiction makes sense if one considers the complexity of motivations and interactions across political actors in a fast-changing political context.

What does the future hold for Turkey and other competitive authoritarian regimes? As the findings in this chapter suggest, the liberal reform coalition in Turkey made limited contributions at the best of times; therefore, expecting a major reform movement from individuals and groups previously associated with the AKP (sometimes referred to as "returning to the spirit of 2002") is unrealistic. It is safe to expect further division inside the current governing coalition, as institutional paralysis has made the country ungovernable and as the spoils of power are shared between an ever-shrinking clique of Erdoğan loyalists. This is likely to provide the opposition with the necessary but not sufficient conditions to become competitive against the AKP. Finally, given the divided nature of opposition parties and civil society groups, bringing together self-designated social democrats, liberals, and the Kurdish political movement to build a pro-democracy opposition bloc is a daunting task; yet such an effort is necessary to establish a pluralistic and democratic political system in Turkey.

Postscript

The coup attempt on 15 July 2016 shook the country. Although the poorly-organized putsch, which was not backed by the majority in the military institution, was defeated within 24 hours, it left behind at least 240 dead. From a normative standpoint, the putsch enjoys no electoral or procedural legitimacy, of course, and the near-total absence of civilian or military support for it shows that the public in Turkey is not convinced that a military takeover can resolve the country's political problems. Yet, the short-lived "festival of democracy" in the wake of the coup attempt cannot hide the fact that the political regime was competitively authoritarian before the coup attempt and remains competitively authoritarian afterwards.[41]

Responsibility for the coup attempt is widely attributed to a small clique of Gülenist officers in the armed forces – Gülen's personal knowledge of the incident is still a matter of contention. The fact that the government's erstwhile allies, once praised by government spokespersons and some liberal intellectuals for their success in ending military tutelage and breaking the Kemalist stronghold in the judiciary, could use conspiratorial and deeply illiberal methods to contest political power confirms this chapter's contention that even the heyday of liberal reformism in Turkey presented limited progress, as the broader governing coalition had little normative commitment to political liberalism, and liberal shifts would often be countered by equally illiberal ones under changing political contexts.

The government's response to the coup attempt only serves to accentuate the increasingly authoritarian character of the regime. The government declared a three-month-long state of emergency on 20 July 2016. In an effort to dismantle all Gülenist networks in the military, judiciary, economy, education sector, and civil society, the government has initiated a widespread purge of military officers, legal professionals, and tens of thousands of public sector employees (many employed in professions with no direct connection to the putsch, like school teachers), denying those suspended or dismissed the right to appeal.[42] Numerous businesses, ranging from high schools to dessert shops, were raided for suspected connections to the Gülen community and some of them were given over to a state fiduciary authority. Furthermore, the government has used the state of emergency and the overall climate of uncertainty to dismiss, arrest and disenfranchise dissidents with no ties to the coup group or the Gülen community. In addition to the more than 28,000 teachers suspended for Gülenist ties, a decree announced under the state of emergency conditions suspended over 11,000 schools, presumably for being PKK members or sympathizers. So-called "intelligence reports" were found to be sufficient evidence for suspension. Of the 2,346 academics dismissed from their university jobs by decree, 41 are known to hold positions sympathetic to the continuation of the peace process and have no connection to the Gülen community. A record number of newspapers, radio stations and TV channels were closed between July and September 2016, among them several leftist, pro-Kurdish and feminist publications, as well as Kurdish-language ones (including *Zarok TV*, a children's channel). Twenty-eight municipalities, 24 of which were governed by HDP mayors, were given over to unelected fiduciary authorities. In sum, the government's effort to eliminate the Gülenist network at all costs, and further weaken opposition groups with non- or even anti-Gülenist stances, has aggravated the situation of human rights in Turkey.

It is by now clear that deepening democratic institutions and strengthening the rule of law to deter future threats against democracy is not the lesson the government has drawn from the coup attempt. The developments after 15 July show that the downward trend in rights protection and institutional safeguards described in this chapter is likely to continue in the near future.

Notes

1. See "Turkey in Turmoil," *The New York Times* (19 June 2013), http://www.nytimes.com/2013/06/20/opinion/turkey-in-turmoil.html, accessed 1 November 2016;

Ian Traynor and Constanze Letsch, "Turkey at a Crossroads as Erdoğan Bulldozes his Way to Lasting Legacy," *Guardian* (2 June 2015), https://www.theguardian.com/world/2015/jun/02/turkish-election-recep-tayyip-erdogan-legacy, accessed 1 November 2016; "Democracy's Disintegration in Turkey," *The New York Times* (7 March 2016), http://www.nytimes.com/2016/03/08/opinion/democracys-disintegration-in-turkey.html, accessed 1 November 2016.

2. The Gülen movement has been portrayed as a religious community, social movement, business network, and political movement by different observers. Led by cleric Fethullah Gülen, the movement is best known for opening Turkish-language charter schools outside of Turkey, and running private tutoring schools to prepare high-school students for the university entrance exam in Turkey. The Gülenists are known to have supported centrist political parties in the past. Their close cooperation with the AKP government enabled the movement to staff the police and judicial institutions with sympathizers in the 2000s. They are held responsible for many of the due-process violations and intelligence leaks associated with judicial and state-security institutions between 2007 and 2013. Disagreements over the status of the tutoring schools are presented as the apparent reason for the fallout between the Gülen movement and the AKP government in late 2013, but it is likely that political and economic rivalry within the governing coalition had deeper roots. Since the fallout, the government and its allies in the judiciary have embarked on an ambitious campaign to eliminate Gülen sympathizers, while online sources suspected of ties with the Gülen movement have publicized numerous recordings of corruption implicating high-ranking AKP leaders, including Erdoğan and his family. For an account of the conflict, see Ruşen Çakır, "Erdoğan-Gülen ilişkisinin dünü, bugünü, yarını", *Vatan* (17–21 February 2012).

3. Keeping in mind the variety of ways in which the word "liberal" is interpreted in Turkey and elsewhere, a caveat is in order: throughout the chapter the words "liberal" and "liberal democratic" are used to refer to the fundamental tenets of political liberalism, understood as limited and constitutional government in which basic rights and liberties are safeguarded.

4. Most accounts argue that this military/judicial establishment was held together by a shared ideology of secularism and Turkish nationalism, namely "Kemalism". While the designation Kemalist lacks definitional precision, I use it interchangeably with secular nationalist throughout this chapter to identify groups that designate themselves as *Kemalist* or *Atatürkçü*.

5. Thomas Carothers, "The End of the Transition Paradigm", *Journal of Democracy*, 13/1 (2002), pp. 5–21; Andreas Schedler (ed.), *Electoral Authoritarianism: The Dynamics of Unfree Competition* (Boulder, CO: Lynne Rienner, 2009); David Collier and Steven Levitsky, "Democracy with Adjectives: Conceptual Innovation in Comparative Research", *World Politics* 49 (April 1997), pp. 430–51.

6. Steven Levitsky, and Lucan A. Way, "Elections without Democracy: The Rise of Competitive Authoritarianism," *Journal of Democracy*, 13/2 (2002), pp. 51–65.

7. Fareed Zakaria, "The Rise of Illiberal Democracy", *Foreign Affairs* 76 (1997), pp. 22–43.

8. Dawn Brancati, "Democratic Authoritarianism: Origins and Effects," *Annual Review of Political Science*, 17 (2014), pp. 313–26. For another account of

maintaining liberal democracy under authoritarian conditions, see: Marina Ottaway, *Democracy Challenged: The Rise of Semi-Authoritarianism* (Washington, DC: Carnegie Endowment for International Peace, 2003).

9. Brancati, Ibid.

10. For an account of how ideas and personal experiences matter in autocrats' choice for liberal reform, see: Calvert W. Jones, "Seeing Like an Autocrat: Liberal Social Engineering in an Illiberal State," *Perspectives on Politics*, 13/1 (2015), pp. 24–41.

11. In fact, the equation of liberal democracy with good governance has been accepted as an article of faith, especially since the collapse of the Soviet bloc. For a critical take on this assumption see: Mick Moore, "The Governance Agenda in Long Term Perspective: Globalization, Revenues and the Differentiation of States," *IDS Working Papers 378* (Brighton: Institute of Development Studies, 2011).

12. For a good summary of the debates on whether liberal democracy performs better than authoritarian regimes in terms of promoting economic development, see: Pranab Bardhan, "Democracy and Development: A Complex Relationship", in Ian Shapiro (ed.), *Rethinking Democracy for a New Century* (Cambridge University Press, 1997).

13. World Bank, "Rule of Law and Development," http://go.worldbank.org/ 9OTC3P5070, accessed 13 April 2016.

14. Needless to say, the West has not been unambiguously and unanimously supportive of democratic regimes in the developing world. Overt and covert U.S. operations against democratically elected governments in Iran, Guatemala, and Chile during the Cold War are examples of the illiberal and anti-democratic influences of international actors. Therefore, I consider foreign governments and organizations as another set of actors who may support liberal or illiberal policies at different times because of ideational and strategic factors.

15. The importance of domestic and international pressure for democratization reform is emphasized in the literature. Nuanced analyses find these pressures to work better in certain structural and institutional contexts. See: Daniela Donno, "Elections and Democratization in Authoritarian Regimes", *American Journal of Political Science*, 57/3 (2013), pp. 703–16.

16. "Electoral Process", "Political Pluralism and Participation", and "Functioning of Government" are subcategories of political rights; "Freedom of Expression and Belief", "Associational and Organizational Rights", "Rule of Law", and "Personal Autonomy and Individual Rights" are subcategories of civil liberties. A country can score between 0 and 4 points for each subcategory question, and each subcategory has between 3 and 4 questions. For a detailed explanation of the methodology used in "Freedom of the Press", see: http://www.freedomhouse. org/report/freedom-press-2013/methodology.

17. "Political rights enable people to participate freely in the political process, including the right to vote freely for distinct alternatives in legitimate elections, compete for public office, join political parties and organizations, and elect representatives who have a decisive impact on public policies and are accountable to the electorate." See: https://freedomhouse.org/report/freedom-world-2012/methodology.

18. "Civil liberties allow for the freedoms of expression and belief, associational and organizational rights, rule of law, and personal autonomy without interference

from the state." See: https://freedomhouse.org/report/freedom-world-2012/methodology.

19. The collapse of the traditional parties of the centre-right and centre-left, accompanied by the peculiarities of the electoral system, created a situation in which the AKP took control of roughly 65 per cent of the parliament with its 34 per cent vote share, and its chief rival CHP captured the rest of the seats with its 19 per cent vote share.

20. Philip Gordon and Ömer Taşpınar, "Turkey on the Brink", *The Washington Quarterly* 29/3 (2006), pp. 57–70, at p. 61.

21. Murat Somer, "Does it take democrats to democratize? Lessons from Islamic and secular elite values in Turkey," *Comparative Political Studies*, 44/5 (2011), pp. 511–45, at p. 514.

22. Political scientist Ziya Öniş refers to AKP as a "conservative-globalist" political movement that holds a favourable attitude towards engagement with global markets, democratization reforms, and progress towards EU membership, while at the same time promoting "defense of traditional values and appeals to the conservative instincts of large segments of voters, cutting across traditional class divisions in the process." Ziya Öniş, "Conservative Globalism at the Crossroads: The Justice and Development Party and the Thorny Path to Democratic Consolidation in Turkey", *Mediterranean Politics*, 14/1 (2009), pp. 21–40, at p. 22.

23. "Excerpts of Turkish Army Statement," BBC News, 28 April 2007.

24. The CHP tended to support the military's secularist posturing uncritically, and rejected a politically negotiated solution to the Kurdish conflict between 1994 and 2010. Since then, it has held considerably more open-minded positions under new leadership.

25. Şener Aktürk, *Regimes of Ethnicity and Nationhood in Germany, Russia, and Turkey* (Cambridge University Press, 2012).

26. Nicole F. Watts, *Activists in Office: Kurdish Politics and Protest in Turkey* (Seattle: University of Washington Press, 2010), pp. 116–17.

27. Yavuz Baydar, "Family of Slain Armenian-Turkish Journalist Boycotts Retrial", *Al-Monitor* (20 September 2013), http://www.al-monitor.com/pulse/originals/2013/09/family-slain-journalist-boycotts-trial.html, accessed 1 November 2016.

28. EU Commission, *Turkey 2006 Progress Report*. Brussels: EU Commission, 2006. Available at: http://ec.europa.eu/enlargement/pdf/key_documents/2006/nov/tr_sec_1390_en.pdf.

29. See: Hakan Yılmaz, "Turkish identity on the road to the EU: basic elements of French and German oppositional discourses," *Journal of Southern Europe and the Balkans Online*, 9/3 (2007), pp. 293–305.

30. Paul Kubicek, "Political Conditionality and European Union's Cultivation of Democracy in Turkey," *Democratization*, 18/4 (2011), pp. 910–31; Murat Somer, "Why aren't Kurds like the Scots and the Turks like the Brits? Moderation and Democracy in the Kurdish Question," *Cooperation and Conflict*, 43/2 (2008), pp. 220–49.

31. Robert Tait, "Turkey's Governing Party Avoids Being Shut down for Anti-Secularism," *Guardian* (30 July 2008), https://www.theguardian.com/world/2008/jul/30/turkey.nato1, accessed 1 November 2016.

32. For a critical account of the Balyoz trial at the verdict phase, see: Simon Tisdall, "Turkey's Sledgehammer Coup Verdict: Justice or Soviet-style Show Trial?"

Guardian (25 September 2012), https://www.theguardian.com/world/2012/sep/25/turkey-sledgehammer-coup-trial-verdict, accessed 1 November 2016.

33. For an overview of the changes, see: "What will the constitutional changes mean for Turkey?", *Hürriyet Daily News* (12 September 2010), http://www.hurriyetdailynews.com/default.aspx?pageid=438&n=what-the-changes-bring-2010-09-12, accessed 1 November 2016.

34. For a brief description of the positions on the referendum, see: "Erdoğan Pulls it off," *The Economist*, 13 September 2010.

35. See, for example: "Darbenin temeli 2010'da atıldı," *Sabah*, 15 March 2015; "Savcıya göre Gülen cemaati, Erdoğan'ın 'Ne istedilerse verdik' dediği dönemden sonra 'silahlı örgüt' oldu," *T24*, 22 December 2014.

36. Ceylan Yeginsu, "Turkish Officers Convicted in 2012 Coup Case Are Released," *The New York Times*, 19 June 2014.

37. Aslı U. Bâli, "The Perils of Judicial Independence: Constitutional Transition and the Turkish Example," *Vanderbilt Journal of International Law*, 52.2 (2012), pp. 235–320; Ergun Özbudun, "Turkey's Search for a New Constitution," *Insight Turkey*, 14.1 (2012), pp. 39–50; Şahin Alpay, "Making Sense of Turkish Politics." *International Spectator: Italian Journal of International Affairs*, 43.3 (2008), pp. 5–12.

38. "Two 'wise men' refuse to attend meeting with Turkish PM over Gezi unrest," *Hurriyet Daily News*, 25 June 2013.

39. Berk Esen, and Şebnem Gümüşçü, "Rising Competitive Authoritarianism in Turkey," *Third World Quarterly* (2016), pp. 1–26.

40. Under the current constitution, the president has real power in terms of vetoing laws and appointing judges and bureaucrats to high courts and administrative positions, but aside from these prerogatives, the presidency had remained a largely symbolic office in Turkey. In addition, the president had been elected by the parliament until the first popular presidential elections of 2014. The direct election procedure and Erdoğan's personal ambition have led to the current paralysis of the parliamentary system.

41. Coup threats are not directed against democracies only; many authoritarian and semi-authoritarian regimes have also suffered coups and coup attempts. See: Jonathan M. Powell and Clayton L. Thyne, 'Global Instances of Coups from 1950 to 2010: A New Dataset,' *Journal of Peace Research*, 48.2 (2011), pp. 249–59.

42. Prime Minister Binali Yıldırım declared the total number of persons suspended from their jobs at 76, 597, and those dismissed at 4,897 four weeks after the coup attempt. "Darbe soruşturması kapsamında toplam 76 bin 597 kişi açığa alındı, 4 bin 897 kişi memuriyetten çıkarıldı," *T24*, 13 August 2016.

CHAPTER 3

ELECTORAL INTEGRITY IN TURKEY: FROM TUTELARY DEMOCRACY TO COMPETITIVE AUTHORITARIANISM

Karabekir Akkoyunlu

Introduction

Turkey's democracy has always been imperfect. But since 1950 elections have been, for the most part, free and fair. The system of military tutelage that was institutionalized after the 1960 coup was primarily designed to limit the impact of elections and the influence of elected governments, rather than manipulating the electoral process or predetermining outcomes. The 10 per cent threshold introduced after the 1980 coup was one of the few direct tutelary interventions into the electoral system and it was intended to concentrate politics in the central mainstream. As the tutelary actors did not participate in elections, they did not risk being voted out.

Military tutelage came to an end during the 2000s but, despite initial hopes and expectations, this did not lead to democratic consolidation in Turkey. A failed attempt at democratization gave way to a competitive authoritarian regime under a personality-driven one-party rule. By 2011, the Justice and Development Party (*Adalet ve Kalkınma Partisi*, AKP) had established itself as the dominant party in Turkish politics. Its efforts to consolidate control over the state and transform Turkey's society intensified socio-political polarization and pushed the regime towards an illiberal path. But unlike the military guardians, the AKP's political hegemony still depended on continuous election victories.

The transformation from a tutelary democracy to a competitive authoritarian regime, via failed democratization, has had a transformative impact on Turkey's electoral institutions. This chapter surveys this transformation by examining the function and integrity of elections under Turkey's tutelary democracy, during its brief "liberal moment" in the 2000s and under the AKP's political hegemony in the 2010s. It also focuses on the repeat elections of 2015 to illustrate how a dominant party operating in an insecure political environment can respond when faced with an election loss.

Elections and Democracy Under Military Tutelage

Established as a parliamentary republic, Turkey officially became a multiparty democracy in 1946 and held its first competitive general election in 1950. That election brought to an end the 23-year single-party rule of the Republican People's Party (*Cumhuriyet Halk Partisi*, CHP). The victory of the Democrat Party (*Demokrat Parti*, DP) signalled a power shift within the young republic's ruling elite from statist military officers and bureaucrats that for over two decades had dominated the CHP, and therefore the country's socio-political life, towards a coalition of economically liberal and socially conservative landowners and entrepreneurs. The 1950 election set two important precedents. The first of these was the acceptance of defeat by the CHP and the smooth transition of power between two political parties, which created democratic path dependence. Ever since that first competitive vote, Turkey's citizens have regularly expressed their will at the ballot box, rewarding or punishing political parties in largely free and fair elections. Despite Turkey's various other democratic deficits, the public on the whole came to trust the voting process and both victors and losers respected the outcomes.

The second precedent was that the 1950 vote set the stage for successive election victories in 1954 and 1957 that would cement the DP's position as the dominant actor in Turkey's politics until it was toppled in a military coup in 1960. The DP became the first in a series of popular "centre-right" parties to achieve spectacular electoral success in Turkish politics in the decades to come. Following on the DP's political tradition and embracing its legacy, the Justice Party of Süleyman Demirel between 1965 and 1971, the Motherland Party (*Anavatan Partisi*, ANAP) of Turgut Özal between 1983 and 1991, and the AKP of Recep Tayyip Erdoğan after 2002 all succeeded in forming single-party governments carrying significant majorities. In contrast, the diverse actors on the "left" of the political divide failed to produce similar electoral outcomes. To date, no self-defined left party in Turkey has been able to form a single-party government on the basis of a simple parliamentary majority.[1]

As the economically liberal, socially conservative centre-right platform repeatedly proved to be the most fertile ground in Turkey's popular politics, parties and politicians occupying this space emerged as outspoken champions of the sanctity of the ballot box. In practice, however, the centre-right's emphasis on elections as the sole source of democratic legitimacy often revealed a majoritarian and procedural understanding of democracy. From the DP to the

AKP, popular parties of this platform have consistently pushed to strengthen the executive branch at the expense of the legislature and the judiciary (as well as non-democratic tutelary actors) and frequently justified non-deliberative approaches to policymaking by invoking the "national will" as manifested through elections.[2]

Belge notes that among the statist officers and bureaucrats who saw their fortunes decline under the DP government, there was a strong belief that the transition to multi-party politics was a mistake that would sabotage the modernizing project launched under the republic's charismatic founder, Kemal Atatürk, by giving power to the people prematurely.[3] The CHP's inability to stem the DP's rising popularity, the DP's gradual relaxation of the strict secular rules imposed previously by the CHP, and the government's increasingly heavy-handed intolerance of dissent, criticism and opposition particularly after the 1957 election reinforced these suspicions and led a group of left-leaning junior officers to stage the republic's first military coup on 27 May 1960.

The 1960 coup was the first in a series of interventions over the next four decades that steadily assembled a system of indirect military-bureaucratic tutelage over electoral politics. Unlike most of its politicized counterparts in Southern Europe, Latin America or Southeast Asia, the Turkish military proved reluctant to rule directly over long periods. While it eventually returned power to civilians after every intervention and allowed for competitive elections, it did so only after legal and institutional adjustments that deepened and expanded the remit of its self-appointed role as the guardian of the republic. Hence, even when it returned to barracks, the military retained significant – but never complete – influence over civilian politics. The resultant system was a hybrid regime; a tutelary democracy where real and meaningful popular contestation of power took place under the vigilant gaze of the guardians.[4]

Electoral Integrity in Tutelary Democracy

In the Turkish tutelary democracy, the guardians on the whole allowed the electoral process to take its own course, without manipulating the vote or tempering outcomes.[5] The military maintained no exclusive institutional link to any single political party (including the CHP, which was outlawed for over a decade after the 1980 coup) but rather sought to cultivate a 'cooperative' relationship with all elected governments. Needless to say, this was an unequal relationship that favoured the guardians over elected politicians. Even in those rare instances when senior generals openly expressed a preference for a party ahead of elections – such as junta leader Kenan Evren's support for the short-lived Nationalist Democracy Party, which was headed by a retired general, in the first competitive general election after the 1980 coup – they did not campaign or attempt to fabricate a victory on their behalf. On the contrary, military statements of party preference often backfired as the electorate routinely voted against the generals' wishes and brought to power those leaders and parties least favoured by the guardians. When faced with undesirable election results, the generals did not contest, annul, or attempt to overturn the outcomes.[6] Elections thus served as an effective popular counterbalance to the tutelage of the military-bureaucratic elite.

In any case, the guardians did not need to manipulate elections as they did not participate in them and run the risk of being voted out. In fact, they had an interest in the maintenance of electoral integrity. Reasonably free and fair elections constituted a central pillar of the Turkish hybrid system, serving a legitimizing function not only for elected governments but also the tutelary actors, which typically justified their interventions as unfortunate but necessary acts to preserve and "restore democracy", in the wake of abuses by self-serving, unpatriotic and inept politicians.[7] These justifications were not only meant for domestic consumption, but also addressed at Turkey's strategic allies in NATO, which supported the military's guardianship role during the Cold War as a bulwark against Soviet expansionism.[8]

The tutelary system was not designed to tamper with or predetermine the outcome of elections, but rather to limit their impact on politics and society by making sure that elected governments acted within the boundaries established by the guardians. The hybrid institutional structure separated the affairs of the state (*devlet*) from the affairs of government (*hükümet*). The latter indicated the realm of everyday socio-economic policy that could be entrusted to elected politicians and debated publicly. Matters pertaining to the country's national security, geopolitical orientation or core constitutional characteristics fell within state affairs, in which the tutelary actors had the first and the final word.[9]

The key institutional mechanisms through which the guardians maintained this hierarchy of power included the National Security Council (NSC), in which the military top brass could present governments with warnings and ultimatums disguised as "recommendations",[10] the presidency, which the 1982 Constitution equipped with veto powers over the legislature,[11] and the Constitutional Court, which had the power to dissolve political parties and ban or imprison politicians on grounds of acting against the constitution.[12] Additionally, in the post-Cold War neo-liberal environment of the 1990s, which rendered direct coups more costly in terms of macroeconomic stability and therefore less politically expedient, the military increasingly turned to nurturing close ties with private media and civil society organizations to manufacture public consent. Instead of a direct military takeover, the so-called 'post-modern coup' of February 1997 featured all of the mechanisms above to oust the Islamist-led coalition government of the time. An intense media and civil society campaign against the government was waged, followed by a presidential warning and an NSC ultimatum, and finally a decision by the Constitutional Court to ban the Islamist Welfare Party.

If the guardians were on the whole uninterested in intervening directly in the voting process, they did not shy away from re-engineering the election system after military interventions. Two examples stand out in particular. The first was the replacement of the winner-takes-all voting system used in the 1950s with the D'Hont method of proportional allocation of parliamentary seats after the 1960 coup.[13] While the former system awarded the first party (in this case the DP) with a considerably higher number of deputies compared to its overall share of the vote, the D'Hont method tended to favour coalitions over single-party governments.[14] The second was the introduction of a 10 per cent national threshold for a party to win seats in the parliament following the 1980 coup. The common justification for setting such a high bar was that it would stabilize parliamentary democracy by preventing party fragmentation. Proportional representation without a national threshold had allowed for a significant pluralization of party politics in the 1960s and the 1970s, enabling smaller parties to gain parliamentary representation and act as kingmakers in volatile coalition governments.

The threshold was intended to weed out "fringe" parties – namely socialist, far-right nationalist, Islamist, and, from the 1990s onwards, regional nationalist (i.e., ethnic Kurdish) parties that the guardians perceived as threats to the regime and sources of instability – and limit government to more "cooperative" mainstream parties. Although junta leader Evren's expressed desire to transform Turkish politics into a two-party system in the US mould did not come to be, with the party spectrum once again fragmenting and leading the way to coalition governments in the 1990s, the threshold has remained a mainstay of Turkish politics.[15]

The End of Military Tutelage and Failed Democratization

The tutelary system that was established gradually after 1960 came undone in the 2000s and the early 2010s. Initially this process took place in the framework of Turkey's accession process to the European Union and the political and economic harmonization packages it entailed. Starting in the late 1990s, there was consistently high public support in Turkey for EU membership, seen as an escape from the cycle of chronic economic crises, political instability and military coups. The "liberal democratization" project was supported by successive governments, the business community, and an increasingly vocal liberal intelligentsia at home, as well as both the EU and the US abroad. Coming to power in a snap election on the heels of a financial crisis that discredited all the major parties of the 1990s, the newly founded Justice and Development Party took on the mantle of change after November 2002.

This process ushered in a "liberal moment", wherein Turkey looked like an increasingly viable candidate for EU membership, with a fast-growing economy, vibrant civil society and a democratically-elected "moderately Islamist" government that seemed capable of steering a process of liberal reform without picking a self-destructive fight with the secular establishment. Many of the key institutional prerogatives of the military – such as its influence over policy-making through the NSC and legal impunity of officers – were rolled back in this process. But the "liberal moment" turned out to be brief and its promise fleeting. The lack of appetite already visible in the EU countries towards Turkish accession in the mid-2000s turned into hostile opposition as socio-economic crisis engulfed Europe after 2008. In tandem with the loss of the EU as the main external engine of Turkey's democratization and the end of the global liquidity boom that had enabled the country's impressive growth, political contestation took a divisive zero-sum turn, played out as a vicious struggle for survival between the elected government and the tutelary actors.

That power struggle defined the second term of the AKP government (2007– 11), featuring a military ultimatum and a constitutional court attempt to block the election of the government's presidential nominee, then foreign minister Abdullah Gül in 2007, the subsequent revelation of two aborted high-level coup plans back in the early 2000s, and a failed case in the Constitutional Court to outlaw the AKP in 2008. In response, the AKP government initiated far-reaching reforms aimed at breaking the hegemony of tutelary actors in the judiciary, including a constitutional referendum in 2010 and two major investigations into coup allegations launched in 2008 and 2010. Carried out through the government's associates in the police force and the judiciary, linked to the Hizmet movement of US-based Sunni cleric Fethullah Gülen,[16] these highly politicized trials saw the arrest and imprisonment of hundreds of acting and retired officers, including, for the first time, a former chief of staff alongside journalists, academics and civil society activists with close ties to the guardians or outspoken opposition to the ruling party.

Coinciding with these trials was the referendum of 12 September 2010, which proposed a wide range of amendments to the junta-crafted constitution of 1982 on issues such as freedom of expression, protection of individual privacy, and labour rights in line with the EU requirements. The reform package provoked controversy mainly over its proposals to restructure the civilian judiciary. The proposed amendments were intended to break the tutelary control over the judiciary by granting greater authority to the president and the parliament in the appointment of judges and prosecutors. This, some critics argued, risked undermining the democratic separation of powers in a non-democratic setting, merely replacing one set of politicized judges and prosecutors with another and enabling single-party governments to pack the courts with their own supporters.[17] Scheduling the referendum on the 30th anniversary of the 1980 coup, the government framed it as a vote between the authoritarian "old Turkey" and the democratic "new Turkey". The package was approved with 58 per cent of the electorate voting in favour on the day.

Although the AKP had largely established itself as the dominant party in Turkey by 2011, the power struggle that enabled this feat had a detrimental impact on Turkey's unconsolidated democratic transition, gradually relegating civil liberties and the rule of law to calculations of political hegemony and revanchism.[18] This trend intensified after 2011, as the ruling party set out to tighten its grip over state institutions, while embarking on a project to transform Turkey's society in the image of its charismatic leader, Prime Minister (now President) Recep Tayyip Erdoğan, who declared his determination to "raise a religious youth".[19]

Advocating a conservative Sunni morality on one side, and thereby increasingly alienating non-Sunni or non-religious citizens, the government pressed on with a construction-based neo-liberal growth agenda on the other.[20] Relying on its parliamentary majority, the AKP decision-makers routinely ignored objections to their policies and passed legislation without engaging in a meaningful dialogue with the opposition parties or civil society organizations. Controversial privatization deals and environmentally damaging mega construction and energy projects were tendered to a small group of contractors close to the ruling circle often despite the opposition of local stakeholders and at times in violation of court rulings.[21]

In the growing absence of a space for public deliberation that could serve as an outlet for critical views, anti-government protests (and heavy-handed police responses) became the norm. The most prominent and internationally visible of these were the nationwide demonstrations triggered after the police attempted to violently disperse a small group of environmental activists protesting the privatization of a public green space at the centre of Istanbul's Taksim Square in June 2013. Spreading across many of Turkey's urban centres, the Gezi Park demonstrations soon turned into a general outpouring of anger at the government's neo-liberal economic and neoconservative social agenda. Framing the events as a coup attempt against his government, Prime Minister Erdoğan took a tough stance against the protestors, calling them "looters and marauders" while praising the security forces, which human rights groups condemned for using disproportionate force on unarmed demonstrators, for their "epic service to the nation".[22] With Gezi, Turkey's simmering socio-political polarization burst to the surface. Far from mending the divide, the violent suppression of the demonstrations deepened this polarization and the growing crisis within a substantial portion of society that felt increasingly disenfranchised and marginalized by the ruling party. At the same time, it further pushed the government along the path of establishing a police state in order to safeguard its interests.

Contributing to this deepening polarization and sense of crisis was the rapid personalization of power within the ruling party by Erdoğan, who handpicked AKP candidates for parliament for the 2011 election and announced his plan to replace Turkey's Parliamentary system with a presidential one. Declaring the institutional separation of powers as the "main obstacle" to political expediency, Erdoğan and his advisors appealed for a "super presidency" equipped with the power to dissolve the parliament, govern through executive decrees and appoint senior judges and bureaucrats without parliamentary approval.[23] Surrounded by loyalists who called him "the Great Master" (*Büyük Usta*) and owed their political status to the leader, a personality cult started to form around Erdoğan that alienated him from his former allies.

In particular, the very public falling out at the end of 2013 between two erstwhile Islamist allies, Erdoğan and Fethullah Gülen, triggered another no-holds-barred battle for survival at the top of the state hierarchy, featuring high-level corruption allegations and indictments, led by Gülen-affiliated police officers and prosecutors, against then Prime Minister Erdoğan's family and key AKP figures, to which the government responded with the purge of suspected Gülenists from the police force and the judiciary to enhance the executive's control over them,[24] as well as a crackdown on businesses and media associated with Gülen's Hizmet movement.[25] The scope and intensity of these arrests and crackdowns grew spectacularly after the failed coup attempt of 15 July 2016, blamed by the government on Gülen-affiliated military officers, in which fighter planes attacked the parliament, more than 300 people were killed, and President Erdoğan himself narrowly escaped capture or worse.

These developments took place against the backdrop of a volatile geopolitical environment that turned steadily against the AKP's regional interests. Initially praised as a potential model for the Middle East after the Arab Spring, the ruling party's ambition to become the order-setting agent in a region where popular Sunni movements came to replace secular dictatorships ground to a halt with the rising sectarian war in Syria and the military coup against the Muslim Brotherhood in Egypt in 2013. The Turkish government's active participation on behalf of various Sunni actors in these countries in turn exacerbated ethnic and sectarian rifts within Turkey and strained its ties with its Western partners. By mid-2015, the Syrian war had crept up inside Turkey with a massive refugee influx, frequent terror attacks in urban centres and a return to intense violence following the collapse of a two-and-a-half-year peace process with the PKK, a Kurdish militant group.[26]

Admitting no responsibility and publicly blaming both the regional turn of events and the domestic setbacks on a sinister plot designed by a "higher intelligence" to stop Turkey's spectacular rise under Erdoğan's leadership,[27] the ruling party abandoned much of what was left of its commitment to the rule of law and civil liberties. After a 13-year hiatus the Kurdish provinces were once again put under a state of exception in 2015, effectively suspending parts of the constitution and democratic rights of the citizens.[28] Following the coup attempt in 2016, these measures were imposed nationwide, without a clear end in sight.

Electoral Integrity under the AKP's Competitive Authoritarianism

A growing number of scholars and observers have noted Turkey's authoritarian slide since 2011, with some arguing that the country under President Erdoğan could no longer be categorized as a democracy, but rather as a rising competitive authoritarianism.[29] Levitsky and Way define as competitive authoritarian those regimes where "although elections are regularly held and are generally free of massive fraud, incumbents routinely abuse state resources, deny the opposition adequate media coverage, harass opposition candidates and their supporters, and in some cases manipulate electoral results."[30] Brownlee observed that the "example of Turkey under premier-then-president Recep Tayyip Erdoğan presents a potentially theory-busting specimen of a highly developed democracy going authoritarian."[31] Freedom House declared in April 2016 that Turkey's democracy was at a "breaking point". Against this backdrop, the coup attempt of July 2016 and the subsequent mass purges and arrests of a diverse range of dissidents under the state of exceptional measures were the straw that broke the camel's back.[32]

Bermeo argues that Turkey under Erdoğan serves as "an illustrative example" of democratic backsliding "legitimized through the very institutions that democracy promoters have prioritized," namely, an elected executive that systematically weakens democratic checks balances and engages in long-term strategic manipulation of the electoral process.[33] Indeed, elections have been integral to both the process of undoing military tutelage and the construction of an illiberal system based on a personality-driven populist one-party rule. In turn, this shift from tutelary democracy to competitive authoritarianism, via a failed attempt at democratization, has had a transformative effect on the function and integrity of elections in Turkey.

Unlike the guardians, the AKP's political hegemony depends on its ability to continually win elections and rule without sharing power. In Erdoğan's popular discourse, the ballot box serves as the source of the "national will" (*milli irade*). Winning elections is deemed the necessary – and, crucially, the *sufficient* – condition to embody this will and speak and act on behalf of the nation, which is exclusively made up of those who support the winning party. In this formulation, the will of the millions who vote for other parties is effectively discounted and the wide range of opposition groups can be labeled as "enemies of the nation's will" or simply "anti-national".[34] If this logic appeared benign, or even "democratizing", when argued from a position of weakness against the interventions of powerful tutelary actors in the 2000s, in a post-tutelary democratic setting, it became the blueprint for establishing a new type of authoritarianism.

Taking place during moments of heightened tension with the military guardians, the referendum of 2010 and the general election victories in 2007 and 2011 served to bolster the AKP's position vis-à-vis their tutelary opponents. In particular, the early election in April 2007 served not only as a verdict on the AKP's first term in government, but also as a plebiscite on the presidential crisis. Securing a larger than expected victory, the AKP re-nominated as its candidate Abdullah Gül, who was subsequently elected by the newly-formed parliament against the guardians' wishes and earlier interventions. An official election monitoring team from the OSCE praised the vote as "a notable achievement against a background of political tensions," demonstrating "the resilience of the election process in Turkey, characterized by pluralism and a high level of public confidence."[35]

Coming on the heels of the so-called "coup trials", the party's third successive election victory in 2011 solidified the elected officials' triumph over the appointed guardians. Yet the zero-sum nature of that power struggle had already started taking a toll on the long-term integrity of elections, in particular with the government assuming an increasingly intolerant stance toward dissenting views represented in the media. While noting the diverse and lively media landscape in Turkey, the OSCE raised concerns over the "high number of arrested and convicted journalists, and the alleged control by the government over some influential media."[36] In October 2012, the Committee to Protect Journalists reported that at least 61 journalists were jailed "in direct reprisal for their journalism". At the end of 2013, the same organization declared Turkey the "world's worst jailer of journalists for the second year in a row."[37]

The picture deteriorated markedly during subsequent election periods, as both Erdoğan's pursuit of political hegemony and the opposition to it took a more intense and irreconcilable turn. Interpreting both the Gezi protests and the corruption investigations of 2013 as a coup attempt against his government, in a similar vein as the Egyptian coup of the same year, Erdoğan apparently decided to leave nothing to chance.[38] For instance, despite being the clear favourite in the race for the presidency in 2014, the prime minister benefited substantially and unfairly from the administrative resources of his office and the lack of an institutional framework to provide transparency and accountability in campaign financing.[39] In the two-week period before the municipal elections of March 2014, the state broadcaster TRT devoted 89 per cent of its airtime to the governing party.[40] TRT's tone and coverage remained steeply biased in favour of Erdoğan and the AKP in the run-up to the 2014 presidential poll and the two general elections of 2015 as well.

Repeat Elections of 2015: The "Fig-Leaf" of Authoritarianism

The June 2015 general election constituted a critical moment not only for the AKP, which faced diminishing popular support in its first campaign without Erdoğan at the head of the party, but also for Turkey's democracy. In a largely unexpected move, the pro-Kurdish leftist Peoples' Democratic Party (*Halkların Demokratik Partisi*, HDP) took the decision to participate in the election as a party, rather than having its members run as independent candidates in order to circumvent the 10-per cent threshold, which remained in place under successive AKP governments. Having previously challenged Erdoğan in the presidential vote, the HDP's charismatic co-chairman Selahattin Demirtaş emerged during this process as a popular figure who was able to combine a message of pluralistic and inclusive democracy and minority rights, with an effective criticism of Erdoğan's single-minded pursuit of power. This was a message that appealed to a wider electorate beyond the Kurdish movement's traditional base. If the HDP managed to pass the threshold and enter the parliament, they could deny the AKP the majority to form a single-party government. If they failed, the AKP could conceivably reach the super-majority necessary to change the constitution and introduce the super-presidentialism Erdoğan had been advocating.

With much at stake, the AKP launched an intensive campaign that targeted the HDP with an aggressive religious-nationalistic rhetoric that would pass as hate speech in a liberal democracy.[41] In breach of his constitutional obligation to act impartially, President Erdoğan personally joined the campaign in favour of the AKP.[42] The electoral playing field was not only tilted against opposition parties in terms of campaign finance and media bias, but also physical security. During the campaign period, the HDP offices and members became frequent targets of physical attacks and intimidation by nationalist mobs. Many of these attacks went unpunished, bolstering the sense among the opposition that critics of the ruling party could be targeted with relative impunity.[43] Reflective of these trends, and of Turkey's deepening social polarization, a nationwide pre-election survey found that public trust in the electoral process had been deteriorating: only 48 per cent of the respondents thought the elections would be conducted fairly (comparable to the trust in elections in Russia), down from 70 per cent in 2007 (on par with the United States).[44] The lack of trust in electoral institutions and the growing fear of fraud among opponents of the AKP led to the rise of popular civic initiatives to monitor the voting process and the vote count on election day.[45]

Although the AKP emerged from the June election as the first party, its share of the vote dropped by nearly 10 per cent from 2011 and the party lost its parliamentary majority for the first time since 2002. Surpassing most predictions, the HDP received 13 per cent and won a record 80 seats in the parliament. The result had two immediate implications. In the first place, it was a major setback for the AKP government and Erdoğan's presidential ambitions. Secondly, it ushered in a new and uncertain era, in which Turkey would once again be governed by coalitions. The fact that the AKP could lose power in an election where no significant manipulation had been detected on polling day initially appeared as a hopeful sign for procedural democracy's persistence in Turkey. But the five-month period that followed the June election proved such assessments false and suggested that elections in Turkey under the AKP had become a "fig leaf" masking an authoritarian one-party regime.[46]

From the outset, President Erdoğan made no secret of his desire to renew elections instead of settling for a coalition government. When the AKP declared after a 60-day period that it had failed to form the government, instead of giving the task to the leader of the second-largest party (in this case, the CHP) as is customary, the president called for fresh elections in November. In the meanwhile, intense fighting resumed between security forces and the PKK, turning Kurdish-dominated urban areas into battle zones reminiscent of neighbouring Syria. At a time when suicide bombings killed hundreds of pro-HDP supporters in Suruç and Ankara, the president, together with a cohort of shadowy ultra-nationalist supporters and the pro-government media, stepped up the campaign to marginalize the HDP, label its supporters as "terrorists" and "traitors" and systematically silence and intimidate critical media and journalists.[47]

Taking place in a "climate of violence and fear,"[48] the November re-election brought the AKP back to power as a single-party government and allowed the president to press on with his ambitions.[49] In a Machiavellian turn of events, the president was able to manipulate conditions of conflict and crisis and then present the AKP as the only solution to these ills, making good of Deputy Prime Minister Yalçın Akdoğan's statement on the day after the June election that "the process ahead will make everyone better understand that the AKP is the only guarantor of security and stability" in Turkey.[50]

Conclusion

Turkey's transition from tutelary democracy to competitive authoritarianism has had a direct and detrimental impact on the function and integrity of its elections. Whereas elections served as the democratic counterbalance to the non-democratic guardianship of the military in the Turkish hybrid regime, in the post-tutelary setting they have become the building block of a one-party dominant system. Under the AKP, the majoritarian view that elections give the winners the right to impose their will on society at large with little regard for the concerns and interests of losers, has proven to be a recipe for socio-political conflict and polarization. Yet Turkey could still qualify as a procedurally democratic country, had Erdoğan and the AKP chosen to abide by this principle even when elections turned out against their interest.

The critical lesson of the repeat elections of 2015 was that, when faced with an unfavourable election result, the Turkish president effectively chose to ignore and suppress the democratic "will of the nation", which he had regularly invoked after every election victory of the AKP since 2002. He did not do this overtly, such as by tempering the vote count or canceling the outcome, but rather through strategic electoral manipulation, which Bermeo has identified as a common feature amongst countries experiencing democratic backsliding. "Strategic manipulation," she notes, "differs from blatant election-day vote fraud in that it typically occurs long before polling day and rarely involves obvious violations of the law. It is 'strategic' in that international (and often domestic) observers are less likely to 'catch or criticize' it."[51]

The repeat elections of 2015 portend a dangerous new era in Turkey's multiparty politics, where elected officials can refuse to share or give up power through the ballot box, thereby violating the most basic requirement of procedural democracy.[52] When key oppositional actors or large sections of a society think that those in power have ceased to play by the basic rules of democracy, the chances of non-democratic interventions into politics also increase. That possibility, in turn, intensifies the siege mentality of the rulers, creating conditions for a self-fulfilling prophecy and give new life to the vicious cycle between illiberal populism and tutelary elitism that has held Turkey's politics captive for over seven decades. A manifestation of this self-fulfilling prophecy, the bloody coup attempt of July 2016 and its heavy-handed aftermath confirm that Turkey has yet to break free from this captivity.

Notes

1. An ever-contested term, "the left" in mainstream Turkish politics has broadly indicated a movement advocating state interventionism to transform society and economy, typically in line with the project of secular nationalization launched under Atatürk and often without an overt reference to Marxism or class struggle. After a decade in opposition, the CHP attempted to remodel itself as a left-of-centre party during the 1960s and the 1970s. Yet even at the height of its popularity as a democratic mass party under the reformist leadership of Bülent Ecevit in the 1970s it was unable to establish the kind of electoral hegemony achieved by the DP, ANAP or the AKP, and had to contend with governing through coalitions with the right.
2. For a critical study of democracy under the DP, see Güliz Sütçü, "Playing the Game of Democracy Through the Electoral Mechanism: The Democratic Party Experience in Turkey", *Turkish Studies*, 12:3 (2011), pp. 341–56.
3. Murat Belge, *Militarist Modernleşme: Almanya, Japonya ve Türkiye* (Istanbul: İletişim, 2011), pp. 617–18.

4. Karabekir Akkoyunlu, "The Rise and Fall of the Hybrid Regime: Guardianship and Democracy in Iran and Turkey", PhD Thesis, London School of Economics (July 2014).
5. For a detailed discussion on defining electoral integrity, see Pippa Norris "Does the world agree about standards of electoral integrity? Evidence for the diffusion of global norms", *Electoral Studies*, 32 (2013), pp. 576–88.
6. In the 1983 election, the MDP came a distant third to Turgut Özal's ANAP. The election victories of the AKP in 2002 and 2007 can also be seen as a snub against the military, which had overthrown the AKP's Islamist predecessor in the so-called "post-modern coup" of February 1997 and published a memorandum against it in 2007.
7. "Turkey's Military Leader Vows to Restore Democracy", *New York Times*, 6 January 1981.
8. Karabekir Akkoyunlu, Kalypso Nicolaidis, and Kerem Öktem, "The Western Condition: Turkey, the US and the EU in the New Middle East", SEESOX Paper Series on Turkey (February 2013) pp. 44–51. Available at https://www.sant.ox. ac.uk/sites/default/files/thewesterncondition.pdf (accessed 31 March 2016).
9. Mikael Wigell, "Mapping Hybrid Regimes: Regime types and Concepts in Comparative Politics", *Democratization*, 15:2 (2008), p. 238.
10. Established after the 1960 coup, the NSC became "the embodiment of the bureaucracy's primacy over the popularly elected parliament". Founded as a governmental advisory body regularly bringing together the military high command and the president with the prime minister and cabinet ministers, the NSC functioned as a key tutelary institution, where the military's recommendations to the government carried the weight of official edicts. Ümit Cizre, "The Anatomy of the Turkish Military's Political Autonomy", *Comparative Politics*, 29:2 (1997), p. 157.
11. Until 2014, presidents were elected by the parliament for a single seven-year term, and until 2007 all presidents were either former military generals, bureaucrats with solid tutelary credentials or civilian politicians whom the generals thought they could control.
12. Established with the 1961 Constitution, the Constitutional Court played a particularly active tutelary role after the 1980 military coup. While between 1963 and 1980 it outlawed only six political parties, 19 parties were banned between 1980 and 2008. Outlawed parties were almost exclusively from the leftist, ethnic Kurdish or Islamist backgrounds. "Anayasa Mahkemesi 44 Yılda 24 Parti Kapattı", *Bianet*, 21 November 2007, http://www.bianet.org/bianet/si yaset/103054-anayasa-mahkemesi-44-yilda-24-parti-kapatti, accessed 1 April 2016.
13. Law 306 dated 25 May 1961 on the Election of Parliamentary Deputies. Despite numerous adjustments and amendments, including the introduction of a nationwide threshold, the D'Hont method has remained in place since 1961.
14. In the 1950 election, for example the DP won 408 of the 487 seats despite securing 53.3 per cent of votes.
15. Burak Cop, "Yüzde 10 barajının öyküsü", *NTV*, http://www.ntv.com.tr/turkiye/ yuzde-10-barajinin-oykusu,3xMZ-FVFNkWjU9mAPgxf9g, accessed 1 April 2016. Ironically, the threshold has also been instrumental in the rise of the AKP as a dominant party that disassembled the tutelary system in the 2000s. The AKP was able to form a single-party government in 2002 securing

two-thirds of the seats in Parliament, despite having won only 34 per cent of the overall vote, as it was one of only two parties (the other being the CHP, which had 19 per cent) that had crossed the 10-per cent threshold, leaving nearly 50 per cent of the electorate who cast their ballot for other parties unrepresented in the new parliament.

16. The Hizmet (Service) Movement represents one of the two main branches of political Islam in Turkey, known as *Nurculuk*. This branch seeks to reconcile Western modernity with Islam, encourages social and economic entrepreneurship over political activism and is sometimes referred to as the pragmatic or 'business-friendly' alternative to the more openly political and ideologically confrontational *Milli Görüş* (National View) tradition, from which Erdoğan and the AKP emerged. The rivalry between the two branches in the 1990s was such that Gülen actually supported the coup against Turkey's first *Milli Görüş*-led government in 1997, even though the coup makers then turned against Gülen himself, who subsequently fled to the US. In the early 2000s, the AKP's declared departure from the political legacy of *Milli Görüş* brought the party and the Gülenists together and Hizmet's cadres in the judiciary and police force proved instrumental in the AKP's battle against the tutelary actors. This marriage of interests, however, broke down amidst a new power struggle soon after the tutelary system had been disassembled.

17. Ersin Kalaycıoğlu, "Kulturkampf in Turkey: The Constitutional Referendum of 12 September 2010", *South European Society and Politics*, 17:1 (2010), pp. 1–22; Can Yeğinsu, "Turkey Packs the Court", *The New York Review of Books Blog*, 22 September 2010.

18. A dominant-party system is one in which there is "a category of parties/political organizations that have successively won election victories and whose future defeat cannot be envisaged or is unlikely for the foreseeable future." Raymond Suttner, "Party Dominance 'Theory': Of What Value?", *Politikon*, 33:3 (2006), p. 277.

19. "Religious youth", *Today's Zaman*, 12 February 2012; "Turkey passes school reform law critics view as Islamic", Reuters, 30 March 2012.

20. "PM Erdoğan unveils long-awaited 'crazy project' as Kanal İstanbul", *Today's Zaman*, 27 April 2011; "Turkish dam threatens town that dates back to the Bronze Age", the *Guardian*, 20 May 2011; "PM announces construction of giant mosque in Istanbul", *Hürriyet Daily News*, 31 May 2012; "İstanbul's new bridge, highway, canal threaten city's northern forests", *Today's Zaman*, 11 August 2013.

21. "Istanbul's income earned by a few construction groups during AKP rule", *Hürriyet Daily News*, 14 April 2014. "Turkish firm must scrap olive grove coal plant, says government", *Guardian*, 11 November 2014.

22. "Erdoğan: Polis Taksim'de destan yazdı", *Milliyet*, 24 June 2013.

23. "Separation of powers an obstacle, says Erdoğan", *Hürriyet Daily News*, 18 December 2012.

24. Constitutional law scholar Ergun Özbudun, who was appointed by the AKP to draft a new democratic constitution back in 2007 but has since turned critical of the government's illiberal policies, notes that "in Turkey the year 2014 can be described as a period when the governing AKP made a sustained and systematic effort to establish its control over the judiciary by means of a series of laws of dubious constitutionality." Ergun Özbudun, "Turkey's Judiciary and the Drift

Toward Competitive Authoritarianism", *The International Spectator*, 50:2 (2015), p. 42.

25. "Turkish opposition newspaper turns pro-government after state takeover", Reuters, 6 March 2016.

26. Cihan Tuğal, *The Fall of the Turkish Model: How the Arab Uprisings Brought Down Islamic Liberalism* (London: Verso, 2016).

27. Mustafa Akyol, "Unraveling the AKP's 'Mastermind' conspiracy theory", *Al Monitor*, 19 March 2015.

28. Much of the Kurdish Southeast had been ruled by a state of exception from 1987 until 2002, when it was finally lifted by the newly elected AKP government.

29. Özbudun, "Turkey's Judiciary and the Drift Toward Competitive Authoritarianism"; Berk Esen and Şebnem Gümüşçü, "Rising Competitive Authoritarianism in Turkey", *Third World Quarterly*, 19 February 2016.

30. Steven Levitsky and Lucan A. Way, "Elections Without Democracy: The Rise of Competitive Authoritarianism", *Journal of Democracy*, 13:2 (2002), p. 53.

31. Freedom House, "Turkey: Proposal to Annul Citizenship Threatens Fundamental Rights", 6 April 2016, https://freedomhouse.org/article/turkey-proposal-annul-citizenship-threatens-fundamental-rights (accessed 7 April 2016).

32. Brownlee's definition of a "highly developed" country is one whose non-oil GDP per capita exceeds USD 8,045. Jason Brownlee, "Why Turkey's authoritarian descent shakes up democratic theory", *Washington Post*, 23 March 2016.

33. Nancy Bermeo, "On Democratic Backsliding", *Journal of Democracy*, 27:1 (January 2016), p. 6.

34. "Erdoğan: The winner of the election is national will and democracy" *Yeni Safak*, 10 August 2014; "Erdoğan: Milli irade istikrardan yana tecelli etti", *Hürriyet*, 2 November 2015; Levent Gültekin, "Milli irade kimin, neyin iradesi?, *Diken*, 30 January 2016, http://www.diken.com.tr/milli-irade-kimin-neyin-iradesi/ [accessed 10 April 2016].

35. OSCE/ODIHR, Election Assessment Mission Report, Republic of Turkey, Parliamentary Elections 2011, http://www.osce.org/odihr/elections/turkey/77703 [accessed 10 April 2016].

36. Ibid.

37. Committee to Protect Journalists, "Turkey's Press Freedom Crisis", Report, October 2012, https://www.cpj.org/reports/2012/10/turkeys-press-freedom-crisis-assault-on-the-press.php. Committee to Protect Journalists, "Turkey worst jailer of journalists for second year in a row", press release, 18 December 2013, https://cpj.org/2013/12/turkey-worst-jailer-of-journalists-for-second-year.php, accessed 10 April 2016.

38. "Like any movement that does not include the nation, the Gezi uprising also fizzled out. When this method failed, they pushed the button for a more sinister operation. The parallel gang of treason [i.e., the Gülen network; KA] targeted in my person the great projects of our country. Mind you, this operation also did not have the nation in it. And so with the help of Allah and support of my nation we overcame this attack too." From Erdoğan's speech to lawyers, "Erdoğan'dan Davutoğlu'na gönderme: Neymiş, akademisyenler tutuksuz yargılansınlarmış!", *T24*, http://t24.com.tr/haber/cumhurbaskani-erdogan-avukatlara-hitap-ediyor,334990, accessed 10 April 2016.

39. OSCE/ODIHR, Election Assessment Mission Report, Republic of Turkey, Presidential Election 2014, http://www.osce.org/odihr/elections/turkey/119672 [accessed 10 April 2016].
40. "TRT'den AK Parti'ye 13 saat muhalefete 48 dakika", *Radikal*, 13 March 2014.
41. Pınar Tremblay, "Could AKP's negative campaign strategy backfire?", *Al Monitor*, 4 June 2015.
42. OSCE/ODIHR, Election Assessment Mission Report, Republic of Turkey, Parliamentary Elections, 7 June 2015, http://www.osce.org/odihr/elections/turkey/153806 [accessed 10 April 2016].
43. Efe Kerem Sözeri, "HDP'ye yapılan saldırılar ve cezasızlık sistemli mi?", *Platform 24*, 17 May 2015.
44. Ali Çarkoğlu and S. Erdem Aytaç, "Public Opinion Dynamics Towards June 2015 Elections in Turkey", Sponsored by the Open Society Foundation, Koç University and Ohio State University, 5 May 2015. http://www.aciktoplum vakfi.org.tr/medya/presentation.pptx [accessed 10 April 2016].
45. Karabekir Akkoyunlu, "Ahead of Turkey's Crucial Election, Citizens Take Action to Protect Their Vote", *Huffington Post*, 20 May 2015.
46. Pippa Norris, Richard W. Frank, and Ferran Martínez i Coma, "Assessing the Quality of Elections", *Journal of Democracy*, 24:4 (October 2014), p. 135.
47. Karabekir Akkoyunlu "Old Turkish demons in new faces?" *Open Democracy*, 23 October 2015. "Prominent Turkish journalist, government critic attacked", *Deutsche Welle*, 1 October 2015, http://www.dw.com/en/prominent-turkish-journalist-government-critic-attacked/a-18753296 [accessed 10 April 2016].
48. Pippa Norris, Richard W. Frank, Alessandro Nai and Ferran Martínez i Coma, "The Electoral Integrity Project: The Year in Elections, 2015", 22 February 2016, http://dx.doi.org/10.2139/ssrn.2753416 [accessed 10 April 2016].
49. OSCE/ODIHR, Election Assessment Mission Report, Republic of Turkey, Parliamentary Elections, 1 November 2015, http://www.osce.org/odihr/electi ons/turkey/186031 [accessed 10 April 2016].
50. "Yalçın Akdoğan: HDP bundan sonra çözüm sürecinin ancak filmini yapar," *Hürriyet*, 8 June 2015. Karabekir Akkoyunlu, "AKP's Machiavellian Victory: How It Happened and What It Means for Turkey", *Centre for Policy and Research on Turkey (Research Turkey)*, 4:10 (November 2015), pp. 26–33.
51. Bermeo, *Democratic Backsliding*, p. 13.
52. Akkoyunlu, "AKP's Machiavellian Victory".

CHAPTER 4

ELECTIONS AND PUBLIC FINANCE IN TURKEY: PUBLIC SPENDING AS A TACITURN ELECTION CAMPAIGN?

Taptuk Emre Erkoç and Abdülkadir Civan

Introduction

The electoral strategies devised by political parties to win elections by reflecting citizens' interests have always been a challenging topic in the literature on political economy. Regarding the decision-making period in the administrative bodies of political parties, particularly during elections, the primary target is to find the best strategy to capture voters' attention towards the policy platform. One of the well-known theoretical explanations for this process is "median voter theorem", which corresponds to policy-making decisions regarding the preferences of the voter in the middle of a ranking of voters within a single dimension. This theorem proposes that, to succeed, a candidate should align him/herself as close as possible to the median voter's preferences.[1]

Although this theorem has certain technical weaknesses, it outlines the process of decision-making within political parties in quite a reasonable way. On the other hand, there are political parties whose discourses and practices in the political arena cannot be solely explained by median voter analysis. The "gate keeping model" in the literature is the most well-grounded theoretical extension to provide an account of the non-median status quo in certain cases. More specifically, the theory holds that gatekeepers pursue a strategy of "closing the gates" to the demands of median voters to sustain the status quo.[2]

In addition to the median voter theorem and the gate-keeping model, researchers in the field have long sought to apply political economy approaches to make sense of the broader economic underpinnings of the political system, including the electoral process. A key conventional wisdom that emerges in the political economy literature is that the power to manipulate public expenditure provides leverage to the incumbent political party to influence the attitudes of the electorate. Accordingly, parties in the opposition face distinct obstacles to attract voters in so far as they lack the economic and financial resources of the state at their disposal. In other words, incumbents may use their legislative or executive power to direct the type and amount of public expenditure in ways that give them an electoral advantage.[3]

This chapter discusses the political economy of elections, focusing particularly on the utilization of public expenditures as an "electoral strategy" in the Turkish case. The strategies of governing parties in Turkey, including the current incumbent Justice and Development Party (*Adalet ve Kalkınma Partisi*, AKP) during elections are assessed in relation to three specific pillars: public expenditure in health and education, local government spending and regional development policies, and government support for agriculture.

The Political Economy of Elections

Political economy approaches in electoral studies have tended to focus on the impact of economic variables on voting behaviour. Alongside several non-economic factors, political economists suggest that citizens cast their votes at the ballot box in accordance with their economic expectations and concerns.[4] In other words, voters' perceptions of the ability of candidates to deliver sought-after economic outcomes play a pivotal role in their political preferences. In this section, the political economic dimension of the electoral process is examined based on three fundamental theoretical frameworks: economic voting; distributive politics; and the political business cycle.

Economic voting: Retrospective and prospective

A wide body of literature has developed that explores the economic underpinnings of the political system, including the electoral process.[5,6] In his seminal work, Downs[7] referred to the fact that individuals make choices in the ballot box based on utility calculations, by comparing the gains they expect from the competing political parties. In a similar vein, a plethora of work on economic voting[8] develops the argument that rational voters can be expected to cast their votes for parties that will deliver the greatest possible economic gains.

Nevertheless, there is no doubt that citizens do not solely rely on considerations of economic conditions when they cast their votes. Ideology, culture, and historical experiences also play a crucial role in their political preferences. Duch and Stevenson have summarized the consensus in the field as follows: "Economic voting is very likely widespread and often important; but, its magnitude and nature across elections is almost certainly variable."[9] In sum, even though economic circumstances are not the only determinants of the voting preferences, their significance should not be underestimated in the study of electoral behaviour either.

In the electoral process, voters weigh the performance of the incumbent party by assessing its track record on economic matters to decide which party to vote for. In this type of *retrospective* economic voting, voters typically weigh the incumbent's previous performance more heavily than any expected future performance. Alternatively, voters might be future-oriented and try to elect the party that is expected to manage the economy well in the following years, which the literature refers to as *prospective* voting.[10] Thus, an electoral outcome may depend on the specific mode of economic voting adopted by citizens as far as economic conditions are concerned.

Distributive politics

Voters' electoral choices are believed to be correlated not only with the general economic competence of the candidate but also the particular economic benefits that have been delivered from the government, either through cash transfers or the provision of public services. This phenomenon is very much linked to the notion of distributive politics, which includes "taxes and transfers, and in particular the decisions about allocations of government goods and services to identifiable localities or groups."[11] Hence, politicians in the government have a strong incentive to utilize distribution channels to retain their privileged status. As Tullock and Buchanan,[12] the founders of the public choice school of political economy, have argued, politicians do not consider the public interest *per se*, but are instead interested in maximizing their own utility via strategies that safeguard their hold on their parliamentary seats.

Studies in the distributive politics literature basically state that government expenditures are expected to induce citizens to show their political support in favour of the incumbent party during the elections. Drazen and Eslava note that voters behave rationally when giving positive responses in the elections to the transfers received from the incumbent, since appropriations offered before the elections act as a good signal of likely behaviour in the post-election period.[13] However, the incumbent party (and possibly parties in the opposition) face a dilemma: to maximize their chances of re-election should they direct the distribution channels towards swing voters or their loyal supporters? This "swing voter vs. core voter" dilemma makes politicians highly sensitive to whether resources need to be allocated to the electorally "delicate" constituencies, or to politically favoured voters through a partisan political agenda.

In Dixit and Londregan's model, the typical voter is expected to change her political preferences in an election if the magnitude of the incumbent party's economic offer surpasses the value of her ideological attachments.[14]

Hence, attractive amounts of distributive allocations are highly "effective" in moving swing voters, and incumbent parties would thus typically prefer to allocate resources in favour of the swing voter group. However, as Cox and McCubbins have shown conclusively, in some cases incumbent parties elect to prioritize their core voters, especially if the political parties are risk-averse and if cultures of political favouritism outweigh any other political and social concerns.[15] The practice of "pork-barrel spending" – where selected members of parliament are more inclined to allocate economic resources according to the tastes of party supporters – follows a similar logic.

Indeed, research has shown that partisan perspectives can have a strong independent effect on government spending decisions. Hibbs' research shows that incumbent parties' spending decisions are often prioritized largely in terms of ideological factors, leaving decisions about the level of government spending hostage to partisan preferences.[16] From a different perspective, Milesi-Ferretti et al. have argued that elected politicians "face a basic trade-off between allegiance to a social constituency and allegiance to a geographic constituency"[17] when deciding on the structure of fiscal policy instruments. Thus, the authors conclude that class interests might conflict with politicians' practical re-election interests, a clash that would materialize in different forms depending on the type of electoral system.

The political business cycle

Another notable theoretical framework in the political economy of elections is the political business cycle (PBC). PBC models also focus on levels of public spending but are distinguished from those mentioned above in their additional focus on the *timing of government expenditure*. In his pioneering work, Nordhaus establishes that "within an incumbent's term in office there is a predictable pattern of policy, starting with relative austerity in early years and ending with the potlatch right before elections."[18] In a similar vein, Rogoff asserts that, before elections, governments tend to boost consumption through cutting taxes and raising transfer spending, and in so doing "incumbent leaders try to convince voters that they have recently been doing an excellent job in administering the government."[19]

Figure 4.1 below presents a summary of the PBC. The period between elections basically comprises two phases through which the magnitude of spending fluctuates based on the timing of elections. To signal the governments' credibility on questions of fiscal management, spending cuts and austerity plans are put into effect immediately after the elections when newly elected governments have accumulated a mandate and a high degree of political capital (and voters presumably have forgotten election promises). Then, as new elections approach and the mind of the government turns to mobilizing the electorate, the incumbent parties ramp up increases in

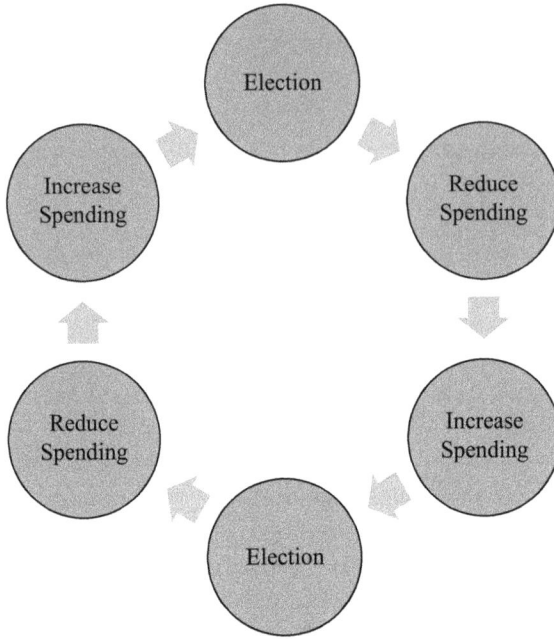

Figure 4.1 The political business cycle.

government expenditure. The elections are held, a new government forms, and the cycle resumes. Although empirical research has yet to find consistent evidence in support of this theory at the cross-national level, research conducted at the national level has found robust and reliable indications that the political business cycle holds, principally in developing countries.[20]

Elections and Economic Voting in Turkey

In line with the arguments mentioned above, Turkey's highly ideologically polarized politics raises a crucial question: Do non-political factors, including economic ones, influence voting preferences in elections in any major way at all? Turkey's long-standing centre-periphery divide, the ever-challenging Kurdish question, the historical secular-religious cleavage and leftist-rightist conflict might be expected, after all, to dominate electoral choices. It is fair to say that those voters with durable secular sensibilities are strongly inclined to vote for the Republican People's Party (*Cumhuriyet Halk Partisi*, CHP) irrespective. Similarly, in cities with significant Kurdish populations, the pro-Kurdish People's Democratic Party (*Halkların Demokratik Partisi*, HDP) almost invariably receives a higher share of the vote. Furthermore, the typical profile of an AKP voter is a highly conservative-religious individual, one who has typically lived his or her life on the periphery of Turkey's economic and political mainstream. The AKP, as is well known, has very successfully appealed to the grievances, demands, and ambitions of this kind of voter. Nevertheless, the literature on Turkey suggests that economic performance also matters for the voters in Turkey.[21]

A Brief History of Elections in Turkey Before the AKP Era

Turkey's first competitive national parliamentary elections were held in 1946, a watershed in the history of Turkish politics. Turkey had, until this time, been run as a single-party regime dominated by the CHP. Since the transition to multiparty politics in 1946, Turkey's political system has "followed a cyclical pattern of transition to democracy and breakdowns of democratic regimes."[22] By the end of the 1960s, Turkey had already passed Samuel Huntington's "two-turnover test",[23] whereby two successive peaceful turnovers of power between incumbent and opposition are achieved. However, Turkish democracy has been subject to regular disruption by military intervention, which has occurred roughly once in every decade since 1950.

Table 4.1 gives a sense of how governments and elections have been distributed across time. Between the military coups of May 1960 and September 1980, 19 governments (an average of nearly one per year) were formed. Through the 1960s and 1970s, an average of almost four distinct governments formed in every inter-election period, indicating the extreme level of instability in domestic politics, foreign policy, and economic development over this period. Indeed, as the following paragraphs will outline, questions of economic stability and development were front and centre in most electoral outcomes throughout the 1980s and 1990s.

As Table 4.1 shows, the 1980s were relatively more stable than previous decades, given that Turgut Özal and his Motherland Party (*Anavatan Partisi*, ANAP) were able to form a majority government between the 1983 and 1987 elections. This stability was largely down to the electoral structure set out in the military-drafted 1982 constitution, which was designed to facilitate the

Table 4.1 Elections and governments in Turkey since 1950

Time Period	Number of Elections	Number of Governments
1950–60	3	5
1960–70	3	11
1970–80	2	8
1980–90	2	4
1990–2000	3	9
2000–10	2	3

formation of a robust "two-party" system and was accompanied by bans on those political parties and personalities who the military viewed as the source of instability in the 1960s and 1970s. Military-sponsored electoral rules allowed ANAP to capture 45 per cent of the votes in the 1983 elections, taking 211 of the 399 seats (53 per cent) in the national assembly to form a strong majority government.

Özal himself has been a key player in economic policy in the late 1970s, when he was appointed as the chief economic advisor to Süleyman Demirel, prime minister in the lead up to the 1980 coup. In this role, he advanced a raft of neo-liberal economic reforms based on International Monetary Fund's (IMF) recommendations. During the military regime of 1980–3, the military appointed him to a key role in implementing these reforms and his expertise in economic issues and his global network (he had worked in both the World Bank and IMF in the 1970s) meant he was looked at favourably by the military when he applied to register ANAP in the run-up to the 1983 elections.[24] In office, however, his government was plagued by an ever-expanding current account deficit and heightening inflation rates, which saw widespread discontent among voters and a gradual decline in ANAP's share of votes in successive elections.

The period of majority ANAP government ended in the 1991 elections and Turkey returned to its tradition of unstable coalition government until 2002. By the late 1980s, Süleyman Demirel had been permitted to return to politics and his True Path Party (*Doğru Yol Partisi*, DYP) won the largest seat-share in the 1991 elections, although falling short of a majority, and formed a coalition government. The DYP came to power at the onset of a very difficult economic period for Turkey. The government was compelled by circumstances to negotiate a very controversial austerity agreement with the IMF, which was announced in April 1994. The austerity package itself tended to have a stabilizing effect on the economy, at least initially, but its measures bit the population hard, and the DYP lost significant support at the 1995 elections.

Largely on the back of skillful instrumentalization of the economic crisis of the 1990s, Necmettin Erbakan's Welfare Party (*Refah Partisi*, RP) swept 21 per cent of the vote in the 1995 elections, emerging with the largest seat-share in the national assembly (ANAP and DYP became the second and third parties, respectively). This was yet another critical juncture in Turkey's electoral history – for the first time, a political party that defined itself as "Islamist" had taken pole position in the party system. The RP formed an uneasy coalition government with the DYP and in mid-1996 Erbakan became Turkey's first Islamist prime minister. However, dismayed and horrified, the secular elite moved against Erbakan and the government was brought down by a military-led intervention in 1997 – the 28 February process. This was followed by three different unstable coalition governments through a succession of economic crises in 2000 and 2001. The 28 February period, subsequent political instability, and economic crisis saw the rise of the AKP on a promise to bring stability and prosperity to Turkey, a commitment the electorate appeared to accept when it swept the party to power in the 2002 elections.

Clearly, then, economic conditions and economic policy played a significant role in Turkey's electoral dynamics, stretching back decades. Beyond the historical narrative, a broad corpus of literature, beginning with Carkoglu's study (before the rise of the AKP) on 21 elections held between 1950 and 1995.[25] He found that support for incumbent parties in Turkey was consistently higher during periods of higher economic growth. Similarly, Akarca and Tansel's electoral research concluded that incumbent parties in Turkey benefited from a strong macroeconomic environment, that is, higher rates of economic growth and diminishing inflation rates.[26] Drawing on the Electorate Tendency Survey, which contains a broader data set on voter preferences, Baslevent et al. argued that *both* economic and non-economic factors shape the choices of voters in Turkey.[27]

Economic Conditions and the AKP's Electoral Performance

From the AKP's watershed 2002 election win until 2015, the party had managed to attract sufficient electoral support to form single-party governments. Although this success cannot solely be reduced to improvements in the economic well-being of the average citizen, its impact cannot be ruled out either. Indeed, the AKP's vote shares between 2004 and 2015 show clearly that AKP's electoral performance has been highly correlated with economic outlook of the country, with vote share and GDP growth rates tracking closely (see Figure 4.2).

Research has tended to confirm this relationship. Akarca's 2010 study found that the incumbent party's slight but clear loss of support in the 2009 local elections was related to poor economic conditions and typical strategic-voting in local elections.[28] Similarly, Yüksel and Civan's research on the 2011 general elections concluded that provincial economic growth positively affects the incumbent party at the province level.[29] More recently, Akarca has argued that the success of the HDP in passing the 10-per cent threshold (and the consequent drop in AKP support) in the June 2015 elections is largely attributable to worsening economic conditions alongside strategic voting,[30] a conclusion reinforced by Kemahlıoğlu's findings that worsening economic conditions shrank AKP votes in the 2015 elections.[31] It is certainly the case that the provinces in which the HDP did best are those under significant socio-economic strain.

In 2015, Onemli et al. conducted a broad-based study that drew on provincial-level data to estimate the impact of economic variables on vote shares of four major parties.[32] Unlike most work on Turkish elections, this study estimates the factors affecting the vote shares not only of the incumbent party

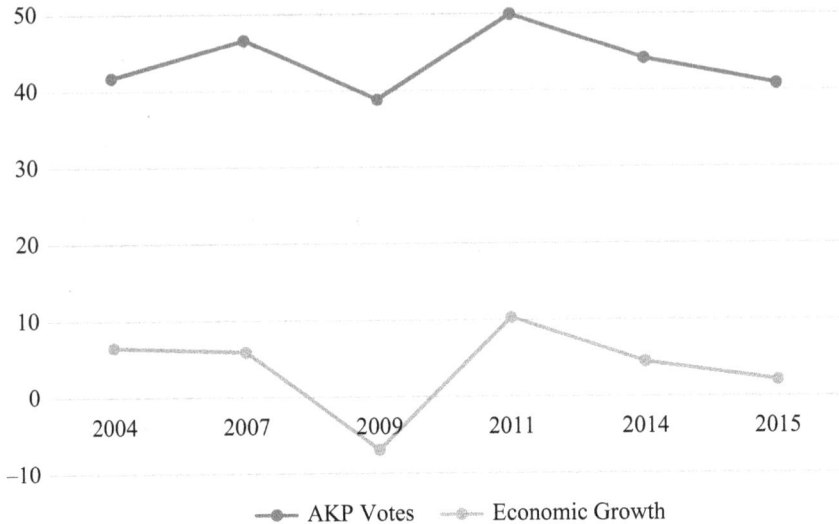

Figure 4.2 AKP votes and economic growth, 2004–15.

but also the opposition parties by applying Spatial-SUR estimations. Moreover, the paper utilizes happiness data and analyses the influence of the non-economic aspects of unhappiness of citizens in their voting behaviours. The authors basically argue that economic variables, including the level of public spending, are intertwined with the political performance of both the incumbent AKP and the opposition parties (CHP, MHP, HDP) in the June 2015 elections.

Public Expenditures, Electoral Success, and the AKP

The "economic school" of electoral analysis assumes that political parties' principal motivation in campaigning for government is the opportunity to decide the level and composition of public expenditures. In winning government, the argument goes, incumbents are at a distinct advantage in retaining office because they can allocate resources in such a way as to maximize political support. This section will explore three dimensions of public spending – social welfare expenditures, local spending and regional development policies, and governmental support to the agricultural sector – to analyse the extent to which, during the AKP era, allocative mechanisms have influenced the electoral support of the incumbent party.

Social welfare spending

The principal salient policy instrument that incumbent governments have at their disposal to cultivate political support to retain office is *social welfare spending*, particularly in the education and health care sectors. As mentioned, significant research on the Turkish case suggests that incumbent parties receive higher votes from those constituencies that are the primary beneficiaries of public expenditures in education and health care services. Indeed, micro-level survey data indicates that 41 per cent of AKP voters in the 2014 elections preferred the party because of its investment in social welfare services.[33] Figure 4.3 shows the significant extent of growth in social spending in Turkey during the AKP period. Nevertheless, as a recent OECD report that drew on 2011 statistics points out, a significant proportion (40 per cent) of new social spending went to the top 20 per cent of households by income level.[34]

A closer look at both health and education expenditures in particular is in order, items given that these services have the highest impact on the average citizen's life. Figure 4.4 shows the dramatic rise in public health spending at all levels in Turkey between 1999 and 2014. While the bulk of these spending increases came from the social security agency, central government spending increases in health services are notable. Moreover, as Figure 4.4 shows, AKP governments elected to make long-term investments in the health sector over this period, indicating that the "political business cycle" was not in play in this area. Significant spending increases were recorded in *both* pre-election and post-election periods. It is clear that AKP governments were committed to the principle that improvements in education and health outcomes require investments that are long-term in nature.

This fact is borne out by the significant improvements in quality metrics recorded in the system over the period. Figure 4.5 shows the number of hospital beds per population available in the health system between 1999 and 2014.

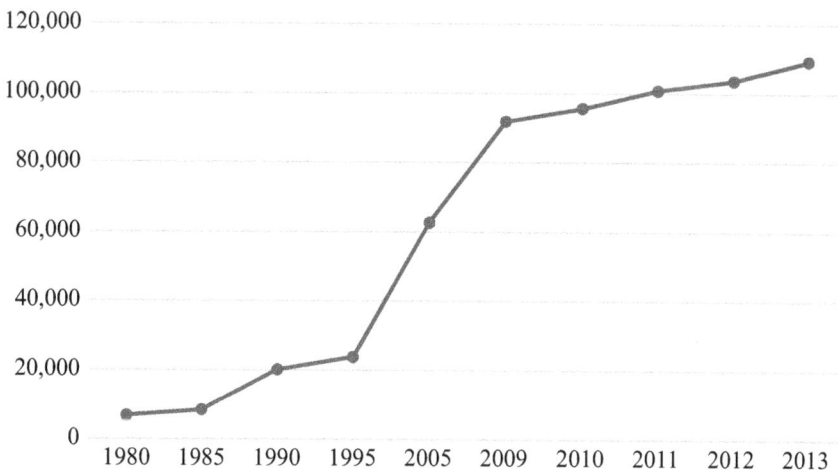

Figure 4.3 Government social expenditures (million Turkish lire, 2005 prices), 1980–2013.

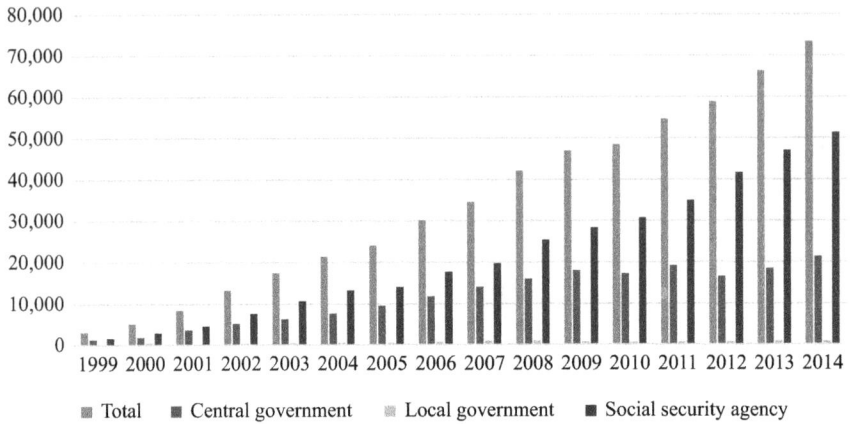

Figure 4.4 Government health expenditures (million Turkish lire), 1999–2014.

During the period of AKP rule, especially in the period immediately after coming into office, the number of new beds available has shown a significant general trend upwards.

AKP governments also appear to have committed to long term significant increases in public education expenditure. This growth in education spending as a share of total government expenditure, especially after 2009, is shown in Figure 4.6.

The consistent increases in spending on education chimes with the suggestion that the AKP has favoured long-term investments in social welfare services instead of opting for the political business cycle. A key policy priority

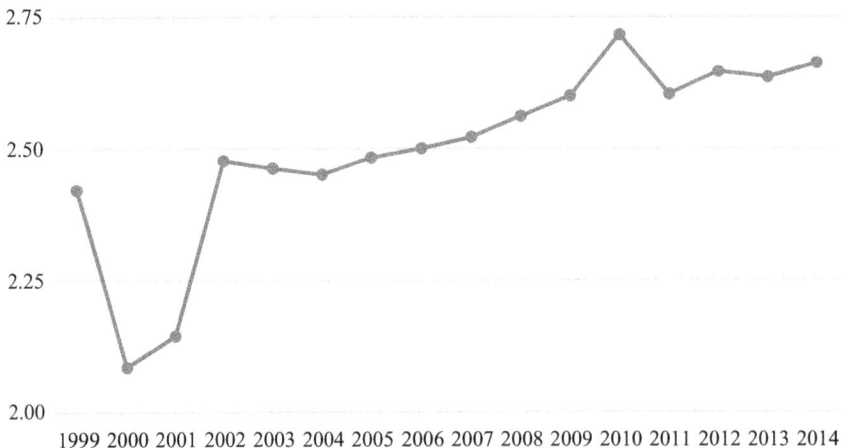

Figure 4.5 Number of beds per 1,000 people, 1999–2014.

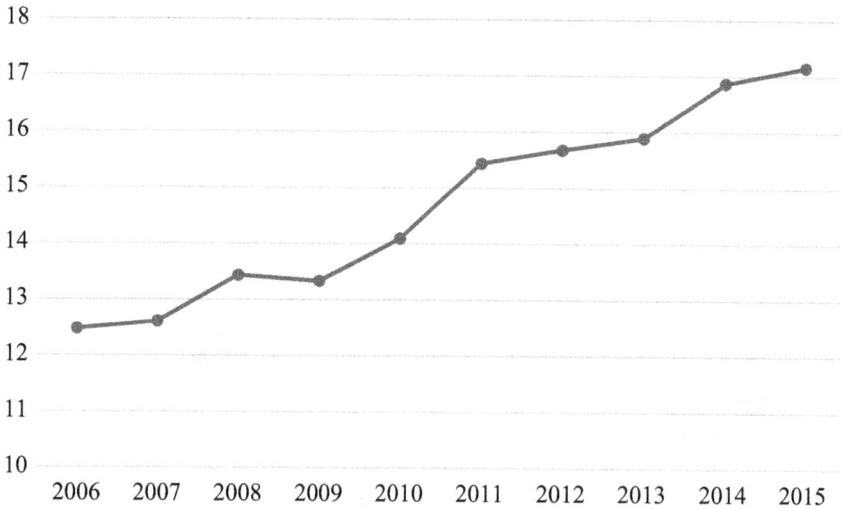

Figure 4.6   Share of education expenditures in public budget (%), 2006–15.

that has contributed to higher spending during the AKP period has been the free provision of books and tablet computers. Furthermore, new school openings have been a significant element in long-term education planning. The number of educational institutions in Turkey tripled between 2002 and 2013, as shown in the Figure 4.7. It is noteworthy in this context that the 2011 elections stand out, seeming to trigger something of a political business cycle approach, with a rapid increase in openings before the elections, and a retrenchment afterwards.

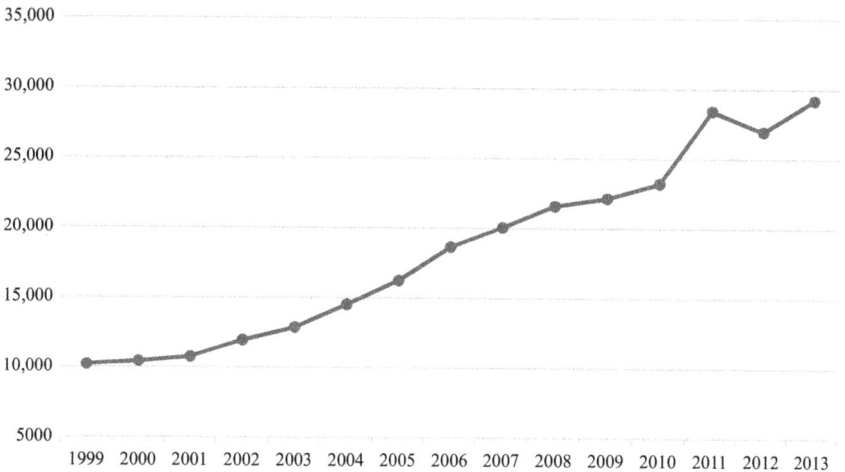

Figure 4.7   Number of educational institutions, 1999–2013.

Local spending and regional development policies

Incumbent governments are also inclined to direct public spending towards regional development policies to attract political support. Incumbent parties in Turkey often prefer local spending as it has a twofold impact on elections. Firstly, provincial candidates of the incumbent party can leverage regional investments during local campaigns, giving them a distinct advantage over other candidates. At the same time, national candidates of the same incumbent party can "double dip", claiming credit as well for these investments during general elections. Therefore, there is something of a "multiplier effect" to regional development policy funding for incumbent parties, which makes this kind of spending particularly attractive.

Figure 4.8 shows the level of local public expenditure by municipal authority in Turkey from 2006 to 2015. What is most striking from this graph is that the total amount of expenditure allocated to local authorities has risen twofold in real terms during the last ten years. Secondly, the number of official metropolitan cities grew to a record 29 in 2015 compared to 2006 and the public money allotted to this category of municipality increased significantly over the same period. Additionally, the gap between transfers to metropolitan authorities and other municipalities started to widen after 2013. Although it may be a speculative conclusion right now, it is nevertheless possible that the increasing amount of public expenditures towards metropolitan authorities could result in more centralized local government because financial support

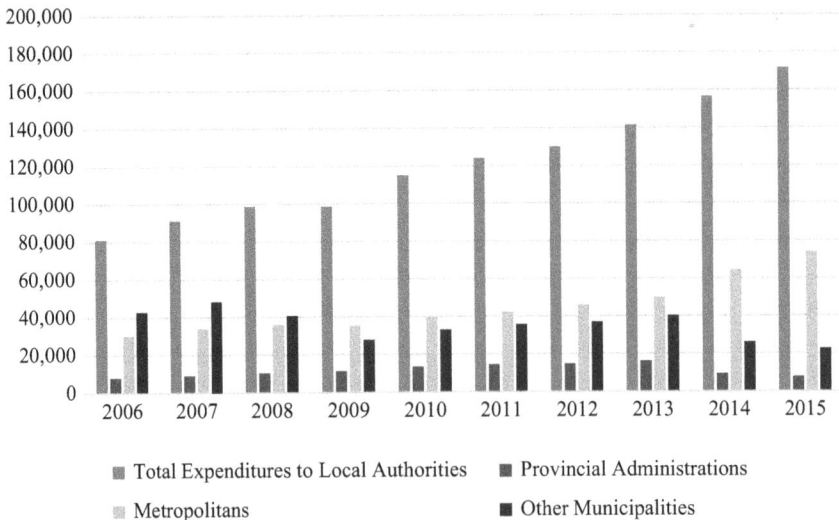

Figure 4.8 Value of local public expenditure by municipal authority (thousand Turkish lire, 2003 prices), 2006–15.

from the central government may create hierarchical superiority over local bodies in terms of local decision-making.

Road construction plays a significant role in regional development as well, particularly in the most underdeveloped cities and regions. Improvements in transportation efficiency are highly correlated with trade growth and thus long-term economic development. One of the AKP's primary transport priorities throughout its time in office has been road construction in the less developed parts of the country, including central Anatolia and eastern Turkey. Between 2006 and 2015 around 30 per cent of the entire state allocation for capital expenditure was spent on road construction. In the lead-up to the 2011 elections, this figure rose to almost 35 per cent, perhaps indicating the influence of the political business cycle in road construction decision-making.

Agricultural support

Nearly 20 per cent of Turkey's workforce is employed in the agricultural sector, a somewhat high figure for a middle-income country.[35] For this reason, agricultural support is a particularly potent tool in any government's efforts at mobilizing Turkey's large rural population. Agricultural producer support estimates (PSE) developed by the OECD measure the level of member states' support for agricultural producers. Drawing on this data, Civan finds that in Turkey the magnitude of PSE across 12 different segments of the agricultural sector shows clear increases before elections.[36] This research confirms a widespread view that incumbent parties in Turkey are highly motivated to gain the political support of powerful interest groups in the agricultural sector.

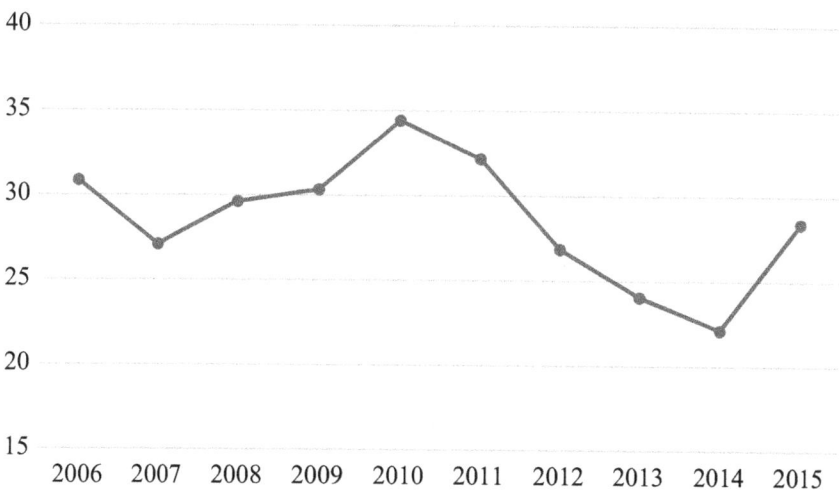

Figure 4.9 Road construction spending (% of total capital expenditure), 2006–15.

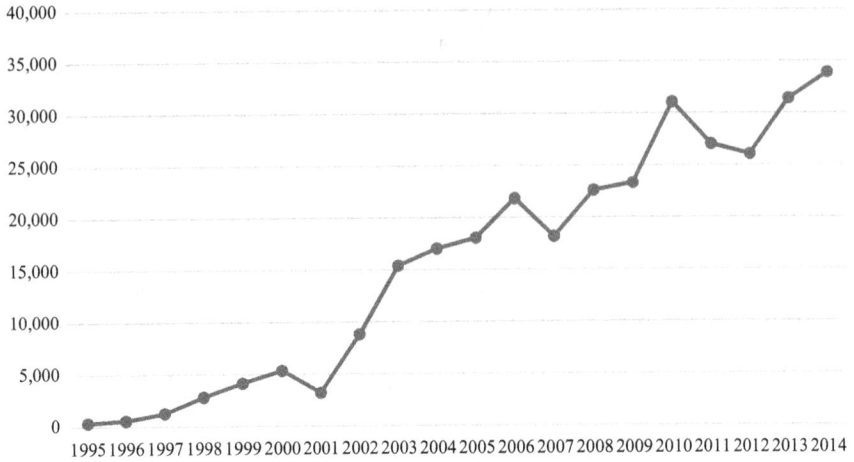

Figure 4.10 OECD Agricultural Producer Support Estimate (PSE), Turkey, 1995–2014.

Evidence of the partisan politicization of agricultural support is provided by Onemli and Korkmaz, who found that agricultural funding followed a distinct Political Business Cycle (PBC) between 1986 and 2011.[37]

The graph above indicates clearly the growth in the level of Producer Support Estimate (PSE) in Turkey under the AKP compared to the pre-AKP period. This pattern is mirrored in the value of direct agricultural transfers by

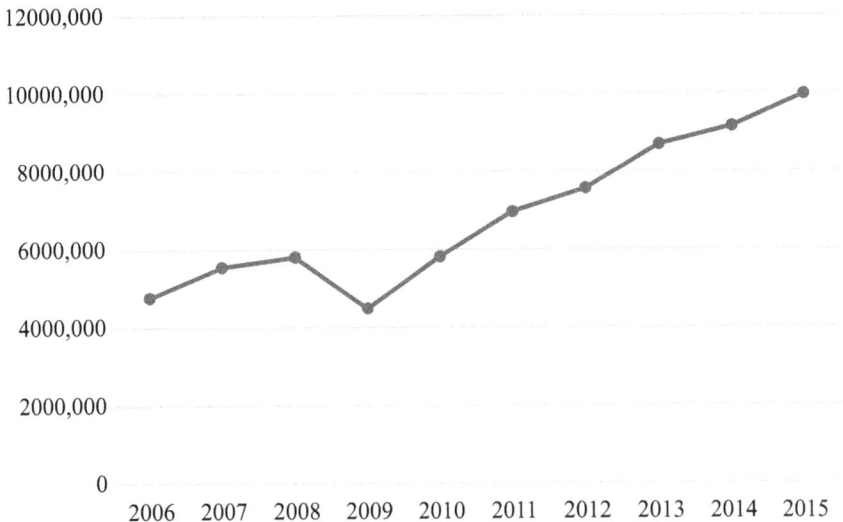

Figure 4.11 Agricultural transfers by government (thousand Turkish lire), 2006–15.

the government between 2006 and 2015 as shown in Figure 6.11 below. Unlike in education and health expenditures, which require long-term investments, in agriculture funding is determined annually and thus can have a significant role in the electoral strategies of the ruling party.

Conclusion

Economic analysis of elections focuses generally on the impact of economic variables on voters' electoral behaviour. The political economy of elections suggests that, alongside the more 'traditional' motivations for electoral behaviour such as ideology and party loyalty, citizens will cast their votes according to their expectations of prospective gains from one party over another. In other words, the voters' expected economic benefit after an election plays a pivotal (if not deterministic) role in electoral preferences.

Incumbency bestows significant power on a political party, the most potent aspect of which is arguably the capacity to direct the level and composition of public expenditure. Incumbent parties thus have a distinct advantage over opposition parties in retaining government through allocating resources to particular sectors and constituencies. This chapter has analysed the connection between the level and type of expenditures and electoral success during the AKP era in Turkey. It has done so through an exploration of three pillars of public expenditure most commonly associated with electoral mobilization: social welfare expenditures, local spending and regional development policies, and government support for the agricultural sector.

Our analysis finds that the AKP appears to prefer long-term investments in health care and education. These budget items have not been subject to overt partisan politicization and have steadily increased during the period of AKP rule. The principal determinant of spending in both these sectors appears to have been to produce concrete improvements in service delivery rather than to "buy" political support in any direct way. Indeed, the number of beds per population and the number of educational institutions increased significantly during the early years of AKP rule.

In addition to the social welfare expenditures, there is an evident fact that the amount of local spending by the government has risen by twofold in real terms during the last ten years. Secondly, the number of official metropolitan cities grew to a record 29 in 2015 compared to 2006 and the public money allotted to this category of municipality increased significantly over the same period. Additionally, the gap between transfers to metropolitan authorities and other municipalities started to widen after 2013. Moreover, the magnitude of agricultural support expenditure in Turkey has increased considerably since the AKP took office. Like the PSE figures, the steady rise in the amount of agricultural transfers by the government between 2006 and 2015 signals the fact that AKP governments have given particular importance to the 20 per cent of the workforce in the agricultural sector and their families, who have significant electoral power.

Our analysis supports the existing body of empirical research that suggests that voting behaviour in Turkey is highly contingent upon the financial support of the incumbent government. Increasing public spending – particularly in education and health – also motivates Turkish citizens to vote for the ruling party, although this is probably not why the AKP has made these kinds of investments. At the same time, the AKP's investment in social services makes most Turkish citizens dependent upon it. Turkish voters therefore make decisions at the ballot boxes that reflect their concern that an AKP loss in the elections might result in real economic deterioration for the household budget.

The AKP's political ambition to consolidate its power has gone hand in hand with increasing support from the public in successive elections, even as Turkey has faced significant challenges both in domestic and foreign affairs. It is fair to conclude therefore that economic policies devised by the AKP have effectively paved the way for the ruling party's authoritarian turn. In other words, mounting authoritarian tendencies are somehow compensated for by public expenditures on social welfare services (among other things). Going forward, however, there is an evident caveat here. To the extent that the oppressive nature of the Turkish state produces political risk that undermines the investment climate and reduces long-term economic growth, Turkish citizens and the AKP alike are in for significant turbulence ahead.

Notes

1. Roger D. Congleton, "The median voter model", *The Encyclopedia of Public Choice* (Springer US, 2004), pp. 707–12.
2. B. R., Weingast and D. A. Wittman, "The reach of political economy" in *The Oxford Handbook of Political Economy* (Oxford: Oxford University Press, 2006), p. 1.
3. R. M. Duch and R. Stevenson, *Voting in Context: How Political and Economic Institutions Condition Election Results* (Cambridge: Cambridge University Press, 2008).
4. Anthony Downs, "An economic theory of political action in a democracy", *The Journal of Political Economy* (1957), pp. 135–50.
5. Duch and Stevenson, *Voting in Context*.
6. M. S. Lewis-Beck and M. Stegmaier, "Economic Model of Voting", In R Dalton and H. D. Klingemann (eds), *Oxford Handbook of Political Behavior* (Oxford: Oxford University Press, 2007), pp. 518–37
7. Downs, "Economic theory of democracy".
8. For a more comprehensive literature, see Duch and Stevenson, *Voting in Context*.
9. Ibid.

10. Burak Onemli, T. E. Erkoç and A. Civan "Economic Voting and June 2015 Elections in Turkey: A Spatial Approach", GERN Microeconomic Research Paper Series, Working Paper 2016-1, January 2016.
11. Miriam A. Golden and Brian K. Min, "Distributive Politics Around the World", *Annual Review of Political Science* 16 (2013), pp. 73–99.
12. J. M. Buchanan and G. Tullock, *The Calculus of Consent* (Ann Arbor: University of Michigan Press, 1962).
13. A. Drazen and E. Eslava, "Pork Barrel Cycles", NBER Working Paper 12190 (2006).
14. A Dixit and J. Londregan "The determinants of success of special interests in redistributive politics", *Journal of Politics*, 58:4 (1996), pp. 1132–55.
15. G. W. Cox and M. D. McCubbins, "Electoral politics as a redistributive game", *Journal of Politics*, 48:2 (1986), pp. 370–89
16. D. A. Hibbs, *The Political Economy of Industrial Democracy* (Cambridge, MA: Harvard University Press, 1987).
17. G. M. Milesi-Ferretti, R. Perotti and M. Rostagno, 2002. "Electoral systems and public spending", *Quarterly Journal of Economics*, pp. 609–57.
18. W. D. Nordhaus. "The political business cycle", *Review of Economic Studies*, 42 (1975): pp. 169–90.
19. K. Rogoff. "Equilibrium political budget cycles", *American Economic Review*, 80 (1990): pp. 21–36.
20. M. Shi and J. Svensson. "Political budget cycles: Do they differ across countries and why?" *Journal of Public Economics*, 90(8–9) (2006), pp. 1367–89.
21. To have a comprehensive understanding of the empirical implications of economic voting in Turkey, see Yüksel and Civan, *The Impact of Economic Factors*; Baslevent and Kirmanoğlu, *Economic Voting in Turkey*.
22. E. Kalaycioğlu. "Elections and party preferences in Turkey changes and continuities in the 1990s", *Comparative Political Studies*, 27(3) (1994), pp. 402–24.
23. Samuel P. Huntington, *The Third Wave: Democratization in the Late Twentieth Century* (Norman, OK: University of Oklahoma Press, 1991) p. 267. He describes the turnover test as follows: "The party or group that takes power in the initial election at the time of transition loses a subsequent election and turns over power to those election winners, and if those election winners then peacefully turn over power to the winners of a later election."
24. Ziya Onis. "Turgut Özal and his Economic Legacy: Turkish Neo-Liberalism in Critical Perspective", *Middle Eastern Studies*, Vol. 40, No. 4 (2004), pp. 113–34.
25. A. Carkoglu. "Macro-economic Determinants of Electoral Support for Incumbents in Turkey, 1950–1995", *New Perspectives on Turkey*, 17, (1997), pp. 75–96.
26. A. T. Akarca and A. Tansel. *Economic Performance and Political Outcomes: An Analysis of the Turkish Parliamentary and Local Election Results between 1950 and 2004.*
27. C. Baslevent, H. Kirmanoğlu, and B. Senatalar. "Empirical Investigation of Party Preferences and Economic Voting in Turkey", *European Journal of Political Research*, 44 (2005), pp. 547–62.
28. A.T. Akarca. "Analysis of the 2009 Turkish Election Results from an Economic Voting Perspective", *European Research Studies*, 13(3) (2010), p. 3.

29. H. Yüksel and A. Civan. "The Impact of Economic Factors on the 2011 Turkish General Election", *Boğaziçi Journal Review of Social, Economic and Administrative Studies*, 27(1) (2013), pp. 53–67.
30. A.T. Akarca. "How Should We Interpret the Outcome of the June 2015 Parliamentary Election in Turkey?" *Ekonomi-TEK*, Vol. 3, No. 3 (2014).
31. Kemahlıoğlu Özge. "Winds of Change? The June 2015 Parliamentary Election in Turkey", *South European Society and Politics*, 20:4 (2015), pp. 445–64, DOI:10.1080/13608746.2015.1115581.
32. Onemli M. Burak, Erkoc T. E., Civan A. *Economic Voting and June 2015 Elections*.
33. 30 Mart Yerel Seçimler Sonrası Sandık ve Seçmen Analizi (2014), KONDA, http://www.konda.com.tr/tr/raporlar/KONDA_30Mart2014_YerelSecimAnalizi.pdf.
34. http://www.oecd.org/els/soc/OECD2014-Social-Expenditure-Update-Nov2014-8pages.pdf.
35. İşgücü İstatistikleri Aralık 2015 Haber Bülteni, http://www.tuik.gov.tr/PreHaberBultenleri.do?id=21569. The corresponding figure for Brazil is 14.5 per cent, for Mexico 13.4 per cent, and for Russia 6.7 per cent.
36. A. Civan. "Türkiye'de Tarımsal Destek Politikaları, Dokuz Eylül Üniversitesi İktisadi ve İdari Bilimler Fakültesi Dergisi", *Sayı* 25(1), pp. 127–46.
37. M. Burak Onemli, and A. Korkmaz (2015) "Political Business Cycle on the Agricultural Supports in Turkey", *Eurasian Journal of Business and Economics 2015*, 8 (15) (2010), pp. 167–84. DOI: 10.17015/ejbe.2015.015.08.

CHAPTER 5

FOREIGN POLICY AS A LEGITIMATION STRATEGY FOR THE AKP'S HEGEMONIC PROJECT OF THE "NEW TURKEY"

Bezen Balamir Coşkun, Salih Doğan and Mustafa Demir

Introduction

By discussing how foreign policy has being instrumentalized by the elites of the Justice and Development Party (*Adalet ve Kalkınma Partisi*, AKP) in Turkey, this chapter aims to contribute to scholarly debates on the role of foreign policy in the legitimization of domestic-level hegemonic projects This chapter argues that during the AKP era Turkey's foreign relations have been framed by the AKP ruling elite to strengthen their hegemony in Turkish politics and society. The chapter also aims to illuminate the role of foreign policy in the search for legitimacy and its function in securing stability and reinforcing the authoritarian trend in Turkey during the AKP's rule. To demonstrate this argument, the chapter examines some of the foreign-policy moves that have taken place during the AKP era and identifies the key discursive frames employed to structure and justify them. The chapter argues that a certain type of foreign-policy rhetoric has been employed by the AKP ruling elite first to build a historical bloc of support, then to get popular consent for their hegemonic project, the so-called "new Turkey".

Foreign policy-making involves a series of steps by state leaders and domestic politics plays an important role. Thus, the "second image"[1] (domestic level) has always been a central focus of foreign-policy analyses in international relations. Even structural realists like Waltz argued that analysis of foreign policy requires examination of "differences of internal composition" as well as examination of "the performance of governments."[2] Waltz's theory of foreign policy analyses political systems and the interpretations of the beliefs of individuals and groups to evaluate the policy outcome. The theory assumes a primary role for the structure of the political system, whether democratic or authoritarian, parliamentary or presidential. Waltz argued that foreign-policy analyses must provide an account of how the various parts are "arranged", the relative power of the parts, and how the arrangements of those parts affect the policy-making process.[3] In this regard, several internal factors – such as power vested in the leader, the leader's acceptability in the domestic system, strategic decision-making, the personality of the leader, rationality, and the impact of interest groups as well as the external environment – can affect foreign policy decisions. From this perspective, Putnam names his model of diplomatic decision-making as a "two-level game". Putnam's model views international negotiations as consisting of simultaneous negotiations at both the domestic level (where negotiators try to build coalitions among domestic interests for a particular foreign policy position) and the international level (where negotiators seek agreements with other nations that produce outcomes that fall within the state's win-set).[4] A quick literature review highlights several core themes on the role of domestic factors in foreign policy-making that recur: the effects of political regime form, the nature of internal political opposition, national political culture, and the role of public opinion and the local media.[5]

Despite the richness of second-image theories of foreign policy, analysis of the role of foreign policy in the legitimization of domestic politics is seldom found in international relations literature. The literature tends to view foreign policy as a dependent variable and regime types as an independent variable; studies that treat *regime types* as independent variables in foreign policy analysis are rare.

The detrimental effects of globalization have been posing challenges to state sovereignty. Certain emerging powers in the international system have found themselves in a crisis of legitimacy both internally and externally. In many cases, we may identify a tendency towards authoritarianism as a key mechanism adopted by leaders in these states to deal with the transnational characteristics of the threats to sovereign power. As a reflection of the legitimacy crisis inside, leaders feel the need to build new historical blocs to consolidate their power. This process of power consolidation typically requires a hegemonic project and the realm of foreign policy offers an abundance of tools to mobilize popular consent in that context. As argued by Stubbs, the legitimacy of political structures is built up over a long period and,

> the ultimate test of a country's political structures [comes] down to the question of whether or not they [can] provide basic necessities, most particularly physical security, social and political stability, and economic prosperity [... This comes] to be termed [...] performance legitimacy.[6]

According to Stubbs, the durability of soft authoritarian governments in Southeast Asia is wholly dependent on performance legitimacy. Besides Stubbs' study on soft authoritarianism and regional affairs in Southeast Asia, several recent studies discuss foreign policy as a tool for legitimizing authoritarian regimes, including Chambers' work on authoritarianism and foreign policy as two pillars of Putin's rule in Russia,[7] Hoffman's study on the international dimension of authoritarian legitimation in Cuba,[8] and Kneurer's study on foreign policy as a legitimation strategy in authoritarian regimes.[9]

This chapter contributes to the literature on the operationalization of foreign policy for domestic purposes. The discussion here is framed from a Gramscian perspective. The AKP ruling elites' foreign-policy rhetoric and action will be discussed as a strategy for the consolidation of their hegemonic rule during the first period of AKP rule (2002–7) and for legitimation of that project during the second period (2007–16).

Organic Crisis in the "Old Turkey" and the Rise of the AKP

For Gramsci, an organic crisis puts the legitimacy of rulers in jeopardy in the eyes of the masses:

> In every country the process is different, although the content is the same. And the content is the crisis of the ruling class's hegemony, which occurs either because the ruling class has failed in some major political undertaking for which it has requested, or forcibly extracted, the consent of the broad masses (war, for example), or because huge masses (especially of peasants and petty-bourgeois intellectuals) have passed suddenly from a state of political passivity to a certain activity, and put forward demands which taken together, albeit not organically formulated, add up to a revolution. A crisis of authority is spoken of: this is precisely the crisis of hegemony, or general crisis of the State.[10]

These kinds of crises represent the moment at which a genuine revolutionary assault on the old order can occur, as the masses are propelled into action to try and resolve the failures of the ruling class.

Since the establishment of the republic, political and ideological arguments over the regime and its legitimacy have occupied political and scholarly debates. At the outset, Turkey was a bureaucratic-military regime. By the mid-1930s, Mihail Manoilesco had classified the one-party rule of Atatürk's Republican People's Party (*Cumhuriyet Halk Partisi*, CHP) as a fascist regime.[11] This moderately mobilizational authoritarian regime, in Linz' terms, transformed itself into a competitive democracy in the late 1940s.[12] During the 1960s, Shils classified Turkey as a tutelary democracy[13] while Rustow[14] and

Dahl[15] adopted the classification "near-polyarchy". Periodic military interventions in Turkish politics put Turkey on the borderline between modern authoritarian regimes and democracy. According to Linz, Turkey is always closer to democracy in terms of its constitutional and ideological conception but closer to some authoritarian regimes sociologically. The pluralistic element is always there, but it is always a limited version of pluralism.[16]

Turkey's first "organic crisis" occurred in the 1960s. The deep division between the political and state elite was brought to a head in the May 1960 military coup. As argued by Bacik and Salur, the 1960 intervention was the reaction of state elites against the "unhealthy" autonomization of economic and political groups at the expense of the Kemalist social contract. After the intervention, the republican elite ushered in the 1961 Constitution to guarantee their social and corporate interests.[17] In this period, the traditional bureaucratic-military state elite assembled a historical bloc, including other actors such as urban intellectuals. To prevent the development of a national-popular movement, this elite coalition excluded peripheral and religious sections of the society, which triggered an organic crisis. The failure of successive republican elite-led governments to make any progress on economic development in the 1960s and the global economic crisis of the 1970s – had severe repercussions for this hegemonic class. In effect, the republican state elite ceded their promise to bring peace, security and prosperity to the people. As claimed by Jean Jacques Rousseau, a social contract is often broken during such times when "a state is in the process of being organized [such that] more resistance would be put up at a time of complete disorder [and] the state would inevitably be overthrown."[18]

These crises have led to the establishment of popular-national movements that consist of previously excluded peripheral and religious groups. Eventually, a historic bloc of peripheral forces, mobilized by a counter-republican political elite, has formed around a succession of populist right-wing parties – the Democrat Party (1946–60), the Justice Party (1961–80), the Motherland Party (1983–2002) and, since 2001, the Justice and Development Party (*Adalet ve Kalkınma Partisi*, AKP). The growth of this historical bloc, especially under the Motherland Party and the AKP, has coincided with the rise of a new socio-political elite. The AKP in particular has benefitted dramatically from the support of the conservative Anatolian proto-bourgeoisie, which emerged from the 1980s. This new historical bloc mobilized both in state and political structures to topple the traditional republican elite.

The AKP was founded in 2001 by a group of reformist politicians of the defunct Welfare Party (*Refah Partisi*, RP), which had been closed by the Constitutional Court in 1998. The RP was merely the last in a long line of political parties with roots in the National Outlook (*Milli Görüş*) movement of Necmettin Erbakan.[19] Erbakan founded his first party in the 1960s, which was subsequently closed by the republican elite, only to be reborn in a new guise a short time later, a pattern that would repeat across the 1980s and 1990s. As Andrew Finkel, a long-time observer of Turkish politics, states "every time the courts shut down a supposedly 'anti-secular' party, another one grew back, and like a pruned tree, stronger than before."[20] However, the cycle was broken when the AKP was founded in 2001.

The reformist wing of the RP that formed the AKP charted a course away from Erbakan's approach, presenting a moderate, modernist, and decidedly economically liberal face. Rhetorically speaking, the agenda and priorities of the AKP stood in stark contrast to the traditional Islamist agenda of its *Milli Görüş* predecessors. As Dağı reminds us, the party explicitly rejected the label "Islamist" and instead presented itself as a "conservative democratic political movement" in the mould of the European Christian Democrat parties.[21] Many intellectuals and academics interpreted this as transformation via "strategic learning induced by the 'February 28 process' of 1997, when the secularist military brought down a coalition government headed by Erbakan [and] closed his Welfare Party."[22] This decisive rhetorical shift helped the AKP to reach out to a wider segment of the society beyond the traditional constituencies of the Turkish centre-right.

Cizre points out the significance of the "soft" 28 February coup as a critical (domestic level) factor in this transformation. Traditional political Islam was clearly the target of this intervention, as she notes, and its impact was felt at the heart of the *Milli Görüş* movement. The closure of the RP by the Constitutional Court in 1998   and, in particular, the banning of Erbakan from politics for five years – presented an opportunity for moderate reformists within the movement to make a break with the past and to attempt to take the movement in a new direction. This was by no means a smooth process. As soon as the Court closed *Refah*, it essentially reformed as the Virtue Party (*Fazilet Partisi*, FP) under the leadership of Recai Kutan, Erbakan's preferred successor (he could not stand as he was banned from politics). When the FP was itself found unconstitutional by the Constitutional Court and then banned on 22 June 2001, reformist moderates led, among others, by Abdullah Gül (later president of the republic) elected to break away to form the AKP as a new, reformist political force. Within 15 months, the AKP swept to power in a landslide election victory, winning a two-thirds majority in the parliament. The main reasons behind the success of AKP was the poor governance of prior political and state elites, who failed to provide "'the safety of the people', and by safety is meant not a bare preservation of life, 'but also all other Commitments of life.'"[23] Hence, the old social contract was broken. By claiming to represent segments of Turkish society which had been ostracized by old historical bloc since the early 1920s, the AKP has attempted to rejuvenate the social contract in Turkey.

Foreign Policy, the New Historical Bloc and the Consolidation of the AKP's Hegemonic Rule

The AKP leveraged both Turkey's "organic" crisis and the broader sense of economic malaise following the 1999 crisis with tremendous skill in its 2002 election campaign. Nevertheless, even the party leadership was taken by surprise by the party's electoral success. Despite winning over 34 per cent of the vote, the party was vulnerable. The counter-hegemonic historical bloc that supported it during the 2002 campaign remained fragile. Thus, the party keenly felt the need to diversify its constituency even further and bring hitherto hostile groups (such as the media and liberal intellectuals) into its fold. The key to consolidating its momentum and power was to construct a "historical bloc" in the Gramscian sense.

In his *Prison Notebooks*, Gramsci defined a historical bloc as a unity between structure and superstructure. At the same time, he deployed the concept to delineate a homogeneous politico-economic alliance without internal contradictions.[24] Building on these insights, Stephen Gill argues that a historical bloc is the product of ideological work undertaken by a conscious social force that intends to establish a new hegemony:

> A historical bloc refers to an historical congruence between material forces, institutions and ideologies, or broadly, an alliance of different class forces politically organized around a set of hegemonic ideas that gave strategic direction and coherence to its constituent elements. Moreover, for a new historical bloc to emerge, its leaders must engage in conscious planned struggle. Any new historical bloc must have not only power within the civil society and economy, it also needs persuasive ideas, arguments and initiatives that build on, catalyze and develop its political networks and organization – not political parties as such.[25]

In the wake of the 2002 elections, the Kemalist bloc was still strongly embedded in all the key state apparatuses, particularly the courts and the military. The 2003 US invasion of Iraq provided the AKP with its first opportunity to draw on a foreign policy event to both gain leverage over the Kemalist state elite (who were in favour of joining the US mission) and to catalyse public opinion around its vision for a "New Turkey". Public opinion was overwhelmingly against joining the US operation and the AKP skillfully leveraged this to its advantage, blocking permission for the US to launch operations into northern Iraq from Turkey in the parliament, to great public acclaim. By speaking about the need for Turkey to consider fresh policy options in relation to its Middle Eastern neighbours, the new prime minister, Recep Tayyip Erdoğan, outlined a new "role conception" for Turkey. In very short order, the political and intellectual elite came on board with the AKP's vision of a new role for Turkey as a uniquely-placed "middle power" bridging Europe and Asia on the stage of global politics, leaving traditional republican foreign-policy orientations (which appeared as both obsolete and pandering to the West) to wither on the vine.[26]

Looking back, we see that from the outset a populist reasoning lay at the heart of the AKP's foreign-policy orientation towards the Middle East. This is seen most markedly through the deployment of both pan-Islamist and quasi-conspiratorial rhetoric as challenging international events have been exploited to divert attention from pressing issues at home. For example, the party has often laid regional crises at the feet of some Western power or other, invoking the long-standing Turkish suspicion of Western hostility towards Turkey or Islam more generally. At other times, blame has been put on some Middle Eastern government for poor dealing or being uncooperative. The pursuit of a belligerent foreign policy to divert popular attention from internal problems is of course a regular pastime of authoritarian elites. As Kneuer notes:

> diversionary action represents a response to internal problems or conflicts. In addition to deflecting the popular attention away from economic or political problems, the intention is to engender a unifying national resilience against external threat, thereby increasing domestic cohesion and support. Hence, diversionary action can be subsumed as a legitimation strategy in foreign policy that begins on the domestic level reacting to inner problems.[27]

The AKP also drew heavily on the external "European anchor" to advance its hegemonic project. The EU was an early and vocal supporter of the AKP's "moderate" approach and, in its early phase, the party skillfully deployed the rhetoric and practice of Europeanization and harmonization with EU norms to enact reforms that undermined military prerogatives and tutelage.[28] The EU reform process has served as the primary mechanism for weakening the Kemalist establishment's institutional stronghold within the Turkish state. "Over-delivering" on EU-accession requirements in the early years was a strategically clever move, because it marshalled EU praise and encouragement to assuage the secular public in Turkey, who had hitherto been very suspicious about the new ruling elite. Moreover, deploying the EU anchor (with its emphasis on democratic norms, transparency, accountability, modernization, and Westernization) caught the Kemalist elite in an ideological-rhetorical "trap", because it allowed the AKP to present *itself* as the true vanguard of Atatürk's historical project of bringing Turkey closer to the ideals of Western civilization, in contrast to the Kemalists, who could be cast as the spoilers. The construction of a set of EU-driven institutional reforms that opened the military's tutelary role to accountability mechanisms was the hallmark achievement of this period.

A closer look at Turkey–Israel relations in the period of AKP rule serves to reinforce the point about the party's use of external events to mobilize popular opinion. Prime Minister Erdoğan's "one minute" intervention at the World Economic Forum in Davos in 2009 and the May 2010 Israeli military assault on a civilian humanitarian flotilla, including the Turkish ship the *Mavi Marmara*, are particularly instructive. These events become game-changing incidents in the AKP's consolidation of its hegemony. Prime Minister Erdoğan's harsh critique of the response of the Israeli leadership to Israeli atrocities in Gaza and the annulment of diplomatic relations and military agreements with Israel attracted widespread acclaim throughout Turkey. Yet this was achieved without any material loss to Turkish economic interests, which is key to the AKP's power consolidation Amidst the diplomatic crisis, the trade volume between Turkey and Israel actually *increased*, rising more than 50 per cent between 2010 and 2015 from \$3.44 billion to \$4.37 billion.[29] This shows how the AKP could *simultaneously* leverage both improving economic relations with Israel and a hostile discourse against it (presaged on the Turkish population's traditional animosity towards Israeli military and settlement policy in the Occupied Territories). By confronting Israeli President Peres so publicly and forcefully, Erdoğan managed to reach the "hearts and minds" of millions of religious Turks, becoming a national hero in the process. AKP officials deployed these two incidents masterfully throughout the 2011 general election campaign, in which the AKP won 49.83 per cent of the votes, thus consolidating its hegemonic rule in Turkey.

In a similar vein, the AKP took a particular interest in relations with the Iraqi-Kurdistan leadership in order to curry favour with Turkey's domestic Kurdish population. From 2009, Iraqi Kurd leader Mesoud Barzani was cast as a "strategic partner" for Ankara. The opening of a Turkish consulate in Erbil, the capital of Iraqi Kurdistan, reflected the shift in relations and a distinct warming and development of economic and diplomatic ties between Ankara and Erbil. In September 2012 Barzani was even invited to address the AKP's fourth party conference, a very important signal to Turkey's local Kurdish population. In his address, Barzani praised the AKP and expressed his gratitude for the AKP leadership's approach to the Kurdish question. While reaching out to Barzani served several important foreign policy purposes, some unrelated to the Kurdish issue, it is nevertheless the case that the public displays of fraternity were crucial to mobilizing Kurdish support for the AKP bloc and for Erdoğan's leadership.

These examples showcase the way in which the AKP skillfully instrumentalized foreign policy and external diplomatic relationships to expand its domestic base of support. Without these moves, its hegemonic position would almost certainly not have been consolidated, at least not as comprehensively as it was.

The party's assiduous construction of its historical bloc was the essential element in its five consecutive general (and three consecutive local) election wins, which saw the AKP transform Turkey into what Sartori called a "predominant party system".[30] In Sartori's classification, a predominant party system is one in which the major party, such as Congress in India or the Liberal Democrats in Japan, is constantly supported by a winning majority of voters and consistently (over at least four legislative elections) wins a majority of parliamentary seats.

Despite dominating Turkish politics for more than a decade, the legitimacy of the AKP has crumbled, particularly after 2011. Indeed, the June 2015 general election was a wake-up call for the AKP, as it was unable to form a single-party government due to the loss of 69 seats. The growing opposition against the hegemony of the AKP had challenged the predominant party system, and the AKP ruling elite has thus realized that they need to overcome the crisis of legitimacy by finding ways and means to marshal consent for their hegemony. As expected, foreign policy has become an important part of the hegemonic project of New Turkey.

Legitimation Crisis, Foreign Policy, and the "New Turkey" as the AKP's Hegemonic Project

> In those Nations, whose Commonwealths have been long-lived, and not been destroyed, but by foreign warre, the Subjects never did dispute of the Sovereign Power.[31]

The empirical focus of this section is legitimation, particularly the strategies that a hegemonic or authoritarian regime will deploy in the quest to cultivate legitimacy, which is considered as a static property of a regime or leader in its relationship to the people or to followers. The particular discussion here will zero in on how discourses and strategies of foreign policy have been deployed by the AKP ruling elite in recent times to marshal legitimacy on the road to authoritarian rule.

Legitimacy as a political concept

Legitimacy is critical to the maintenance of power and stability of all political systems. Any power needs to justify itself by attempting "to establish and cultivate the belief in its legitimacy."[32] This is as true of authoritarian regimes as it is of their democratic counterparts, even though it is more difficult for authoritarian regimes. The central problem of autocracies is to secure stability, which is not possible without public support. Although repression (or the threat of it) remains an important source of stability in an authoritarian system, the ruling elite must still draw on additional modes of recognition. This recognition is essential not only among the population at large, but also to maintain the support of the groups within the historical bloc. In this regard, Lipset views output legitimacy or "performance legitimacy" as crucial.[33]

To sustain its hegemony within the society, the leadership must make considerable efforts to convince these different groups that they can solve problems and "deliver" tangible benefits. Hence, the output dimension of legitimation is essential for any regime that wishes to justify its non-democratic practices. "Law and order" arguments to establish public safety; "justice" arguments that imply the promise of improved distribution of public goods, "restoration" arguments against the more egalitarian aims of the revolutionary masses, and finally the "development" argument for improved economic progress are typically deployed to serve this purpose.[34] Naturally, this produces expectations for concrete outputs. The fulfilment of those expectations requires a systematic performance. Keuner argues that this performance has both external and internal dimensions, which are linked. Foreign policy is part of the output dimension of legitimacy since it "can be symbolic, declaratory, or concrete. Second, foreign policy reinforces domestic economic or security aspects."[35] By referring to identity concerns and cultivating a sense of belonging, foreign policy can also generate internal solidarity.

The role of the "hegemonic project" in the legitimation of authoritarianism

To expand and/or legitimize the hegemonic rule of a certain political elite, a "hegemonic project" is usually introduced that can anchor the exercise of power. The social bases of the hegemonic power are heterogeneous – that is to say, different social forces vary in their degree of commitment. There also exists:

> a considerable variation in the mix of material concessions, symbolic rewards, and repression directed through the state to different social forces. These variations in support and benefit are typically related to the prevailing hegemonic project (if any) and its implications for the form and content of politics.[36]

Hegemony organizes class-relevant forces under the political, intellectual, and moral leadership of a class or fraction. Jessops views the development of a specific "hegemonic project" as the key to the exercise of such leadership to resolve the conflicts between particular interests and the general interest. A hegemonic project thus involves the mobilization of support behind a concrete "national" and "popular" programme of action which asserts a general interest in the pursuit of objectives.[37] Hegemonic projects are concerned with various non-economic objectives including military success, social reform, political stability, or moral regeneration. They are also typically oriented to broader issues grounded in both economic relations and civil society.[38] In this regard, hegemonic projects concern themselves with the "national-popular", understood in the Gramscian sense.

Foucault's lectures on security, territoriality and population focus on the way in which contemporary governance is no longer about "the safety of the Prince and his territory but the security of population."[39] Hence, the safety of the state (the Prince) is contrasted with the security of population. In this context, ongoing terror attacks and the rise of critiques over the inability of government to protect its citizens has become one of the soft spots of AKP leadership. These internal conditions are accompanied by totalitarian trends in international politics resulting from "a limitation, a reduction, and a subordination of the autonomy of the state."[40] Foucault calls this trend "state phobia".[41] The obvious reflection on state phobia is the erosion of sovereignty which also has detrimental effects on the powers of the ruling/governing elite.

The "New Turkey" as the AKP's hegemonic project

The AKP's "New Turkey" constitutes such a hegemonic project. An imprecise formulation that is heavily rhetorical and symbolic, it nevertheless focuses on military strength, social reform, political stability in the face of threats from within and without, and a general moral and social rejuvenation of the society. It has been constructed by the AKP ruling elite to overcome the detrimental effects of state phobia among liberal sections of the society. "New Turkey" rhetoric has gained momentum after the Gezi protests, as a response to increasingly vocal anti-government movements. The foreign policy aspect of the New Turkey project is crucial and has been skillfully deployed to cultivate legitimacy by the AKP's ruling elite. Three discursive and strategic elements stand out in this context: broad-based Sunni politics in the Muslim World, humanitarian foreign policy (particularly towards Africa), and a values-based foreign policy orientation.

Prior to the Arab uprisings that broke out in 2011, the AKP had pursued a foreign-policy orientation that was based, broadly speaking, on economic and trade relations. The Arab Spring not only shook the region and regional balances, but also deeply affected Turkey's foreign policy orientation. Political crisis in Egypt and Syria provided an opportunity for the AKP (and Erdoğan in particular), to promote Turkey as the "saviour" of Sunni Muslims in the region. This stance strengthens the hegemonic bloc since Sunni politics in the region is of utmost concern among pious Sunni Muslims in Turkey. Even though sectarianism had been a driving force in Turkish foreign policy since 2009, this aspect became more salient after 2011. Taking a clear sectarian stance, however, cost Turkey dearly. Its role as trade partner and "neutral party" in regional conflicts has been undermined, and Turkey has become increasingly sidelined diplomatically. Additionally, while Sunni politics could mobilize pious Sunni support to the AKP's hegemonic bloc, it also produced harsh criticism from both secular and ultra-nationalist sections of the society. During the 2013 crisis in Egypt, the AKP and Erdoğan emerged as the fiercest international critics of Morsi's overthrow. Turkey–Egypt relations soured dramatically following the killing of hundreds of Morsi supporters in the *Rabaa al-Adawiya* Square in August 2013. Erdoğan called on the UN Security Council to convene for an urgent response to what he described as a massacre.

Erdoğan's support for the Muslim Brotherhood in the Arab world has two important motives. First, his Islamist supporters continue to admire Morsi and the Muslim Brotherhood in Egypt,[42] and the "Rabba sign" was adopted as a symbol of the "New Turkey" project.[43] Erdoğan famously keeps the symbol by his desk and has consistently referenced it as a key element of the "New Turkey" project: "One nation, one flag, one state, one homeland." Second, Erdoğan's anti-coup foreign policy towards Sisi was related to his policy of further weakening the Kemalist military bloc as a legitimating contrast with the AKP's hegemonic bloc, since no sensible Turkish citizen, even ultra-secular ones, would wish to be identified as a supporter of military coups. Anyone who criticizes this sectarian strand in Turkish foreign policy had been accused of being insensitive towards the pain of oppressed Muslim brothers and sisters. Critics have also been accused of lacking the humanitarian values that "New Turkey" purportedly champions.

Indeed, the second pillar of foreign policy dimension of new Turkey rhetoric is humanitarianism. Until his reassignment in May 2016 Ahmet Davutoğlu was an enthusiastic advocate of humanitarian diplomacy and foreign policy. Together with Erdoğan and Davutoğlu, İbrahim Kalın, a close and longstanding confidante of Erdoğan, played a significant role in the development of public diplomacy rhetoric which has given legitimacy to Ankara's "soft" involvement in the old Ottoman territories. As in other pillars of the hegemonic "New Turkey" project, the AKP elite has constantly underlined the distinctive features of the Turkish model of humanitarian assistance. Even arms transfers to Syria (for Turcoman rebels fighting the regime) was justified with a humanitarian logic. Turkey, so the rhetoric went, is a strong country with a responsibility to offer a helping hand to its brethren in need. Critics were silenced under pain of being accused of being insensitive towards ethnic Turks in Syria. The dominant discourse about Erdoğan as the saviour of the Turcomans in Syria and Iraq intended to contribute in the construction of the image of him as a leader on the world stage, something which "New Turkey" can be proud of.

In 2012 Turkey ranked as the fourth-largest government donor of humanitarian relief, which became an oft-cited fact in official statements at home and abroad. Turkey's humanitarian engagement was an indication of the ruling elites' desire to play a greater role globally. Turkey's growing engagement in the humanitarian field has become a legitimation tool for the AKP ruling elite as well. African humanitarian assistance has played a crucial role here, strengthening a perception that Turkey is on the rise. At the same time, Turkey's "humanitarian generosity" has been used by ruling elite to cover up internal and external failures in the eyes of Turkish public. The rhetoric glorifying Turkey's success in the humanitarian arena is always accompanied by a harsh critique of either the EU or the UN (or both). President Erdoğan's constant emphasis on the idea that the "world is bigger than five" is directed almost entirely at a domestic audience. By pointing out the incapacity of leading international organizations to bring stability and peace in the system, Erdoğan's discourse conceals both Turkey's failed foreign-policy adventures abroad and the growing authoritarian tendencies inside. In a threatening and anarchic system, so the rhetoric goes, Turkey must do whatever it takes for survival, even if at the cost of democracy and human rights.

Moreover, in such a system, stability and strength are the primary requirements of Turkish policy at home and abroad, which further plays into the rhetoric that everyone must "rally around" the government: to criticize is to put Turkey's stability and peace at risk. This discourse of "obligatory solidarity" thus excludes (or at least marginalizes) all social and political opposition to the AKP. In this regard, foreign policy is easily instrumentalized by the AKP to justify authoritarian tendencies inside. As Scharpf states, by imposing a sense of normative obligation rulers "ensure the voluntary compliance with undesired rules or decisions of governing authority"[44] and citizens conclude that it is a duty to make sacrifices for the sake of the state's survival and the power of the regime. In demanding such sacrifices to consolidate the power of the ruling elite, the AKP leadership (and President Erdoğan in particular) have raised their voice to criticize powerful actors of the international system. In this context, the tensions over the shooting down of a Russian jet and over the German parliament's approval of the resolution on the "Armenian Genocide" have been skillfully used by Erdoğan to persuade his domestic constituency about the strength of New Turkey in the interests of consolidating their power at domestic level.

Conclusion

This chapter has sought to highlight the critical role of foreign policy as a strategy of legitimation for hegemonic rule by the AKP. The basic assumption is that foreign policy can serve as such a strategy when foreign-policy action is linked to domestic constraints or interests. In the Turkish case, foreign policy has been utilized as a tool to legitimize the AKP's hegemonic rule in Turkey and to undergird its hegemonic project of the "New Turkey", which steadily introduces nationalist-authoritarian elements into Turkish politics.

One could be forgiven for thinking that Erdoğan, as the leader of a historical bloc, has taken a page straight from the playbook of Machiavelli's advice to the Prince:

> A prince must [...] encourage his citizens to be able quietly to practise their trades, in commerce, in agriculture and in every other human occupation [...] at the appropriate times of the year he should keep his people occupied with feast-days and spectacles [...] he should [...] offer himself as an example of humanity and munificence.[45]

Since Erdoğan's famous "one minute" intervention at Davos, the AKP leadership has found a fertile ground in foreign policy to highlight the "grandeur" of the "New Turkey". Even when Turkey was relatively isolated from regional affairs, this was presented as "precious loneliness." The hegemonic project of the AKP has had both domestic and international dimensions: political stability and economic growth on the domestic level and a proactive and leading state on the international level. The ruling elite, and particularly Erdoğan, have skillfully utilized the rhetoric of Turkey as a strong actor in the international community that attracts the envy of other states at moments of insecurity about domestic legitimacy. Serious domestic legitimacy crises, such as the Gezi protests, terror attacks, and big mining accidents, have been accompanied by intensified foreign visits by senior leaders – the president, prime minister and minister of foreign affairs. Public speeches abroad have targeted both domestic and international audiences.

Erdoğan's repeated criticisms of the UN and the EU have been intended to highlight the unfairness of the international system towards Turkey and to gin up domestic constituencies in that context. In this sense, those messages have been targeted almost exclusively at a domestic audience, even as they have been broadcast on the world stage. Particularly in the wake of the destabilizing Gezi protests, the AKP leadership has sought even more extensive legitimation strategies to compensate for growing authoritarian tendencies. Thus, foreign policy rhetoric underlying the security threats posed by external actors and the networks of conspiracies against Turkey supposedly coming from within have been deployed to consolidate power and to expand both the state's and the ruling elite's power over society.

Notes

1. The "first image" in international relations focuses typically on human nature or on the beliefs of individuals; the "second image" involves the nature of the state, its social system and domestic politics; the "third image" focuses on the general characteristics of the international system as a whole, as well as the more specific aspects of a state's external environment.

2. Kenneth N. Waltz, "International Politics is not Foreign Policy", *Security Studies*, 6 (1996), pp. 54–7.
3. Ibid., *Theory of International Politics* (Reading, MA: Addison–Wesley, 1979), p. 81.
4. Robert Putnam, "Diplomacy and Domestic Politics: The Logic of Two-Level Games", *International Organization*, 42 (1988), pp. 427–60.
5. Among all see Graham Allison and Morton Halperin, "Bureaucratic Politics: A Paradigm and Some Policy" in John A. Vasquez (ed.), *Classics of International Relations* (New Jersey: Prentice Hall, 1996), pp. 172–8; Abdulkadir Baharcicek, "Psychological Environment of Foreign Policy Making", *Foreign Policy*, 26:1 (2001), pp. 81–8; Ryan K. Beasley, "Domestic and International Influences on Foreign Policy: A Comparative Analysis", in Ryan K. Beasley et al., *Foreign Policy in Comparative Perspective: Domestic and International Influences on State Behaviour* (CQ Press, 2001), pp. 321–45: Christopher Hill, "What is Left of the Domestic? A Reserve Angle View of Foreign Policy" in Michi Ebasa (ed.), *Confronting the Political in International Relations* (London: MacMillan Press, 2000).
6. Richard Stubbs "Performance Legitimacy and Soft Authoritarianism" in Amitav Acharya et al. (eds), *Democracy, Human Rights and Civil society in South East Asia*, (Toronto: Toronto University Press, 2001), p. 39.
7. Luke Chambers, "Authoritarianism and Foreign Policy: The Twin Pillars of Resurgent Russia", *Caucasian Review of International Affairs*, 4:2 (2010), pp. 112–75.
8. Marianne Kneuer, "The Quest of Legitimacy: Foreign Policy as a Legitimation Strategy in Authoritarian Regimes", Unpublished Paper Presented at ISPA-ECPR Conference, Sao Paolo, 16–19 February 2011.
9. Bert Hoffmann, "The International Dimension of Authoritarian Legitimation: The Impact of Regime Evolution", GIGA Working Papers 182 (2011).
10. Antonio Gramsci, *Selections from the Prison Notebooks of Antonio Gramsci*, (New York, International Publisher 1971), p. 210.
11. Mihail Manoilesco, *Le Siecle du Corporatisme* (Paris: Felix Alcan, 1936).
12. Juan J. Linz, *Totalitarian and Authoritarian Regimes* (Boulder, CO: Lynne Rynner, 2000).
13. Edward Shills, *Political Developments in New States*, (The Hague: Mouton, 1960).
14. Dankwart Rustow, "Succession in the twentieth century", *Journal of International Affairs*, 18 (1964), pp. 104–13.
15. Robert Dahl, *Polyarchy: Participation and Opposition* (New Haven, CT: Yale University Press, 1971).
16. Linz, *Totalitarian and Authoritarian Regimes*, p. 160.
17. Gökhan Bacık and Salman Salur, "Coup-Proofing in Turkey", *EJEPS*, 3:2 (2010), pp. 163–88.
18. Jean-Jacques Rousseau, *The Social Contract* (Translated by Christopher Bates) (Oxford: Oxford University Press, 1994), p. 85.
19. Banu Eligür, *The Mobilization of Political Islam in Turkey* (Cambridge: Cambridge University Press, 2010).
20. Andrew Finkel, "Pining For Morsi in Istanbul", *New York Times*, Opinion, August 2, 2013, http://latitude.blogs.nytimes.com/2013/08/02/pining-for-morsi-in-istanbul/?_r=3, accessed 1 November 2016.
21. Ihsan Dagi, "Turkey's AKP in Power", *Journal of Democracy*, 19:3 (2008), pp. 25–30.

22. Dagi, "Turkey's AKP".
23. C. B. McPherson," Introduction to Leviathan" in Thomas Hobbes, *Leviathan* (Oxford: Penguin, 1984).
24. Gramsci, *Prison Notebooks*.
25. Stephen Gill, *Power and Resistance in the New World Order*, (Palgrave, Macmillan, 2002), p. 58.
26. Bülent Aras and Gorener, A., "National Role Conceptions and Foreign Policy Orientation: The Ideational Bases of the Justice and Developments Party's Foreign Policy Activism in the Middle East", *Journal of Balkan and Near Eastern Studies*, 12:1, (2010), pp. 73–92.
27. Maria Kneuer, "The Quest of Legitimacy. Foreign Policy as a Legitimation Strategy in Authoritarian Regimes", Unpublished Paper Presented at ISPA-ECPR Joint Conference, Sao-Paulo, Brazil, 16–19 February 2011.
28. Evren Balta Paker and I. Akça, "Beyond Military Tutelage: Analysing Civil-Military Relations under the Justice and Development Party", in Ebru Canan Sokullu (ed.), *Debating Security in Turkey: Challenges and Changes in the Twenty-First Century* (Lanham, MD: Lexington Books, 2012), pp. 77–93.
29. Ministry of Economy, TUIK.
30. Giovanni Sartori, *Parties and Party Systems: A Framework for Analysis* (Essex: ECPR Press, 2005).
31. Thomas Hobbes, *Leviathan* (Oxford: Penguin Books, 1984), p. 107.
32. Max Weber, *Economy and Society: An Outline of Interpretive Sociology* (Berkeley, CA: University of California Press (1922), 1978).
33. Seymour Martin Lipset, *Political Man: The Social Bases of Politics* (2nd ed.) (London: Heinemann, 1983).
34. Kneuer, "The Quest of Legitimacy".
35. Ibid., p. 5.
36. Bob Jessops, "Accumulation strategies, state forms, and hegemonic projects", *Kapitalistate*, 10 (1983), pp. 89–111.
37. Jessops, "Accumulation strategies".
38. Ibid.
39. Mitchell Dean, *The Signature of Power: Sovereignty, Governmentally and Biopolitics* (London: Sage, 2013), p. 71.
40. Ibid., p. 55.
41. Ibid., pp. 52–6.
42. Soner Cagaptay, "Erdoğan's Empathy for Morsi", *The Washington Institute*, September 2014, http://www.washingtoninstitute.org/policy-analysis/view/erdogans-empathy-for-morsi, accessed 1 November 2016.
43. The *Rabaa* or *Rabbi'ah* sign is a hand gesture and a symbol (in the mould of the V-symbol that became infamous among social movements in the wake of the global financial crisis of 2008–9), which first appeared during the August 2013 protests in Egypt. It has been used by the Muslim Brotherhood and its supporters in Egypt in the wake of Morsi's ousting as a symbol of protest and resistance.
44. Fritz W. Scharpf, *Legitimacy in the Multilevel European Polity*, MPIfG Working Paper 09/1 (Cologne: Max Planck Institute for the Study of Societies, 2009), http://www.mpifg.de/pu/workpap/wp09-1.pdf.
45. Niccolo Machiavelli, *The Prince* (Translated by William J. Connell) (Boston: Bedford/St Martins, 2005), p. 111.

CHAPTER 6

POWER AND ISLAM IN TURKEY: THE RELATIONSHIP BETWEEN THE AKP AND SUNNI ISLAMIC GROUPS, 2002–16

Emrah Çelik

Introduction

Since the elections in 2002, the Justice and Development Party (*Adalet ve Kalkınma Partisi*, AKP) has gone from strength to strength, winning local and general elections (and a constitutional referendum) by a landslide. The AKP came to power as a conservative outfit rooted in political Islam and was thus expected to protect the rights of religiously observant people. The 2002 elections marked the first time in Turkish history that the country's Sunni Muslim groups were united in common cause and they have been a decisive factor in the party's political victories since this time. Over the years, religious groups have mobilized their religiously observant followers by employing the power of their visual and written media and personal and institutional charisma. This has created great anxiety among secularist citizens of the country and has raised the question as to whether the AKP's success should be seen as a victory of Islamism over secularism. To address it, we need to examine the history of Islamism and Islamic groups in Turkey, as well as the current motivation and discourse of both the AKP and Islamic groups. What have been the characteristics of the relationship between Islam and the Turkish state from the late Ottoman period to the beginning of the Republic? How has Islamism been understood and shaped in the country in terms of power? What are the factors behind the extraordinary and historically unprecedented post-2002 alliance of political and socio-religious forces in Turkey? In discussing these questions, I also wish to analyse more fully the contemporary power struggles in both Islam and Turkey by looking at three factors. The first is the theological, historical and sociological background to the current relationship between Islamic groups and the state. The second is the understanding of state and opposition held by Islamic groups in Turkey. Finally, I will explore the relationship between power, political Islam, and secularism.

State and Islam in Turkey

The social and intellectual divide between Islamists and Westernizers that we see today is historically constituted, having its roots in the mid to late nineteenth-century Ottoman Empire, when the modernization and Westernization of Turkey began.[1] This division and conflict continues still, under a variety of designations: progressive versus reactionary, society versus the state,[2] the forces of tradition against the forces of modernity,[3] Islamists against Kemalists,[4] and so on. During the *Tanzimat* period of Ottoman reform between 1839 and 1871, the scope of Islamic law (*shari'a*) was limited almost completely to family matters, new secular laws were adopted, and modern institutions were created. Secular schools were founded and education partly secularized. Along with political and institutional reforms came cultural change. As a result of new relationships with the West, significant change occurred in the daily life of both the elites and the masses, the introduction of Western-style clothing being the most noticeable example.[5] The process was not smooth. As Zürcher states: "The reform policies of *Tanzimat* had never been based on popular demand,"[6] and this kind of reform inevitably met with opposition from segments of society, and especially traditionalist Muslims. Westernizing secular reforms were resisted by tradition-alists and the religious political opposition throughout the final period of the Ottoman Empire and into the new Turkish Republic, especially in its early years. We witness the tension of this polarization even in the political and social problems of today.

With the secularizing reforms of the Turkish Republic after 1923, conflict between Islam and secularism took a different form. The leaders of the newly founded Turkish state, in order to modernize society, embraced six fundamental policy principles which became part of the Constitution in 1937: republicanism (*cumhuriyetçilik*), nationalism (*milliyetçilik*), populism (*halkçılık*), secularism (*laiklik*), statism (*devletçilik*) and reformism (*inkılapçılık/devrimcilik*). Among these principles, secularism has played a crucial role in the process of creating modern Turkey.[7] To achieve the vision of a modern nation state, various reforms[8] were made, particularly in the areas of law, education and culture, aimed at breaking with the Ottoman past, weakening the influence of Islam in society, secularizing the country, and becoming much closer to Western civilization.[9]

Compared to other Muslim countries[10] in the twentieth century, which embraced modern and unitary state law, "only the Turkish Republic rejected the *Shari'a* outright and declared an entirely secular legal system.

Even advocating the application of *Shari'a* became an offence in Turkish law."[11] The state adopted secularism as a modernizing ideology and, as Shankland points out, "the early republican governments attempted to relegate religious conscience as much as was humanly possible to the sphere of the private individual."[12] Kuru describes Turkish secularism as "assertive",[13] in line with Göle's point that the state's ideology "became a 'didactic secularism': moralistic and pedagogical, teaching and imposing a modern way of life."[14] Accordingly, the secular public sphere was to be controlled by the state, and Islamic groups and activities were pushed out of the public and political areas and put under the control of the Directorate of Religious Affairs (*Diyanet İşleri Başkanlığı*, Diyanet), founded in 1924.[15] Keyman argues that elites of the state have used the secular state to control religion with the intention of de-linking it from the Ottoman heritage.[16] As a result, in the new social order of the republican period, the power of Islamic institutions, scholars, and leaders was lost.[17]

As Keyman points out, "the state's top-down act of creating a secular national identity by initiating strict political and institutional regulatory mechanisms on religious communities has been challenged by Islam and its powerful symbolic and cultural role in the constitution of societal relations and social identity formations of Turkish people."[18] This challenge encompassed a great number of Islamic Sufi orders, Islamic NGOs, Islamist political parties, and Islamic social movements.

Islamic Groups

Islamic religious groups in Turkey are generally categorized either as *tarikat* (religious or Sufi orders) or *cemaat* (religious communities). *Tarikat* groups focus on Sufism and the spiritual aspect of religion. The *Nakşibendilik*,[19] *Mevlevilik*, and *Kadirilik* are the best known of these religious orders in Turkey. Their roots date back to the eleventh century, and they grew mainly in the Seljuq and Ottoman periods. They have continued to be active down to the present, despite secularist reforms, which included the closing of religious shrines (*türbes*) and dervish convents (*tekkes*) in 1925.

Cemaat groups are especially concerned with politics, education, relief of distress and other social matters. Most *cemaats* arose originally from *tarikats*, particularly from the *Nakşibendilik*. The *Nurculuk*,[20] the Gülen movement,[21] the *Milli Görüş* movement, the *Süleymancılık*,[22] the *İskenderpaşa*, the *Erenköy*, and the *İsmailağa* are the foremost examples of this kind of group in the country. They were all founded during the republican period. Compared to *cemaats*, *tarikats* have more traditional characteristics. Although the main features of the *cemaats* reflect their roots in the traditional *tarikats*, they have evolved and developed in ways that very much reflect the demands and needs of modern traditions and societies.[23]

As mentioned, from the beginning of the republican period, all kinds of Islamic groups lost their official status and power, and many of them their legal status. Although there are numerous Islamic groups in Turkey, from the beginning of the republic until recently none of them was openly active. The groups faced a choice: either work with the secular tools of the newly-founded republican order or go underground. As Toprak argues: "Overtly religiously observant people were not accepted into the political, social, or intellectual elite circles. The republic marginalized them, caricaturized [sic] them as fanatics, and considered them uncivilized. It was these marginalized groups that later formed the backbone of political Islam."[24] Suppression began in the 1920s and 1930s and political projects launched by Islamic groups and individuals were suppressed by military coups, and through interventions of the Turkish Constitutional Court.[25]

A most significant Kemalist reform was the abolishment of the Caliphate in 1924. The Caliph was the political and religious head of the whole Muslim community (*ümmet*). Even though, by common assent, the Caliphate did not perform its unifying function well in the late Ottoman period, it nevertheless remained powerful in some parts of the empire. Therefore, the abolition of the Caliphate and the revival of the Islamic movements are closely related.[26] However, it would be a mistake to argue that the abolition of the Caliphate was the only reason for the rise of the movements. Even in the Ottoman Empire there was Islamic opposition to the state, and the Caliphate came close to losing political and religious power in Turkish society.

Islamic movements and opposition grew much stronger in the 1980s and 1990s because of the socio-economic and cultural characteristics of the period.[27] It is useful to summarize the conditions of this period in Turkish history. To weaken leftist and certain armed political organizations, the state reinforced Islam in various ways, demanding the creation of a synthesis of Turkish identity and Islam. The numbers of religiously-based Imam-Hatip schools, Qur'an courses, and mosques dramatically increased and religious groups could act much more freely. Instruction in Islam was made compulsory even in secular primary and secondary schools. Turgut Özal (Prime Minister 1983–9; President 1989–93) opened the ranks of state cadres to religiously observant citizens, and encouraged religiously observant businessmen to grow their businesses. Religious TV and radio channels, newspapers, magazines, and books were allowed in this period, and Islamic religious groups and their activities spread all over the country, especially through the agency of university students. In this period, as Şimşek notes: "An important number of those young people served as ready votes for the *Refah Partisi* (RP, The Welfare Party), which was extremely ambitious with its motto of *Adil Düzen* (just order). The rest of these young people participated in various religious movements and organizations such as that of Fethullah Gülen."[28]

Parallel to the growing role of religion in public life, the purposes of Islamic religious groups have increasingly been discussed in Turkey, both in the political and the social domain. The Turkish state saw them originally as a threat to its secular nationalist ideology and was troubled by even the display of minor symbols.[29] The main concern of secularists about religiously observant people has been fear of pressure for a restoration of *shari'a* or Islamic law and – another, related, term used widely by the military and secularists – *irtica* (going back or reaction). What is the real objective of religious groups and individuals? Why are there so many events, organizations, and institutions? Have they a hidden agenda? Do they seek to overthrow the secular state and establish an Islamic one? Are they sincere in their declarations in favour of democracy and liberty? These questions have been posed often by secularists, secularist political parties and government bodies.[30]

The Islamic Theology of Power

Islam is an expansionist religion that claims to be the only true religion addressing all of humanity and that holds that its message should be spread all over the world. This belief in theological supremacy imposes a duty on Muslims to call both Muslims and non-Muslims to acknowledge the pillars of the Islamic faith and to practice the principles of the religion. This duty is called *da'wah* in Islamic terminology, and all political terms and acts are connected to this and derive legitimacy from it. *Jihad* is a term used to refer to the Islamic conquests of the pre-modern period, and even some wars against Islamic sects seen as deviant. *I'la kalimatullah* (the exaltation of God's word) is an expression connoting the bringing of the message of Islam to all whilst seizing political power. The expansion of Islam and the practice of its principles are seen as only possible with *da'wah*. Islamic literature cites this as one of the binding duties of all Muslims. In political and social matters, as in every other respect, the Prophet Muhammad is the exemplar for all Muslims. Muhammad (AD571–632) was both the prophet of Islam and head of state in Medina. Religion and politics were from the time of the Prophet intimately associated, and having power in every area of social and political life has been considered necessary in order to practice and spread Islamic teachings freely. This can be seen even in classical Islamic civil law, according to which, whilst Muslim men can marry non-Muslim wives, whereas a Muslim woman can only marry a Muslim. Karaman explains this restriction for women compared to men by citing the latter's prescribed dominant role, arguing that male dominance was thought to guarantee the protection of Islam and the education of children in the family.[31]

This type of interpretative tendency led Muslim jurists to divide the world into three conceptual categories: *dar al-Islam* (house of Islam: territories belonging to Muslims); *dar al-harb* (house of war: territories belonging to enemies); and *dar al-sulh* (house of peace or non-belligerence: territories considered neutral or non-hostile).[32] This categorization reveals that Muslim jurists of the pre-modern period saw the world from the perspective of Islamic politics, since "classical juristic discourse was developed when Islamic civilization was supreme."[33] Lewis reads this categorization as demonstrating the inherent hostility of Islam or Muslims towards non-Muslims, particularly the West.[34] Some Muslim thinkers object to this interpretation, arguing that this perception is not relevant to the majority of contemporary religious Muslims with regard to relations generally with non-Muslim countries.[35] Nevertheless, debate over *dar al-Islam* and *dar al-harb* between Turkish Islamic groups was heated even 20 years ago in Turkey. The main question was whether the Republic of Turkey's secular character rendered it *dar al-harb* or whether its Islamic Ottoman past and the possibility of practising religious duties made it *dar al-Islam*.

The political concepts of *da'wah*, *jihad*, and *i'la kalimatullah* are still relevant in the discourses and principles of Islamic movements in and outside of Turkey. The relationship between the AKP and Islamic groups cannot be grasped properly if the significance of these concepts is not taken into consideration. Bulaç emphasizes the close connection between Islamic political theology and the struggle for political power in Turkey, and support of the party by religious groups and individuals. Concerning political Islamists, particularly the AKP government, he argues: "Those who say Islam is right (*haq*), the rest is wrong (*batil*), hence the government should exclusively be in the hands of Muslims, use the superiority of Islamic faith to other beliefs as a pretext, in reality, of a political theology of monopolizing the resources inherent to power."[36] Similarly, Bilici argues that the idea of the superiority of Muslims over non-Muslims was contingent on the state having the apparatus of "sovereignty". Originally, this was because the Bedouin tribes needed the predominance of sovereignty in order not to fall under domination. For Bilici, the necessity of Muslims dominating the rulership of a state, no longer applies, modern states and societies being essentially altered in their make-up and in the thinking that underlies them.[37]

Islamism

In relation to the dynamics of contemporary political Islam, "Islamism" has become one of the most prominent terms encountered in the social and political sciences. However, there is no agreement among scholars on its definition. While some advocate defining all Islamic movements as Islamist, others favour reserving the term for those Islamic organizations having political aims as a principal *raison d'être*. For Göle, for instance, "Muslim" implies a religious identity, and "Islamist" denotes a distinctive social and political consciousness and agenda.[38] Although some theologians object to these definitions,[39] the term "Islamism" is generally used with socio-political connotations.[40] However, the term does vary in meaning from country to country and from one Islamic movement to another. This is reflected in the political agenda of the revivalist movements in Sunni and Shi'i sects. Likewise, because of their relationship with politics, Islamic movements embrace different agendas with respect to the different conditions – the particular internal and external problems– of each Muslim country, and to the nature of their relationship with modernity.[41] As Fuller argues, there are different kinds of Islamists, being "either radical or moderate, political or apolitical, violent or quietist, traditional or modernist, democratic or authoritarian."[42]

Each group distinguishes itself with its own ways of thinking, strategies, methods and other characteristics, and has its own approach to the Islamic sources (the Qur'an and the Sunna), politics, modernity, and religiosity. Depending on their different interpretations of the main Islamic texts and their different positions in the face of modernity and the secular state, some have concentrated on political and economic issues, others on social, educational, and cultural matters. Accordingly, Bulaç classifies "Muslimhood" in Turkey in three interacting categories: political Muslimhood, social Muslimhood, and intellectual Muslimhood.[43]

Power struggles related to Islamism in Turkey have become visible mostly in the political area, generally associated with certain political parties along with small radical Islamist groups. In the aftermath of the multi-party elections in 1946, some Muslims utilized the democratic system to oppose the secularist Kemalist system through party politics. Gole focuses on how political Islam in Turkey has thereby attempted to resist the secular, nationalist, authoritarian and exclusionist politics of the state.[44] The first Islamist political party, the National Order Party (*Milli Nizam Partisi*, MNP), was established in 1970. Among the supporters of the party were conservative peasants and artisans in the provinces, and religious Sufi orders.[45] As De Leon, Desai, and Tuğal argue: "Formerly conservative subjects were reinterpellated [sic] as Islamic subjects. Had the centre-right parties kept these sectors in their orbit through the necessary concessions and maneuvers, the Islamist challenge in Turkey would never have been as serious."[46] While the MNP was closed down by the military for secularist reasons in 1971, it was reopened in 1972 as the National Salvation Party (*Milli Selamet Partisi*, MSP). It remained a small party for a decade until being shut down along with other political parties by the military government in 1981. In 1983 the party once again reformed, this time as the Welfare Party (*Refah Partisi*, RP).

As Arat indicates, political Islamism changed considerably in the 1980s.[47] *Refah* was radicalized mainly because of both the Iranian Revolution in 1979 and the 1980 military intervention in Turkey. It was also formed as a response to the neo-liberal economic programme of Turgut Özal's Motherland Party (*Anavatan Partisi*, ANAP) government, which came to power in 1983. Although *Refah* became radicalized in this period, it is generally stated that it moderated the radical Islamist population in the country by mobilizing them to act via democratic politics rather than by attempted insurrection. As De Leon, Desai, and Tuğal argue,

> The RP came to be an articulation of competing strands, with emphasis on further politicization of religion (against the desires of the Sufi orders) combined with moderation (against the desires of the radical intellectuals). The incorporation of radical cadres resulted not only in an indecisive radicalization of the party, but also in the moderation of the radicals.[48]

Although Islamic Sufi groups were politicized, supporting the RP in the 1980s and 1990s, they remained moderate in their aspirations. The relationship between Islamic groups and political Islamism was crucial, as the RP received considerable support from the Sufi orders. It did not, however, succeed in uniting the Islamic movements. Some, especially the Gülen movement, remained distant from political Islam throughout the 1980s and 1990s, since there had always been a disagreement and tension between "political" Islamists and "social" Islamists such as Gülen.

The RP concentrated on achieving redistributive social justice, promoting the ideal of a commercial market dominated by morality.[49] Because of this discourse and successful mobilization, White argues that the Turkish political Islamist movement in the 1990s and after put the community and its values at the centre of its politics, rooted in local culture and interpersonal relations, uniting people from different backgrounds around the same ideals. She describes this process as the party becoming "intimate": "It did so," she argues, "by interacting with constituents on an individual level through known, trusted neighbours, building on sustained, face-to-face relationships, and by situating its political message within the community's cultural codes and norms."[50] Having been the leading party in the 1994 municipal elections, the RP increased its popularity and emerged as the largest party after the 1995 general election. The increasing success of the Islamist party discourses and policies excited secularist anxiety in the country, leading to protests by secularist middle-class organizations. They called implicitly (and even openly) for military intervention, and the military obliged by driving the RP from power in 1997. The party was later banned from politics in 1998. This ban divided the *Milli Görüş* movement, and later gave birth to three new political parties. The first two were the traditionalist (*gelenekçi*) Virtue Party (*Fazilet Partisi*, FP), formed in 1998, and its successor the Felicity Party (*Saadet Partisi*, SP), which was founded in 2001. The third, and soon to be victorious, was the AKP, which was also founded by *Milli Görüş* leaders but differed from the former two in its decidedly reformist (*yenilikçi*) outlook.

The 28 February Period

The military intervention of 28 February 1997 (known as *28 Şubat*) badly affected religiously observant people and institutions. In February 1997, the military members Turkey's National Security Council delivered an ultimatum to the government, bringing about the resignation of the governing coalition, dominated by the RP. The main target of the ultimatum was what the military called *irtica* (reaction), which they saw as "Islamist tendencies" in government agencies. The 28 February military intervention, in Silverstein's words, "came to be used as a euphemism for the beginning of a crackdown led by the military against 'political Islam.'"[51] The National Security Council's demands included: a strict headscarf ban in all universities; compulsory primary school education extended from five years to eight, making it almost impossible for a child to attend religious Imam-Hatip high school; a great number of Qur'an courses shut down, and *tarikats* repressed. The current president of Turkey, Recep Tayyip Erdoğan, who was mayor of Istanbul at that time, was given a prison sentence and banned from politics forever for publicly reading a nationalist poet whose work nevertheless included Islamic words.

The 28 February period was thus a turning point for political Islam and the role of religion in the country, for polarization of religious and secular people and for the political strategies of religious groups and the relationship between Islam and the state. The consequences of this period have continued to deeply effect Turkish society, politics and the economy through to the present. During and since the 1997 intervention, religious people, Islamic groups and political parties have felt they must struggle to prove that they are sincere in wanting an independent, powerful, liberal-democratic state, and are not hankering to introduce the *shari'a* law into the country as state law. This huge pressure on all the Islamic movements brought great changes to their discourses and strategies, often apparently radical ones. When Recep Tayyip Erdoğan established the AKP out of the ashes of the RP in 2001 he announced that the party had "removed the shirt of *Milli Görüş*",[52] meaning that it had renounced the traditional aims and discourses of political Islamism and embraced secular democracy in its place. When journalists remind him of his old Islamist statements against secularism and the European Union, he replied: "Now I am the leader of a party that has been established with new and reformist ideas. My thoughts have changed. I am the new Tayyip, not that Tayyip."[53] He persuaded many, in and outside the country, of the genuineness of his change of direction. Shankland said before the presidential elections in 2007, for instance, "even though

Erdoğan's Justice and Development Party [...] derives directly from Erbakan's Welfare Party, it represents a division or wing of the Refah Party which sought a moderate presentation of Islam."[54] This kind of change was not limited to Erdoğan. During the first years of AKP rule, there were no Islamist street demonstrations. The proportion of people saying they wanted an Islamic state decreased from around 20 per cent throughout the 1990s to 9 per cent in 2006.[55]

The AKP built its party programme on democratization, freedom, market reforms, and European Union accession. In the first years, Erdoğan visited Western countries and even tried to establish close ties with some European leaders. With this remarkable change of course and strategy, and despite the obstacles that had appeared after the 28 February intervention, Erdoğan and his party went on to great success in parliamentary elections, winning 34.26 per cent of the vote in 2002, 46.58 per cent in 2007, 49.83 per cent in 2011, 40.87 per cent in June 2015, and no less than 49.50 per cent in November 2015. This is read by some as a success story for Turkish democracy,[56] and by others as a victory for Islamism against secularism.[57]

Islamic Groups and the AKP

One of the most important developments since the 28 February period has been the AKP's great success in uniting almost all Islamic groups.[58] This kind of unity was a first for Turkey; neither Turgut Özal, nor Necmettin Erbakan, both of whom drew heavily on the support conservative-religious Turks, managed to achieve this feat. Even the relatively apolitical groups, such as the Gülen movement, supported the AKP through their communications media and formal and informal networks. Islamic groups mobilized their followers and played an important role in persuading the conservative, religious, right-wing (and even nationalist) electorates, in and out of the country, to support the party. Except for some Islamic groups that opposed the AKP, such as the Gülen movement (after 2013), *Yeni Asya*, and *Furkan Vakfı*, most of the *tarikats* and *cemaats* have supported the party during the whole period of the AKP rule. Among these supporting groups are *Menzilciler, İskenderpaşa Cemaati, İsmailağa Cemaati, Erenköy Cemaati, Yahyalı Grubu, Kadiriler, Halveti Şabaniye Grubu*, the Kurdish sheikhs of Tillo and Norşin, *Işıkçılar*, the Kurdish Islamists, *Hazneviler, Adnan Hocacılar, Galibiler*, and the *Süleymancılar*. In addition, the *Nurcu* groups, such as *Okuyucular, Yazıcılar, Kırkıncı Hoca*, and the close friends of Said Nursi, such as Mehmet Fırıncı and Said Özdemir, have been strong supporters. Although the percentage of support for these groups in the elections is relatively small, they shape and influence the Islamic understanding and practices of religious people.

This support has, of course, been mutually beneficial. Islamic groups have provided personnel for the AKP to fill civil service posts. Placing cadres into public office made it easier for these groups to expand, both financially and politically. Although AKP recruited a variety of people from different backgrounds and outlooks to the civil service in the first years of power, the majority were associated with either a *tarikat* group or a *cemaat* group, particularly the *Milli Görüş* and the Gülen movements. This ratio slightly increased between 2002 and 2016. Indeed, the pioneer cadres of Erdoğan and the AKP were old friends of Necmettin Erbakan, the long-standing leader of the *Milli Görüş* movement. As Şahin indicates, it is well known that there are both MPs and ministers in the AKP who are associated with Islamic groups.[59] Foremost among them are the former Minister of Energy and Natural Resources Taner Yıldız and the former Minister of Health Recep Akdağ – who both hail from the *Menzil Cemaati* – and former Prime Minister Ahmet Davutoğlu, Deputy Prime Minister Numan Kurtulmuş, former Minister of National Education Ömer Dinçer, and current Prime Minister Binali Yıldırım – all who come from the *İskenderpaşa Grubu*.[60]

Erdoğan's popularity has remained constant among his religious or conservative constituency. Serious allegations of corruption in December 2013[61] did not erode public support or confidence. This united and unwavering support for the AKP was not only a religious matter. It was a multi-dimensional situation that needs to be examined closely. Apart from the successful economic programmes that stabilized the financial markets after the economic crisis of 1999, there are several other key factors behind this support. First, religious groups and middle-class people felt a strong need to consolidate their hard-won rights from the strict secularist state and the secularist elites. With the help of the AKP government, they could freely act and grow. Policies of the AKP relieved Islamic groups from many onerous and irksome restrictions. Following the 2002 election, legislation was enacted removing restrictions on religious Imam-Hatip high schools, removing the ban on wearing the headscarf in universities and public institutions, and the restrictions on religious propaganda and activities.[62]

Another army takeover in the mould of the 28 February process has remained a great fear in the back of people's minds. During my research at the Gezi Park protests in 2013, one of my interviewees was someone who supported the main objectives of the protestors from a distance but did not go to the park because of the activities and statements of some protestors. She spoke of the "trauma" for religious people brought about during the 28 February period:

> Because of the headscarf bans, I had to wear a wig in the last year of high school and at university. I experienced many difficulties, had really very big troubles. It is still affecting me. Because of this, I still relive the trauma when I hear the sound of pots and pans being banged, and my tweets change immediately. All my thoughts, views, attitudes, keeping my

balance, change! That period of the 28 February was also a trauma for a lot of friends of mine, like me. We are a generation that experienced these difficulties. Consequently, we work to avoid being reminded of these traumas.[63]

This feeling was the same for the Islamic groups that faced the possibility of closure of all their institutions, and the religious businesspeople who were under scrutiny and pressure from the secularist media and state institutions.

As a populist and talented leader, Erdoğan successfully connects with his electorate, invokes their collective memories of social adversity and cultural victimization, and translates collective symbols (from the headscarf problem to the Palestine–Israel conflict) into political support. Moreover, he has a close familiarity with the ideals, problems, and vulnerabilities of the conservative-religious population. His campaign displayed remarkably effective political management, creating a smoke-screen of victimhood to obscure scandalous allegations. Especially after the Gezi Park protests in May and June 2013 and the corruption allegations that surfaced between 17 and 25 December 2013, "Erdoğan," as Toktamış and Çelik point out, "emerged as a victim of historically-embedded coup attempts and supposed 'international' conspiracies, evoking this shared sense of victimhood, marginalization and ostracization with his public."[64]

It is also critical to note that the AKP has engaged in extreme power struggles beyond those with the secular establishment. Islamic groups – the Gülen movement in particular – have been in the line of fire. The Gülenists were the most prominent Islamic group related to the AKP between 2002 and 2011.[65] The movement's close cooperation with the party grew until the *Dershane* (privately-run university preparation schools) crisis in November 2013. This was followed in short order by serious corruption allegations and subsequent dramatic police and court action against Erdoğan and his family and members of the government. The *Dershane* crisis occurred when the government proposed a law to close the preparation schools, many owned by the Gülen movement. Sound recordings of corruption probes subsequently released (and viewed widely on YouTube and other social media) were alleged by Erdoğan to have been faked by members of the Gülen movement. Since then, the movement has been a highly critical opponent of the party, and in turn the party has declared the Gülenists to be a threat to the government and the entire state. According to Erdoğan, the Gülen movement had attempted to found a "parallel state" to seize power through a gradual secret infiltration of vital public institutions by its supporters, engaging in unauthorized phone-tapping, staging the anti-corruption operations as a preparation to overthrowing the AKP government, and finally attempting the failed military coup of 15 July 2016. The Gülen movement rejects this reading of things. The government stopped the anti-corruption operations, firing many police officers and judges, or assigning them to other places. Erdoğan has had success in persuading his supporters of his innocence, and in moving against the movement's newspapers, TV channels, banks, study centres, colleges, various companies, business associations, businesspeople, universities, and members of the movement in employed in government agencies. The government has put the leader of the group, Fethullah Gülen, on a list of wanted terrorists, offering a reward of 4 million Turkish lira (US$1.5 million) for anyone who can "produce" his return to Turkey and surrender to the authorities.[66] Gülen's organization has been declared a terrorist organization, labeled variously the Fethullahist Terrorist Organization (FETÖ) and Organization of the Parallel State (PDY), and journalists, businessmen, public servants and others associated with the group have been imprisoned. Moreover, the authorities have seized many companies, particularly operating in educational services and media, including the country's best-selling daily newspaper, *Zaman*.

This break between two major forces of Islamic mobilization in Turkey has created two significant results in the relationship between Islamic groups and the AKP. Since this clash, the government has designated people associated with Islamic groups that are siding with the AKP government for preferential treatment. This has created an opportunity for these groups in government institutions. Islamic groups are now vitally important actors in the contemporary business life of Turkey. They do business in a wide range of sectors, from media to banking and education. Since closing the doors to the Gülen movement, the government has promoted the other Islamic groups to make investments in these spheres.

The second result is that other groups now lie in fear of the AKP's overweening power. Although they are still free to pursue growth and activity in all areas, the consequences of any opposition to the regime are now all too clear. The bringing to heel of the once-powerful Gülen movement has been a lesson to others. This lesson has led them to be silent in some situations and be obedient to the government.[67] Atay speaks of "the fear of Erdoğan".[68] Given that many of these groups own major businesses, he explains this as fear of loss of wealth, as much as anything. Now that the AKP government can declare an individual or group in Turkey illegal with ease, the experience of the Gülen movement is seen as the likely response to other groups that step out of line. Atay reports a statement of one of his interviewees: "As long as Erdoğan exists, there would be no power of the tarikats and cemaats in Turkish politics." The interviewee then elaborates this point in striking terms, saying "Erdoğan is the only party, the only state and the only man," and that he "is both the only tarikat and the only cemaat" in Turkey.[69] None of this cowering should be read as suggesting that religious groups are in any way dissatisfied. Indeed, it is fair to argue that they are in fact generally very content – and proud of the growing power of the AKP government – and remain genuinely loyal to Erdoğan.

Bulaç explains the power struggle between political Islamists by reference to what he calls the "political codes" of Muslims and Turks. According to these codes, he argues, the founding ideology of the state is religion (Islam), and the state get its legitimacy from activities to empower religion – religion only exists with the state, and it exists as long as the state exists.[70] This is the same for the relationship between the AKP government and Islamic groups. Government statements support this argument. When tension between the Gülen movement and the AKP was high, the then deputy prime minister, Bülent Arınç, referred to religious groups by saying, "We guarantee everything. You exist as long as we exist. You cease to exist when we cease to exist."[71]

Is the AKP an Islamist Party?

In their first years, the AKP declared that they had left behind their political Islamist ideas and had instead embraced conservative democratic ideas. They indeed struggled to persuade people of the authenticity of this change. Then, after the 2011 elections (and increasingly during and after the Gezi Park protests), the party gradually abandoned liberal and democratic discourse, increasingly using a religious one boldly and openly. Parallel to the political crisis in and outside the country, the AKP has become increasingly intolerant of its opponents, flaunting its Sunni Islamic identity, and using the concept of *da'wah* more frequently in its political discourse.

The questions of whether the party is Islamist or not, and whether Turkey is now "Islamized" have been much discussed in recent years. It is not easy to correlate directly the Islamist images of the government with the fact that Islam has been becoming more and more visible and prominent in the society. The government has taken several concrete actions and engaged in very public debates regarding the place of religion in the country, particularly in the cultural, economic and educational spheres. As Buğra and Savaşkan point out, "The place of religion in the society has been shaped repeatedly by both the activities of the government and the roles played by numerous organizations that use Islamic references in their organizational strategies."[72] The following are some examples that may be taken as evidence of the Islamic identity of the AKP and Islamization of the country. Since 2002, *Diyanet* has had an increasingly significant role in both the state and the society.[73] The place of *Diyanet* in state protocol has changed as well; it rose from fifty-first in the hierarchy of bureaucratic agencies before the AKP came to power to tenth in 2012.[74] The numbers of mosques built also increased, from 77,151 in 2004 to 86,101 in 2014.[75] Furthermore, the number of Qur'an courses has shot up dramatically, from 3,811 in 2003[76] to 16,958 in 2014.[77] Events in the Islamic religious *Kutlu Doğum Haftası* (Holy Birth Week), initiated in 1989, have come to prominence in the AKP period. Despite lawsuits, and several rulings by the

European Court of Human Rights, religious lessons remain compulsory in the curriculum of primary and secondary schools. In 2012, lessons on the Qur'an and the life of the Prophet Muhammad became elective in primary education.[78] The importance of Imam-Hatip religious schools in the Turkish education system has also grown. In 2012 then Prime Minister Erdoğan declared: "Imam-Hatip schools will be the apple of society's eye."[79] The number of these schools rose from 450 in the 2002–3 school year to 537 in the 2011–12 school year and student enrolments in Imam-Hatip school increased from 64,534 in the 2002–3 school year[80] to 546,443 in the 2014–15 school year.[81] Likewise, the political strength, prestige, and number of Islamic organizations and institutions have dramatically increased during the AKP period.

Conclusion

Since the first electoral success of the AKP, tension has increasingly arisen in Turkey with secular people suspicious of the newly-ascendant Islamic party and Islamic groups. Until recently, Islamists were the ones who felt repressed by secularist elites, especially by the military. Now it is the turn of secularists to express anxiety at the Islamist threat to their preferred form of society. Since the AKP came to power, particular secular intellectuals have referred to themselves as "anxious moderns" because of the speed of cultural and social transformation,[82] the growing power of the AKP in the legislature, executive and judiciary,[83] the hastening of the conservative tendency in Turkish society and, finally, because of the ineffective opposition of the secular political parties, the CHP and MHP.[84] Shankland reported on this anxiety before the presidential elections of 2007: "there are pent-up feelings, movements under the surface, in Turkey that give rise for grave concern and are hardly likely to be resolvable in the short term."[85] To a significant extent, the Gezi Park protests that occurred in 2013 grew out of these anxieties regarding Islamic authoritarianism and interference with people's secular lifestyles.[86]

After 14 years in government, the power the AKP has accrued shows that, in terms of the Islamist–secularist divide in the foundations of the Republic, Islamists have won and the secularists have lost. If the AKP does not lose its electoral majority, and becomes yet more powerful by replacing the parliamentary system with a presidential system, new questions will arise about the characteristics of what the AKP calls "New Turkey." What Islamists understand about the terms "Islamic" and "Islamization" will shape the near future of Turkey.

Notes

1. Binnaz Toprak, "Secularism and Islam: The Building of Modern Turkey", *Macalester International*, Vol. 15 (2005), pp. 27–43.

2. Niyazi Berkes, *Türkiye'de Çağdaşlaşma* [The development of secularism in Turkey], Yapı Kredi (Istanbul, 2002).
3. Mahmood Monshipouri, "Secularization", in *Encyclopedia of Islam and the Muslim world*. Ed. R. C. Martin, Vol. 2, pp. 615–16, Macmillan Reference (New York, 2004).
4. Berna Turam, 'Between Islamists and Kemalists: Ordinary Secular Citizens in Turkey', *ISIM review*, Vol. 21, Spring (2008), pp. 40–1.
5. Erik Jan Zürcher, *Turkey: A Modern History*, I.B.Tauris (London, 2003).
6. Ibid., p. 66.
7. Fuat Keyman, "Modernity, Secularism and Islam: The Case of Turkey", *Theory, Culture & Society*, 24(2) (2007), pp. 215–34.
8. Among related reforms made in the early republican period, the Sultanate was abolished in 1922, as were religious courts (*Şer'iyye mahkemeleri*), the Caliphate, and religious schools (*medreses*) in 1924, the year in which the Directorate of Religious Affairs (Diyanet) was established, and the education system unified (*Tevhid-i Tedrisat*). In 1925, religious shrines (*türbes*) and dervish convents (*tekkes*) were closed, and the turban and fez prohibited and replaced by the Western-style hat or cap. In 1926 the Italian penal code was adopted, religious marriages and polygamy were abolished and the Swiss civil code was adopted along with the Western clock and the Gregorian calendar. Western numerals and the Latin alphabet were adopted in 1928, and the constitution amended to remove Islam as the official state religion. Women were progressively enfranchised in the years 1930, 1933 and 1934, and Western weights and measures adopted in 1931. Language reform was instituted in 1932, removing some Arabic and Persian words and making changes to the rules of grammar. The traditional Arabic *ezan* (call to prayer) was replaced with a Turkish one in 1932. All courtesy titles (*Bey, Effendi, Pasha*) were abolished, except in the army, in 1934, and the use of family names was mandated. In 1935 the official day of rest was changed from Friday to Sunday. And in 1937 the principle of laicism or secularism was inserted into the constitution.
9. Şerif Mardin (1981) "Religion and Secularism in Turkey", in Kazancıgil, A. and Özbudun, E. (eds), *Atatürk: Founder of a Nation State*, CT: Archon, pp. 191–219 (Hamden, 1981).
10. In the late eighteenth century, just before its collapse, the Ottoman Empire roughly consisted of Anatolia (modern-day Turkey), most of the Arab world (with the modern states of Syria, Lebanon, Jordan, Israel, Iraq, Kuwait, parts of Saudi Arabia, Egypt, Libya, Tunisia and Algeria) and the Balkans (with modern-day Serbia, Bosnia, Kosovo, Macedonia, Albania, Greece, Bulgaria and large parts of Romania). These newly established countries embraced different state ideologies, most of which were secular to various degrees.
11. Sami Zubaida, *Law and Power in the Islamic World*, I.B.Tauris (New York, 2003). p. 158.
12. David Shankland, "Islam and politics in Turkey: the 2007 presidential elections and beyond", *International Affairs*, 83 (2007), pp. 357–71, p. 360.
13. Ahmet T. Kuru, *Secularism and State Policies toward Religion: The United States, France, and Turkey*, Cambridge University Press (Cambridge, 2009). p. 236.
14. Nilüfer Göle, "Secularism and Islamism in Turkey: The Making of Elites and Counter-Elites", *Middle East Journal*, 51(1) (1997), pp. 46–58, p. 49.

15. İştar Gözaydın, *Diyanet: Türkiye Cumhuriyeti'nde Dinin Tanzimi*, İletişim (İstanbul, 2009).
16. Keyman, "Modernity, Secularism and Islam: The Case of Turkey", p. 234.
17. Gökay Bülent and Aras Bülent, "Turkey after Copenhagen: Walking on a Tightrope", *Journal of Southern Europe and the Balkans*, 5(2) (2003), pp. 147–64.
18. Keyman, "Modernity, Secularism and Islam: The Case of Turkey", p. 216.
19. *Nakşibendilik*, founded by Muhammad Bahauddin Naqshband (1317–89), is one of the most widespread and effective religious groups in Turkey. Öktem explains the fundamental principle of this Sufi order as: "the inner purification of the soul, which must be realized under the direction of a shaykh or chief abbot, called the Perfect Guide (*murshid-i kamil*)" (2002: 389). Compared to others, it gives more importance to the Sunni tradition, Islamic law, and politics. Two prime ministers of Turkey, Turgut Özal (1927–93) and Necmettin Erbakan (1926–2011) were members. *Nakşibendilik* has many publications and radio channels, and student residences in almost every city in Turkey. Nowadays there are numerous *Nakşibendi* groups in the country: *İskenderpaşa Cemaati*; *Menzil cemaati*; *Mahmut Efendi cemaati*, to name only a few.
20. Said Nursi (1876–1960) was one of the most influential Islamic scholars and leaders in the history of the Turkish Republic. Active in politics until the age of 40 (he called this period "the first Said period"), he then changed his focus to engage in more purely intellectual activity. Most of his substantial literary oeuvre (*Risale-i Nur Külliyatı*), of more than 6,000 pages, dates to this second period. It consists mostly of Qur'anic commentary and theological (*Kelam*) reflections. As with the *Nakşibendi* groups, there are many subgroups under the umbrella of the *Nurculuk* movement. *Yeni Asyacılar*; *Yeni Nesil grubu*; *Okuyucular*; *Yazıcılar*, and *Med-Zehra grubu* are among them. These groups each have their publications, events, and student dormitories in which they provide residents with religious education informed by the Risale-i Nur Collection. Each of these groups interprets the thoughts of Said Nursi in different ways, and every group has a different understanding and approach to politics, religious propaganda (*tebliğ*), and the methods to be pursued in serving religion.
21. Fethullah Gülen is an interpreter of the ideas of Said Nursi and has made significant contributions to the movement, establishing primary and secondary schools all over the country and indeed the world; as well as nursery schools, university preparation courses, universities, student residences and houses, NGOs, businessmen's associations, newspapers, magazines, TV and radio channels, publishing companies, and charities. One of the distinguishing features of the Gülen movement is that the activities of the group are not limited to Turkey. Most of the activities are worldwide, in almost every country. The movement does not use Islamic discourse in its works, including in schools. The Gülen movement is far more popular and effective than any other religious group in Turkey (Kömecoğlu, 2000). According to the Andy-Ar research, 61 per cent of the Turkish population know of Fethullah Gülen; and the British *Guardian* newspaper presented him as "Turkey's most powerful man" (Butt, 2008).
22. *Süleymancılık*, founded by Süleyman Hilmi Tunahan (1888–1959), for instance, is quite effective in social and political life. This group has established more than 1,000 student residences, and accommodates almost 100,000 students,

from secondary school to university (Öktem, 2002: 393). It is also well established in Europe, particularly with mosques and Qur'an courses.

23. Tayfun Atay, "Parti Tarikat Cemaat 1 – Cemaatlerde hükümet korkusu", *Cumhuriyet Daily*, 22 May 2015.

24. Binnaz Toprak, "Secularism and Islam: The Building of Modern Turkey", *Macalester International*, Vol. 15 (2005), pp. 27–43, p. 32.

25. İsmail Kara, "Mevcut Dindarlık Anlayışı Türkiye'yi Taşımaz", *Yeni Safak*, 5 June 2011.

26. Bobby S. Sayyid, *A Fundamental Fear: Eurocentrism and the Emergence of Islamism*, Zed Books (New York, 1997).

27. For details, see: Zürcher, Erik Jan, *Turkey – A modern history*, I.B.Tauris (London, 2003); Toprak, Binnaz, "Secularism and Islam: The Building of Modern Turkey", *Macalester International*, Vol. 15 (2005), pp. 27–43.

28. Sefa Şimşek, "New Social Movements in Turkey Since 1980", *Turkish Studies*, Vol. 5, no. 2 (2004), pp. 111–39, p. 121.

29. Nilüfer Göle, *Modern Mahrem – Medeniyet ve Örtünme* [The Forbidden Modern – Civilization and Veiling], Metis Yayınları (İstanbul, 1998).

30. In my ethnographic research in Istanbul in 2012, I found that religious groups, rather than threatening the secular state, are bringing religion, religiosity and religiously observant people into the public sphere, while securing for religious Muslims suitable alternatives to "unsuitable" secular spaces, social relations and leisure activities. They seek to educate the new generation in Islamic values, teaching them Islamic beliefs and principles. Private schools and universities established by religious groups aim to respond to the needs of religiously observant people, giving a quality science and religious education. Religious groups are nevertheless achieving their aim of creating social surroundings suitable for practising religion, by providing opportunities for socializing through their institutions and events. At the same time, they make a significant contribution not only to the mobilization but also the modernization of Turkish society. In addition, there has been strong resistance to the groups' privatization of religion, and moves to restore it to the political and public spheres (Çelik, Emrah, *Between Religion and Secularity – An Ethnographic Enquiry into the Understandings and Experiences of University Students in Turkey* (Completed PhD Thesis), Keele University (Keele, 2015)).

31. Hayrettin Karaman, "Müslüman Kadının Gayr-i Müslim Erkekle Evlenmesinin Caiz Olmaması", available at http://www.hayrettinkaraman.net/sc/00100.htm (accessed 10 March 2016).

32. Khaled Abou El Fadl, "Islamic Law and Muslim Minorities: The Juristic Discourse on Muslim Minorities from the Second/Eighth to the Eleventh/Seventeenth Centuries", *Journal of Islamic Law and Society* 22/1 (1994).

33. Khaled Abou El Fadl, "Islam and the Theology of Power", *Middle East Report*, No. 221, Winter (2001), pp. 28–33, p. 31.

34. Bernard Lewis, *The Crisis of Islam: Holy War and Unholy Terror*, Modern Library (New York, 2003).

35. Heiko Henkel, "Rethinking the dar al-harb: Social Change and Changing Perceptions of the West in Turkish Islam", *Journal of Ethnic and Migration Studies*, Vol. 30, No. 5 (2004), pp. 961–77.

36. Ali Bulaç, "Toplumsal Meşruiyet!", *Zaman Daily*, 5 June 2014.

37. Mücahit Bilici, 17 April 2016, 'LGBT'lerle nasıl eşit olacağız?', *Yeni Yüzyil Daily*, available at: http://www.gazeteyeniyuzyil.com/makale/lgbtlerle-nasil-esit-olacagiz-2023 (accessed on 17 April 2016).
38. Nilüfer Göle, "Secularism and Islamism in Turkey: The Making of Elites and Counter-Elites", *Middle East Journal*, 51(1) (1997), pp. 46–58.
39. Jenny B. White, "Turkish Muslimhood replacing Islamism", *Today's Zaman* [online], available at http://www.todayszaman.com/news-285170-anthropologist-turkish-muslimhood-replacing-islamism.html (accessed on 1 June 2012).
40. Western colonialism, despotic and corrupt Muslim governments, nationalization of the classical Islamic institutions, and political and military conflicts in Muslim countries such as the Palestine–Israel conflict are among the contributing factors. In addition, according to El Fadl, "Perhaps most importantly, Western cultural symbols, modes of production and social values aggressively penetrated the Muslim world, seriously challenging inherited values and practices, and adding to a profound sense of alienation" (El Fadl, Khaled Abou, "Islam and the Theology of Power", *Middle East Report*, No. 221, Winter (2001), pp. 28–33, p. 31).
41. P. L. Berger, "The Desecularization of the World: A Global Overview", in: *The Secularization of the World: Resurgent Religion and World Politics*, Ed. by P. L. Berger, Ethics and Public Policy Centre (Washington, 1999).
42. Graham E. Fuller, "The Future of Political Islam", *Foreign Affairs* 81(2) (2002) pp. 48–60, p. 49.
43. Ali Bulaç, "Islamcılar kendileriyle yüzleşmekten kaçıyor mu?", *Zaman Daily*, 5 June 2011.
44. Nilüfer Göle, *Seküler ve Dinsel: Aşınan Sınırlar*, Metis (İstanbul, 2012), p. 16.
45. Ali Y. Sarıbay, *Türkiye'de Modernleşme, Din, ve Parti Politikası: Milli Selamet Partisi Örnek Olayı*, Alan (İstanbul, 1985).
46. Cedric De Leon, Desai, Manali, and Tuğal, Cihan, "Political Articulation: Parties and the Constitution of Cleavages in the United States, India, and Turkey", *Sociological Theory*, 27(3) (2009), pp. 193–219, p. 207.
47. Yeşim Arat, *Rethinking Islam and Liberal Democracy: Islamist Women in Turkish Politics*, State University of New York Press (Albany, 2005).
48. Cedric De Leon, Desai, Manali, and Tuğal, Cihan, "Political Articulation: Parties and the Constitution of Cleavages in the United States, India, and Turkey", *Sociological Theory*, 27(3) (2009), pp. 193–219, p. 208.
49. Necmettin Erbakan, *Adil Ekonomik Düzen*, Semih Ofset Matbaacılık (Ankara, 1991).
50. Jenny B. White, *Islamist Mobilization in Turkey – A Study in Vernacular Politics*, University of Washington Press (London, 2003). p. 7.
51. Brian Silverstein, *Islam and Modernity in Turkey*, Palgrave Macmillan (New York, 2011), p. 106.
52. Fatma S. Yüksek, 26 December 2003, "AKP'nin Yeni Zarfı", *Radikal Daily*, available at http://www.radikal.com.tr/haber.php?haberno=100157 (accessed on 2 April 2012).
53. "Dedim, ama artık değiştim" (22 August 2001), *Radikal Daily*, available at http://www.radikal.com.tr/haber.php?haberno=11866 (accessed 1 February 2016).
54. David Shankland, "Islam and politics in Turkey: the 2007 presidential elections and beyond", *International Affairs*, 83 (2007), pp. 357–71, p. 361.

55. Ali Çarkoğlu and Binnaz Toprak, *Religion, Society and Politics in a Changing Turkey*, TESEV Publications (Istanbul, 2007).
56. Binnaz Toprak, "Secularism and *Islam*: The Building of Modern Turkey", *Macalester International*, Vol. 15 (2005), pp. 27–43.
57. Metin Toprak and Nasuh Uslu, "The headscarf controversy in Turkey", Journal of Economic and Social Research 11(1) (2009), pp. 43–67.
58. Ömer Şahin, "Erdoğan-Gülen kavga ediyor peki ya diğer dini gruplar?", *Al-Monitor*, available at http://www.al-monitor.com/pulse/tr/originals/2014/12/turkey-erdogan-gulen-war-benefit-lesser-known-islamic-groups.html# (accessed 30 December 2014).
59. Ibid.
60. Tayfun Atay, "Parti Tarikat Cemaat 6 – ''Küyerel'leşen Nakşilik: Menzil Cemaati", *Cumhuriyet Daily*, 28 May 2015.
61. The 17–25 December 2013 investigation was into allegations concerning several key people in the AKP government, including cabinet ministers, the director of the state-owned Halkbank, and the Iranian businessman Reza Zarrab, of corruption, money laundering, bribery, fraud, and gold smuggling.
62. Ömer Şahin, "Erdoğan-Gülen kavga ediyor peki ya diğer dini gruplar?", *Al-Monitor*, available at http://www.al-monitor.com/pulse/tr/originals/2014/12/turkey-erdogan-gulen-war-benefit-lesser-known-islamic-groups.html# (accessed 30 December 2014).
63. Emrah Çelik, *Between Religion and Secularity – An Ethnographic Enquiry into the Understandings and Experiences of University Students in Turkey* (Completed PhD Thesis), Keele University (Keele, 2015).
64. Kumru Toktamış and Emrah Çelik, (5 April 2014), "Exploring Erdoğan's Unwavering Support in Turkey", available at https://www.opendemocracy.net/kumru-toktamis-emrah-celik/exploring-erdo%C4%9Fan%E2%80%99s-unwavering-support-in-turkey (accessed 5 April 2014).
65. Ömer Şahin, "Erdoğan-Gülen kavga ediyor peki ya diğer dini gruplar?", *Al-Monitor*, available at http://www.al-monitor.com/pulse/tr/originals/2014/12/turkey-erdogan-gulen-war-benefit-lesser-known-islamic-groups.html# (accessed 30 December 2014).
66. "En çok arananlar listesinde 676 terörist" (14 December 2015), *TRT Haber*, available at http://www.trthaber.com/haber/turkiye/en-cok-arananlar-listesinde-676-terorist-222486.html (accessed 14 December 2015).
67. A. Emrah Şenel, (12 January 2016), "Cemaat hizmeti verilecekse onu da biz veririz", *Yeni Asya Daily*, available at http://www.yeniasya.com.tr/a-emrah-senel/cemaat-hizmeti-verilecekse-onu-da-biz-veririz_379175 (accessed 12 January 2016).
68. Tayfun Atay, "Parti Tarikat Cemaat 1 – Cemaatlerde hükümet korkusu", *Cumhuriyet Daily*, 22 May 2015.
69. Ibid., "Parti Tarikat Cemaat 7 – 'Erdoğan tarikat cemaat takmaz!'", *Cumhuriyet Daily*, 29 May 2015.
70. Ali Bulaç, "Din-u devlet arasında İslamcılar", *Zaman Daily*, 2 July 2015.
71. "Arınç Cemaate Seslendi: Biz varsak siz de varsınız" (26 January 2014), *Milliyet Daily*, available at http://www.milliyet.com.tr/arinc-o-merkez-tespit-edildi/siyaset/detay/1827535/default.htm (accessed 26 January 2014).
72. Ayşe Buğra and Osman Savaşkan, *Türkiye'de Yeni Kapitalizm: Siyaset, Din ve İş Dünyası*, İletişim Yayınları (İstanbul, 2014), p. 105.

73. A. Erdi Öztürk, "Turkey's Diyanet under AKP rule: from protector to imposer of state ideology?", *Southeast European and Black Sea Studies* (2016), DOI: http://dx. doi.org/10.1080/14683857.2016.1233663.
74. "Devlet Protokol Listesi Değişti" (14 May 2012), *Zaman Daily*, available at http://mobil.zaman.com.tr/politika_devlet-protokol-listesi-degisti_1287400. html (accessed 14 May 2012).
75. "İstatistiksel tablolar" (1 March 2016), *Diyanet.gov.tr*, available at http://www.di yanet.gov.tr/tr/kategori/istatistikler/136 (accessed 1 March 2016).
76. Çakır, Ruşen ve Bozan, İrfan, *Sivil, Şeffaf ve Demokratik Bir Diyanet İşleri Başkanlığı Mümkün mü?*, TESEV, p. 86 (İstanbul, 2005).
77. "İstatistiksel tablolar" (1 March 2016), *Diyanet.gov.tr*, available at http://www.di yanet.gov.tr/tr/kategori/istatistikler/136 (accessed 1 March 2016).
78. "Ve Kur'an Seçmeli Oldu" (30 March 2012), *Vatan Daily*, available at http:// www.gazetevatan.com/ve-kuran-secmeli-ders-oldu-439998-siyaset/ (accessed 30 March 2012).
79. "İmam-Hatipler Milletin Gözbebeği Olacak" (25 April 2012), *Hürriyet Daily*, available at http://www.hurriyet.com.tr/imam-hatipler-milletin-gozbebegi-olacak-20419310 (accessed 25 April 2012).
80. Çakır, Ruşen ve Bozan, İrfan, *Sivil, Şeffaf ve Demokratik Bir Diyanet İşleri Başkanlığı Mümkün mü?*, TESEV, p. 86 (İstanbul, 2005).
81. "MEB İstatistikleri" (2015), *sgb.meb.gov.tr*, available at http://sgb.meb.gov.tr/ istatistik/meb_istatistikleri_orgun_egitim_2014_2015.pdf (accessed 10 March 2016).
82. Fuat Keyman, "Endişeli Modernler", *Radikal Daily*, 24 October 2010.
83. "AKPli Milletvekillerinden Canlı Yayınca Skandal Diyaloglar" (6 April 2016), *Cumhuriyet Daily*, available at http://www.cumhuriyet.com.tr/haber/ siyaset/510316/AKP_li_milletvekillerinden_canli_yayinda_skandal_diyaloglar__ Oglan_bizim_kiz_bizim.html (accessed 6 April 2016).
84. Ayla Göl, "The Identity of Turkey: Muslim and Secular", *Third World Quarterly* 30(4) (2009) pp. 795–811.
85. David Shankland, "Islam and politics in Turkey: the 2007 presidential elections and beyond", *International Affairs*, 83 (2007), pp. 357–71, p. 358.
86. Emrah Çelik, "Negotiating Religion at Gezi", *Everywhere Taksim: Sowing the Seeds for a New Turkey at Gezi*, edited by David, I. and Toktamış, K., Amsterdam University Press (Amsterdam, 2015b).

CHAPTER 7

TURKS AS A MINORITY: THE EFFECTS OF MINORITY STATUS ON ELECTORAL BEHAVIOUR

Samim Akgönül

Introduction

Minority is not a *sui generis* concept. There are no minorities "by themselves". All minorities are the result of a double process: the creation of minority status as quantitative process and as qualitative process. A minority is thus defined by its difference to the majority and is constructed in relation to the latter's chosen self-definition. Of course, all nations are constructed based on a range of criteria, such as language, ethnicity, history, culture and religion (and many others). But depending on the social and political history of each nation, one of these criteria is always dominant. Thus, sociologically speaking, in societies where the main criterion of belonging to the majority is territoriality (as in France, which is adopted as a comparative case study in this chapter) those who are believed to come from outside (immigrants and especially their descendants) are classed as minorities. In other societies where ethnicity is the main criterion (as in Germany), minorities are ethnic. If a majority defines itself primarily by the language, we have linguistic minorities, and so on.

The Turkish nation, as other nations, has been constructed based on several complex (and flexible) criteria. But the main criterion, since the beginning, has been religious belonging, due to the *millet* system.[1] In other words, people from outside of Anatolia, or people who are not Turkish speakers have been accepted as "deserving" of assimilation if they were Muslims but not autochthonous and/ or Turkish-speaking non-Muslims. Thus, Turks living in France (because they are seen to come from outside) or in Germany (because they don't belong to the German ethno-linguistic group) form a minority even if they are born, raised and socialized in the countries where they live. And, on the other hand, the only minorities identified in Turkey are non-Muslims, even if other groups, such as Kurds and Alevis, are sometimes given "minority" status.

Minority is not an issue of numbers. It's an issue of consciousness of difference, the will to protect this difference (and especially from being dominated by it), at least having the impression that the group is itself dominated because of its difference. Minority status is directly related to a specific political behaviour. Minorities are, on the one hand, protected in a reflexive sense. They are inclined to read all political decisions and social facts according to the effects on minority "interests". On the other hand, precisely because they are dominated and/or they perceive themselves as dominated, they maintain an ambivalent relationship with "power". Power (state power, financial power, judicial power and of course "government") is simultaneously a source of legitimation and source of domination.

This chapter analyses the voting patterns of Turkish citizens living in selected Western European countries and will explore the extent to which these patterns played a role in the rise of the Justice and Development Party (*Adalet ve Kalkınma Partisi*, AKP) in Turkey. It will argue that, even if Turkish voters living abroad are low in number, they have had a symbolic and political role in the legitimation of the AKP, especially in Western Europe. The AKP's discourse has for the most part been directed internally. In other words, there has been no specific discernible project from the party that has sought to directly touch the Turkish diaspora. But the proactive and self-confident discourse of the AKP, and especially of its leader Recep Tayyip Erdoğan, satisfies European voters who feel disparaged by their minority status in their host countries. Electoral behaviour thus may be framed as a kind of "settling of scores" against the majority societies they find themselves living in and at the same time serves to legitimize the AKP within Turkey. As the AKP is very popular among Western voters, even in the absence of a programme that directly concerns them, we may say that European Turks vote according to who they are and not according to what the AKP says. Thus, "who are they" is a more important factor than who they vote for.

Turks in Europe: Issues of Multi-Belonging and the Perpetual First Generation Strategy

The "Turks in Europe" is undoubtedly an ideal-type category. No formal structure identifies any group of "Turks in Europe", "Turks of Europe", or "European Turks" *per se*. Instead, the reality consists in several legal (Turkish citizen, dual citizen, European citizen, refugee, asylum seeker ...), generational (immigrant, immigrant child, child of one immigrant and one Turk born in Europe, descendant ...), social (worker, middle class, student, imported bride and groom ...), ethnic

(Turk, Kurd, Armenian ...) and religious (Sunni, Alevi, Non-Muslim, Atheist, secular ...) forms of identification or identity-construction.

But it is also true that a "specification"[2] of the Turkish communities in Europe has been rendered in an ongoing fashion over time. These communities are considered more resistant to multi-belonging, seem more nationalist and more attached to the "homeland" (even if the homeland in question is largely imaginary, at least for the second and third generation). The generational issue is also subject to criticism. Some observers[3] criticize "the second and third generation" concept because it "starts life" in Europe and conceals previous generations of future emigrants. In contrast, my criticism framed in terms of the "strategy of perpetual first generation," which as shall be detailed further below is one of the principal dynamics in intergenerational identity-formation for Turkish communities in Europe.[4]

In the case of minorities, particularly the Turks, religious loyalty is considered the guarantee and proof of national loyalty. The transfer of national identity, and consequently religious identity, is directly correlated to the transfer of the collective memory to new generations. The transfer of the collective memory for the purposes of ensuring unity and integrity rests on three identity pillars: the longing for and loyalty to "the motherland" (Turkey in general and a hometown or village in particular); transfer of the Turkish language to younger generations despite French being the official language and; the continuation of customs and traditions believed to be rooted in religion. The reason the community is so fervently attached to these three topics is their desire that the Turkish children born in Western Europe share the same sentiment of "Turkness" that existing generations do. Various methods are employed by the community to transfer these three elements to new generations. The leading method has been what I call "the perpetual first generation strategy." What is meant by this is the marriage of young French, German, Belgian, and so on people of Turkish descent to Turkish brides and grooms who preferably live in Turkey, and even more preferably are brought to Europe for marriage from the region of the European family's hometown. In other words, young Europeans of Turkish origin seldom marry people who are native to the country they are resident in or to any other nationality living there. Moreover, they seldom marry even other members of the Euro-Turkish community. Thus, a second or third generation of ethnic Turks, in the sense of children born in Europe from both parents born in Europe, has not yet arisen in Europe. From a statistical point of view, one of the parents (usually the mother) of Turkish (and Kurdish) children born in Europe is typically a new arrival in Europe. The "fresh blood" is received as the representative of a genuine "Turkness" (particularly in terms of language and religion) who will help to correct the apparent degeneration in the "Turkness" of ethnic Turks who have lived in Western Europe for too long.

The loyalty of the ethnic Turks in Europe to Turkey becomes manifest even in how they refer to Turkey as the "motherland." The pillars of identity-building in the community are language (Turkish and/or Kurdish) and religion (Sunni or Alevi). But the two pillars need a hinterland. The hinterland is primarily Turkey, but expands in concentric circles from the home village and town of the immigrant, then out further to the province, region, and so on. The ties with their country are both physical and mental. Physical ties are the result of frequent travel to Turkey (whether for business, school or leisure) but also close following of developments in Turkey (via newspapers, television and other media) and contact with the country by phone or the internet. These three methods of contact have developed significantly in the last two to three decades. Air travel has become both relatively cheap and readily accessible, the number of national and local television stations available outside Turkey has boomed and interpersonal contact has become ever easier as the internet provides a means to communicate at minimal cost and international phone tariffs plummet. All of these enable the ethnic Turks in Europe to keep in very close contact with Turkey. Interaction with Turkey is now ubiquitous.

It is more difficult to grasp the emotional or mental ties with Turkey. My view is that these ties emerge in two critical dimensions.

(1) First, ethnic Turks in Europe are more interested in Turkish politics than the local affairs of the countries in which they live. In fact, they pay close attention to the political environment in Turkey and opinion-formation dynamics tend to fall out in precisely the way they do with compatriots in Turkey. From this perspective, the change in the discourse of Euro-Turks regarding the accession of Turkey to the EU is noteworthy. Although they desire Turkey and the resident country to share EU membership for emotional and practical reasons, they too have begun to voice the anti-European discourse recently on the rise in Turkey. Meanwhile, none of the Turkish associations or organizations in Europe have attempted to block Turkey's accession to the EU. They support Turkey's membership for two somewhat irrational reasons. The first is the desire for the Turkish state to attain a better future and position. The second is the hope that the accession of Turkey will legitimize their presence in France and improve their image in the eyes of the European public. This attitude points to the fact that people of Turkish origin have evolved into a "diaspora" as defined by Kim Butler. According to Butler, members of the diaspora continue to be interested in the politics of the root nation. The interest is not necessarily supportive, at least not unconditionally. On the contrary, a section of the diaspora may even side with the opposition. But it is *interest* that matters, not its direction.[5]

(2) These irrational ties may be explained in terms of Benedict Anderson's concept of the "imagined community".[6] In other words, the Turks in

Western Europe associate themselves with the other individuals comprising their community (even if they do not know all of them personally) and root for the success and victory of other Turks in a setting where they feel they are in "competition" with the majority in their own resident country, brought about by being in the minority.

For its part, until recent times the motherland itself took a rather irrational approach in relation to ties with the Turks in Europe. For years, every administration tried to prevent European Turks from acquiring citizenship in the host country, even if they had been born there. Successive governments feared that by acquiring a different nationality, European Turks would detach from "Turkness" and Turkey. Legal attachment to the motherland seemed more important than emotional and identical loyalty. This was partly influenced by Germany's denial of dual-citizenship status. It should be remembered that the nationalist mindset considers national identity one and singular. As Max Weber suggested, nationalism is a system of belief over all,[7] and just as a person may be loyal to only one religion among monotheistic faiths, so must an individual choose to be loyal to only one nation. Multiple national loyalties are, in this perspective, condemned severely. Nevertheless, a recent radical change occurred in Turkey's approach to the issue. From the late 1990s, but particularly after 2002, European Turks have been expected to acquire the citizenship of their country of residence. This is presumably because it will give them a voice in the national and local politics of their respective countries, and allow them to lobby in favour of Turkey.

The radical shift is indicated by comparison with the traditional approaches of the Turkish state in this regard. At the origins of mass emigration from Turkey, Turkish governments took a rather ambivalent position. The emigration of Turks to Western Europe from the 1960s certainly helped to expand the concept of external Turks. As migrant workers began to settle more or less permanently from the mid-1970s onwards, successful groups among them (simultaneously scorned by the elite and cherished for their accumulation and capital transfer) emerged as the backbone of the "Turks abroad." After 20 years of relative neglect, this group became a key focus in the wake of the regime established by the 1980 junta and was framed within the "omnipresent father-state" that emerged as a hegemonic discourse in that period. One purpose of this framing was to prevent European Turks from following "the wrong path." The wrong path, of course, was paved with leftist movements and dissenting religious organizations.

The real danger, from the perspective of the post-1980 regime, was assimilation – and the consequent forgetting of "Turkness" and loss of loyalty to Turkey. So while this group was exposed to Turkish propaganda by print, media and imams and teachers commissioned from Turkey, they were strongly discouraged from forming any kind of multiple loyalty. As nation states whose strength is dubious are want to do, there was a kind of reflexive approach whereby the perpetual first generation strategy was imposed upon generations born in Europe. The objective was to ensure that ethnic Turks born in Europe were at least as loyal to country as those who came from Turkey, and the strategy was adopted and implemented by European Turk communities themselves. The rejection of multiple loyalties applied to the change in legal affiliation – acquiring citizenship of the country of residence.

Administrations in Turkey thus considered change in citizenship or an additional citizenship dangerous for decades. Turks who acquired the citizenship of their country of residence, it was feared, would make compromises with Turkness, and their loyalty would weaken. So they were expected to remain purely Turkish. Yet from the 2000s, this policy was abandoned in a dramatic shift. The relief brought by globalization led Turkish officials to believe that European Turks were no longer under threat of assimilation and came to the view, instead, that these communities could be mobilized as a strong lobby for Turkey's position in Europe. The improvement and expansion of communication technologies removes the threat of assimilation that came with adopting, say, French or German citizenship. The state thus began to actively encourage them to acquire the citizenship of their countries of residence. The instrumentalization that inheres in this shift should be clear: these groups are still viewed as tools at the disposal of the Turkish state.

Another way of seeing this instrumentalization is to conceptualize the diaspora as like a vanguard army of soldiers (envoys) for Turkey. Whereas prior to 2000 the soldier's duty was to be a Turkish citizen, the troops are now instructed to become French or German citizens. Moreover, as it was in the 1970s, wealth accumulation by migrant workers is still cast as a remedy for economic problems at home. Significantly, the long-standing sentimental discourse around homesickness and loyalty to the motherland remains – the extent of sheer emotional exploitation that was on display at a recent Paris rally attest to that. All of these dynamics make it clear that the motherland's view of the migrant communities has not changed radically.

Although multiple *legal* affiliation has now clearly become acceptable, this is not the case in *cultural* loyalties. Multiple cultural loyalties are still viewed as dangerous and even treasonous. It was mentioned that cultural loyalty was built on two pillars: language and religion. When in the minority, teaching the language to new generations becomes particularly difficult. Naturally, the language of the majority immediately becomes the dominant language in a social environment. Furthermore, France in particular insists on fluency in the official language as a prerequisite for integration, and this has come to be accepted by the majority as well as the minority, who had previously resisted the idea. Fluency in French is the most important measure of virtuous integration. Thus, lack of fluency in Turkish no longer poses a threat to loyalty to Turkness. Meanwhile religious loyalty, being sacred therefore immune to intervention, gained great importance and took priority. In a contradictory way, this type of loyalty became an indispensable and paramount element of Turkness for both Sunni and Alevi Turks in Western Europe.

The shifting to religion from language as a principal factor gave rise to several issues in the French case. The French system is built on the principle of laicism and Turkish immigrants have diverse cultural and social backgrounds. A recent official survey on the backgrounds of immigrant populations in France.[8] confirmed this "exception". First, I am in general sceptical of identity-based statistics since they can be misused in culturist and essentialist ways. The characteristics of a given group are not related to its identity (Turkish, Muslim, etc.) but are the product of multi-dimensional social, educational, economic and cultural parameters. This recent study on trajectories and origins is not limited to the dimension of identity but also considers differences related to social class. Second, in France, identity-based statistics are forbidden because the French understanding of nationhood does not support identity-based divisions. This study is not on "Turks" or "Algerians" but on people who were born outside France and people who have at least one parent who was born outside France. The data presents the characteristics of French people who were born in Turkey or French citizens whose parents hailed from Turkey. Finally, I have some concerns about the concept of "generation", not only regarding first-generation French-Turks who came to France many years ago, but also their children who were born in France. As discussed above, the kinds of intergenerational difference one might normally expect to find among other immigrant groups do not hold among European Turks – in fact, what we have is a perpetual first generation, whereby the transmission of identity from parent to child is skewed between French-Turkness and "pure" Turkness.

With these caveats in mind, we can start to analyse some data on French-Turks. The study shows that there are currently three-and-a-half million immigrants in France and three million descendants of immigrants (people born in France to at least one immigrant parent). However, the study sample comprised people between 18 and 60 years of age. Thus, the total number of both groups must in fact be around double the sample size due to the fact that the immigrants of 1960 would be over 60 years old today, and children up to the age of 18 with a foreign parent or immigrant status themselves must also be large in number.

The same observation can be made of French-Turks. According to the study, there are 212,000 Turkish immigrants in France and 63,000 descendants of Turkish immigrants, but we know that because of the failure to count children under 18 and adults over 60, there are approximately 600,000 people of Turkish birth or parentage. Turkish authorities put the figure at 613,000 in 2013.

These French-Turks are mostly concentrated in Paris and Alsace (north-eastern France near Germany). Even in cases where French-Turks migrate from rural areas in Turkey, they very rarely end up living in rural areas of France. Most French-Turks tend to live in areas with high levels of industry.

For young people born in France to Turkish parents, the study shows that they have the highest school dropout and failure rates. Some 44 per cent repeat at least one year at primary school, while the same is true for 34 per cent of French-Tunisians and 33 per cent of French-Algerians. This ratio must have a linguistic and social explanation. Parents of Algerian or Tunisian origin master the French language better than Turkish parents because of the colonial past and existence of French as a second language in their countries. Five per cent of French-Turks leave education after high school, while 64 per cent of French-Turk parents are uneducated. Only 14 per cent of the French population at large has an uneducated parent. A total of 68 per cent of French-Turks have been raised in families with four or more children, and 87 per cent say they never had any help from their parents with their homework. In addition, 27 per cent of French-Turks don't have *Le diplôme national du brevet* (the French national diploma awarded to children at the end of middle school). Only 31 per cent of French-Turks obtain a bachelor's degree compared to 55 per cent of French-Tunisians and 46 per cent of French-Algerians. In the French population as a whole the figure is 64 per cent.

Only 21 per cent of French-Turks start higher education, while 47 per cent of French-Tunisians and French-Algerians do so. According to the survey, because of the number of craftsmen and merchants among Turkish immigrants, Turkish parents push their children to cut their studies short and start a trade career as soon as possible. But also, we must add, students with a Turkish or African background are the biggest victims of academic segregation, being "streamed" into basic, vocational education of short duration. Finally, French–Turks get married much earlier than their peers, pushing young people (especially girls) to abandon school. Among all the groups in the survey, the French-Turk group was the only one in which girls had lower middle school graduation rates than boys (39 per cent for boys and 35 per cent for girls). All in all, descendants born and raised in France by at least one Turkish immigrant parent seem to be less well-educated than other groups in the study with immigrant backgrounds, and certainly much less educated than most French people.

According to the survey, the French-Turks sample is in a bad shape in employment too. Twenty-six per cent of male French-Turks and 44 per cent of female French-Turks experienced unemployment at least once during the first seven years of their professional lives. It is the highest ratio among all descendants of immigrants. At the time the survey was carried out, 19 per cent of French-Turks were unemployed and 26 per cent of women were. Let me reiterate that the survey's sample is based on people between 18 and 60 years old; in other words, the active population. At that time the unemployment rate of French-Turks was much higher than of French-Algerians or French-Tunisians. However, I must emphasize the fact that many French-Turks work informally in family businesses and do not declare their working activity to keep their unemployment benefits. This fact may also mean the real unemployment rate is much lower.

Obviously French-Turks are not attracted by the public sector as only two per cent attempted the civil service exam. This is the lowest ratio and the quasi-absence of people originating from Turkey in the public administration should be taken as a clear sign of integration difficulties (to feel at home and to participate in public life). This can be explained also by a lack of self-confidence, by the low rate of academic graduation and also by real or perceived discrimination that prevents young French-Turks from entering the public service. According to the study, young French-Turks remain within a Turkish network for their working lives, creating a perception of "ethnic-business" in a "connected vessels" framework. Actually, an ethnic (or religious) business is never that closed and is certainly a part of the general economy. Having said that, the communitarian reflex is more often linked to a lack of any other ready identity. It is at the same time an attempt to protect the identity of the group (the minority reflex) and an obligation in the face of discrimination in professional life: 35 per cent of French-Turks think potential employers ask 'inappropriate questions' during job interviews. There is no doubt that this is an issue, but also minorities frequently use this kind of self-victimization discourse to hide other weaknesses.

Furthermore, there is also a social class issue. Having two immigrant parents increases substantially the likelihood that one will remain within a lower socio-economic milieu. Indeed, 70 per cent of French-Turks are the children of workers, 28 per cent are of artisan or merchant families and only 2 per cent of intermediary professions. No doubt, French-Turks are the children of the working class. Moreover, their parents were most likely also from the lowest socio-economic class in Turkey. Sixty per cent of immigrants have or had parents who were labourers in Turkey and the parents of a further 18 per cent were farm labourers. In fact, this piece of information shows that the rural origin of immigrants is largely a myth. Those who migrated from Turkey to France from the 1960s onwards are, to a significant extent, the children of factory workers and not children of the rural poor. Having said that, this rural-migrant Turkish class make up the largest such group in France – the ratio of rural parents of Portuguese immigrants is 17 per cent and only 9 per cent for the French majority. The French-Turks born in France certainly have poor grandparents, but not to the extent commonly believed. Nevertheless, it is the largest group of this kind in France.

What is most striking in this survey is the weakness of social mobility. According to the survey, 59 per cent of immigrants from Turkey are manual workers and, among their children born in France, the ratio is 62 per cent. This is the only social-identity group in France where the social class of parents and their children is equal. Some 12 per cent of French-Turks are merchants but among their immigrant parents, 19 per cent are merchants. This group form the "visible" part of the community in some French cities, workers in factories being "invisible"). A further 6 per cent of French-Turks are "white-collar" workers while only 1 per cent of their parents are – here we see a small degree of social mobility. Additionally, 14 per cent are of intermediary professions (17 per cent for immigrants from Turkey) and 6 per cent are lower-level employees (4 per cent for their parents). In general, we may say that the social ladder in which the French display such pride is broken for French-Turks.

These results confirm a general knowledge that specialists have maintained for at last a decade: There is an "inflation of identity" among Turks born in Europe, especially in France. At least at the discursive level, French-Turks are "too Turkish" to advance socio-economically. For example, to the question "Do you feel French?" only 42 per cent of French-Turks answer "Totally agree". This is the lowest percentage among the descendants of immigrants in France (the figures are 64 per cent among French-Moroccans and French-Tunisians; 68 per cent among French-Algerians; 75 per cent among French-Portuguese and 85 per cent among French-Spaniards and French-Italians). A total of 47 per cent of French-Turks answer "Totally agree" to the question "Do you feel Turkish?" – the highest score among descendants of immigrants – and French-Turks have the highest incidence of dual-nationality (48 per cent). Thus, French citizenship does not tend to produce identification with France as a self-ascription.

French-Turks also say they are religious, but not much more than the other group of immigrants of Muslim descent (62 per cent declare themselves "religious"). The figure is 61 per cent for French-Algerians and 55 per cent for French-Tunisians. However, other groups are far more likely than French-Turks to dare to declare themselves atheists.[9] Only 15 per cent of French-Turks say they are atheists. Even if this data is high compared to Turkey (2 per cent of Turks report being atheist, according to the latest Gallup survey), it is very low compared to French-Algerians and French-Tunisians, of whom 30 and 22 per cent say they are atheist, respectively. Forty-five per cent of French people say they are atheists or agnostic. Once again, it's important to highlight that this is self-reporting: French-Turks, whether or not they are in fact religious, are under great social pressure to identify this way publicly.

According to the same survey, French-Turks display high levels of endogamy or marriage within the group (as opposed to exogamy, marriage between people of different identity groups). Most strikingly, some 90 per cent of French-Turks born in France have two Turkish parents. This is highly unusual in France, where "mixed" marriages are very common, even among immigrants. But what is more striking in my opinion (confirming my previous research) is the fact that French-Turks born, raised and socialized in France seem to repeat the same pattern by marrying within the group, but especially with people born and raised in Turkey. This fact, called "the importation of grooms and brides," confirms my hypothesis of a of a perpetual first-generation strategy among Euro-Turks.[10]

The perpetual first-generation strategy concept that I have developed is related to the affirmation of everything emanating from Turkey itself, which is deemed to be "authentic" in its Turkishness. This also includes popular cultural products. There too, the study confirms my previous observations. For example, 73 per cent of French-Turks say they watch Turkish TV channels. The corresponding figures are 50 per cent for French-Moroccans, 38 per cent for French-Algerians and 37 per cent for French-Tunisians. The TV in the Turkish household is much like the fish tank in many American homes – it is there to be seen and heard almost all day long. Thus, while French-Turks live in France they are constantly receiving cultural messages and programming from Turkey. Here, we observe a kind of "sacralization" of the root Turkish identity. For example, 90 per cent of Turkish immigrants say that they visit Turkey, while the figure stands at 96 per cent for French-Turks. Territorial roots seem to be continually transmitted.

Data on language habits is also interesting. Ninety per cent of Turkish immigrants still use Turkish within the family and the neighbourhood and some 95 per cent of French-Turks report being able to speak Turkish fluently. This is again a record among all descendants of immigrants in France. Use of the language of origin is also related to patterns of family life, and cohabitation with parents in particular. Indeed, 60 per cent of French-Turks between the ages of 18 and 30 report that they live with their parents and 50 per cent state that they live near their parent after marriage. This is the highest score in France among immigrant groups. All in all, during their daily life French-Turks have more opportunities to speak in Turkish than in French.

Other interesting data show that French-Turks see marriage as essential: 60 per cent of French-Turks between the ages of 18 and 60 are, in fact, married. Moreover, unmarried cohabitation, while almost completely non-existent among immigrants, appears common among French-Turks – 36 per cent of men report living with a girlfriend. The figure for French-Turkish women, however, is only 5 per cent of women, which suggests that French-Turkish men are happy to pursue cohabiting relationships with French women, but are inclined to marry only Turkish women. Here, too, the "perpetual first generation" strategy is at play. Actually, they do not marry within the community but "import" their spouses and views from the micro-identity:

39 per cent of male French-Turks get married with women from the same region of their origin and 74 per cent of female French-Turks. It is the highest score by far among descendants of immigrants. French-Turks also have children very early, with the average first maternity being 25 years old.

As these three last articles show, there is a "Turkish exception" in France due to social class, origin and culture and this "exception" seems to be transmitted to the generation born in France. The study must be repeated in 20 years to see if the generation born from parents themselves born in France repeats the same pattern. But as the ratio of Turks coming from Turkey for marriage is very high, the transmission of cultural features originating from Turkey remains strong.

Euro-Turks and Voting Patterns

It is true that the French case cannot be generalized across Europe. National contexts change attitudes and belonging categories slightly, as many comparative studies have shown,[11] but for political preferences, there is a general similarity in Western Europe. Euro-Turks (with all the problems that this term implies) reproduce the political preferences of their parents and grandparents towards Turkey even if in Europe they have other (often paradoxical) political belongings.[12] Descendants of immigrants are, statistically speaking, close to the left-wing parties in the countries where they live (especially because of immigration and integration issues) but in Turkey they are largely supportive of the Islamist and right-wing parties.

As Aslı and Başer have noted, since the mid 1980s a distinct shift in the posture of the Turkish state on the issue has been occurring:

> Turkey, as an emigration country now for more than five decades, enfranchised its expatriates in a rather limited way in 1986. Even though Turkish citizens abroad had been claiming and putting pressure on political authorities in Turkey for the introduction of out of country voting since the 1990s, the introduction of the set of legislative and administrative measures effectively enabling external voting had to wait until 2012. Expatriates were given the option of voting from their countries of residence for the first time in the August 2014 presidential elections.[13]

As a matter of fact, for many decades Ankara considered the diaspora vote to be a threat. This was because diaspora voters in Europe were overwhelmingly likely to vote for Kurdish and Islamist parties (especially of the *Milli Görüş* movement)[14], which were for most of the period counter-hegemonic. For this reason, governments of all persuasions were generally reluctant to encourage voting rights for Turkish citizens living abroad. Critically, parties of the

Table 7.1   Distribution of border votes in the general elections 2002–11

Election Year	AKP	CHP	MHP	Other
2002	37,525	26,232	11,368	38,910
	33%	23%	10%	34%
2007	128,694	40,255	33,417	24,418
	56.75%	17.75%	14.74%	10.76%
2011	78,875	33,552	10,503	4937
	61.69%	26.24%	8.21%	3.86%

Source: Figures compiled by Aslı Okyay and Bahar Başer based on the Turkish Supreme Election Board's official election results.

Milli Görüş movement sought to circumvent this by bussing voters to the Turkish border to capture the Islamist slice of the vote abroad – this "border vote" was very beneficial to the party (see Table 7.1).[15] Since 2002, the AKP – a party with origins in the *Milli Görüş* movement – has been on the ascendency within Turkey and so the context has shifted. In 2014 the right to vote was extended to Turkish citizens living abroad, something that has emerged as a natural outgrowth of the nature of the Turkish voter in Europe. It is worth pointing out that this voting extension entails a "double legitimation" process: conservative Turks living in Western Europe are legitimized as citizens capable of playing a role in internal Turkish politics and the AKP is legitimized as the only movement able to represent them inside Turkey.

   Before analysing the results of three elections where Turks abroad took part, I must underline some structural problems of this voting system. During the three elections where the Turkish diaspora could vote, Turkish citizens voted according to the preoccupations concerning Turkey but in a self-legitimation process in their country of residence. Thus, if at the beginning of the Turkish immigration to Western Europe, political belongings were carbon copies of the existing movements in Turkey, "they acquired later their own dynamics, discourses and actions, while remaining connected with homeland politics."[16] But it is true that the right to vote and the possibility to effect Turkish internal politics during the 2014 presidential elections and 2015 general elections re-concentrated the diaspora's belonging in Turkey far from acquired local discourses. Thus, we may say that there too an exception was in play. Voting patterns analysed by Jean Michel Lafleur on, among others, the Italian and Mexican diasporas show that they tend to vote by mixing their internal and external preoccupations.[17] In the Turkish case, however, during the last three elections, dynamics seem to be exclusively external (related to Turkey) if we leave aside the internal revenge and legitimation sentiment.

   During the presidential elections of 2014 (the first in which the office was directly elected by citizens) Turkish citizens living abroad had the chance to

Table 7.2   Election turnout, 2014 and 2015 elections in Turkey

Elections	Average voter turnout abroad	Voter turnout in selected Western European countries		Voter turnout in Turkey
10 August 2014 Presidential (appointment system)	8.32 %	Germany	8.15 %	74.13 %
		France	8.35 %	
		Belgium	6.31 %	
		The Netherlands	7.21 %	
		UK	6.41 %	
		Switzerland	9.90 %	
7 June 2015 General (consulates)	32.53 %	Germany	34.44 %	86.38 %
		France	36.97 %	
		Belgium	35.24 %	
		The Netherlands	31.51 %	
		UK	28.45 %	
		Switzerland	39.34 %	
1 November 2015 General (Consulates)	39.90 %	Germany	40.78 %	87.40 %
		France	44.78 %	
		Belgium	41.66 %	
		The Netherlands	46.46 %	
		UK	38.25 %	
		Switzerland	44.60 %	

vote for the first time. The voting system was based on an individual appointment at consulates or embassies and lasted four days. This system has been criticized because it is seen as violating the principle of the secret ballot. During the general elections of 2015, Turkish consulates welcomed electors anonymously over a three-week period in order to correct this situation. But in both cases, as electoral districts were extremely vast, the voter turnout remained under expected knowing that generally, participation in Turkey is much higher than in many Western European countries.

For the three pre-mentioned elections, ballots were not counted on the spot but ballots but were transferred in Ankara to be counted with other national ballots. Here, the preservation of ballots and their transfer in Turkey was hard to ensure. In addition, this kind of transfer is against the principal than an elector may follow her own vote and assist in ballot counts. As a matter of fact, the only objection during the ballots counts for the 1 November 2015 election occurred while counting diaspora votes in Ankara.

For Western European countries where citizens abroad have the right to vote – such as France or Italy – overseas electoral divisions are created and citizens are represented by a representative/deputy at the assembly from those divisions and thus have a clear set of candidates to choose from when selecting a representative. No such condition obtains in Turkey. It is true that during the presidential elections of 2014, Turkish voters abroad selected among three candidates: Recap Tayyip Erdoğan, Ekmeleddin Ihsanoğlu – jointly nominated by the Republican People's Party (*Cumhuriyet Halk Partisi*, CHP) and the Nationalist Action Party (*Milliyetçi Hareket Partisi*, MHP) – and Selahattin Demirtaş (Kurds and leftist movements). However, for the two following general elections, voters could select only among *parties* and not among *candidates*. In other words, Turkish citizens abroad voted without knowing for whom they were voting insofar as their votes have been distributed in all Turkey.

As mentioned, the only two political parties that have consistently drawn large vote shares abroad are the two erstwhile "counter-hegemonic" ones – the AKP and the HDP – and the leaders of these two movements, Recep Tayyip Erdoğan and Selahattin Demirtaş, are the only ones who deigned to hold public meetings in Western Europe in front of diaspora electors. But there too, the content of their speeches in three different elections was directly related to the internal policy of Turkey. They never built a policy towards their electors, thus attaching them to the elections sentimentally but not politically. In other words, during two elections Turkish citizens vote ideologically and/or dogmatically rather than politically in the noble sense of the term (i.e., related to a life lived within the *polis*).

Multi-belonging, when legitimized, allows interest and involvement in more than one political context. For many decades, Turkish citizens living abroad were unjustly and unfairly denied basic citizen's rights to multi-belonging. At the same time, in the countries where they live, the majorities constantly deny the possibility of multi-belonging, pushing local-born Turks towards a "Turk abroad" identity. Recent elections have thus trapped the Turks of Western Europe even more in their Turkish identity, leaving them with fewer reasons now to be interested in the political life of the countries where they live. Accordingly, the lack a true connection with *both* the Turkish and the local *polis* (those who have only Turkish citizenship, are prohibited from voting in local elections in many countries, including France). For young generations born in Western Europe, the ability to vote in Turkey's elections thus poses the very real risk of imprisoning them in their Turkness.

After these few general remarks, we can analyse the results the last three elections where Turks living in a minority situation voted (see Figures 7.1–7.3). The observation is straightforward: In Western European countries where Turkish citizens are concentrated, there is an overrepresentation of right-wing Islamist votes and an overrepresentation of the Kurdish vote.

Exceptions are also revealing. As Figure 8.1 indicates, in those states where the Turkish presence is a result of historical bilateral guest-worker agreements (Germany, France, Belgium, the Netherlands, Switzerland) the presidential

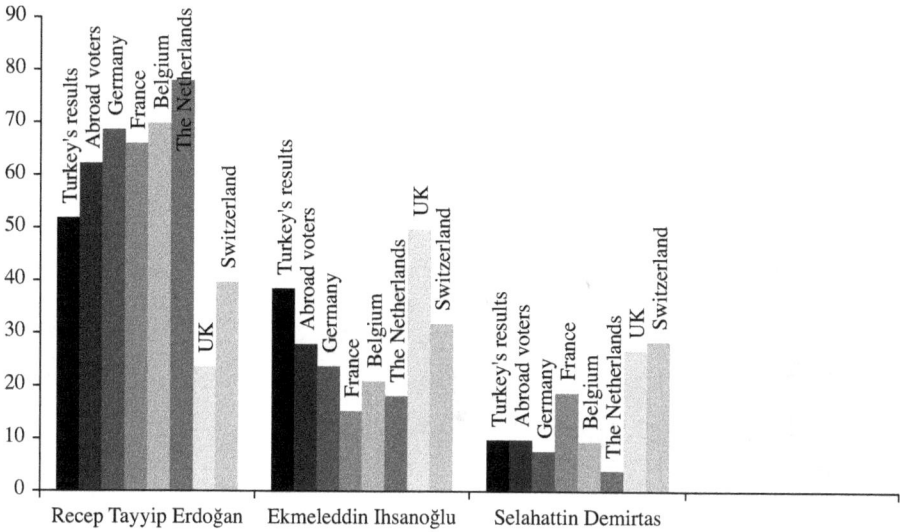

Figure 7.1 Candidates' vote share in the 2014 Turkish presidential elections by location of voters (% of votes).

candidate of political Islam (Erdoğan) attracted a high vote share. However, in the United Kingdom – where the profile of the immigrant Turk has typically been less working-class and less rural – the joint CHP-MHP candidate faired best and the Kurdish-leftist candidate came in second. In the US, where Ekmeleddin

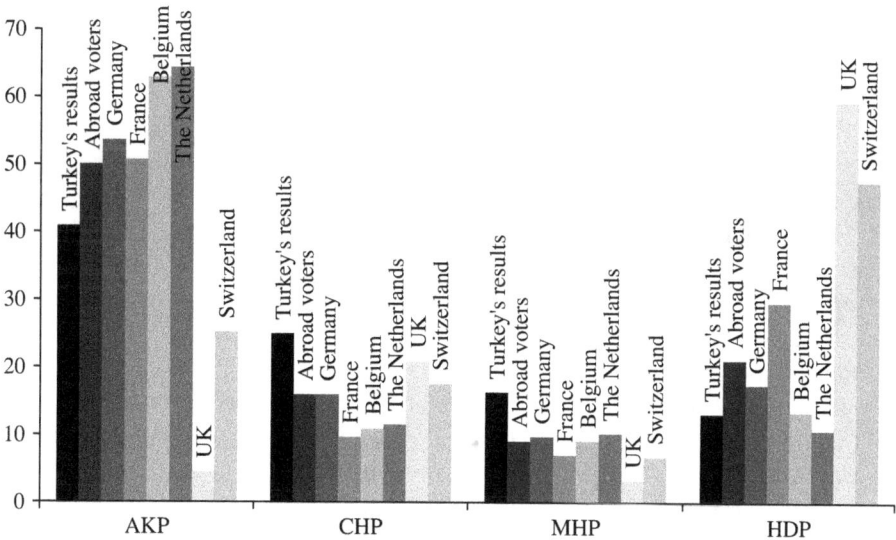

Figure 7.2 Candidates' vote share in the June 2015 parliamentary elections by location (% of votes).

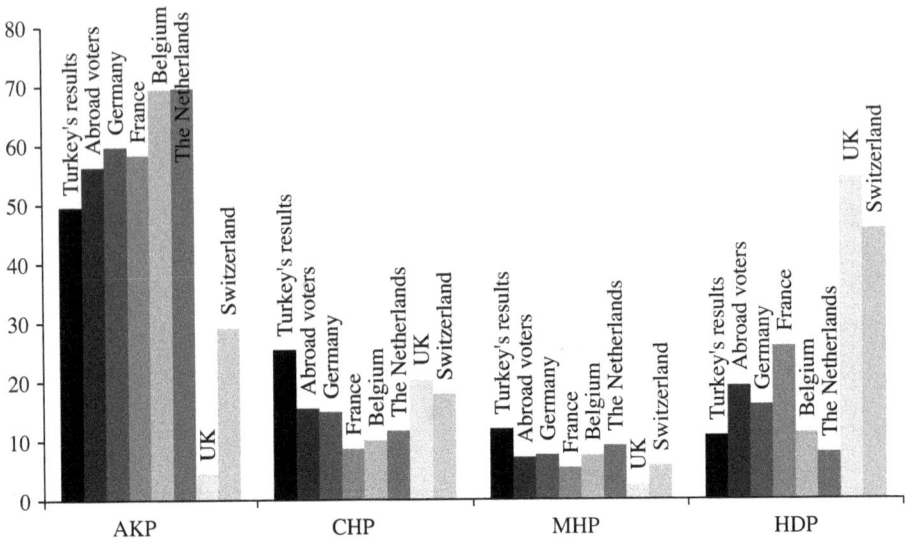

Figure 7.3 Candidates' vote share in the November 2015 parliamentary elections by location (% of votes).

Ihsanoğlu obtained 77 per cent, and Ireland (65 per cent), the trend is even more pronounced. On the contrary in countries where the Turkish community has already formed a strong minority (as in Austria where Erdoğan took 80 per cent of the vote) religious preoccupations are sharper. But there is a difference between new minorities (Turkish communities resulting from migration processes) and old minorities (Turkish minorities remaining in the Balkan countries after the collapse of the Ottoman Empire). In countries like Greece and Bulgaria the religious vote and nationalist vote are much closer. Thus, we may say that in the presidential elections, minority dynamics played an important role in three different categories: old minorities (mixed vote), new minorities (popular conservative vote) and no minority dynamic (elitist CHP and MHP vote).

Here, too, except for the United Kingdom and Switzerland (because of the Kurdish and Alevi presence, especially in the UK), the AKP's vote is overrepresented everywhere compared with Turkey itself. The AKP also seems to siphon off the traditional nationalist votes abroad from the MHP, which is underrepresented everywhere.

The June 2015 elections were widely seen as a failure for the ruling party, provoking something of a political crisis. The ruling party refused to share power and stalled coalition negotiations while simultaneously conducting a rhetorical campaign highlighting security threats and violence throughout the country as a pretext for new elections. Turkey therefore entered the November 2015 elections on a "war footing", the main purpose of which was to delegitimize the HDP and "sell" the AKP as the party of stability.

The AKP's "crisis" rhetoric political strategy was not as successful abroad as it was within Turkey itself, except in Germany. The variations between the two elections within and outside Turkey are interesting to observe (see Table 7.3).

Thus, the AKP's strategy worked everywhere but less so in Europe (except for Germany) than in Turkey. The CHP remained stabilized and very weak in Western Europe. The HDP lost votes but remained above the threshold of 10 per cent. The MHP lost its nationalist votes to the AKP.

These results show that in Western Europe only the AKP with its sharp conservative-nationalist Islamic rhetoric and the HDP with its message of Kurdish self-determination and leftist programme remain powerful electoral forces. The CHP and MHP appear to be more or less spent. Western European Turks, besides the fact that there is neither representation nor a programme concerning them directly, have voted for these two parties to influence Turkish internal politics in a classical minority reflex.

Conclusion

Turks living abroad are diverse and dynamic. But for several reasons as an identity category, they are still strongly involved in Turkish internal politics. Since 1970, Western Europe has been a relatively free context for the development of political currents, which were seen until comparatively recently as "threatening" within Turkey. Thus, Islamist movements (especially the *Milli Görüş*) on one side, and banned and oppressed leftist movements, on the other, had the opportunity to flourish in Western Europe. This also had a class dimension. Those who migrated to Western European countries followed three different paths. The first was economic migration which began in the 1960s and was dominated by conservative Anatolian young men identifying themselves strongly in terms of popular Islam. The second "wave" came in the form of "political" migration (refuges and others who left Turkey due to political oppression), which began with leftists after the 1980 coup and involved and Kurds from the 1980s and into the 1990s. The final aspect of outward migration has been "family" migration since the 1990s and into the 2000s in the strategy of "perpetual first generation" mentioned above.

Kemalists and "seculars", having until recently dominated the upper echelons of Turkish society, didn't generally follow these three trends, or, when they did, managed to slip more easily into majority societies, which meant they did not act as a distinct political and/or ideological category. As a result, it is understandable, sociologically speaking, that we see an overrepresentation of Islamist right-wing or leftist/Kurdish concentration in Western Europe. As mentioned, the Turkish state recognized this as "threatening" from its origins and sought to develop – principally through Turkish consulates in Europe – aspects of the state apparatus, such as government-oriented

Table 7.3 Change in vote share, June and November 2015 parliamentary elections (% change in total vote)

	Turkey	Abroad	Germany	France	Belgium	The Netherlands	UK	Switzerland
AKP	+ 8.63	+ 6	+ 9.4	+ 7.6	+ 6.5	+ 5.3	+ 5.8	+ 4
CHP	+ 0.37	− 0.5	− 1.1	− 1.04	− 0.9	+ 0.01	+ 0.6	+ 0.3
MHP	− 4.39	− 2.2	− 2.22	− 1.78	− 1.73	− 1.13	− 0.57	− 1.13
HDP	− 2.36	− 2.3	− 1.5	− 3.8	− 2.2	− 2.8	− 3.9	− 1.9

non-government organizations (GONGOs), the activities of the Diyanet abroad, Turkish cultural associations, and so on to circumvent this. The aim was to "protect" Turks living abroad from subversive Islamist and leftist movements. However, from the late 1990s and early 2000s political Islam (the *Milli Görüş* and after 2002 the AKP) essentially co-opted this apparatus in its own interests. Instead of restructuring this apparatus, the AKP has conquered and expanded it to ideologically frame Turkish politics for those Turks living abroad. Thus, the Turkish "state apparatus abroad" now largely "works" on behalf of the AKP and its hegemonic ideological project in Turkey. In these circumstances, it is not surprising to see the success of Recep Tayyip Erdoğan in person and the AKP as a state-party in the diaspora.

On the other hand, starting with the Gezi movement in Turkey in June 2013, a new opposition narrative has been built, mainly by Kurds but also by liberals, former leftists and democratic civil society. This coalition has had quite an impact not only on Kurdish voters in Europe but also younger generations of Turkish born there who are somehow "primed" for a liberal democratic discourse but for whom the old Kemalist "republican-democratic" discourse is a dead letter. As we have seen, the HDP vote share is not only overrepresented in Western Europe but has also been stable between the recent parliamentary elections in which Euro-Turks could freely vote. That said, given the authoritarian turn in Turkey and the AKP's increasingly aggressive anti-HDP rhetoric, it is not at all clear how this vote share will hold going forward.

Notes

1. The *millet* system was a structure of social categorization in the Ottoman Empire based on religious belonging that can be qualified as a "non-territorial autonomy". For a classical view on this system see Stanford Shaw, "The Dynamics of Ottoman Society and Administration", in Shaw Stanford, *History of the Ottoman Empire and Modern Turkey, Volume 1, Empire of the Gazis: The Rise and Decline of the Ottoman Empire 1280–1808* (Cambridge, Cambridge University Press, 1976), pp. 112–68. For a critical point of view see Taş Latif, "The Myth of the Ottoman Millet System: Its Treatment of Kurds and a Discussion of Territorial and Non-Territorial Autonomy", in the *International Journal on Minority and Group Rights*, Vol. 21, No. 4, 2014, pp. 487–526.
2. Related to "integration" issues, the Turkish "exception" in Europe has been a controversial topic since the 1990s. Michèle Tribalat's book *Faire France – Une enquête sur les immigrés et leurs enfants* (Paris, La Découverte, 1995) underlines the Turkish "exception", and has been criticized for adopting a culturalist and essentialist approach instead of a social class approach. Since its publication, many academic works have tried to confirm or disprove this idea of Turkish specificity, including my own. See Akgönül Samim, *Religions de Turquie, Religions des Turcs: nouveaux acteurs dans l'Europe élargie* (Paris, L'Harmattan, 2005). In contrast, Nermin Abadan Unat defends the transnational (and thus

multi-belonging) aspect of Euro-Turcs. See Abadan Unat Nermin, *From Guest Worker to Transnational Citizen* (London, Berghamm Books, 2011).

3. See for example, De Tapia Stéphane, *Migrations et diasporas turques: circulation migratoire et continuité territoriale* (Paris, Maisonneuve et Larose, 2004).

4. The idea of "perpetual first generation" that I summarize here is discussed in detail in Samim Akgönül, *The Minority Concept in the Turkish Context, Practices and Perceptions in Turkey, Greece and France* (Leiden, Brill, 2014).

5. Butler Kim, "Defining diaspora, refining a discourse" in *Diaspora: A Journal of Transnational Studies 10*, No. 2, 2001, pp. 189–219.

6. Anderson, Benedict, *Imagined Communities: Reflections on the Origin and Spread of Nationalism* (London, Verso, 1991 (2nd edition)), pp. 6–7.

7. Norkus Zenonas, "Max Weber on Nations and Nationalism: Political Economy before Political Sociology" in *The Canadian Journal of Sociology / Cahiers canadiens de sociologie* Vol. 29, No. 3 (Summer, 2004), pp. 389–418.

8. Beauchemin Cris, Hamel Christelle, Simon Patrick, *Trajectoires et origines: Enquête sur la diversité des populations en France* (Paris, INED, 2016).

9. Atheism is generally treated as a form apostasy in Islam and is considered an egregious affront to the religion.

10. This is discussed in greater detail in Akgönül, *Minority Concept*.

11. See for example Kentel Ferhat, Kaya Ayhan, *Euro-Turks. A Bridge or a Breach Between Turkey and the European Union: A comparative study of German-Turks and French Turks* (Bruxelles, Centre For European Policy Studies, 2005).

12. See Erdoğan Murat, Akgönül *Samim, Fransa'daki Türkiye Kökenlilerin Güncel Konulardaki Görüş ve Düşünceleri* (Ankara, HUGO, 2013).

13. Okyay Aslı, Başer Bahar, "How does expatriates' enfranchisement reconfigure transnational politics? Analysing the recent external voting experience of Turkey and its diaspora(s)", Aix AFSP Congress 2015, http://www.congres-afsp. fr/st/st5/st5okyaybaser.pdf.

14. The main political Islam movement in Turkey, *Millî Görüş*, was born in 1960's in Turkey under the leadership of its historical and symbolic founder Necmettin Erbakan. Its main ideology is the union on Sunni Islam in a very centralized State, against Western civilization and in favour of a national industrialized economy. For a general analyse of Turkish Political Islam see Jenkins Gareth, *Political Islam in Turkey: Running West, Heading East?* (New York, Palgrave Macmillan, 2008).

15. Akgönül Samim, "Millî Görüş", in Peter Frank, Ortega Rafael (eds), *Islamic Movements of Europe: Public Religion and Islamophobia in the Modern World* (London, I.B.Tauris, 2014), pp. 139–44.

16. Başer Bahar, *Diasporas and Homeland Conflicts* (Farnham, Ashgate Publishers, 2015).

17. Lafleur Jean Michel, *Transnational Politics and the State. The External Voting Rights of Diasporas* (London, Routledge, 2013).

CHAPTER 8

RECASTING THE PARAMETERS OF FREEDOM OF RELIGION IN TURKEY: NON-MUSLIMS AND THE AKP

Anna Maria Beylunioğlu

Introduction

Looking at developments since the founding of the Republic of Turkey in 1923, most recent scholarly literature takes the 2002 general elections as a turning point for the democratization process. Within this process, there have been noticeable improvements in the field of freedom of religion and particularly the treatment of non-Muslim minorities. It would be fair to argue that EU reforms aiming to enhance the conditions of non-Muslim minorities, which gained speed after November 2002, received considerable support from those non-Muslim communities that have survived decades of exclusionary state policy since 1923. However, as a former representative of a minority community contends, since the Gezi Park protests in June 2013 the momentum in the negotiation process of issues with regard to non-Muslims has declined significantly.[1] As a response to the government's foot-dragging, it is not surprising that non-Muslims have largely withdrawn their support for the government's policies. But more importantly, they have publicly protested the ongoing extrajudicial activities of the state. Within this context, the resistance at *Kamp Armen* led by the *Nor Zartonk* Armenian youth movement, which aimed to block the demolition of a summer camp for Armenian children, signalled a new era in which the state approach towards non-Muslims and the implementation of the reform process has come under serious question by civil society organizations.

In fact, the questioning of the restrictive attitude towards non-Muslim minorities began in the 1980s, along with a general political transformation at the time, and continued intensively during the process right after the 1999 Helsinki summit, during which Turkey gained EU candidate status. Freedom of religion in relation to religious minorities has been monitored through progress reports and three harmonization packages introduced up to November 2002, which sought to enhance general human rights standards in line with the Copenhagen criteria. However, the democratization process, and particularly reforms regarding non-Muslims, intensified when the Justice and Development Party (*Adalet ve Kalkınma Partisi*, AKP) came to power and signalled a commitment to the EU reform agenda. Indeed, the five reform packages passed in the parliament up to 2004 included significant steps with regard to enhancement of the conditions of non-Muslim minorities. With the introduction of the initial reforms, it became possible to establish associations on the basis of race, ethnicity, religion, sect, region, or minority group affiliation[2] and to construct sanctuaries other than mosques.[3] Moreover, additional reforms sought to address issues concerning board elections in Christian foundations.[4]

Although the pace of the democratization process slowed down with the beginning of the accession negotiations, it would be fair to argue that the "golden age of Europeanization"[5] lasted longer for non-Muslim minorities. The government pursued reforms in relation to non-Muslim minorities and passed a new law on foundations in 2008 (with an amendment in 2011)[6] that led the way for non-Muslim communities to reacquire, register and restore their properties. Private schools affiliated with non-Muslim communities were also aided by new regulations to overcome the long-standing difficulties faced by administrators.[7] Apart from these legal arrangements, a dialogue process initiated with non-Muslim community representatives signaling a change in the state approach towards non-Muslims citizens was opened. Within this context, non-Muslims began to be presented as "first class" and "equal" citizens of the republic[8] and evaluated through an emphasis on "richness" deriving from "different faiths and cultures" in the AKP's election manifesto.[9]

The opening of communication channels between the government and the non-Muslim representatives had a positive impact on non-Muslims' manifestation of their religion in teaching, practice, worship and observance, which resulted in increasing support for the AKP among non-Muslim citizens. Although it is difficult to find resources to estimate the voting behaviour of non-Muslim communities even today, the comments of prominent non-Muslim figures in newspaper articles at the time suggested that minority communities were "backing the AKP" for their "less nationalistic approach towards minorities".[10] Recent research conducted on the *Rum*, Jewish, and Armenian communities also revealed that these three communities gave considerable support to the AKP up to 2014 due to the negative image of the previous governments engrained in the memory of the older generations[11] who had battled extremely restrictive practices for decades.

However, it is too early to be optimistic about the AKP's relatively positive attitude towards non-Muslim minorities due to the limitations experienced both in formal rule adaptation and in practice during the period of reform activity. As of writing, although important steps have been taken in order to improve the conditions of Turkey's non-Muslims, key issues remain unresolved and the reform process has not been cemented in a robust legal framework. For example, the suspension of board elections in non-Muslim foundations continues to leave them vulnerable to possible closure attempts. Additionally, community foundations are still deprived of legal personality. Moreover, the newly-introduced and recently-amended laws remain insufficient to eradicate restrictive attitudes towards freedom of religion for non-Muslim minorities. Coupled with the AKP's emphasis, especially after 2011, on consolidating a conservative society these limitations and shortcomings cast positive developments in a dark shadow.

Against this background, in the remainder of this article I will focus on the parameters that have shaped the relationship between the AKP and non-Muslim minorities since 2002. Questioning the motives and the limitations of the transformation of religious freedoms during AKP rule, I will argue that the main explanation of the AKP government's relatively friendly approach towards non-Muslims (and reciprocal support) was the AKP's dissatisfaction with the long-standing Kemalist parameters of freedom of religion. In particular, a shared sense of being victims of Kemalist restrictions on freedom of religion since the founding of the republic opened up common ground between the AKP and non-Muslim minorities. However, the government's increasing emphasis on the superiority of Islamic values after the AKP's authoritarian turn in 2011 and the failure to cement a legal framework for religious freedom based on equality and human rights has placed a brake on the prospect of transformation. Therefore, I suggest that the recent developments that are germane to non-Muslim minorities should be considered as a part of a *recasting* of freedom of religion rather than a *transformation* of it.

Freedom of Religion, Kemalism and Non-Muslims

Although the Republic of Turkey was built on the principle of secularism, it has adopted a selectively secular approach, which included a restrictive attitude towards freedom of religion of some groups and individuals belonging to these religious communities. This is mainly due to the traditional approach towards religion and activities of religious groups and individuals, which were kept restricted not only in political but also in social and private spheres. This conventional approach towards freedom of religion took shape around the idea of *laicité* as a part of the Kemalist ideology introduced by (and named after) Mustafa Kemal Atatürk following the collapse of the Ottoman Empire.

The main objective of the introduction of *laicité* principle was to separate religion and state. This particular Kemalist principle extended the moderniz-ation and secularization processes initiated during the late Ottoman Empire[12] and aimed to create a country similar to the "advanced states of the world".[13] As a part of this project, the republic was founded as a secular state and one of the very first acts of the new regime was to disestablish religion, particularly Islam, from social and political spheres. Within this context, the office of *Şeyhülislam* and the Caliphate were abolished, religious brotherhoods (*tarikats*) were banned, and religious schools for training Imams were closed. More remarkably, the promotion of religious ideas in a political context and the public display of piety were marginalized and sometimes even prohibited.[14]

The reflection of the principle of secularism in the Turkish context however has been twofold. As it has been implemented, *laicité* has not only displayed a partly antagonistic attitude towards religion but also included contradictory features within itself, which left some religious groups and individuals in a disadvantaged position by failing to meet their basic needs as religious people. In line with the authoritarian characteristic of the Kemalist establishment, which is intolerant against any public entity that would weaken its "vision of an ideal society",[15] the new regime left no room for any religious activity and aimed to clear the public sphere of both the traditional Islamic culture[16] and non-Muslim faiths. At the same time, rather than separate religion completely from the state, Kemalists somewhat contracted the *laicité* principle by electing to bring religion closely under the state apparatus. To achieve this end, the office of *Şeyhülislam* was replaced with the Presidency of Religious Affairs (*Diyanet İşleri Başkanlığı, DİB*) after the collapse of the Ottoman Empire, which instead of acting upon the religious diversity in the country promoted a controlled version of Sunni/Hanefi Islam[17] and excluded both folk Islam and non-Muslim faiths. Although free exercise of worship and equality of citizens "regardless of one's language, race [...] religion, sect [...] etc"[18] was guaranteed in the constitution, in practice individuals belonging to certain religious groups were subjected to unequal treatment. Among those groups, Islamists in particular were ostracized by the system and prohibited from expressing religious ideas in a political context but also from joining the public sphere more generally.[19]

The introduction of the multiparty system and the policies of the Democrat Party (DP), which brought changes such as lifting the ban on religious instruction and broadcasting,[20] loosened the pressure on Islamists for a while but nevertheless maintained a hard line against radical Islamist groups.[21] The liberal 1961 Constitution opened up a space for the rise of parties with political-Islamist tendencies during the 1970s. These parties were shut down by the

Turkish Constitutional Court – often in the wake of military coups – which found their activities to be contrary to secular principles. After the 1970 coup, the Turkish-Islamic synthesis opened a new avenue for the use of Islam to reinforce Turkish nationalism, but kept a tight rein on expression of Islam in state institutions such as the army and the universities in line with the standard principles of Kemalism.[22] Alevis were also restricted from expressing their religious freedoms and the state apparatus denied their non-Sunni identity continuously.[23] Despite their strong support of the secularizing reforms of the Kemalist establishment,[24] massacres in *Dersim* (1936–8), *Maraş* (1978) and Sivas (1993), and the *Gazi* events of 1995 cast a spotlight on the discrimination Alevis have faced since the founding of the republic.

Within this picture, non-Muslim minorities – whose numbers are estimated to make up fewer than 1 per cent of the Turkish population – have faced the most negative effects of the state-led policy towards religion. Over the decades they have encountered extreme difficulties with regard to the practice of religion, worship and teaching. Their properties have been confiscated and they have also been assaulted, forced to emigrate and subjected to extrajudicial practices, which has led to a steady decrease in their population. This is despite the fact that the articles of the Treaty of Lausanne (Articles 37–43) signed after Turkey's war of independence (and still technically in force today) provide a comprehensive framework with regard to the protection of religious minorities. However, considering the lack of tolerance of the Kemalist establishment towards non-Muslims[25] it would be fair to argue that the Turkish state has gone to great lengths to reduce the practical scope of the Treaty to the greatest extent possible.

In the period since World War I, a lingering "suspicion" of non-Muslim subjects as traitors has prevented the secular ideal of a "religion-blind" approach to take effect. First, the non-Muslim population was not included in the definition of Turkishness that underpinned the formation of the republic. The subsequent Turkification policies, which according to Ayhan Aktar meant the "domination of Turkish ethnic identity in every sphere of life from the spoken language in the streets, history learnt in schools; from education to industry, from trade to state personnel administration, from private law to settling policies", [26] placed an intense burden on non-Muslim citizens. It is possible to observe the traces of these policies in the deportation of Armenian subjects of the Ottoman Empire in 1915.[27] This process was followed by the population exchange between Greece and Turkey in 1923, which resulted in a tremendous decrease in the size of the *Rum* Orthodox population.[28]

This process of exclusion continued until the end of 1960s under a range of Turkification measures, including the Turkification of economic capital via expropriation of property, prohibition of education in Greek in Imbros (*Gökçeada*) and Tenedos (*Bozcaada*),[29] displacement of the Jews in Trace in

1934,[30] and the "Citizen! Speak Turkish" campaign organized in 1927 to encourage people to use Turkish in their daily lives. Somewhat later, a capital tax implemented in 1942 (ostensibly to raise funds for the war effort) fell heavily on non-Muslims.[31] The September 1955 pogrom against the properties of non-Muslim citizens in Istanbul and elsewhere and the expulsion of Greeks in 1964[32] were devastating for non-Muslim populations.

Apart from the Turkification policies, non-Muslims have also encountered numerous difficulties and extrajudicial practices limiting their religious freedoms. In the first place, the Turkish republic has not recognized the legal personality of these religious communities. The Law on Foundations, the Turkish Civil Code, and the Municipality Law included provisions restricting the properties that Christian communities could possess and prevented them from legating their properties to religious foundations and interfered with the election procedures of both administrative authorities and religious bodies. Moreover, the registration of children at schools affiliated with minority communities[33] and provision of education in (non-Turkish) native languages were also prohibited.[34] Religious minorities have also encountered obstacles in practising their religion, most notably prohibitions against building new sanctuaries. Moreover, despite the fact that proselytizing or propagation of one's religion is perfectly legal in Turkey, Christian spiritual activities – including the ecumenicity of the Patriarchate and the missionary activities of Protestant communities – have always been perceived as a threat to the state's project of the homogenization of society.[35]

Teaching religion has also been restricted for non-Muslim minorities in Turkey. While the *Rum* Orthodox Theology School was closed by the state in 1971, Syriacs, Protestants and Catholics have been denied a clergy school throughout the entire republican period. Last but not least, religious minorities have faced general discrimination within society. While the existence of state agencies dedicated to "monitoring" the activities of religious minorities[36] and the legal requirement to identify one's religion on the national identity card[37] are the most egregious examples, religious minorities have also been subject to discrimination in many other fields from university entrance exams to recruitment in government institutions.[38]

These authoritarian and discriminatory policies of the Kemalist establishment attenuated briefly during the DP administration of the 1950s and the *Anavatan Partisi* (ANAP) government in the 1980s, during which short-term enhancements of freedom of religion for non-Muslim minorities were implemented.[39] This did not, however, result in any substantive transformation process. It was only after the intensification of Turkey–EU relations after the Helsinki Summit that governments began to introduce a substantive reform agenda. Within this context, changes made to the Law on Associations and the Law on Foundations, as well as several articles of the Turkish constitution around the turn of the century were critical. Moreover, highly symbolic steps taken by the government, such as inviting expatriate Syrian Orthodox citizens of Turkey to return to their homeland,[40] signalled a substantial shift from the Turkish state.

For most non-Muslim representatives, therefore, EU candidacy has been the cornerstone of efforts to enhance their religious freedoms and the EU is seen as having acted as the main facilitator of the changes occurring during this first stage of EU candidacy.[41] Despite the EU's pressure, many state authorities maintained a traditional Kemalist suspicion towards non-Muslims,[42] and often disregarded or ignored formal legal changes and failed to develop an efficient system of implementation. As the EU's impact remained largely limited to formal legislative changes,[43] non-Muslims have not, as a matter of practical reality, noticed substantive improvements in the position of their churches in the broader context, or in their religious freedoms when compared to previous decades.

Freedom of Religion under AKP Rule: Towards Superiority of Islamic Values?

When the AKP came to power in November 2002, the party's ideological past, which was rooted in political Islam, raised doubts not only among secularists but also other fractions of Turkish society including nationalists, civil society organizations and the army. Religious minorities were not immune from these concerns either. The commitment to the EU reform agenda declared by the new AKP prime minister,[44] however, promised a continuation of the EU accession process. However, reviewing the official discourse toward non-Muslim minorities, it would be fair to argue that AKP's interest in the EU remained instrumental and heavily based on a desire to dismantle a number of aspects of the Kemalist project. Following Ertuğ Tombuş's suggestion that the AKP has governed in two distinct phases – a "polemical phase" geared towards disestablishing the Kemalist authoritarian regime, and a "ruling phase" focused on developing its own authoritarian control[45] – the remainder of this section suggests that two distinct approaches towards freedom of religion in general (and non-Muslims in particular) may be observed under the period of AKP rule. In the early years, discourses dominated by more universalist themes of "human rights", "fraternity", and "cultural richness" were deployed in relation non-Muslims. This formed part of a larger process to destabilize the Kemalist project. In the wake of the AKP's "authoritarian turn" around 2011, this phase yielded to a discourse coloured more in terms of the superiority of Islamic values.

Inheriting the EU reform agenda from the previous coalition government, the AKP demonstrated a clear intention to champion the EU reform process further. The AKP party platform[46] evinced a strong commitment to international human rights standards, including those enshrined in the European Convention of Human Rights. A series of reform packages subsequently passed, including changes with regard to non-Muslims. This paved the way for formal accession negotiations, which commenced in 2005. However, the reforms outlined in the EU harmonization packages were somewhat limited, and several non-Muslim scholars have criticized the government's approach, declaring that the rights of non-Muslims should not be held "hostage"[47] to the politics of Turkey's potentially lengthy European accession process.

The role of EU conditionality (i.e., "push" factors) as an impetus for enhanced conditions for non-Muslim minorities is undeniable. That said, scholars also urge that attention be paid to domestic level ("pull") factors,[48] which I argue are a necessary part of understanding why the reform agenda with regard to non-Muslims continued even after 2005, when a general slowdown in the Europeanization process was observed in Turkey. As a party born of Turkey's Islamic movement, the AKP came to power with an abiding resentment towards Kemalist secularist policies, which have sought to exclude pious Muslims from the political system since the founding of the republic. For the AKP, the EU's standards for human rights and religious freedom appeared as a powerful corrective to the Kemalist approach. The AKP's party platform incorporated many elements drawing on European norms that challenged the status quo. The platform thus provided a strong corrective to the classic Kemalist interpretation of religion as a threat to the state, and presented human rights as the basis of an alternative model for relations between the state and religion.[49] Government representatives also highlighted the EU as a model of the peaceful coexistence of different cultures and religions.[50]

Despite the fact that the EU reform agenda provided only limited change and the ongoing challenge of developing a robust legal framework for the protection of non-Muslim rights, the AKP's special interest in recasting the parameters of freedom of religion was nevertheless appreciated by the vast majority of non-Muslim minorities. Compared with the long Kemalist tradition of (often narrow-minded) opposition to the enhancement of the rights of non-Muslims,[51] the AKP's positive emphasis on "richness" deriving from "different faiths and cultures" was noteworthy and appealed to a non-Muslim audience.[52] The AKP's approach towards freedom of religion, however, took a remarkable turn after a series of homicides targeting non-Muslims in 2007. These attacks were widely attributed, including by the AKP government, to elements connected to the Turkish deep state. In a year (2007) in which the AKP and the Kemalist establishment reached a final and dramatic "showdown", many saw the real motive behind these murders as an attempt to undermine the AKP as a political force.[53]

At this point the government thus began to embrace and empathize with Turkey's non-Muslims by defining freedom of religion as a problematic field in which *both* non-Muslims and Muslims had suffered since the founding of the republic.[54] Non-Muslims were cast explicitly (and for the first time) as "first-class citizens" and their equality in the Turkish society was highlighted on several occasions.[55] Despite proving insufficient as a comprehensive solution to problems minority foundations have faced historically, the introduction of a reformist Law on Foundations (against stern criticism from the Kemalist opposition) was notable. The government's conciliatory approach towards Turkey's non-Muslims was even reflected in parliamentary debates, during which an AKP parliamentarian criticized the longstanding principle demanding 'reciprocity' from the Greek government in dealing with the rights of religious communities of Greek heritage in Turkey and stated that what had been intended in the Treaty of Lausanne was not reciprocity but "parallelism".[56] For the first time, then, the argument was put that Turkey should proceed with liberalization of religious minority rights simply because it is the right thing to do, rather than as a *quid pro quo* for policy reform on the Greek side.

It would, however, be naive to consider the AKP's approach towards freedom of religion in general (and non-Muslims in particular) to be fully compatible with the EU's human rights-centric framework. First of all, old state reflexes did not disappear altogether. Government representatives did not publicly condemn *DİB*'s clear stance against Christian organizations' (perfectly legal) missionary activities,[57] nor did they accept a "minority report" prepared by the Prime Minister's Human Rights Advisory Board containing a roadmap to minority and cultural rights, including the rights of non-Muslims. More to the point, they described the report as 'intellectual rubbish'.[58] The Prime Minister's emphasis on "kin" in referring explicitly to *Muslim* Turks in Europe also suggested that the government's rhetoric about Turkishness as a "rich" and "diverse" concept had not been fully embraced.[59] Many scholars also underlined that hate speech against non-Muslim minorities continued to appear in the statements of government representatives.[60] Secondly, the AKP's approach to the EU model of freedom of religion remained explicitly unconditional. In fact, the AKP found cause to criticize the European approach when the European Court of Human Rights' (ECtHR) *Leyla Şahin* decision found Turkey's ban on headscarves consistent with the principle of freedom of religion.[61] This decision roundly disappointed AKP members, who had expected the EU to champion an idea of freedom inclusive of public Islamic identity.[62] Following the *Leyla Şahin* ruling, the AKP began to censure the EU more openly. Mehmet Ali Şahin, a minister of state at the time, criticized the EU's demands with regard to the restitution of Christian properties saying that "Equating freedom of religion only with the restitution of the properties makes me uncomfortable."[63] Finally, the statements of AKP politicians signalled that the EU was merely one of a range of alternatives seen as a model to replace the Kemalist edifice. On many occasions AKP parliamentarians took a more chauvinistic stance, referencing Turkey's glorious Ottoman heritage[64] and referring to the *millet* system as one in which different religious traditions were tolerated and coexisted.[65] This approach was also reflected in the parliamentary debates on the new Law on Foundations in 2008. A parliamentarian reminded the assembly that Turks "are the children of a great civilization" and argued that "Everybody in our land is under the protection of this country [...] Let us remember the Byzantines and the tolerance of our ancestor who said 'I would rather see an Ottoman turban in the midst of the city than the Latin mitre.'"[66]

References to Ottoman heritage at times signalled a religion-based attitude towards religious minorities and its usage carried the potential to "other" non-Muslims[67] because the Ottoman *millet* system was based ultimately on the superiority of Islam over other religions. This frame simply had not appeared in the early years of AKP rule. At that time, EU standards for freedom of religion were ubiquitous, despite the severe criticism directed towards the EU at times. In several speeches government representatives indicated the instrumental role of the EU to achieve basic rights and liberties including freedom of religion.[68] Nevertheless, the "Ottoman turn" in AKP discourse in the later period was not perceived wholly as a step backwards because it was cast as a supplement to, rather than a replacement of, European approaches. While Ottoman chauvinism certainly created discomfort among non-Muslims in general,[69] the combination of the Ottoman tolerance model with the EU's human-right based approach at the discourse level was actually welcomed by some non-Muslim minorities, who took the view that a government with religious sensitivities would never harm other genuinely religious people.[70]

Government representatives continued to refer to human rights and equality among citizens regardless of faith in speeches for some time after the AKP's transition to its "ruling" or authoritarian phase after 2011. However, an increase in the emphasis on Islamic values was clear for all to see. This shift in government discourse did not have an immediately negative effect on the dialogue process, however. On the contrary, the number of meetings between government representatives and non-Muslims increased considerably. Non-Muslim representatives continued to witness positive changes, such as amendments to the Law on Foundations in 2011 and 2013, the introduction of a new private school regulation in 2012, and the restitution of several non-Muslim properties. Moreover, some symbolic gestures were offered. Non-Muslim citizens, for example, were invited to apply for public service positions, from which they have been traditionally discouraged and excluded.[71] Significantly, during the inaugural visit of the *DİB* leadership to the Ecumenical Patriarchate in 2011, the president of religious affairs declared his support to reopen the *Halki* Seminary.[72] However, declining emphasis on European norms in regard to non-Muslims and increasing criticism of the EU in general implied a clear shift away from the EU-centred approach to religious freedom towards the

Ottoman model. Government representatives spoke increasingly, as Jenny White has argued, of a "deep-rooted past",[73] and highlighted more and more the Ottoman Empire's tolerant approach towards non-Muslims.

Most strikingly, a discourse emphasizing the superiority of Islam over other religions came to the fore. As the government declared its absolute priority to be "Islam, Islam, Islam",[74] Muslim youth were increasingly defined as the "real descendants of the Turkish nation". Within this context, it is hardly surprising that pejorative labeling of non-Muslims as "traitors" and "exploiters"[75] became more evident or that non-Muslims were increasingly subject to hate speech, even by the prime minister who took public umbrage at having been "insulted" by being referred to as "Armenian" on one occasion.[76] Last but not least, the controversial proposal to turn the *Ayasofya* museum in Istanbul into a mosque returned to the top of the agenda. The prospect that this idea would become reality was cast into sharp relief when the identically named museums in *Iznik* and *Trabzon* were in fact converted, feeding the perception that the AKP is intent on prioritizing Islam over other religions.[77]

This trend eventually led to a slackening in the momentum of reforms addressing non-Muslims' religious freedoms. Arguably the most remarkable indicator of this was the government's return to the conventional nationalist argument of reciprocity in relation to the status of Muslim imams in Greece, which has traditionally been made conditional on the reopening of the *Halki* Seminary.[78] For this reason, the reopening of the *Halki* Seminary was omitted from the 2013 democratization package, a noted disappointment to many. Moreover, a new regulation for board elections of non-Muslim foundations, which had been suspended by the state in early 2013, was postponed indefinitely. Coupled with obstacles put in the way of restitution of non-Muslim foundations' property, non-Muslims again felt excluded from the system, as had been the case during the many decades of Kemalist hegemony. In the wake of the AKP's "authoritarian turn", revealed most pointedly during the 2013 Gezi Park protests, non-Muslims now increasingly see the AKP as a party aiming to create an Islam-based conservative society.[79] The party has thus forfeited its potential as a champion of the interests of non-Muslim individuals and communities within a general framework of plural human rights.

Conclusion: Where to From Here?

As the above discussion has suggested, the AKP has been reconfiguring the parameters of freedom of religion in Turkey for more than a decade. The role of the EU in this recasting process, both as a push factor and as a source of inspiration, is undeniable. Yet, at the end of the day the policies of the AKP in government and the discourse of the party's politicians with regard to non-Muslim issues clearly show that the party has not been seeking to establish a human rights-based framework for freedom of religion in Turkey as was once hoped. Rather, a particular selective blending of EU norms and Ottoman models has given way over time to a more chauvinistic approach implying the superiority of Islamic values.

Non-Muslims have been following this shift in the perception of freedom of religion in Turkey with deep concern. The party's eagerness to open up the debate and its decision to take concrete steps on questions of freedom of worship and other issues in the early years of AKP rule were broadly welcomed by non-Muslim citizens. Yet the failure to establish a comprehensive and robust legal framework for the protection and advancement of religious rights has resulted in disappointment and a gradual diminution of support for the AKP among non-Muslim groups. Non-Muslims today are uncomfortable with the fact that in the absence of a robust legal structure supporting the existence of religious entities, the only recourse to protect their fundamental rights is through costly and uncertain appeals to the courts. More importantly, churches and monasteries continue to be threatened by the prospect of unlawful confiscation by the state. While government representatives prefer to keep silent where this kind of extrajudicial practice takes place, they continue to reinforce through rhetoric and discourse a traditional Turkish mindset that treats non-Muslim citizens as foreigners. As the sense among non-Muslim representatives that governments can be relied upon to advance religious-rights reform as part of the normal governing agenda has largely evaporated, the view has emerged that the only way to transcend Turkey's longstanding "dominant vs. subordinate nation approach" towards non-Muslims is a new democratic constitution that would enshrine universal human rights and freedoms.[80]

As the wellspring of dialogue between the government and non-Muslim representatives becomes ever more poisoned, it nevertheless remains the case that increasingly self-assured civil-society organizations and younger generations of non-Muslims raised with a common sprit of resistance have developed a determination to keep alive the demand for equal treatment as citizens of Turkey. Indeed, those non-Muslim representatives who have repeatedly sat down at the negotiation table with the AKP government are confident enough to urge all religious communities to "define their identity for themselves" and "voice loudly the demand to be included in a possible new constitutional order".[81]

Within this context, non-Muslims have become increasingly visible in the public sphere through channels such as the newspaper *Agos* and the Association of Protestant Churches, which were established around the turn of the century to voice the problems of their communities and "to struggle for reinforcing freedom of religion in Turkey in parallel to international Human Rights Law".[82] Newer organizations are flourishing as well. *Nor Zartonk*, a civic youth initiative, was established in 2008. Since 2011, organizations such as *RUMVADER* and *Sabro* have begun to initiate high-profile projects in order to "struggle for a common, equal, and free life."[83] Many other initiatives that seek to bring issues related to non-Muslims and their freedoms to the table have moved into the public square. Moreover, just as these channels are expected to proliferate in the near future, non-Muslim youth – as they did in *Kamp Armen* – continue to refuse to accept the extrajudicial and discriminatory practices of the state. In the context of a formal reform process that appears to have stopped dead in its tracks, these actions offer a glimmer of hope that the future of religious freedom for non-Muslims in Turkey will be brighter than the past.

Notes

1. Interview with a former representative of a minority community, 3 July, 2015, Istanbul.
2. Official Gazette (2004a), "Law on Associations", No. 25649, 23 November.
3. Ibid. (2003), "Zoning Law", No. 25192, 7 August.
4. Ibid. (2004b), "Regulation of the Methods and Principles of the Boards of Non-Muslim Religious Foundations", No. 25585, 16 September.
5. Ziya Öniş, "Turkey-EU Relations: Beyond the Current Stalemate", *Insight Turkey*, 10/4, (2008).
6. Official Gazette (2008), "Law on Foundations", No. 26800, 27 February; Official Gazette (2011), "Law on Foundations", No. 28038, 27 August.
7. Official Gazette (2007), "Law on Private Schools", No. 26434, 14 February.
8. "Egemen Bağış'tan Paskalya Tebriği" [Greetings from Egemen Bağış for Easter], *Agos*, 10 April 2012; "Gayrimüslimlere de 3 Çocuk Çağrısı" [Non-Muslims also called on to have three Children], *Radikal*, 14 February 2012.
9. *AKP* Election Manifesto (2002). Available at http://kurzman.unc.edu/files/2011/06/AKP_2002.pdf (Accessed 10 May 2016).
10. Yigal Schleifer, "Turkey: Religious Minorities Watch Closely as Election Day Approaches", available at www.eurasianet.org/departments/insight/articles/eav071907a.shtml (accessed 10 May 2016); "Ermeni cemaati AK Parti'ye eğilimli [Armenian community have a tendency towards the *AKP*]", *NTV*, 11 June 2007. available at http://arsiv.ntv.com.tr/news/410682.asp (accessed 10 May 2016).
11. Özgür Kaymak, "The Socio-spatial Construction of Istanbul's Rum, Jewish and Armenian Communities", Istanbul University, Department of Political Science and Public Administration, unpublished Phd Thesis (2016).
12. Binnaz Toprak, "Islam and Democracy in Turkey", *Turkish Studies*, 6/2 (2005), pp. 167–86.
13. Suna Kili, *Kemalism* (Robert College, Istanbul, 1969), p. 40.
14. Hakan Özoğlu, "Exaggerating and Exploiting the Sheikh Said Rebellion in 1925 for Political Gains", *New Perspectives on Turkey*, 41(2009) pp. 181–210; Binnaz Toprak, "Religion and Politics", in M. Heper & S. Sayarı (eds), *The Routledge Handbook of Modern Turkey* (Routledge, London and New York, 2012), pp. 217–26.
15. M. Hakan Yavuz, "Cleansing Islam from the Public Sphere", *Journal of International Affairs*, 54/1 (2000), p. 25.
16. Şerif Mardin, "Turkish Islamic Exceptionalism Yesterday and Today: Continuity, Rupture and Reconstruction in Operational Codes", *Turkish Studies*, 6 (2005), pp. 145–65.

17. Ruşen Çakır & İrfan Bozan, *Sivil, Şeffaf ve Demokratik Bir Diyanet İşleri Başkanlığı Mümkün Mü? [Is a Civil, Accountable, Democratic Presidency of Religious Affairs Possible?]* (TESEV, Istanbul, 2005); İştar Gözaydın, *Türkiye'de Diyanet [Diyanet in Turkey]*, (Yeni Yüzyıl, Istanbul 1995); İştar Gözaydın, *Diyanet: Türkiye Cumhuriyeti'nde Dinin Tanzimi [Diyanet: Regulation of Religion in the Republic of Turkey]* (İletişim, Istanbul, 2009).
18. Article 12 and 19 of the 1961 Constitution and Article 10 and 24 of the 1982 Constitution.
19. M. Hakan Yavuz, "Political Islam and the Welfare (Refah) Party in Turkey", *Comparative Politics*, 30/1 (1997), pp. 63–82.
20. See the works of Prof. Binnaz Toprak (Toprak, Islam and Democracy) for more on the changes implemented in the Democrat Party period.
21. Hugh Poulton, *Top Hat, Grey Wolf, and Crescent: Turkish Nationalism and the Turkish Republic* (New York University Press, New York, 1997), p. 171.
22. Pınar Tank, "Political Islam in Turkey: A State of Controlled Secularity", *Turkish Studies*, 6/1 (2005), pp. 3–19.
23. İştar Gözaydın, "A Religious Administration to Secure Secularism: The Presidency of Religious Affairs of the Republic of Turkey", *Marburg Journal of Religion*, 11/1 (2006).
24. Ali Çarkoğlu and Nazlı Çağın Bilgili, "A Precarious Relationship: The Alevi Minority, the Turkish State and the EU", *South European Society and Politics*, 16/2 (2011), pp. 351–64; Karin Vorhoff, "'Let's Reclaim Our History and Culture!': Imagining Alevi Community in Contemporary Turkey", *Die Welt des Islams*, 38/2 (1998), pp. 220–52.
25. James G. Mellon, "Islamism, Kemalism and the Future of Turkey", *Totalitarian Movements and Political Religions*, 7/1 (2006), pp. 67–81.
26. Ayhan Aktar, *Varlık Vergisi ve Türkleştirme Politikaları [Capital Tax and Turkification Policies]*, (İletisim, Istanbul, 2000), p. 101.
27. Baskın Oran, "Osmanlı'dan Cumhuriyet'e Mülkiyet Politikaları ve Gayrimuslimler: 1936 Beyannamesi [Ownership Politics and non-Muslims From Ottoman to Republic: 1936 Declaration]", *Türkiye'de Azınlık Hakları Sorunu: Vatandaşlık ve Demokrasi Eksenli Bir Yaklaşım* (TESEV, Istanbul, 2005).
28. Alexis Alexandris, *The Greek Minority of Istanbul and Greek-Turkish Relations: 1918–1974*, (Centre for Asia Minor Studies, Athens, 1992).
29. Oran, "Osmanlı'dan Cumhuriyet'e".
30. Aktar, "Varlık Vergisi".
31. Oran, "Osmanlı'dan Cumhuriyet'e".
32. Alexandris, "The Greek Minority of".
33. "Ermeni Azınlık Okullarında Karma Evliliklerden İlk Jenerasyon [First Generation of Mix Marriages in Armenian Schools]", available at http://hyetert.blogspot.com/2011/01/ermeni-aznlk-okullarnda-karma.html (accessed 20 April 2016).
34. "Azınlık Okulları da Sorunlu [Minority Schools are Problematic As Well]" (*Radikal*, 15 September, 2002).
35. Esra Özyürek, "Convert Alert: German Muslims and Turkish Christians as Threats to Security in the New Europe", *Comparative Studies in Society and History*, 51/1 2009), pp. 91–116.
36. "İşte O Gizli Karar [Here is That Secret Decision]", *Hürriyet*. 24 February 2004).
37. Anna Maria Beylunioglu, *Religion-State Relations in Greece and Turkey: The Identity Cards Controversy*, (VDM Verlag, 2009).

38. "Sınavda Din Sorusu Kafa Karıştırıyor [Religion Question in the Exam Creates Confusion]", *Agos*, 8 February 2013.
39. It is also important to note the recent research that shows that most of the non-Muslims that compare *Kemalist* practices with the policies of the DP and ANAP, also tend to vote for centre-right parties in any case (Kaymak, "The Socio-spatial").
40. "Nazi Tarzı Yasak [Nazi Style Ban]", *Milliyet*, 14 June 2001.
41. Interview with the principal of a minority school, 24 March 2014, Istanbul.
42. Interview with a former representative of a minority community, 3 December 2013, Istanbul.
43. Interview with a representative of a minority community, 14 January 2014, Istanbul.
44. "6 Güvence [6 Guarantees]", *Hürriyet*, 4 November 2002.
45. Ertuğ Tombuş, "Reluctant Democratization: The Case of the Justice and Development Party in Turkey", *Constellations*, 20/2 (2013), pp. 312–27.
46. AKP Party Program (2002), available at http://www.tbmm.gov.tr/eyayin/ GAZETELER/WEB/KUTUPHANEDE%20BULUNAN%20DIJITAL%20KAYNAKLAR/ KITAPLAR/SIYASI%20PARTI%20YAYINLARI/200205071%20AK%20PARTI%20 DEMOKRATIKLESME%20VE%20KALKINMA%20PROGRAMI%202002/20020 5071%20AK%20PARTI%20DEMOKRATIKLESME%20VE%20KALKINMA%20 PROGRAMI%202002%200000_0116.pdf (accesed 20 May 2016).
47. "Azınlıklar Bildirisi: Rehine Değiliz [Minority Notice: We are not Hostages]", *Radikal*, 26 September 2006.
48. Gözde Yılmaz, "It is Pull-and-Push that Matters for External Europeanization! Explaining Minority Policy Change in Turkey", *Mediterranean Politics*, 19/2 (2014), pp. 238–58.
49. "AKP Party Program".
50. See Erdoğan's "Monthly Address to the Nation" speech, December 2004.
51. Interviews with representatives of minority communities, 26 March 2013; 14 January 2014, Istanbul.
52. Ibid.
53. "Suikast Cephaneliği [Assasination Armoury]", Taraf. *Taraf*, 20 December 2009.
54. "AKP'nin Kestirilemezliği [Unpredictability of the AKP]", *Radikal*, 24 March 2010.
55. Erdoğan's speech at the *AKP* group meeting on 6 May 2008.
56. See the parliamentary speech of *AKP* MP Hayati Yazıcı on 31 January 2008 (23. Term 57. Session).
57. "Kahvaltılı Basın Açıklaması [Press Release]", of the Presidency of Religious Affairs on 16 October 2003, available at www.diyanet.gov.tr/tr/icerik/kahvaltili-basin-toplantisi/6381?getEnglish=accessed 15 April, 2016.
58. Baskın Oran. "Azınlık Hakları ve Kültürel Haklar Raporu'nun Bütün Öyküsü [Minority Rights and the Whole Story of Cultural Rights" Report]", *Birikim*, 188, (2004), pp. 17–25.
59. See Erdoğan's speech "Address to Our Citizens and Kin" on 25 October, 2007 in Bucharest, Romania.
60. Ahmet İnsel, "Özür Dilemek Artık Bir Zorunluluk [Apologizing is a Necessity Now]", *Radikal*, 16 November, 2008b.
61. Leyla Şahin v. Turkey (10 November 2005), App.no: 44774/98, ECtHR, Strasbourg.
62. Marcie J. Patton, "AKP Reform Fatigue in Turkey: What Has Happened to the EU Process?", *Mediterranean Politics*, 12/3 (2007), p. 348.

63. "AB'nin Aklı Mülkte [EU is Interested in Property]", *Radikal*, 25 June 2005.
64. See Erdoğan's "Monthly Address to The Nation" Speech, November 2003.
65. See Erdoğan's speech in the opening ceremony of "Garden of Faiths" on 8 December 2004, Antalya.
66. See the parliamentary speech of *AKP* MP Avni Erdemir on 31 January 2008 (23. Term 57. Session).
67. Zeynep Gambetti, "Halkımızın "Gerçek" Değerleri [The "Real" Values of Our People]", *Taraf*, 26 October 2010.
68. Erdoğan's speech at the *AKP* group meeting on 27 March 2007.
69. Interview with a representative of a minority community, 20 November 2013, Istanbul.
70. Interview with a representative of a minority community, 24 March 2013, Istanbul.
71. "Gayrimüslimlere Polis Olma Daveti [Non-Muslims Invited to Become Policeman]", *Hürriyet*, 14 October 2013.
72. "'Her İnanç Kendi Din Adamını Yetiştirebilmeli', ['Every Faith Should Train Its Own Clergy'], " *Agos*, 5 July 2012.
73. "Başbakan'ın Paskalya Mesajı [Easter Message of the Prime Minister]", *Agos*, 1 April 2013.
74. "Erdoğan: Bizim Tek Derdimiz Var, İslam, İslam, İslam [Erdogan: We Have Only One Concern, Islam, Islam, Islam]", available at http://bianet.org/bianet/siyas et/166454-erdogan-bizim-tek-derdimiz-var-islam-islam-islam (accessed 31 July 2015).
75. "Ders Kitaplarında Ermeniler Yine Hedef [Armenians are Targetted in Textbooks Again]", *Radikal*, 25 September 2015; "Din Kültürü ve Ahlak Bilgisi Ders Kitaplarında Ayrımcılık Sürüyor [Discrimination Continues in Religious Culture and Ethics Textbooks]", *Radikal*, 26 September 2015.
76. "Bir Gün Senden Daha İyisini Yapabileceğimizi Gösterene Kadar Dalgana Bak [Make Fun Until We Will Show We Can Do Better Than You]", *Agos*, 8 August 2014.
77. Vangelis Kechriotis, "Hayali Osmanlı Otoritesinin Bitmeyen Osmanlı İnadı [The Imaginary Ottoman Authority's Insistence over Ayasofya]", *Agos*, 16 December 2013.
78. "Erdoğan Türkiyeli Azınlıkların Hakları İçin Atina'yı Bekliyor [Erdoğan Waits Athens for the Rights of Minorities of Turkey]", *Agos*, 7 October 2013.
79. Kaymak, "The Socio-spatial".
80. See the articles by the representatives of non-Muslim minority communities in the recent book published: Rober Koptaş and Bülent Usta (eds), "Yok Hükmünde: Müslüman Olmayan Cemaatlerin Tüzel Kişilik ve Temsil Sorunu [*Yok Hükmünde*: Legal Personality and Representation of non-Muslim Communities]", *Aras*, Istanbul, 2016; See also: Laki Vingas, "From the Margins to the Centre of Social Life: Non-Muslim Minorities in Modern Turkey", *Turkish Policy Quarterly*, 13/1 (2014), pp. 111–19.
81. Tuma Çelik's article in "Yok Hükmünde".
82. "Protestan Kiliseler Derneği Tüzüğü [Charter of Association of Protestant Churches]", available at http://www.protestankiliseler.org/?page_id=693 accessed 20 March 2015).
83. "Hakkımızda [About Us]", *Sabro*, available at http://www.usabro.net/hakkimi zda/ (accessed 11 January 2015).

CHAPTER 9

KURDS AND ELECTIONS UNDER THE AK PARTY'S RULE: THE SHIFTING INTERNAL AND EXTERNAL BORDERS OF THE KURDISH POLITICAL REGION

Cuma Çiçek

Introduction

Maps of Greater Kurdistan produced by both Kurds and non-Kurds have changed since the nineteenth century. In her book *Trapped Between the Map and Reality: Geography and Perceptions of Kurdistan*,[1] O'Shea illustrates that many maps of Kurdistan produced by Kurds and their sympathizers neither explain nor justify their methodology adequately.[2] Despite the existence of many maps of Greater Kurdistan showing the geographies where the Kurds constitute the majority, the debates concerning the borders of the Kurdish homeland are still ongoing both among ordinary Kurds, Kurdish political groups and non-Kurdish actors.

A similar debate also is ongoing in Turkey, where most Kurds live and the largest proportion of the presumed territory of Kurdistan is located. Precisely what are the boundaries of the Kurdish region within Turkey? Does it include 15 provinces? Twenty? Twenty-five? These questions remain the subject of ongoing debate in Turkey. Several different maps of Kurdistan exist to indicate the region where the Kurds constitute the majority. It is fair to say that it will not be possible to draw the border of the Kurdish region and complete this ongoing debate without a general census, including information about the population living in the area in question. A general census held in a democratic and liberalized atmosphere could quite easily put an end to this debate.

However, the problem is not just about the number of the people who live in a region. Three other issues must be highlighted. First, the populations of the regions and the provinces and districts within them are not static, but dynamic. Socioeconomic, cultural, and political shifts have seen a remarkable movement of people among and between districts, provinces and regions in Turkey for decades. These movements have had significant effects on the ethnic/national composition of the population in the settlement areas.

Secondly, the self-perception and the self-image of the people are also tremendously dynamic. Those whose parents perceive and define themselves as Kurdish, for instance, may perceive and define themselves as non-Kurdish, often as Turkish. Besides, an increasing proportion of people report multi-national origins due to mixed marriages between Kurdish and non-Kurdish people. Most of them do not perceive and define themselves solely as Kurdish but also as Turkish, Arabic, or Armenian.

Finally, people who perceive and define themselves as Kurdish also attribute a range of different meanings to their idea of "Kurdishness". For some Kurds, Kurdishness is just an issue of cultural origin and does not have any particular importance in daily life. Others see it as the basis of their ethnic identity, but do not consider it as an important element in the socio-political sphere. Unlike the first two groups, some Kurds understand Kurdishness as a political identity beyond the ethnic/cultural identity and give it a priority in the socio-political sphere, as can be seen among the Kurds supporting the leading Kurdish movement in Turkey.

Given the apparent fluid and various meanings and parameters of Kurdishness, in this chapter the Kurdish region is considered neither as a given nor a stable space, but as a socio-politically and historically constructed one with dynamic internal and external borders. Departing from this point, the chapter analyses the construction process of the Kurdish political region under the rule of the Justice and Development Party (*Adalet ve Kalkınma Partisi*, AKP). At this point, the chapter makes a distinction between the "Kurdish cultural region" and the "Kurdish political region". The former signifies the region where Kurdishness is essentially a cultural identity, while the latter denotes the region where Kurdishness refers to a political identity and where a remarkable socio-political and socio-cultural mobilization is in existence. The Kurdish cultural region includes roughly 24 provinces,[3] while the Kurdish political region includes the provinces in which the leading Kurdish movement (KM) is the most or the second-most powerful political movement. Although both regions refer to historically constructed areas, the former refers to a more stable area in comparison with the latter.

The external and internal borders of the Kurdish political region have dramatically changed since 2002 when AKP rule began. With the rise of the pro-Kurdish People's Democratic Party (*Halkların Demokratik Partisi*, HDP), the hegemony of the KM has both deepened and widened. The HDP has expanded the Kurdish political region to 20 provinces overall. In the 7 June 2015 elections, the HDP marginalized the AKP in most Kurdish provinces, a circumstance that persisted in the 1 November 2015 elections.

How can we analyse the HDP's achievement in overcoming the ten-per cent election threshold, after the failure of previous parties to do so after more than two decades of socio-political mobilization by the pro-Kurdish legal parties? In this chapter, I argue that the HDP's success is essentially based on three principal dynamics. First, it is a result of the ongoing process of constructing a Kurdish political region in Turkey. Second, the rising pro-Kurdish politics beyond Turkey's borders has facilitated and accelerated the KM's socio-political advancement in Turkey. Finally, it is a consequence of the HDP's integrationist political discourse and actions during the peace process.

To illustrate the construction process of the Kurdish political region, I first present a brief theoretical debate about the socio-political and historical constructing process, with particular reference to the geographic boundaries of Kurdistan. Second, I analyse election results between 1991 and 1999 to show the border of the Kurdish political region in the 1990s. Third, I examine the changes in the borders of the Kurdish political region between 1999 and 2014. Finally, I illustrate the dramatically changed borders of the Kurdish political region after the foundation of the HDP and discuss its unprecedented success.

Geography: A Socio-Political and Historical Construct

Constructivist approaches argue that reality is "socially constructed"[4] and that "all human 'knowledge' is developed, transmitted and maintained in social situations."[5] We can argue that like all "realities" and all "human knowledge", geographical reality and geographical knowledge are likewise socially constructed. Being socially constructed means that reality and knowledge are context-dependent; that is, dependent on time, space, and the agents involved. In other words, social constructivism highlights that any reality or human knowledge is contextual and cannot be understood adequately without taking the given circumstances into consideration.

David Harvey, a distinguished professor of anthropology and geography, argues that four structural components of geographical knowledge stand out: cartographic identification, the measure of space-time, place/region/territory, and environmental qualities and the relation to nature.[6] Analysing the dialectical relationship between geographical knowledge and political-economic and socio-ecological changes, Harvey asserts that the geography is "a mode of understanding [that is] formulated, used and applied in different institutional settings (for example the military, Greenpeace, the state apparatus, multinational corporation, and so on)."[7] In other words, "different institutions [...] create a demand for different kinds of geographical knowledge."[8] Although "empty" or "biased" geographical knowledge are produced in the name of universal goodness and reason, they are commonly constructed, maintained, and mobilized for political purposes in different institutional settings varying according to distinctive institutional requirements, cultures, and norms.[9] It is important to note that geographical knowledge produced within an institutional setting also changes significantly over time.[10]

Studies on map-making and cartography, the first of Harvey's four structural components of geographical knowledge, show how geographical understandings change according to time, space, and actor. Although some essentialist approaches argue that "all maps are abstractions of reality,"[11] different actors have diverse (even contentious) perceptions about the reality in each context. For instance, O'Shea illustrates how the reality about maps of Greater Kurdistan is based on Kurdish and non-Kurdish actors' perceptions, and changes over time and space. She notes that "all maps of Kurdistan are based on distant perceptions, which are shifting over time."[12]

"Propaganda cartography,"[13] "persuasive cartography"[14] and "the map as discourse"[15] are three critical concepts that serve to highlight the contextual, relative and plural qualities of "reality", on the one hand, and the relationship between geographical knowledge and the actors' political purposes within an institutional setting on the other. On this issue, Pickles contends that "all map presentations show a bias towards a particular historical interpretation."[16] Similarly, Harley asserts that "both in the selectivity of their content and in their signs and styles of representation maps are a way of conceiving, articulating and structuring the human world."[17] He underlines the relationship between power and map-making, and illustrates how cartography can be used for political purposes, such as global empire building, preservation of the nation state, and the assertion of local property rights.[18] Therefore, "the map is never the reality; it helps to create a different reality [...] Without our being aware of it, maps can reinforce and legitimate the status quo."[19] O'Shea shows that the powerless (e.g., Kurds) are often as capable as the powerful to use map-making or cartography to realize their political projects. She asserts, "maps are the most effective and visible means of disseminating the concept of Kurdistan amongst both Kurds and non-Kurds."[20]

As a key concept of the geographical realities and knowledges of place/city/ region/territory, space is also a socio-political and historical construct. It is years now since Lefebvre taught us that the space is a social product.[21] Bayat points out that "space is also culturally constructed."[22] Likewise, as Amoros asserts: "There is no natural space. All space is social space; it implies, contains and dissimulates social relations. Social relations have a spatial existence; they are projected in space and are inscribed upon it by producing it."[23] Underlining the direct relationship between the social change and the production of space, Lefebvre argues that "the analysis of production shows that we have passed from the production of thing in space to the production of space itself."[24] Within capitalism and neo-capitalism, according to Lefebvre, space has several functions, such as a means of production, an object of consumption and a political instrument. It is also important to note the class struggle intervention in the production of space. Lefebvre concludes that "in the current mode of production, social space is considered among the productive forces and the means of production, among the social relations of production and, especially, their reproduction."[25]

It is also important to note that there exists a direct relation between the formation of the state, power relations, local or national identity, and the construction of geographical realities and knowledges. Lefebvre asserts that the state accords primary importance to space as a political instrument and "uses space in a way that ensures its control of places, its strict hierarchy, the homogeneity of the whole, and the segregation of the parts."[26] Similarly, Harvey argues that the formation and articulation of the certain kinds of geographical understandings play a constructive role in the formation of the state and identities both at local/regional and national levels.[27] Highlighting "the conflict between institutionalized knowledge directed towards govern- mentality and localized knowledges",[28] Harvey points out that the state is a major site for orchestrating the production of space, the definition of territoriality, the geographical distribution of population, socio-economic activities, wealth, well-being, and local and national identities.[29]

In sum, geographical realities and knowledges and their structural components – the cartography and space in particular – are contextual and dependent on the time, space, and actors. There exists a direct relationship between social change and the geographical understanding and construction of space. Besides the interaction and integrity of social change, geographical understanding and space construction are embedded in asymmetrical power relations. Both powerful and powerless actors construct different geographical realities and knowledges according to their different political purposes.

Following this theoretical framework, in what follows I analyse the construction process of the Kurdish political region in Turkey. To do this, I examine the legislative elections held after 1991, when the People's Labour Party (*Halkın Emek Partisi*, HEP), the first pro-Kurdish political party in Turkey, competed in elections for the first time. The subsequent section concentrates on the period between 1990 and 1999.

The Emergence of the Kurdish Political Region in the 1990s

In the legislative election of 1991, the pro-Kurdish HEP formed an electoral alliance with the Social Democratic Populist Party (SHP). SHP came third overall, taking 20 per cent of the votes and winning 88 seats in the 450-seat parliament. Among its 88 MPs, 22 hailed from the HEP, who were mostly elected from the provinces in the Kurdish cultural region.[30] These provinces were Adıyaman (1 MP), Batman (3 MPs), Diyarbakır (6 MPs), Mardin (3 MPs), Muş (3 MPs), Siirt (2 MPs), Şırnak (3 MPs), and Van (1 MP).[31] Although the HEP won 22 seats in eight provinces, the influence of the SHP–HEP electoral alliance resonated heavily within the broader Kurdish cultural region of 24 provinces. SHP was the first party in 11 provinces and won 42 seats from the Kurdish cultural region (See Figure 9.1 and Table 9.1).[32]

Unlike the 1991 election, in the subsequent polls in 1995 the pro-Kurdish People's Democratic Party (*Halkın Demokrasi Partisi*, HADEP), the successor of the HEP, participated independently under its own name, despite the risk of doing so due to the 10-per cent election threshold. In this election, the HADEP took 4.2 per cent of the votes and came first in 23 seats. Despite this, the party was unable not enter Parliament due to the election threshold.[33] HADEP emerged as the first party in five provinces (Batman, Diyarbakır, Hakkari, Iğdır, Van), the second party in five provinces (Mardin, Muş, Siirt, Şırnak, Tunceli), and took a remarkable vote-share in four other provinces (Adıyaman, Ağrı, Bitlis, Şanlıurfa). We can argue that the provinces in which the pro-Kurdish party came first or second constituted the Kurdish political region in the 1995 legislative election. The province of Ağrı can be added to the Kurdish political region since there was only a single percentage point difference between the HADEP and the second party (See Figure 9.2 and Table 9.1).[34]

In the legislative election of 1999, the HADEP took 4.8 per cent of the vote and came first in 34 seats in the expanded 550-seat parliament.[35] Yet, the threshold again resulted in its seats being awarded to other parties and the party finished with no parliamentary representation. Despite this setback, the HADEP had emerged as the first party in 11 provinces, and garnered overwhelming support in four of them (Bingöl, Bitlis, Şanlıurfa, and Tunceli) within the Kurdish cultural region (see Table 9.1).[36] Given the fact the party had come first in only five provinces in the previous legislative election, this was a stunning result and a clear sign of the enlargement of the Kurdish political region and the expanding influence of the pro-Kurdish party in the region (see Figures 9.2 and 9.3).

Drawing on Gramsci's concept of "hegemony",[37] we can divide the Kurdish political region into three sub-regions. The first sub-region covers the provinces where the pro-Kurdish party is a "hegemonic power". The second sub-region refers to the provinces where the pro-Kurdish party plays the role of "hegemonic power balancer". The third sub-region covers the provinces where the pro-Kurdish party is a "powerful opposition". Given the fact that the Kurdish cultural region indicates a larger area than the Kurdish political region, there exists a non-political Kurdish cultural sub-region where the pro-Kurdish parties are marginalized political powers.

Figure 9.1 The Kurdish political region in the 1991 legislative election.

Provinces where the pro-Kurdish party candidates were elected to Parliament

Table 9.1 Legislative elections and the Kurdish Cultural Region in the 1990s

Provinces	SHP's Performance in the 1991 Election		HADEP's Performance in the 1995 Election		HADEP's Performance in the 1999 Election	
	Vote rate (%)	Party rank	Vote rate (%)	Party rank	Vote rate (%)	Party rank
Batman	52	1	37	1	44	1
Diyarbakır	49	1	46	1	46	1
Hakkari	19	3	54	1	46	1
Ağrı	15	4	17	3	34	1
Iğdır	-	-	21	1	29	1
Mardin	53	1	21	2	25	1
Muş	41	1	16	2	32	1
Siirt	39	1	26	2	22	1
Şırnak	61	1	25	2	24	1
Van	22	4	27	1	35	1
Bingöl	17	3	7	4	12	3
Bitlis	21	3	9	4	13	4
Kars	31	1	6	7	17	1
Şanlıurfa	20	3	13	4	16	3
Tunceli	57	1	16	2	13	4
Adıyaman	27	1	9	5	7	6
Ardahan	-	-	6	7	7	7
Elazığ	15	4	3	6	4	7
Erzincan	33	1	1	8	1	9
Erzurum	8	4	5	5	6	5
Gaziantep	28	1	6	7	5	7
Kahramanmaraş	18	3	2	6	1	8
Kilis	-	-	0	7	0	8
Malatya	26	2	2	7	2	9

Note: Ardahan and Iğdır provinces were counties of Kars, and Kilis province was a county of Gaziantep in the 1991 Election. Source: Data from www.secim-sonuclari.com.

In the 1990s, the pro-Kurdish party was clearly politically dominant in the Diyarbakır and Hakkari provinces. The pro-Kurdish party was the first party in Diyarbakır in three consecutive legislative elections, while it consolidated its power in Hakkari in the subsequent elections in 1995 and 1999. Since there existed a clear difference (over 12 percentage points) between the votes of the pro-Kurdish party and the second party in these provinces,[38] we can argue that

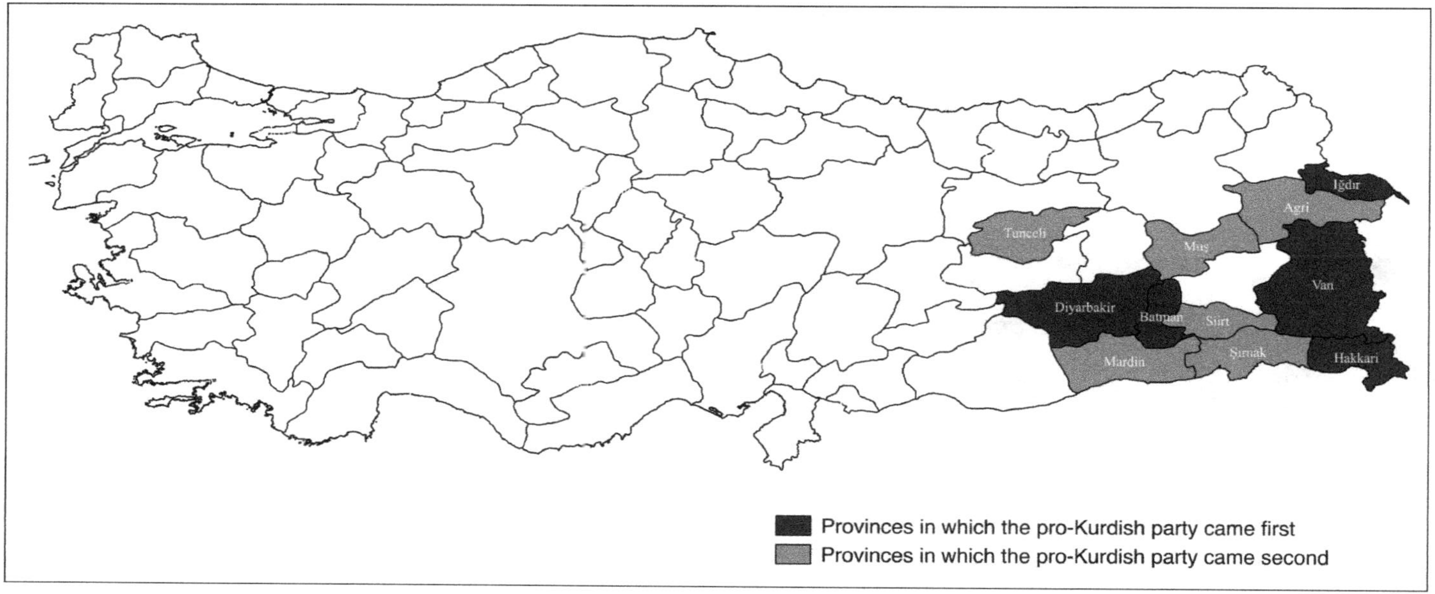
Iğdır
Agri
Tunceli
Muş
Van
Diyarbakir
Batman
Siirt
Şırnak
Mardin
Hakkari
Provinces in which the pro-Kurdish party came first
Provinces in which the pro-Kurdish party came second

Figure 9.2 The Kurdish political region in the 1995 legislative election.

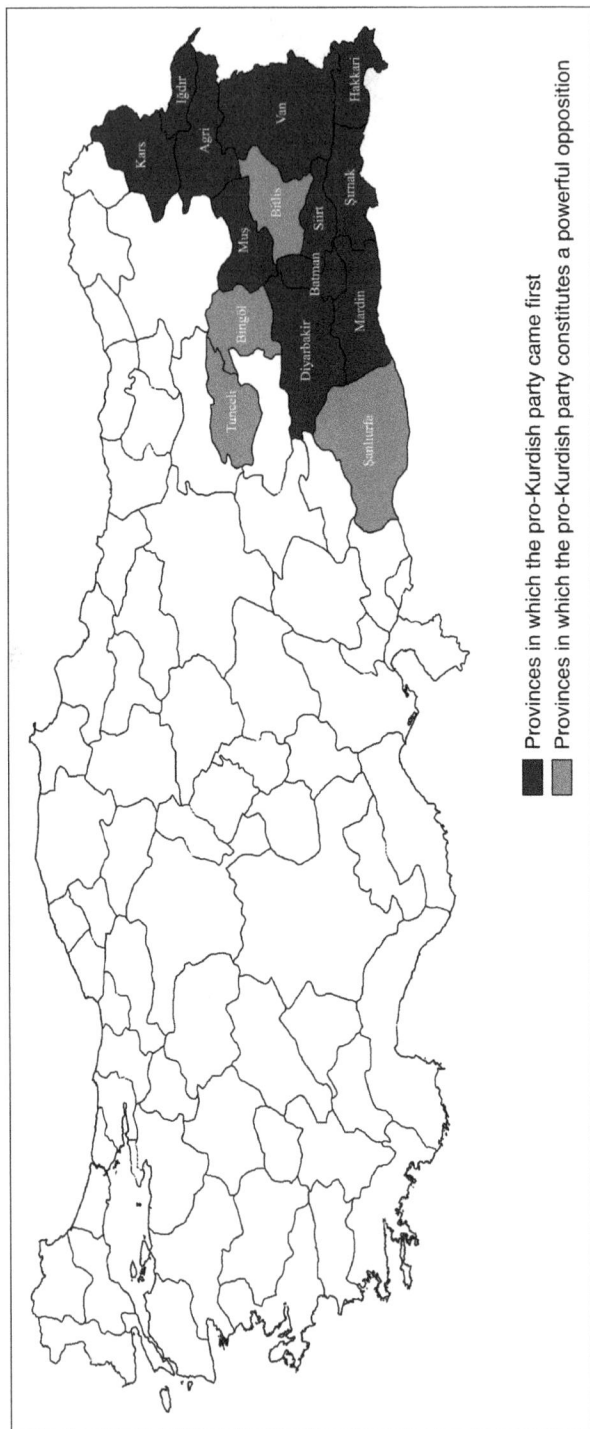

Figure 9.3 The Kurdish political region in the 1999 legislative election.

the party was a hegemonic power in these provinces. Therefore, the first sub-region included Diyarbakır and Hakkari in the 1990s.

The second sub-region covered the province of Batman only. In this province, the pro-Kurdish party lacked clear hegemony and other parties could challenge it. The third sub-region included Ağrı, Iğdır, Bingöl, Bitlis, Kars, Mardin, Muş, Siirt, Şırnak, Şanlıurfa, Tunceli, and Van. In this region, the pro-Kurdish party was neither a hegemonic power nor a hegemonic power balancer. It represented, however, a significant force of opposition. Finally, the non-political Kurdish cultural sub-region covered nine provinces: Adıyaman, Ardahan, Elazığ, Erzincan, Erzurum, Gaziantep, Kahramanmaraş, Kilis, and Malatya. Among these provinces, in Erzincan, Kahramanmaraş, Kilis, and Malatya the vote of the pro-Kurdish parties was less than 1 per cent (See Figure 9.4 and Table 9.1).

Consolidation of the Kurdish Political Region After 2002

The 2002 legislative election was held in a different context. As I have noted in previous work,[39] after 1999 the Kurdish issue shifted sharply and dramatically due to three significant and interrelated events. The first was the capture of Abdullah Öcalan on 15 February 1999. This event caused significant ideological, political, strategic and institutional changes within the KM in Turkey. The PKK withdrew its armed groups out of Turkey and announced that it would use democratic measures and methods to advance cultural rights for Kurdish society in a "democratic republic". During the next five years, the KM, including both legal and illegal forces, was reorganized at ideological, political, and institutional levels, according to new strategic goals, which centred on democratization, multiculturalism, and Kurdish cultural identity.[40] Addition-ally, the reorganization of pro-Kurdish politics more generally saw a turn towards promoting democratic measures and methods, facilitated and accelerated thanks to the significant success of pro-Kurdish parties in the local election held on 18 April 1999.[41] This new local government experience of the KM enlarged the political sphere for pro-Kurdish politics at multiple levels. Lastly, Turkey was recognized as a candidate state for EU accession at the Helsinki European Council in December 1999.[42] Turkey's accession process to the EU was unquestionably a transformative event in relation to politics and policy changes concerning the Kurdish issue.

In the 2002 legislative election, the Democratic People's Party (*Demokratik Halk Partisi*, DEHAP), the successor of HADEP, formed a coalition with two left-leaning parties to form the "Labour, Peace, and Democracy Bloc."[43] DEHAP took 6.22 per cent of the votes nationally and thus failed to pass the election threshold.[44] However, it made remarkable gains in the Kurdish region: it came first in 13 provinces, second in two provinces, and third in a further four.

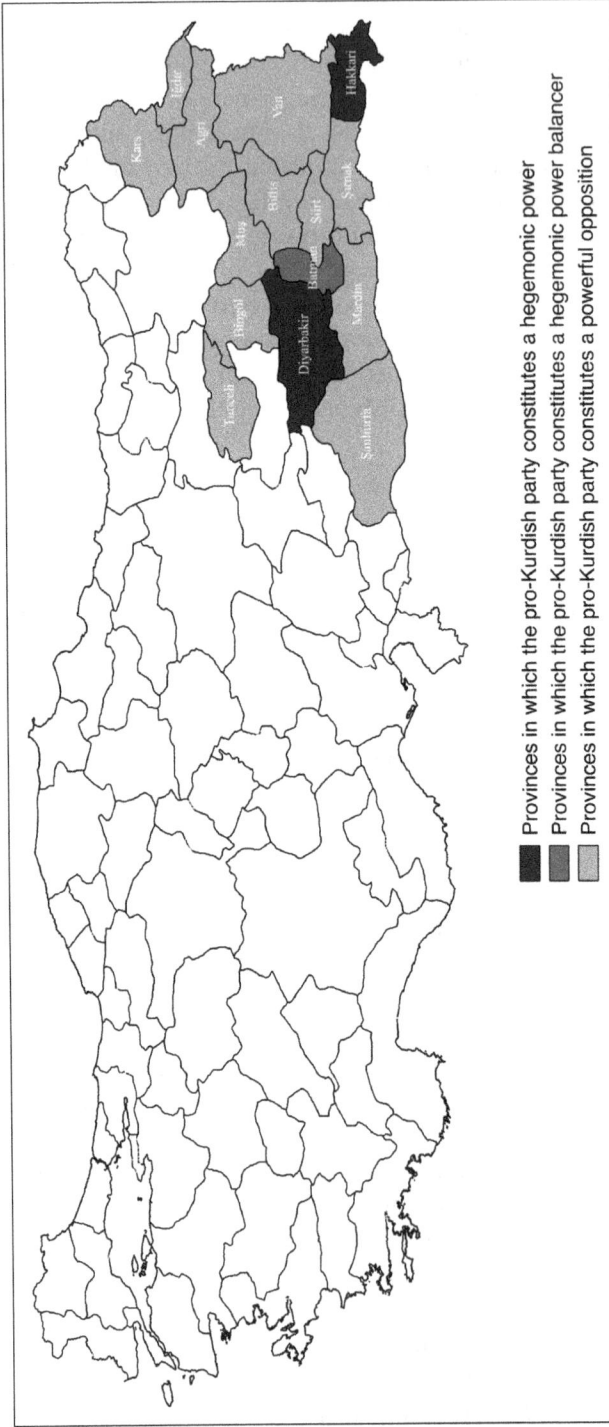

Figure 9.4 The Kurdish political region and sub-regions in the 1990s.

Provinces in which the pro-Kurdish party constitutes a hegemonic power

Provinces in which the pro-Kurdish party constitutes a hegemonic power balancer

Provinces in which the pro-Kurdish party constitutes a powerful opposition

However, among these four provinces, it exceeded 10 per cent of the vote in only two provinces. This election thus saw the Kurdish political region enlarged from 15 to 17 provinces (See Figure 9.5).[45]

Having failed to pass the electoral threshold in successive elections, the leading pro-Kurdish party took a different tack in the 2007 elections and put up its candidates as independents instead.[46] DEHAP's successor party, the Democratic Society Party (*Demokratik Toplum Partisi*, DTP) again formed a pact with left-leaning parties, with some success: 22 MPs were returned to the parliament. Apart from two MPs elected from Istanbul, the rest were elected in the Kurdish political region, as follows: Diyarbakır (4 MPs), Mardin (2), Batman (2), Muş (2), Van (2), Şırnak (2), Bitlis (1), Hakkari (1), Iğdır (1), Siirt (1), Şanlıurfa (1), and Tunceli (1).[47] The number of provinces in which it was the first party fell significantly to six, and it came second in a further eight. It was third in four provinces, of which only in Kars did it exceed 10 per cent.[48] These poor results in comparison to the previous election were quite a setback for the Kurdish movement. The borders of the Kurdish political region shrank from 17 provinces to 15. On top of this, the vote share of the pro-Kurdish party fell significantly in ten provinces. It lost supremacy in seven provinces compared with the previous election (See Figure 9.6).

Without getting to far into the weeds in relation to all the electoral dynamics in this disappointing result, two critical points are worth mentioning. The first is that the pro-Kurdish party's decision to compete for the first time with independent candidates in this legislative election (in an attempt to reverse 16 years of failure to pass the threshold) proved, in the end, a poor strategy. Second, the AKP achieved an electoral landslide across Turkey in general and in the Kurdish political region in particular. In the wake of the 2007 showdown with the Kemalist establishment, the AKP took 46.58 per cent of the votes and won 341 seats in the 550-seat parliament.[49] In the Kurdish political region, the AKP marginalized other Ankara-centred political parties, united different socio-political tendencies under its institutional roof, and became the main political bloc opposing the KM in the Kurdish region.

Despite the disappointing results in pushing its slate of candidates as independents in 2006, the DTP's successor party, the Peace and Democracy Party (*Barış ve Demokrasi Partisi* BDP) stuck with the strategy in the 2011 legislative election. It again formed an electoral alliance with different opposition groups – the "Labour, Democracy, and Freedom Bloc" – and won 36 seats in the parliament. Except five MPs (1 from Adana, 1 from Mersin, and 3 from Istanbul), 31 MPs were elected in the Kurdish political region: Ağrı (1), Batman (2), Bingöl (1), Bitlis (1), Diyarbakır (6), Hakkari (3), Kars (1), Iğdır (1), Mardin (3), Muş (2), Siirt (1), Şırnak (3), Şanlıurfa (2), Van (4).[50] This represented a significant improvement off the back of the 2007 disappointment. Its vote in 13 provinces improved markedly and it came first in seven provinces, second in

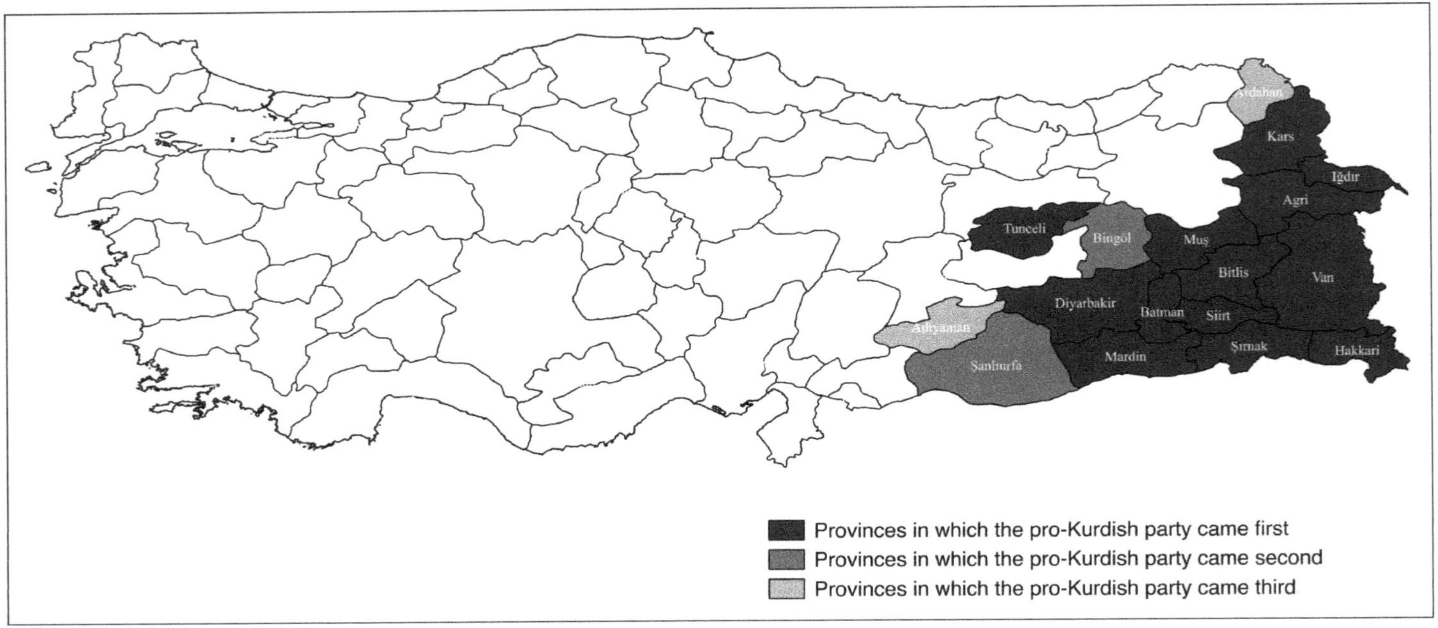
Ardahan
Kars
Iğdır
Agri
Tunceli
Bingöl
Muş
Bitlis
Van
Diyarbakir
Batman
Siirt
Adiyaman
Şanlıurfa
Mardin
Şırnak
Hakkari
Provinces in which the pro-Kurdish party came first
Provinces in which the pro-Kurdish party came second
Provinces in which the pro-Kurdish party came third

Figure 9.5 The Kurdish political region in the 2002 legislative election.

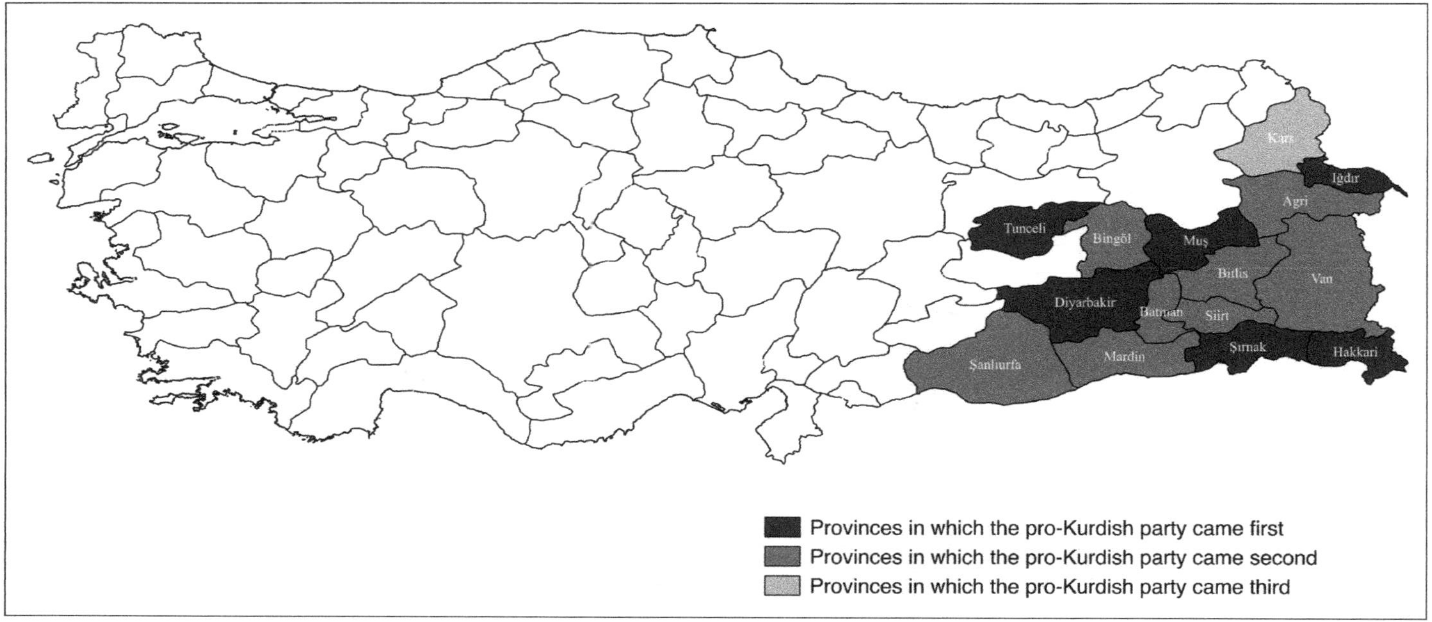

Figure 9.6 The Kurdish political region in the 2007 legislative election.

a further eight. The BDP was third in three provinces, in one of which (Ardahan) the pro-Kurdish party achieved 12.49 per cent of the vote. Thus, in 2011, the Kurdish political region expanded again, from 15 to 16 provinces. Yet, the most important achievement was not the enlargement of the region, but a deepening of the pro-Kurdish party's power in the region (see Figure 9.7 and Table 9.2).

Compared with the 1990s, the borders of the Kurdish political region expanded and the hegemony of the pro-Kurdish party both enlarged and deepened in the 2000s. It is thus fair to say that the Kurdish political region *emerged* in the 1990s, and *consolidated* in the 2000s. The Kurdish political region comprised 15 provinces in the 1990s. In 2000s, Ardahan province was added to the region. In the 1990s, the pro-Kurdish party established itself for the first time as a hegemonic power in two provinces – Diyarbakır and Hakkari. In the following decade, the pro-Kurdish party became hegemonic in Mardin and Şırnak as well. Alongside Batman, in Muş, Tunceli, and Van the party also shifted from an opposition power to a hegemonic power balancer. It sustained itself as a powerful opposition in a further eight provinces, while remaining a marginalized power in the eight provinces of the non-political Kurdish cultural sub-region (compare Figure 9.4 and Figure 9.8).

It is important to note that the power of the pro-Kurdish party also deepened in each sub-region. In the first sub-region, its vote range improved from 46–54 per cent to 47–62 per cent in Diyarbakır, from 46–54 per cent to 56–80 per cent in Hakkari, from 21–5 per cent to 40–61 per cent in Mardin, and from 24–5 per cent to 50–72 per cent in Şırnak. In the second sub-region, vote range rose from 16–41 per cent to 38–46 per cent in Muş, from 13–16 per cent to 22–60 per cent in Tunceli, from 22–35 per cent to 33–50 per cent in Van. There was a similar deepening of political strength in the third sub-region. For instance, the pro-Kurdish party's vote range increased from 13–16 per cent to 19–27 per cent in Şanlıurfa, from 9–13 per cent to 22–40 per cent in Bitlis, and from 6–17 per cent to 16–20 per cent in Kars (compare Table 9.1 and Table 9.2).

The HDP's Success and the New Borders of the Kurdish Political Region After 2014

The "Labour, Democracy, and Freedom Bloc" coalition that was established before the 2011 legislative election became the organizational basis for the next phase of political mobilization for the KM. The establishment of the Peoples' Democratic Congress (*Halkların Demokratik Kongresi*, HDK) as an umbrella organization of various leftist groups – with the HDP as its national parliamentary wing and the Democratic Regions Party (*Demokratik Bölgeler Partisi*, DBP) as its municipal/regional counterpart – was a major turning point for the movement in Turkey and represented a new "dual strategy" in Turkey

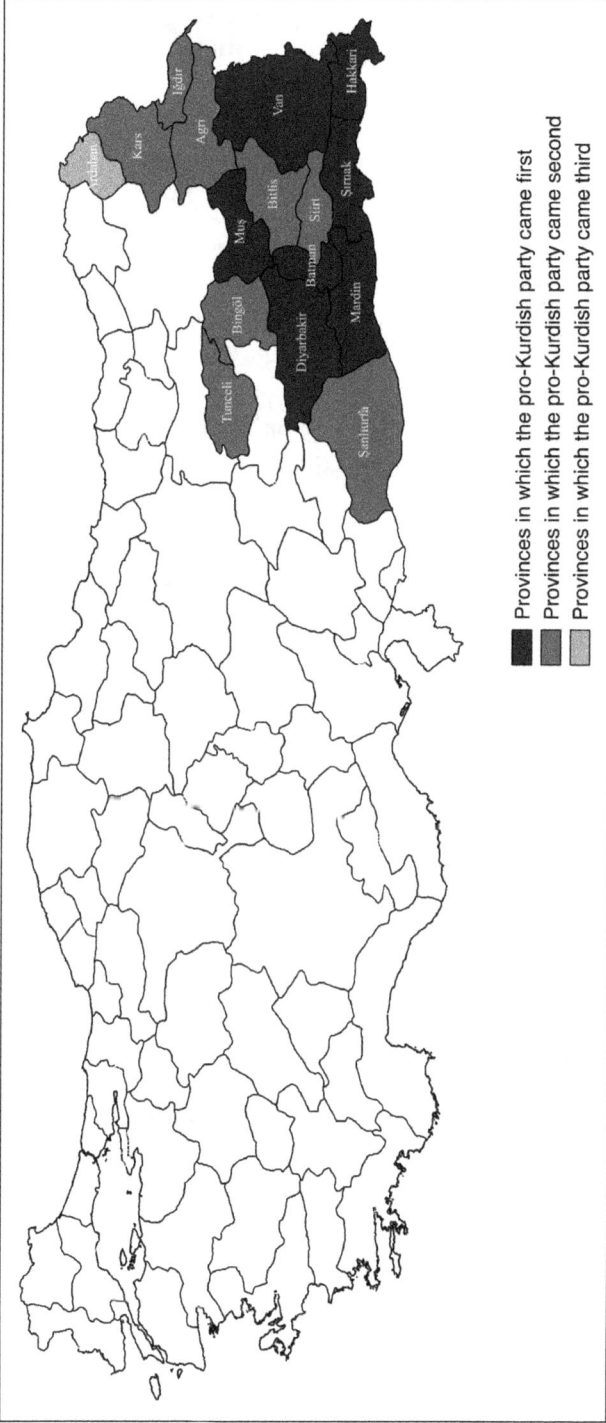

Figure 9.7 The Kurdish political region in the 2011 legislative election.

Table 9.2 Legislative elections and the Kurdish cultural region in the 2000s

Provinces	DEHAP's Performance in the 2002 Election		DTP's Performance in the 2007 Election		BDP's Performance in the 2011 Election	
	Vote rate (%)	Party rank	Vote rate (%)	Party rank	Vote rate (%)	Party rank
Diyarbakır	56.13	1	47.01	1	61.69	1
Hakkari	45.10	1	56.24	1	79.82	1
Mardin	39.58	1	38.77	2	60.85	1
Şırnak	45.94	1	51.83	1	72.31	1
Batman	47.10	1	39.42	2	51.48	1
Muş	38.09	1	45.81	1	44.26	1
Tunceli	32.55	1	59.96	1	22.22	2
Van	40.85	1	32.60	2	49.47	1
Ağrı	35.06	1	24.36	2	43.42	2
Ardahan	15.93	3	9.27	3	12.49	3
Bingöl	22.18	2	14.28	2	23.90	2
Bitlis	29.55	1	21.77	2	40.22	2
Iğdır	32.68	1	40.53	1	31.48	2
Kars	19.58	1	15.63	3	19.21	2
Şanlıurfa	19.28	2	20.14	2	26.97	2
Siirt*	34.23	1	39.51	2	42.45	2
Adıyaman	11.97	3	8.04	3	6.56	3
Elazığ	7.12	4	3.06	6	-	-
Erzincan	1.81	8	-	-	-	-
Erzurum	9.84	3	5.37	3	8.14	3
Gaziantep	8.00	3	5.05	4	5.39	4
K.maraş	3.19	6	-	-	0.54	7
Kilis	2.26	8	-	-	-	-
Malatya	4.18	5	1.83	4	1.26	4

Note 1: The 2002 Election in Siirt was canceled due to an objection lodged by the AKP, and it was rescheduled. DEHAP, however, could not participate in the rescheduled election because of the election threshold.

Note 2: The cells without figures indicates that the pro-Kurdish party did not nominate an independent candidate. Source: Data source: http://www.haberturk.com/secim/secim2011/genel-secim; http://www.haberturk.com/secim2007; http://www.haberturk.com/secim2002.

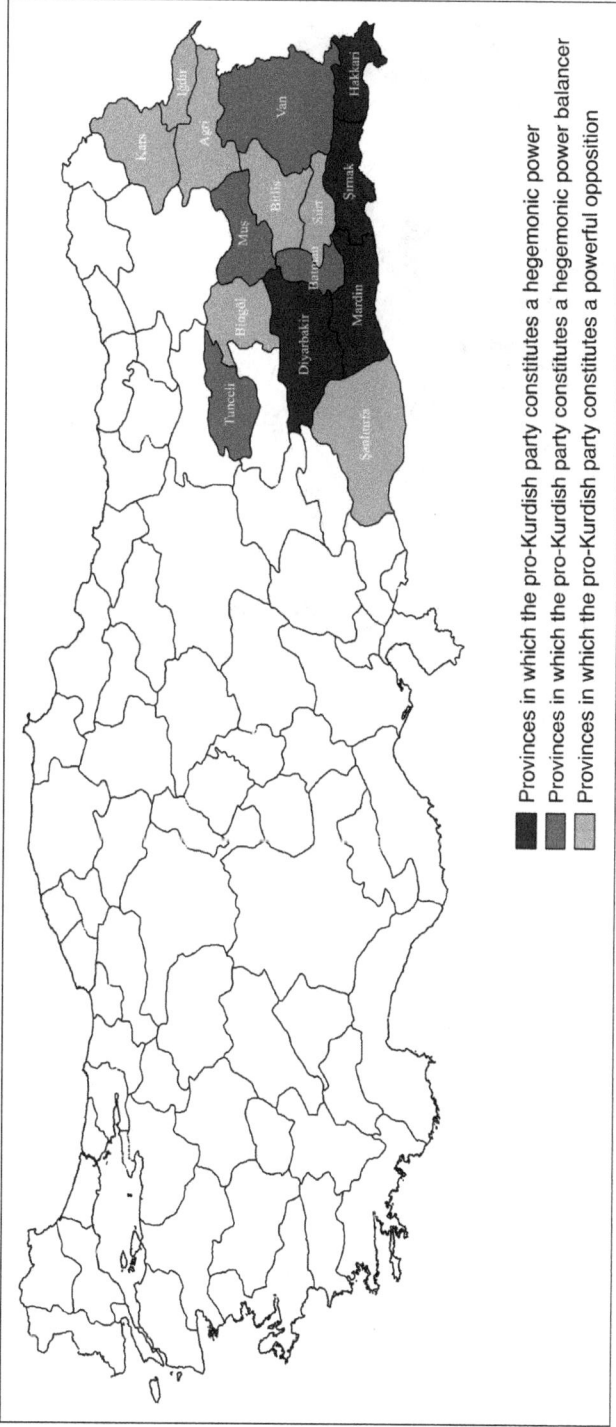

Figure 9.8 The Kurdish political region and sub-regions in the 2000s.

Provinces in which the pro-Kurdish party constitutes a hegemonic power

Provinces in which the pro-Kurdish party constitutes a hegemonic power balancer

Provinces in which the pro-Kurdish party constitutes a powerful opposition

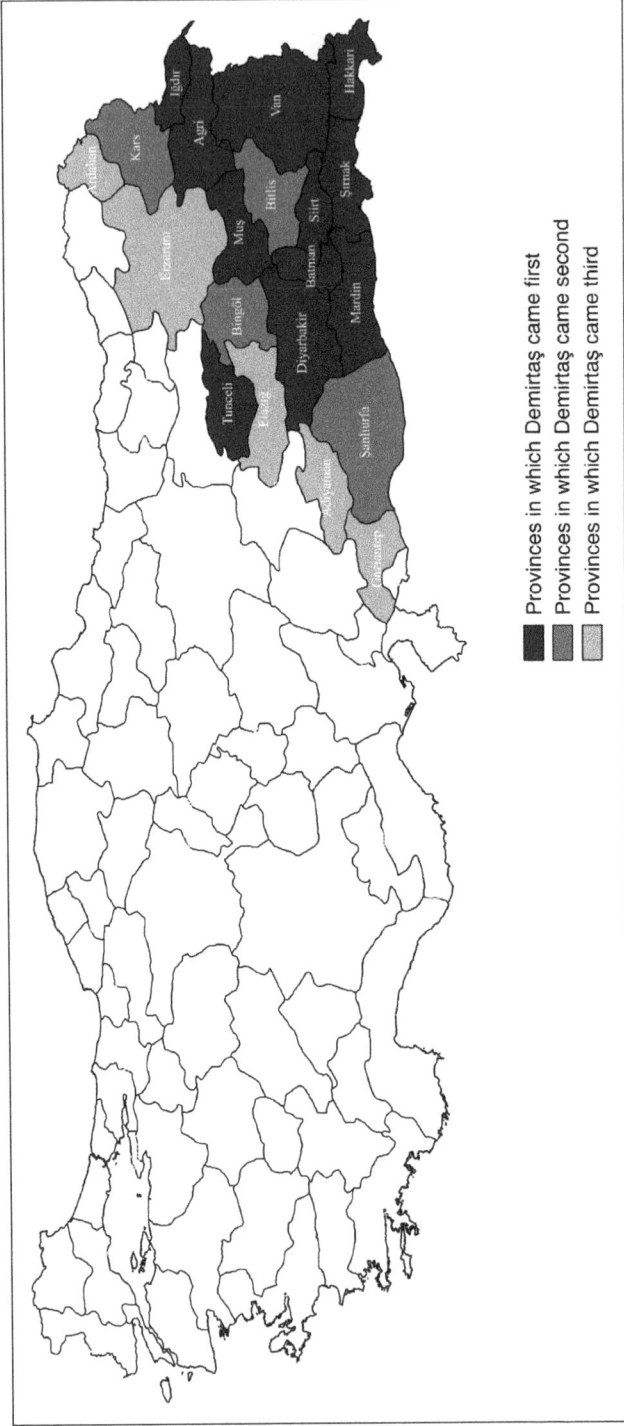

Figure 9.9 The Kurdish political region in the 2014 presidential election.

that aimed to fundamentally recreate Turkish politics in a progressive-democratic direction.

The BDP now acts as a regional party to advance an autonomous political and administrative space in the Kurdish region. Its national representatives transferred to the HDP, while keeping local governments under its party structure. At this local level the BDP functions under the umbrella of the Democratic Society Congress (*Demokratik Toplum Kongresi*, DTK), a confederation of civil society organizations, political parties, and individual members of diverse ethnic, political, and religious groups. The BDP and DTK have been evolving in accordance with eight "democratic-autonomy" organizing themes – political, legislative, self-defence, cultural, social, economic, ecological and diplomatic. The KM defines this "democratic-autonomy" project as a socio-political venture aimed at advancing the Kurdish people's capacity for self-government in their homeland[51]. The eight stars in the DBP's flag symbolize these aspects of the project. The reconstruction of the DBP and DTK at the regional level and the reshaping of the political agenda based on Kurdish self-government in the Kurdish region can be conceptualized as a strategy of "Kurdistanization".

At the national level, both the HDK and the HDP act as two arms of the KM in its vision of coalescing left-wing democratic opposition Turkey-wide. While the DBP and the DTK signify the Kurdistanization of the leading Kurdish movement, the HDP and the HDK denote its "Turkey-ization". Reaching out to different left-wing, feminist, and ecological groups, parties and movements, and ethnic and religious minorities that have not been in the past been all that close to the Kurdish issue, the HDP and the HDK have attempted to unify and represent all oppressed groups in terms of class, ethnicity/nation, religion and gender in Turkey with a left-wing populist political agenda.

Turkey's first direct elections for the office of president were held on 10 August 2014. S. Selahattin Demirtaş, the co-president of the HDP, ran as a candidate alongside Erdoğan, and Ekmeleddin Mehmet İhsanoğlu, who was supported jointly by the Republican People's Party (*Cumhuriyet Halk Partisi*, CHP) and the Nationalist Action Party (*Milliyetçi Hareket Partisi*, MHP). Although the leading legal pro-Kurdish parties typically take no more than 6 per cent of the vote in a general election, Demirtaş achieved a vote share of 9.77 per cent. In the Kurdish political region, Demirtaş won the presidential election in 11 provinces and took over 60 per cent in seven of them, between 50–60 per cent in three, and 43 per cent in one province. In four provinces, Demirtaş was the second candidate by taking between 26–44 per cent of the votes, and the third candidate in five provinces by taking between 10–23 per cent of the votes (see Figure 9.9).[52]

Although the KM competed in the election with independent candidate because of the election threshold, following the presidential election, the HDP decided to participate in the 7 June 2015 legislative election as a party. With its new radical democracy programme[53] and discourse,[54] and its candidates representing the different oppressed groups at multi-levels in Turkey, the HDP represented a new focus of left-wing opposition beyond pro-Kurdish mobilization in this election. The result was a doubling of the leading pro-Kurdish parties' vote, such that for the first time the threshold was breached. In the past, as mentioned, Kurdish parties had struggled to get above 4–6 per cent of the votes. As the results poured in on the evening of 7 June, the HDP achieved a glorious success, taking 13.12 per cent of the votes and winning 80 seats in the 550-seat parliament.[55]

In the Kurdish political region, the HDP emerged as the first party in a total of 14 provinces, and took at least 60 per cent of the votes in 12 of these. That means that it bested the second party in these provinces by at least 20 percentage points. In three provinces, the HDP was the second party, taking between 23 and 41 per cent of the votes. Finally, it was the third party in two provinces (15–18 per cent of the votes), and the fourth party in five provinces (4–15 per cent of the votes). Among the last five provinces, in Gaziantep, the HDP took 15.32 per cent of the votes,[56] meaning that the HDP took over 15 per cent of the votes in a total of 20 provinces. In other words, the KM achieved an enlargement of the Kurdish political region from 16 provinces to 20 (See Figure 9.10).

A coalition government could not be established after the 7 June election so new legislative elections were held on 1 November 2015. In this election, the HDP took 10.75 per cent of the votes and won 59 seats. In the Kurdish political region, the HDP was the first party in 12 provinces, taking over 50 per cent of the votes in 11 of them. In four provinces, the HDP was the second party with 14–34 per cent of the votes. Finally, it was the third party in four provinces by taking 11–22 per cent of the votes. Obviously, this was a retrenchment compared to the previous election – a clear political decline of the HDP in the Kurdish political region. However, given the 20-year electoral experience of the pro-Kurdish parties in Turkey, it was still a remarkable achievement (see Figure 9.11).

Simply put, the HDP has dramatically expanded the political map of the Kurdish region and the hegemony of the pro-Kurdish party has both enlarged and deepened through the 2010s. The KM could once lay claim to preeminent support in 16 provinces, and remained a not insignificant political movement in the remaining 9 provinces within the Kurdish cultural region. Since 2015, the HDP has expanded this "political region" to 20 provinces overall, achieving a remarkable political rise in Erzurum, Elazığ, Adıyaman, and Gaziantep provinces, which it has now added to the Kurdish political region.

The pro-Kurdish party was a hegemonic power in the sub-region based on Diyarbakır, Hakkari, Mardin, and Şırnak in the 2000s. With the HDP, this

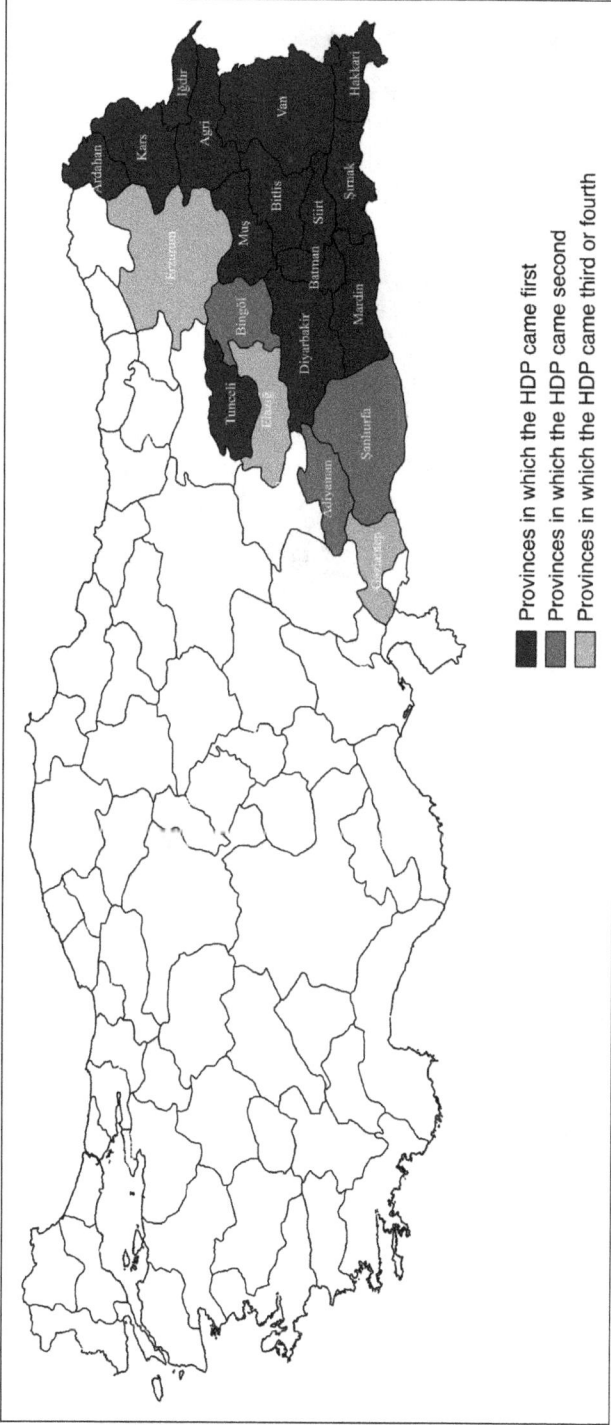

Figure 9.10 The Kurdish political region in the 7 June 2015 legislative election.

Provinces in which the HDP came first

Provinces in which the HDP came second

Provinces in which the HDP came third or fourth

Ardahan

Kars

Iğdır

Ağrı

Van

Hakkari

Erzurum

Muş

Bitlis

Siirt

Şırnak

Bingöl

Batman

Mardin

Tunceli

Elazığ

Diyarbakır

Adıyaman

Şanlıurfa

Gaziantep

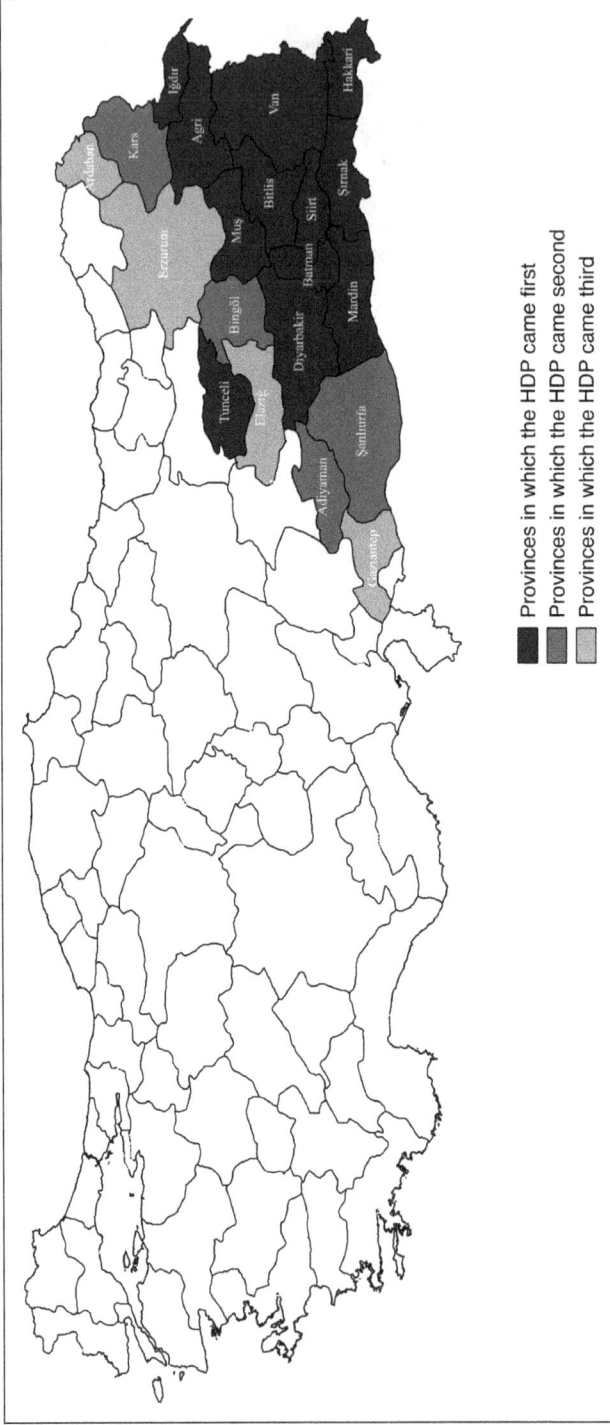

Figure 9.11 The Kurdish political region in the 1 November 2015 legislative election.

sub-region has enlarged to 11 provinces such that where it was once a hegemonic power balancer it is now a hegemonic power. The second sub-region includes two provinces: Kars and Bitlis. In these provinces, the pro-Kurdish party can challenge other parties and can now act as a hegemonic power balancer. The third sub-region includes seven provinces: Adıyaman, Ardahan, Bingöl, Elazığ, Erzurum, Gaziantep, and Şanlıurfa. The KM represents a significant opposition power in these provinces (see Figure 9.12).

Alongside the enlargement of the borders of the Kurdish political region, it is important to note that the power of the pro-Kurdish party has deepened within each sub-region. Compared to the 2000s, in the first sub-region it increased its votes from 47–62 per cent to 64–78 per cent in Diyarbakır, from 56–80 per cent to 82–6 per cent in Hakkari, from 40–61 per cent to 61–72 per cent in Mardin, and from 50–72 per cent to 83–4 per cent in Şırnak. In the second sub-region, the votes increased from 16–20 per cent to 33–44 per cent in Kars and, from 22–40 per cent to 44–60 per cent in Bitlis. There was a similar political rise in the third sub-region. For instance, the pro-Kurdish party's votes increased from 19–27 per cent to 26–38 per cent in Şanlıurfa, from 9–16 per cent to 22–30 per cent in Ardahan, from 14–24 per cent to 30–41 per cent in Bingöl, and from 5–8 per cent to 11–15 per cent in Gaziantep (compare Tables 9.2 and 9.3).

Despite falling back somewhat since the 7 June 2015 election, the KM is still more powerful than it was in 2013. We might argue that the 13.12 per cent vote share won on 7 June was an "extraordinary peak" (a result of tactical voting by HDP supporters, support from one of the principal mainstream media groups for the HDP, the influential election campaign and a stellar campaign performance by Demirtaş) and that the 10.75 per cent vote share won on 1 November represents the "true" political position of the KM in Turkey. In other words, this figure may well represent the KM's "structural" vote in the wake of the transformations within Kurdish society that have occurred since the 1990s.

The leading pro-Kurdish parties had not achieved to overcome the 10-per cent election threshold until the last years. The success in the presidential election in 2014 created a hope to overcome the election threshold and the HDP decided to enter the election as a party in the last two elections. After two-decade-long legal party experience, the overcoming the election threshold in the last two elections signifies a qualitative transformation of the KM and its societal support.

Second, the HDP still is the first party in the 12 provinces and a hegemonic power in the 11 ones. In this sub-region that has a population of over five million, the pro-Kurdish party will maintain its hegemonic power in the near future. That means it will be very difficult to challenge the pro-Kurdish party in this region for other political groups including the AKP and the CHP. Besides, in two provinces (Bitlis and Kars), the HDP is a hegemonic power of balance. That is to say, the

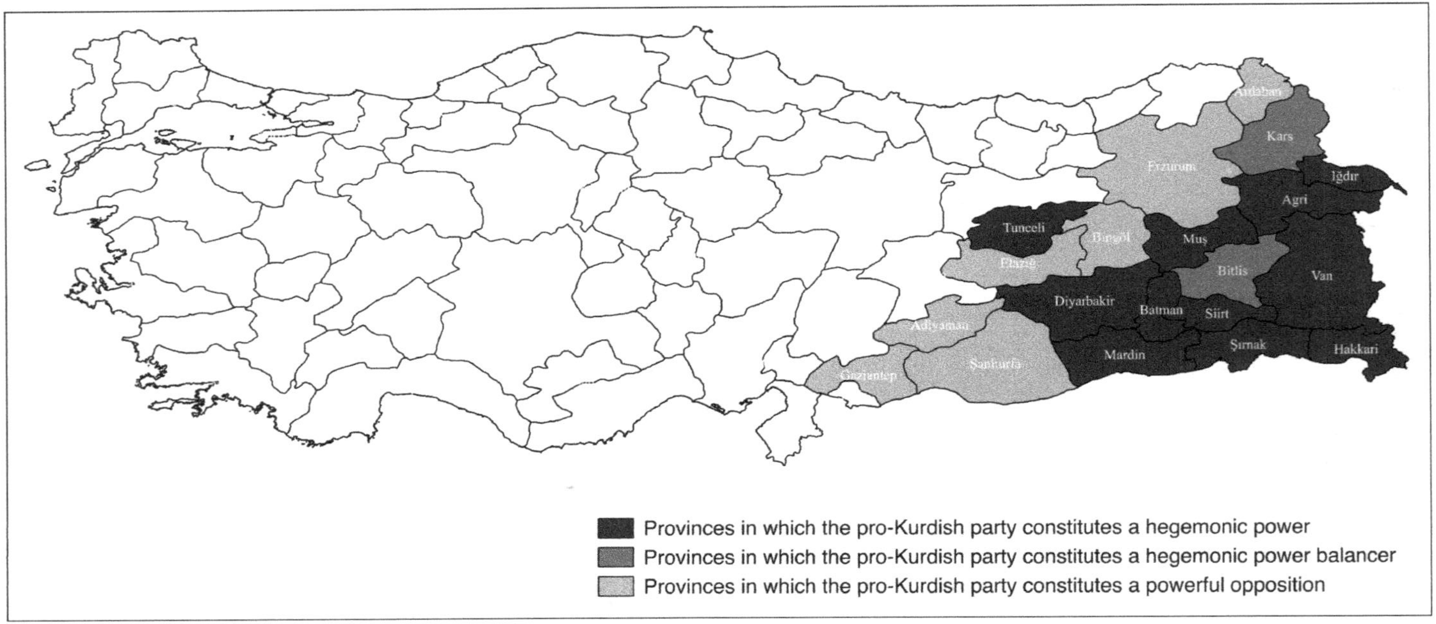
Ardahan
Kars
Erzurum
Iğdır
Agri
Tunceli
Bingöl
Muş
Elazığ
Bitlis
Van
Diyarbakir
Batman
Siirt
Adıyaman
Şırnak
Hakkari
Mardin
Şanlıurfa
Gaziantep
Provinces in which the pro-Kurdish party constitutes a hegemonic power
Provinces in which the pro-Kurdish party constitutes a hegemonic power balancer
Provinces in which the pro-Kurdish party constitutes a powerful opposition

Figure 9.12 The Kurdish political region and sub-regions in the 2010s.

Table 9.3   Elections and the Kurdish cultural region in the 2010s

Provinces	Demirtaş's Performance in the 2014 Presidential Election		HDP's Performance in the 7 June 2015 Legislative Election		HDP's Performance in the 1 November 2015 Legislative Election	
	Vote rate (%)	Candidate Rank	Vote rate (%)	Party rank	Vote rate (%)	Party rank
Adıyaman	15.27	3	22.63	2	14.31	2
Ağrı	61.28	1	76.91	1	66.80	1
Ardahan	23.09	3	30.15	1	22.08	3
Batman	60.00	1	71.20	1	66.81	1
Bingöl	30.57	2	40.52	2	29.67	2
Bitlis	43.72	2	59.73	1	48.61	1
Diyarbakır	64.17	1	77.73	1	71.27	1
Elazığ	10.88	3	15.36	3	11.16	3
Erzincan	4.06	3	5.85	4	3.49	4
Erzurum	13.07	3	17.81	3	13.32	3
Gaziantep	10.56	3	15.32	4	10.66	3
Hakkari	81.60	1	85.98	1	81.96	1
Iğdır	42.94	1	59.92	1	51.72	1
Kahramanmaraş	4.29	3	5.49	4	3.80	4
Kars	32.89	2	43.46	1	34.02	2
Kilis	3.79	3	4.07	4	2.00	4
Malatya	5.31	3	8.20	4	5.94	4
Mardin	60.90	1	72.07	1	67.02	1
Muş	61.24	1	70.18	1	60.63	1
Şanlıurfa	26.24	2	38.07	2	28.18	2
Siirt	54.07	1	65.05	1	57.20	1
Şırnak	83.18	1	83.90	1	83.63	1
Tunceli	52.25	1	59.91	1	54.85	1
Van	54.55	1	73.50	1	64.26	1

Source: This table draws on data from http://www.cnnturk.com/cumhurbaskanligis ecimi/, http://www.cnnturk.com/secim7Haziran2015/, and http://www.cnnturk. com/secim2015/.

pro-Kurdish party has built a region, including 13 provinces and having over a 5 million population, which is relatively autonomous from the rest of the country in terms of the socio-political tendencies. Moreover, in the seven provinces, it represents a remarkable power of opposition. The pro-Kurdish party has a noteworthy political potential to enlarge its power in this sub-region.

Finally, a remarkable part of the right-wing conservative Kurds have separated their paths from the AKP and participated in the KM. It is a mostly shared point that the HDP realized the glorious success in the last years thanks to mostly the right-wing conservative Kurds. Among the three million voters that newly supported the HDP in the 7 June election, there were at least two million right-wing conservative voters. Although voters chose to return the AKP on 1 November election, the HDP kept most of them. The newly participated right-wing conservative Kurds in the HDP have been playing a significant role in the building of the KM's hegemony in the Kurdish political region.

Conclusion: Understanding the Rise of Kurdish Politics in Turkey[57]

How can one analyse this success? Several trends must be noted. First, several Kurdish national movements have arisen in the Middle East since 2003, when the Iraqi Kurdistan Region was established. In 2012, the Kurds in Syria managed to establish three cantons in Rojava (Kurdistan regions in Syria) and still control their homeland. These events have changed the geopolitical equation of the Kurdish issue in the region and affect Kurds from all over the world, particularly in Turkey.[58] Moreover, the punishing war between Kurdish forces and ISIS both in Iraq and Syria has been mobilizing Kurds from all over the world since the summer of 2014.

Indeed, the leading Kurdish movement did not increase its societal support just in the last elections; rather, it has gradually expanded and deepened its hegemony in Turkey over the last decade. One can easily note the resurgence of the KM not just in local government and the national parliament, but also in civil society networks, in the media and in the streets. In brief, HDP success cannot be understood without taking into consideration the ongoing Kurdish spring in Iraq, Syria and Turkey over the last decade, for the last two years in particular.

In this respect, the war between the Kurds and ISIS in Kobani must be particularly noted. The Kobani war has become a "national" event mobilizing the Kurds and growing their national feelings and thoughts all over the world. The AKP's sectarian and nationalist policies in Syria and Rojava in particular, and its position during the Kobani war came as a shock to most of the Kurds supporting the AKP.

Second, we must underline the positions of the KM and the AKP concerning the peace process in Turkey. The KM's positive stance regarding the peace process and the rise of a legal democratic politics have strengthened the HDP. The open, sincere, reassuring, and stable role of the HDP in the ongoing peace process increased the party's credibility throughout society. Conversely, the AKP and President Erdoğan in particular, adopted a narrow, insecure, and unstable position during the peace process, and this has disappointed most of those who believed that the AKP would build peace and find a democratic and fair solution to the Kurdish issue. In this respect, President Erdoğan's statements saying that there was no negotiation table and opposing the monitoring committee for the peace process during recent months must be strongly underlined.[59]

Third, the HDP's integrationist policies in approaching socio-economic, ethnic/national, religious/sectarian, and gender-based inequalities and in advocating equality, liberty, and pluralism at many levels way beyond the Kurdish national struggle elicited a remarkable response in many parts of the society. The Kurds who mostly live in the metropolises and have already well integrated into Turkey welcomed this political position in particular. This position also convinced non-Kurdish liberal, democrat, left-wing, feminist, democrat Muslim voters.

Fourth, the HDP libertarian secularist position criticizing state control over religion, and emphasizing religious rights as well as the equality of religions has considerably undermined the AKP's influence over pious Kurds and banished the suspicions that arose from governmental allegations to the effect that the HDP is an anti-religious party. Besides, the HDP's intellectual Muslim candidates, including several women wearing a headscarf, notably influenced people and convinced them regarding the party's libertarian secularism.

The AKP has lost remarkable societal supports from the Kurds for the last two years Its political stance regarding Rojava and the Kobani war in particular and the last peace process initiated in 2013 and failed in 2015 must be principally noted in this political setback among the Kurds living both in the Kurdish region and the western part of the country. Yet, in the Kurdish political region, the AKP still is a hegemonic power of balance. In fact, except Dersim and Ardahan provinces, it is the only party that has been challenging the KM in the Kurdish political region for the last decade. In Dersim, the CHP takes the place of the AKP, while in Ardahan the CHP constitutes third hegemonic power alongside the AKP and the HDP.

At the level of the Kurdish political region, the leading Kurdish movement and the AKP constitute two principal hegemonic powers representing nearly three million voters and a population of five million people. Yet, it is important to note their societal supports differ in sub-regions in the Kurdish region. Except for two provinces, where two political movements represent a hegemonic power balance, the Kurdish political region comprises roughly two sub-regions. In each sub-region, there is a powerful hegemony of one of the political movements. The AKP is a hegemonic power in the seven peripheral provinces in the Kurdish political region, which are neighbours in the western provinces of the country. The rest is under the hegemonic power of the KM.

Notes

1. Maria Theresa O'Shea, *Trapped Between the Map and Reality: Geography and Perceptions of Kurdistan* (New York & London, 2004).
2. Ibid., p. 156.
3. The provinces that constitute the border between the Kurdish cultural region and the rest of Turkey are Ardahan, Kars, Erzurum, Erzincan, Malatya, Kahramanmaraş, Antep, and Kilis. Ardahan and Kars are ethnically cosmopolitan provinces, including Kurds and Turks. Besides, the Kurdish cultural region border passes within Erzincan, Erzurum, and Kahramanmaraş provinces.
4. Peter L. Berger and Thomas Luckmann, *The Social Construction of Reality: A Treatise in the Sociology of Knowledge* (New York, 1966), p. 13.
5. Ibid., p. 15.
6. David Harvey, *Space of Capital: Towards a Critical Geography* (Edinburgh, 2001), pp. 219–29.
7. Ibid., p. 209.
8. Ibid.
9. Ibid., pp. 211–12.
10. Ibid., p. 214.
11. Arthur H. Robinson et al. (eds), *Elements of Cartography* (New York, 1984), p. 7.
12. O'Shea, Ibid., p. 157.
13. O'Shea, Ibid., pp. 156–61; Judith A. Tyner, *Persuasive Cartography* (Los Angeles, 1974).
14. Judith A. Tyner, "Persuasive Cartography", in M. Monmonier (ed.), *The History of Cartography Volume Six: Cartography in the Twentieth Century* (Chicago, 2015); P. J. Mode, "Persuasive Cartography", *The PJ Mode Collection*. Available at https://persuasivemaps.library.cornell.edu (accessed 30 January 2016).
15. O'Shea, Ibid., pp. 7–8.
16. John Pickles, "Text, Hermeneutics and Propaganda Maps", in T. J. Barnes and J. S. Duncan (eds), *Writing Worlds: Discourse, Text, and Metaphor in the Representation of Landscape* (London, 1992), p. 199.
17. J. Brian Harley, "Maps, knowledge, and power", in D. Cosgrove and S. Daniel (eds), *The Iconography of Landscape* (Cambridge, 1988), p. 278.
18. Ibid.
19. J. Brian Harley, "Deconstructing the Map", in T. J. Barnes and J. S. Duncan (eds), *Writing Worlds: Discourse, Text, and Metaphor in the Representation of Landscape* (London, 1992), p. 247.
20. O'Shea, ibid., pp. 159–60.
21. Henri Lefebvre, *La production de l'espace* (Paris, 1974). For English version see *The Production of Space* (Oxford, 1991).
22. Asef Bayat, "Politics in the City-Inside-Out", *City & Society* 24/2 (2012), p. 113.
23. Miguel Amoros, "Kentsel Mücadeleler ve Sınıf Mücadelesi", in S. Torlar and Ö. Kulak (eds), *Mekan Meselesi* (Ankara, 2014), p. 129.
24. Henri Lefebvre, *State, Space, World: Selected Essays* (Minneapolis & London, 2009), p. 186.
25. Ibid., p. 189.
26. Ibid., p. 188.
27. Harvey, ibid., p. 217.
28. Ibid., p. 217.

29. Ibid., p. 213.
30. Eyüp Demir, *Yasal Kürtler: HEP'ten HDP'ye Kürt Siyaseti* (İstanbul, 2000), pp. 118–22.
31. Ibid.
32. Seçim Sonuçları, "1991 İl Oylarının SHP Göre Dağılımı ve Milletvekili Sayısı", available at http://www.secim-sonuclari.com/sosyaldemokrat-halkci-parti/1991.parti (accessed 3 February 2016).
33. Demir, ibid., p. 330.
34. Seçim Sonuçları, "1995 İl Oylarının HADEP Göre Dağılımı ve Milletvekili Sayısı", available at http://www.secim-sonuclari.com/halkin-demokrasi-partisi/1995.parti (accessed 3 February 2016).
35. Demir, ibid., pp. 339–400.
36. Seçim Sonuçları, "1999 İl Oylarının HADEP Göre Dağılımı ve Milletvekili Sayısı", available at http://www.secim-sonuclari.com/halkin-demokrasi-partisi/1999.parti (accessed 3 February 2016).
37. Antonio Gramsci, *Selection From The Prison Notebooks* (New York, 1971), pp. 245–6.
38. See: www.secim-sonuclari.com
39. Cuma Çiçek, *Ulus, Din, Sınıf: Türkiye'de Kürt Mutabakatının İnşası* (İstanbul, 2015), p. 70
40. For debates on this transformation see Cengiz Gunes, *The Kurdish National Movement in Turkey: From Protest to Resistance* (London & New York:, 2012); Ahmet Hamid Akkaya and Joost Jongerden, "Reassembling the Political: The PKK and the Project of Radical Democracy", *European Journal of Turkish Studies (Online) 14* (2012). Available at https://ejts.revues.org/4615 (accessed 10 February 2016); Joost Jongerden, Ahmet Hamdi Akkaya and Bahar Şimşek, (eds), *İsyandan İnşaya: Kurdistan Özgürlük Hareketi* (İstanbul, 2015).
41. Seçim Sonucu.com, "Yerel Seçim Sonuçları", *Seçim Sonucu*, available at http://www.secimsonucu.com/YerelSecimSonuclari.asp?SY=1999 (accessed 10 February 2016).
42. Ministry For EU Affairs, "Turkey – EU Relations: Brief History", *Republic of Turkey Ministry For EU Affairs*, 15 December 2015, available at http://www.ab.gov.tr/index.php?p=111&l = 2 (accessed 10 February 2016).
43. Demir, ibid., p. 488.
44. Yuksek Seçim Kurulu, "Gümrük Oyları Dahil Türkiye Geneli Seçim Sonuçları", available at http://www.ysk.gov.tr/ysk/docs/2002MilletvekiliSecimi/gumrukdahil/gumrukdahil.pdf (accessed 12 February 2016).
45. Haber Türk, "Genel Seçim 2002", http://www.haberturk.com/secim2002 (accessed 14 February 2016).
46. Bianet, "Bağımsız Milletvekili Adaylarının Tam Listesi", *Bianet*, 5 July 2007, available at http://bianet.org/bianet/siyaset/98781-bagimsiz-milletvekili-adaylarinin-tam-listesi (accessed 15 February 2016).
47. Demir, ibid., p. 523.
48. Haber Türk, "Genel Seçim 2007", available at http://www.haberturk.com/secim2002 (accessed 14 February 2016).
49. Ibid.
50. Demir, ibid., pp. 531–2.
51. I discussed the democratic autonomy project in different works. See Cuma Çiçek, "Demokratik Özerklik: Bir Ulusal ve Sosyal İnşa Projesi mi?", *İktisat Dergisi 525* (2014), pp. 35–48; Cuma Çiçek, "Etnik ve Sınıfsal İnşa Süreçleri

Bağlamında Kürt Meselesi: Bölgesel Eşitsizlik ve Bölgesel Özerklik", *Praksis 28* (2012), pp. 11–42.

52. CNN Türk, "2014 Cumhurbaşkanlığı Seçim Merkezi", available at http://www. cnnturk.com/cumhurbaskanligisecimi/ (accessed 17 February 2016).

53. HDP's party program is accessible on the Internet. See HDP, "Halkların Demokratik Partisi Programı", available at http://www.hdp.org.tr/parti/parti-programi/8 (accessed 17 February 2016).

54. HDP's election manifesto represents very well this new discourse. See HDP, *HDP 2015 Seçim Bildirgesi: Büyük İnsanlık Çağrısı*, available at https://drive.google. com/file/d/0Byrzr4UgN9-0QzV1ZnJfcXMwaVE/view (accessed 17 February 2016).

55. CNN Türk, "7 Haziran 2015 Genel Seçim Merkezi", http://www.cnnturk.com/ secim7Haziran2015/ (accessed 17 February 2016).

56. Ibid.

57. This part has been written on the basis of another work that I wrote for the openDemocracy. See Cuma Çiçek, "HDP: focus of left-wing opposition beyond pro-Kurdish mobilization", *openDemocracy*, 15 June 2015, available at https:// www.opendemocracy.net/cuma-çiçek/hdp-focus-of-leftwing-opposition-beyond-prokurdish-mobilization (accessed 21 November 2015).

58. For a more sophisticated discussion on this issue see: Çiçek, ibid.

59. For a more sophisticated discussion the peace/solution process see: Necmiye Alpay and Hakan Tahman (eds), *Barış Açısını Savunmak: Çözüm Sürecinde Ne Oldu?* (İstanbul, 2015).

CHAPTER 10

VANGUARDS OF VIOLATION: FREEDOM OF ASSEMBLY AND NOTES ON THE TURKISH POLITICAL REGIME

Kıvanç Atak

Introduction

20 April 1990. About one thousand superannuation pensioners gather in front of the headquarters of the Confederation of Turkish Trade Unions (TÜRK-İŞ) in Ankara to relay their resentment with the superannuation policy and the government's proposal to redress the pensioners' material losses. Unsatisfied with the message they receive from the union leadership, the group heads to the Ministry of Labour and Social Security and stages a sit-down in front of the ministry's premises to protest İmren Aykut, the minister, and calls for her resignation. The police forces intervene but do not force the crowd to disperse. After two hours, the pensioners decide to go back to TÜRK-İŞ headquarters to negotiate with the unionists again and leave with the promise that their demands will be delivered to the prime minister, Yıldırım Akbulut.

5 August 1995. The central square of Ankara, Kızılay, hosts around 100,000 trade unionists and political activists staging a mass demonstration upon the call by TÜRK-İŞ to protest the government's position concerning the collective bargaining process in the public sector. The demonstrators gathered in Tandoğan Square about three kilometres away and marched to Kızılay for a stationary meeting where the union leaders addressed the crowd and held speeches. The protest proceeded and ended in a peaceful atmosphere with negligible distortions of public order.

More than two decades after these two separate protest events, even the most credible actors within Turkish civil society would be unable to organize a public demonstration on Kızılay Square. Permission to do so would simply never be granted. Likewise, any protest attempt near government premises would most probably experience the taste of pepper spray or the smell of tear gas – or perhaps even the cold touch of the baton charge. The situation would be quite similar in Istanbul where mass demonstrations are pushed away from the most central locations of the city to deserted yards on the outskirts, well out of the public eye, the curious citizen, and bystanders. What does this spatial contraction of the exercise of the right to protest imply for a political regime?

This chapter addresses the trajectory of the political regime in Turkey through the lens of freedom of assembly. The freedom to assemble, demonstrate, and protest peacefully is a necessary condition for a democratic polity – one that goes far beyond its minimalist definition in the Schumpeterian sense. Since political participation entails much more than casting votes, its exercise free from arbitrary restrictions and interference by the state is a litmus test of the democratic qualities of a regime. In the last few years, this question has grown in significance due to the mass mobilization of citizens against austerity policies, financial suppression, corruption, and authoritarian rule across the world. Turkey also joined in this wave of mass protests when uprisings broke out in the middle of Istanbul in June 2013. In fact, the country has a notorious past as to the infringement of citizens' right to organize peaceful protests. The question of the extent and direction of change in the last decade under the resilient rule of the Justice and Development Party (*Adalet ve Kalkınma Partisi*, AKP) therefore goes begging for an answer.

In this chapter, I lay out a narrative of continuity rather than change. Drawing on a multiplicity of sources, I suggest that authoritarian *practices* at the expense of the freedom of assembly have not waned but have been perpetuated during the ongoing AKP period. A controversial framing of unlawful assembly, I argue, lays bare a pervasive authoritarian "mentality" that goes together with a lack of institutional reform within the police. The contrast between Turkey's vanguard position with respect to the relative resource priority given to policing and its weak performance in public social spending and protection, I further claim, adds another layer to the story and feeds into what I call an "authoritarian equilibrium". The empirical material I use to base my argument comes from case law and statistical data from the European Court of Human Rights (ECtHR), the Cingranelli-Richards Human Rights Database (CIRI), data on government spending, legislative documents, police and interior ministry reports, and judicial records.

Authoritarian Rule, Civil Liberties, and Repression

What makes a government authoritarian? In his seminal work *Totalitarian and Authoritarian Regimes*, Juan Linz elaborates on the characteristics of authoritarian political systems and suggested that limited political pluralism together with systematic constraints on civil liberties and suppression of political opponents constitute one of the defining features of the authoritarian "mentality" that pervades the exercise of power in such regimes.[1] Beyond dispute, the right to freedom of peaceful assembly – one of the main pillars of democratic participation (albeit one usually considered as unconventional) – is most likely to be endangered by restrictions on and violations of civil rights and liberties.

It is probably wise to make a distinction between authoritarian *practices* and authoritarian *regimes*. For it is not only under certain regimes that we observe infractions of democratic rule and flirtations with authoritarian forms of government. Democracies also "kill", as Davenport phrases it, not only when political challenges are perceived to be threatening and posed by "unaccepted" groups who resort to "unacceptable" forms of action but also when repression is facilitated by democracies' "highly decentralized structure [...] the fact that they engage in the worst activity before the polity is politically 'opened' [...] relevant behaviour takes place within areas that were created to be isolated from the rest of the society (both psychologically as well as physically)."[2] In his most recent book, *War, States and Contention*, Sydney Tarrow also carves out his critical observation that the present-day politics in the United States veers away from a historically-rooted "devotion to rights" to a despotic machinery fighting against social movements under the rubric of national security.[3] Hardly any report or index classifies the US today as an authoritarian regime; on the contrary, the American political regime consistently registers peak scores in various democracy indexes. But authoritarian *practices* have surely been ingrained deeply in US history as well, and have expanded since 9/11 with international consequences.

Still, it is legitimate to ask under what conditions states tend to clamp down on civil liberties and citizen mobilization on the streets. Two separate but partially related literatures offer us some convincing answers to this question. Research on state repression, particularly extensive work done by Christian Davenport and his colleagues, has verified that below a certain and actually quite high threshold, democratic advancement does not necessarily bring about a significant decrease in the traces of state repression. It is only above the threshold of "domestic democratic peace" that there seems to be a linear and negative relationship between the level of democracy and repressive under-takings of the state.[4] Even though this relationship is nuanced by the presence or absence of civil conflict in society, the participatory/competitive aspect of democracy (*voice*) proves to be more influential in pacifying repression than executive constraints on political administration (*veto*).[5] The major inference that can be drawn from these studies is that repression and human rights violations are more intrinsic in, albeit not limited to, non-democratic settings.

This conclusion complements the proposition that systematic restrictions on civil liberties are pervasive in regimes that may not fully qualify as autocracies but which also fall short of the more substantial traits of a democratic polity; that is, *hybrid regimes*.[6] In the past two decades, the literature on hybrid regimes has grown almost exponentially. These regimes have been scrutinized under numerous labels ranging from illiberal democracies to competitive authoritarianism.[7] Here, I do not pay much attention to the type of hybrid regime but show more interest in the fact that all those regimes in the political grey zone typically fail to protect and often violate civil liberties, particularly the right to freedom of peaceful assembly. That is why I concur with Schedler's claim that regimes in which regular elections are held with *some* level of competition (real but not fair) but civil liberties are regularly flouted despite *some* level of institutional guarantees (written in law but not respected) "do not represent limited, deficient, or distorted forms of democracy" but should be characterized as "instances of authoritarian rule".[8]

How does Turkey fit into this debate? Would it count as a democracy, an authoritarian or a hybrid regime? Given the (latest) persecutions of journalists, academics, activists and so on, what would be an informed answer to these queries? For one thing, the country has never been a paragon of civil rights and liberties and has, in fact, a remarkably poor record in this regard. For another, Turkey has a tumultuous and contested history of democratization together with a fairly long constitutional tradition that dates back to the late nineteenth century. But its history of democratization can be simultaneously characterized as a history of "de-democratization" in Tilly's words, due to the periodic interruptions by military veto players to civilian affairs in politics. In some accounts, the "statist tradition" or the grip on "stateness" inherited from Ottoman times has contributed to the development of a political culture that virtually precludes any democratic consolidation in the country.[9] The literature on hybrid regimes has curiously neglected Turkey, labeling it as a "vague" case or exhibiting perfunctory interest (at best) in its military tutelage and periods of democratic breakdown without significant effort to understand its dynamics in a comparative framework. At any rate, there is little doubt that Turkish democracy has always floated on the fringes of authoritarian rule – thereby earning its reputation as a "democracy in danger".[10]

How much has changed under the single-party rule of the AKP since 2002? Its march into power certainly was not welcomed within the Kemalist milieu because of an "imminent" threat to the so-called *laik* foundations of the republic. But its relatively moderate Islamist face – initially coupled with a zealous devotion to rapprochement with the European Union and commitment to a series of political reform packages – convinced many sceptics that the AKP was in the vanguard of an emerging period of liberal and democratic progress in Turkey. For better or worse, these reforms and harmonization with the EU removed some of the remnants of a woefully illiberal past. However, as the AKP seized an expansively dominant position in Turkey's multi-party system, its political geography evolved into a "progressive land of repression" where "there is a growing disjuncture between those who promote modern-day Turkey as a democracy and those who experience Turkey as a land of arbitrary detentions, political repression and military destruction".[11] Few would deny that "the AKP has led a determined struggle against the far-reaching powers that the military High Command enjoyed under the old regime; but this has increasingly taken the form of replacing Kemalism with a new police state".[12] The wholesale celebration by the intellectual elite of the political defeat of military tutelage, however favourable for democratization, arguably risked a "reductionist reading of the Turkish state," a reading that underpinned "an inability to analyse it as a differentiated set of institutions and social actors with now overlapping, now conflicting concerns and interests".[13]

The question of how to define the political regime in Turkey under the consecutive governments of the AKP is indeed a compelling one. As I suggest, any plausible answer cannot be detached from the constellation of *practices* that underlie how the regime functions or that simply exists on the ground. That is why I specifically discuss the Turkish variety of freedom of assembly and how it has looked during the reign of the AKP.

Why Freedom of Assembly?

In his book *Liberty's Refuge: The Forgotten Freedom of Assembly*, John D. Inazu juxtaposes three main elements to summarize his interest in the historical role of assembly.[14] First, groups invoking the right of assembly have usually been those that dissent from the majoritarian standards endorsed by the government. Second, claims of assembly have insisted on a political mode of existence that is separate from the politics of the state. Finally, practices of assembly have themselves been forms of expression – parades, strikes, and meetings, but also more creative means of engagement like pageants, religious worship, and the sharing of meals.

Inazu tells us an American story of the gradual demise of the freedom of assembly particularly in the second half of the twentieth century and how it has been "forgotten", subsumed (to a significant extent) within the territory of free speech in legal documents and court decisions, and increasingly confined strictly to political protests and demonstrations. His attention to the three eminent qualities of assemblies, though, can surely be extended beyond the

American context. And to some extent, assembly as a "political mode of existence" is most relevant for protest as an empowering tool. Half a century ago, Martin Lipsky identified protest as a key political resource of relatively powerless groups – an assertion that roughly overlapped with the heyday of the civil rights movement in the US.[15] In hindsight, after several decades of research on social movements and contentious politics, we need perhaps a more nuanced view on this assertion. For it is not only the disenfranchised, vulnerable groups, and progressive forces who take to the streets seeking social justice and the expansion of rights and freedoms for themselves as well as for others; reactionary forces and those who push for a less pluralistic and inclusive and a more exclusionary social and political imagery use this resource also. Thus protest has the capacity to empower collective actors with incompatible and opposite visions some of which might be "shocking" for some sections of society. Nevertheless, what it should not empower and entitle are acts and expressions of hate-speech which inflict harm upon people and generally "hurt more".[16]

The recognition of the freedom to peacefully assemble as a *right* dates back to the late eighteenth and early nineteenth centuries in most parts of Western Europe and the United States.[17] And if we endorse Tilly's "shorthand" differentiation between reactive and proactive forms of collective action, the demonstration as "sponsored public meeting" and a proactive performance, entered in our repertoires in the nineteenth century and "began to thrive with the arrival of mass electoral politics".[18] Assembly was considered as a means for people to "redress grievances", and in some jurisdictions (notably the American ones) closely tied to the right to petition. In democratic theory, freedom of assembly is an integral part of political participation and simultaneously an act of expression as it allows a person to publicly raise her voice. Even in most democratic regimes not all ideas and political visions are adequately represented. What is more, democratic institutions cannot always absorb and efficiently channel those ideas and visions. Therefore, assembly – especially if we concentrate on protests and demonstrations – gives political subjects a space to claim "I do exist" whether or not she is actually delivering an articulate message to the authorities and ruling elites. It is both a positive freedom to protest and a negative freedom from the arbitrary interference of the state.

Historically speaking, there is also a tight connection between rights and social struggle which often takes advantage of the street. Here, I once again look to Charles Tilly's model to explain the origins of rights many people enjoy today.[19] Citizenship rights, in Tilly's telling, emerged because relatively organized members of the general population bargained with state authorities for several centuries – first over the means of war, then over enforceable claims that would serve their interests outside of war. This bargaining enlarged the obligations of states to their citizens, broadening the range of enforceable claims citizens could make on states even more than it expanded the population who held rights of citizenship.

Tilly's account of rights is one of struggle and resistance and what he calls "white-hot bargaining". Politics in the street, if we consider it as an aspect of assembly, definitely occupies a sizeable space in the history of social struggles and movements. One may argue that new avenues of political action on the internet, that is, social media, have reduced the importance of street politics to a certain extent. Instead of taking such line of thinking at face value, I would rather espouse the view that these avenues enrich the (non-physical) space of action. Whichever view one takes, one thing remains certain; namely that suppressing the right to freedom of peaceful assembly would be equal to cutting down one of the most effective tools of seeking rights in society.

(Un-)Freedom of Assembly in Turkey: Quo Vadis?

On 13 October 2013, the local branch of the Education and Science Employees Union (Eğitim-Sen) staged a protest in front of the courthouse in Adana, a populous city in southern Turkey. The protesters, who numbered around 45 individuals, delivered a press declaration and demanded the establishment of day care centres in their respective institutions. The protest was conducted in a peaceful manner all the way through. The district police authorities, however, issued a 143 TRY (€40) fine to Mr Akarsubaşı, the applicant to the ECtHR, on the grounds that the protest took place on the stairway in front of the courthouse – an act which reportedly violated the November 2009 decision by the provincial governorship on the conditions and public places where press declarations are permissible and not permissible. In May 2011, the local court in Adana upheld the fine and its ruling was not open to appeal since, according to the domestic law on misdemeanors, fines below 3,000 TRY are not eligible for appeal. The ECtHR accepted the application by Mr Akarsubaşı and convicted Turkey for violating Article 11 of the European Convention on Human Rights (ECHR) on freedom of assembly and association. While acknowledging the signatory states' right to regulate this freedom on the basis of public order and national security, the ECtHR reasoned that the ruling of the local court completely ignored the peaceful nature of the protest, which did not pose any observable risk to public order and law enforcement in the vicinity of the courthouse. In addition, the fine could also be interpreted as an unfair means to deter anyone who is a member of a trade union from exercising her right to freedom of peaceful assembly.[20]

The above case is but one example of the (soft) violation of the right to freedom of peaceful assembly in Turkey. In other cases, violations might turn much more severe especially when they come together with physical means of coercion. Extensive use of police force throughout the Gezi Park protests was emblematic in that sense. Part of the reason as to why it startled so many is because it literally took place in the middle of Istanbul. On the contrary, state violence which occurs in the peripheries of the public gaze, to invoke Davenport, often goes unnoticed. After this short remark, we are left with the following question: is this a negligible issue or a serious question in Turkey? And, to reiterate one of the queries formulated above, how much has changed, for better or worse, under the single-party rule of the AKP?

What the Numbers Say

Figures from the annual reports of the Turkish National Police (TNP) show that each year several thousand "events" take place in the streets of the country. In the period between 1993 and 2000, the numbers ranged from 4,385 (1993) to 12,495 (1997), and in the period between 2001 and 2013 from 5,261 (2004) to 38,079 (2013). A compilation of police records of protest events and judicial records of suspects and convictions concerning the Law No. 2911 on public assemblies, by the same token, shows a discernible fluctuation in the number of suspects and convictions per event in the last two decades. What is noteworthy is that the conviction rate increased considerably from less than one conviction per 100 events in the early 1990s to almost 15 in 100 in 2002 (see Figure 10.1).

These numbers give us a sense of the scope of contentious activity and street mobilization in Turkey but they hardly inform us about the extent to which the Turkish state *fails* to protect its citizens' right to peacefully assemble. The picture looks much clearer if we take a comparative and long-term perspective. Figure 10.2 presents figures from the ECtHR and summarizes the violations of Article 11 of the Convention on freedom of assembly and association by respective signatory states under the court's jurisdiction. There is obviously an outstanding state in the bar graph and that outlier is Turkey. The illustration covers a large period from 1959 to 2015, but note that Turkey officially accepted the court's jurisdiction only at the end of the 1980s.[21]

This is undoubtedly a grim picture. The fact that in 2010 Turkish citizens were, for the first time, granted standing before the Turkish Constitutional Court (CCT) might eventually see the number of applications to and convictions by the ECtHR fall in the future. This does not necessarily mean, however, that the violations of the Turkish state would follow suit. Recent rulings by domestic courts, albeit unevenly, reaffirm that freedom of assembly in Turkey remains at risk. In a January 2015 decision, for instance, the CCT, by majority vote, laid down that in two separate occasions protesting educational reform, organized in İzmir in 2012, the applicants' right to public demonstration and assembly was infringed despite constitutional guarantees of the protection of this right.[22]

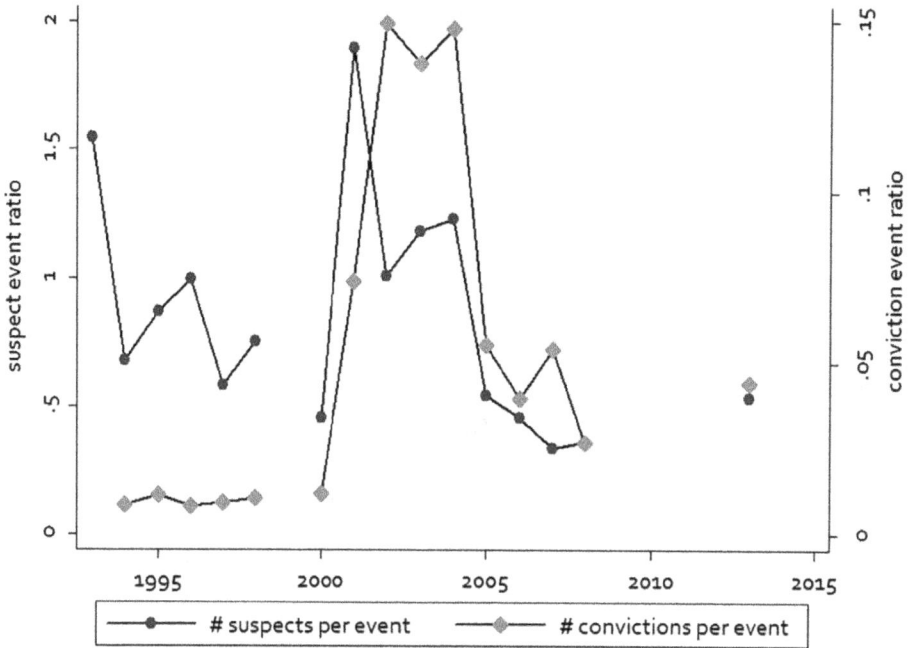

Figure 10.1 Ratio of suspects and convictions (law on public assemblies) to police recorded (protest) events, 1993–2013. Source: TNP,[23] General Directorate of Judicial Records and Statistics.[24]

In a long-term perspective, the picture does not truly seem to have improved in the last decade either. Drawing on the Cingranelli-Richards Human Rights Database, Table 10.1 illustrates three selected indicators of human rights violations between 1981 and 2011 in Turkey. The database shows that even though disappearances ceased to be a severe question in comparison with the 1990s, both restrictions on freedom of assembly and association and political imprisonment remain dire, except for a few consecutive years in the 2000s in the case of freedom of assembly. These data confirm that Turkey under the AKP continues to be a consistent violator of its citizens' right to stage peaceful protests.

Law Matters

Where does the problem lie then? One explanation would suggest that this is a question of legislation or the legal code (laws-in-effect). The political regulation of the right to assembly in Turkey dates to the *İçtimaati Umumiye Kanunu* (General Assembly Law) in 1909 and *Tecemmuat Hakkında Kanun-u Muvakkat* in 1912, a provisional clause about spontaneous gatherings. The former was abolished in 1946 and replaced with Law No. 6761 in 1956. Because

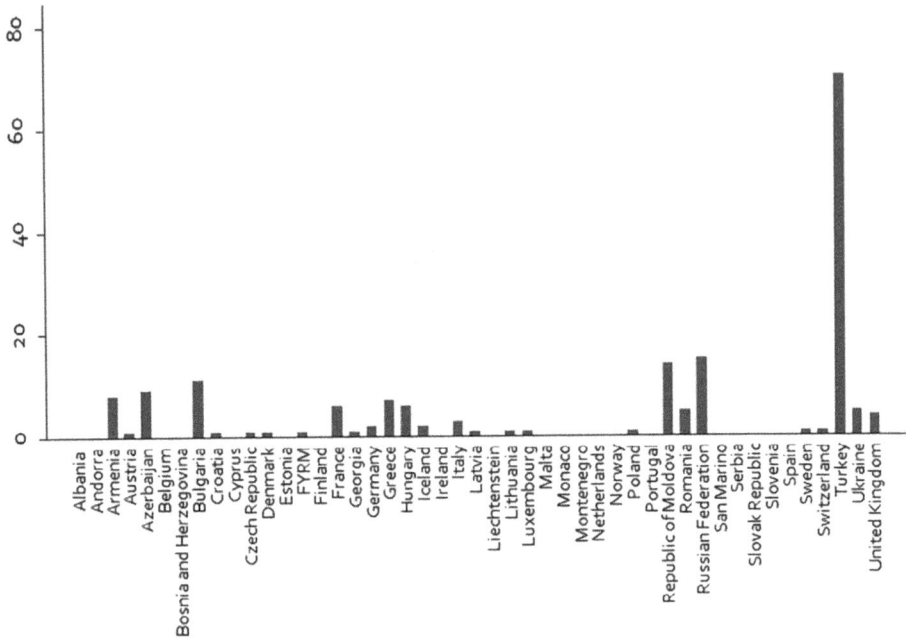

Figure 10.2 Number of violations of Article 11 of the ECHR on freedom of assembly and association, 1959–2015. Source: European Court of Human Rights.[25]

of the military intervention in 1960 and the constitutional order laid down in its aftermath, Law No. 171 was introduced and remained in force until the suspension of democracy, once again, by the armed forces in 1980. In 1983, Law no. 2911 on public assemblies and demonstrations was enacted under the new constitution and has in the period since been amended several times. The clauses of these laws surely reflected the political context in which they were drafted. Hence, the direction of changes has oscillated between a more liberal and more restrictive path, though often biased in the second direction (see Table 10.2).

The development of public order management systems in the twentieth century brought about more refined "time-place-manner" regulations with respect to the implementation of public assembly laws across the world. Despite considerable variation among countries, such regulations in Western Europe and the United States, for instance, include specific clauses on what constitutes an assembly, a march and a stationary meeting, on the terms of prior notification, restricted areas, banned symbols, wearing of masks, carriage of arms, and so forth.[26] It is true that there has been a growing trend on a global scale, especially since 9/11, to curb civil rights and liberties including the freedom of assembly. In the UK, Orsolya Salát notes, "recent decades have seen

Table 10.1 Selected indicators of human rights violations in Turkey, 1981–2011

Year	Political imprisonment			Disappearances			Freedom of assembly and association		
	many	few	none	frequent	occasional	none	severe restrictions	limited restrictions	virtually unrestricted
1981	+					+	+		
1982		+				+	+		
1983		+				+	+		
1984	+					+	+		
1985	+					+	+		
1986	+					+	+		
1987	+					+	+		
1988	+					+	+		
1989	+				+		+		
1990	+				+		+		
1991		+			+		+		
1992		+			+			+	
1993	+			+			+		
1994	+				+		+		
1995	+			+			+		
1996	+			+			+		
1997	+				+			+	
1998	+				+			+	
1999	+					+	+		
2000	+				+			+	
2001	+				+			+	

Table 10.1 *Continued*

	Political imprisonment			Disappearances			Freedom of assembly and association		
	many	few	none	frequent	occasional	none	severe restrictions	limited restrictions	virtually unrestricted
	+					+		+	
	+					+		+	
2005	+					+		+	
	+					+		+	
	+					+	+		
	+					+	+		
2010	+					+	+		
	+					+	+		

Source: Cingranelli-Richards Human Rights Database.[27]

Table 10.2 Selected clauses of the public assembly laws in Turkey, 1950s–2000s

	1950s	1960s	1970s	1980s	1990s	2000s
Law in effect	No. 6761	No. 171	No. 171	No. 2911	No. 2911	No. 2911
Year of enactment/amendment	1956	1963	1973	1983	1998	2002; 2003; 2008; 2010
			1976			
Type of authorization	permission from the prefect	notification of the prefect	same applies	same applies	same applies	same applies
Notification of authorities prior to event	48 hours	48 hours	96 hours	72 hours	72 hours	48 hours
			48 hours			
Minimum size of the organizing committee	3 persons	same applies	same applies	7 persons	7 persons	7 persons
Details of notification	place-day-hours; objectives, roads, directions of the rally and its dispersion; proof of identity and residence of leaders and speakers	place-day-hours; objectives, roads, directions of the rally and its dispersion in compliance with provincial regulations; proof of identity and residence of the organizers	same applies	place-day-hours; objectives; roads, directions of march and dispersion in compliance with provincial regulations; proof of identity, residence, profession and workplace of the organizers	same applies	same applies

Table 10.2 *Continued*

	1950s	1960s	1970s	1980s	1990s	2000s
Duration (for open air events)	from sunrise to sunset	same applies		from sunrise to one hour prior to sunset	same applies	same applies
Banned places	Highways, parks, sanctuaries, public institutions	Highways, parks, sanctuaries, public institutions and their extensions, less than 1 km from the parliament	same applies	Highways, parks, sanctuaries, public institutions and their extensions, less than 1 km from the parliament, intercity roads	same applies	same applies
Justification for postponing the event	No clause	No clause	public order	public order, indivisibility of the state and the nation, national security, public good, general health and morality	public order, indivisibility of the state and the nation, national security, threats to the Republic's foundations, general health and morality	same applies	public order, national security, general morality and health, prevention of crime, protection of rights and freedoms of others
Terms of postponement	No clause	No clause	30 days	10 days	60 days	same applies	30 days

Justification for proscribing the event	No clause	No clause	No clause	Same clauses as for postponement	same applies	Same clauses as for postponement
Coercive dispersion after	Oral warning	Oral warning (no warning in case of physical offense)	same applies	same applies	same applies	same applies
Law enforcement agent	Police (+ army)	Police	Police	Police	Police (+ army)	Police (+ army)
Means of control	All equipments + resort to arms if necessary	No clause	No clause (specified in the Code)	No clause (Specified in the Directive)	same applies	same applies
Definitions of unlawful assembly	P: violation of procedures; M: means (carriage of arms); O: objectives (if they extend specified ones); C: criminal propagation	M: extended (further arms included) O: extended (objectives proscribed by law)	same applies	M: extended (banners, posters, placards, pictures, tools, slogans proscribed by law)	M: extended (symbols of illegal organizations)	same applies

Source: adapted from Atak (2013).

an extraordinary mushrooming of legislative restrictions on freedom of assembly from public order laws to terrorism and antisocial behaviour legislation; even harassment provisions are applied to restrict protest."[28] Similar observations concern the US where such restrictions intertwine with a more subtle and protracted process that feeds into the spatial contraction of permissible protest.[29]

The current legislation in Turkey has several similarities with legislation in Western-democratic countries. It has also joined many democracies in the "restrictive turn" as described above. In fact, political reforms and alignment with the European Union in the first half of the 2000s led to a handful of cosmetic changes in the public order provisions and Law No. 2911. Yet these changes left some of the most restrictive aspects of the law intact. Turkey retains a relatively broad definition of the circumstances under which an assembly becomes unlawful. The law criminalizes public demonstrations – regardless of their peaceful nature – when procedural conditions are not met (Article 23). This applies in particular to the rule of *prior notification*: an assembly or public demonstration that is held without notice is ubiquitously considered unlawful. Furthermore, the police are entitled to disperse such a gathering even if it is peaceful (Article 24). To nobody's surprise, such police powers are conducive to further human rights violations, not least infringements of the right to personal integrity or freedom from torture. All in all, this runs counter to the provisions in the Turkish Constitution (Article 34), the ECHR (Article 11) and several ECtHR and domestic rulings in Turkey. It has been recurrently stated that prior notification might be a *duty* but its lack thereof does not necessarily render a gathering illegal if it adheres to peacefulness. States are expected to show a certain level of tolerance to such assemblies because (1) they have a *positive* obligation to facilitate the exercise of the right to freedom of peaceful assembly and; (2) a *negative* obligation not to arbitrarily interfere with this right. Yet Turkey seems to be consistent in its disrespect of these principles.[30]

Underlying this disrespect, I argue, is the authoritarian "mentality" Juan Linz has referred to in his regime definition – one that he distinguished from ideology, which he associated with totalitarian systems. Inspired by the German sociologist Theodor Geiger's notion of *Subjectiver Geist* (subjective mind), Linz considered mentalities as "ways of thinking and feeling [that] provide noncodified ways of reacting to different situations".[31] The disrespect as *practice* constructed with the help of a controversial legal framing of unlawful assembly, I claim, reflects a particularly authoritarian "way of thinking" which treats the state as a sacred but fragile entity to be protected from the citizen (voice and dissent), and rights and civil liberties as potential threats to the survival of the state (*devletin bekası*, in its well-known Turkish formulation).

Lack of Institutional Reform

Yet it would be misleading to boil down authoritarian practices to legal framing alone. There is also an institutional aspect that adds to the story. Violations of freedom of assembly typically involve police actions. Ironically, already in the second half of the 1990s politicians realized that there was something wrong with the crowd management strategies of the police at public events. After the May Day incidents in Kadıköy and the disturbances in the Gazi neighbourhood in Istanbul 1996, the TNP launched a project to address problems of public order policing. Since the riot police were at the heart of the criticisms this unit has become the main subject of scrutiny.[32] These efforts culminated in an extensive 2002 report on the riot police, which paid utmost attention to the severe working conditions and lack of sufficient equipment, training, and knowledge experienced by the officers and the rank-and-file personnel deployed in this unit. These factors negatively affected and impinged on how crowd situations were (mis-) handled.[33]

In 2014, the interior ministry published the results of a project with an aim to explore several obstacles to the exercise of the right to organize public assemblies and demonstrations in Turkey. Presumably, it was due to the Gezi Park protests the year before that the project was put in place. In any case, it is remarkable that several points raised by the police officers interviewed are strikingly similar to what was said 12 years ago. The report found that the riot police are perceived as a sink unit, rank-and-file are not well-informed about their tasks and the crowds they face, and they work long hours without a break, officers do not receive enough in-service training, and so forth.[34] Reminiscent of the conclusions from the previous report, all these factors create conditions under which police officers are highly stressed, work under high pressure, and tend to overreact or mismanage situations.

The inference I draw from this narrative is that the recurrence of problems indicates a lack of solutions. In other words, the fact that there is such a big overlap between the issues diagnosed before and those identified now shows that urgent police reform has never come. Whether it is due to a lack of political will or institutional incapacity to reform, this undermines the possibility of instituting a better system of managing crowds at public demonstrations, one that is not inherently predisposed to infringe the citizens' right to peaceful protest.

Resource Allocation: A Tale of Contrasts

The problem may also lie in – or, if you will, be disguised by – the way the Turkish state allocates its own resources in a way that can be linked to the discussion above.

As I said, in comparative perspective Turkey stands out for its long record of violating the right to freedom of peaceful assembly and this is therefore a perennial question. Interestingly, Turkey stands out in yet another aspect as well. Figure 10.3 presents the share of resources allocated to the police services as percentage of total government expenditure in respective European countries in 2014. The figures show that among these states Turkey registered the highest share (more than five per cent), which is two and a half times higher than the EU average.

If we look at the share as a percentage of GDP, on the other hand, the picture seems only slightly different. In the last ten years, even though certain countries ranked higher than Turkey in this regard, it has nevertheless moved up in to that group of countries that do spend the most as a proportion of GDP. This share has steadily increased, reaching a point almost 50 per cent above the European Union average by the end of the period 2006–15 (see Figure 10.4).

Turkey's outstanding profile concerning the relative weight of its resources for police services is somewhat perplexing when we turn our gaze to public social spending and expenditures on social protection. A rough comparison of Turkey with European Union and OECD countries presents a striking picture.

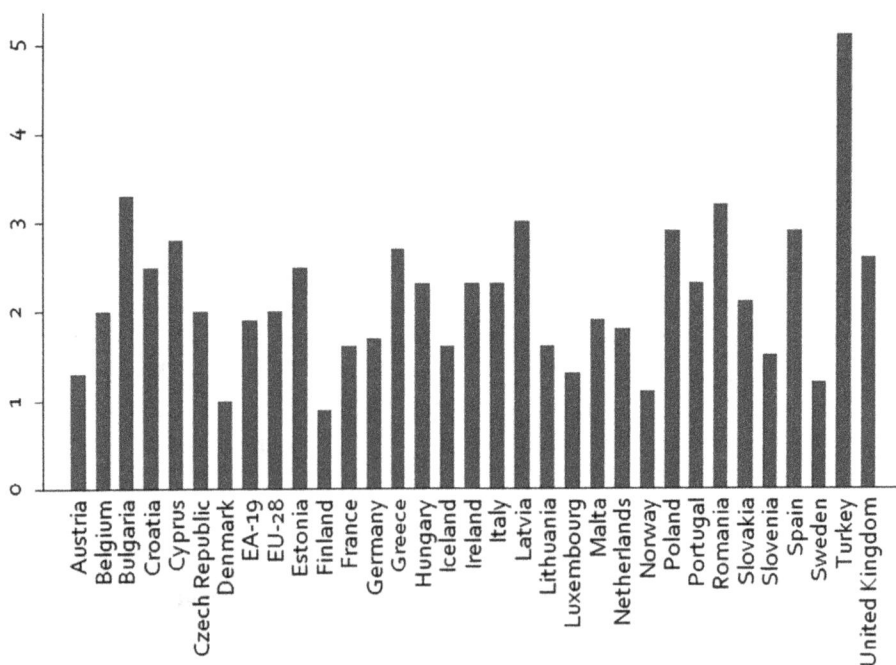

Figure 10.3 Share of resources allocated to police services (% of total expenditures), 2014. Source: Eurostat[35] & Ministry of Finance of Turkey.[36]

In terms of social spending and expenditure on social protection as a proportion of GDP, Turkey's outlays are far below the EU and OECD norm (see Figure 10.5).

It is true that in the past decade Turkey's social spending has increased, as they have in the European Union and in the OECD, at large. However, the growth in spending on public order and security services has been much higher than the growth in social spending and protection in the same period (see Figure 10.6).

The mere fact that a country directs a relatively high amount of its resources to policing and security does not unambiguously make that country authoritarian. After all, policing is also a public service and governments may have legitimate reasons to deliver it in an efficient way and hence to allocate resources for it. But the key issue that deserves attention here is the sharp contrast between Turkey's generous spending when it comes to the police and security services, and its rather poor performance in the field of social spending and protection. I believe that this contrast does not challenge the picture described above, but rather complements it. Turkey is a state that repeatedly violates its citizens' right to assemble peacefully *and* fails to fulfil its positive and negative obligations to safeguard the exercise of this right. Such a contrast may

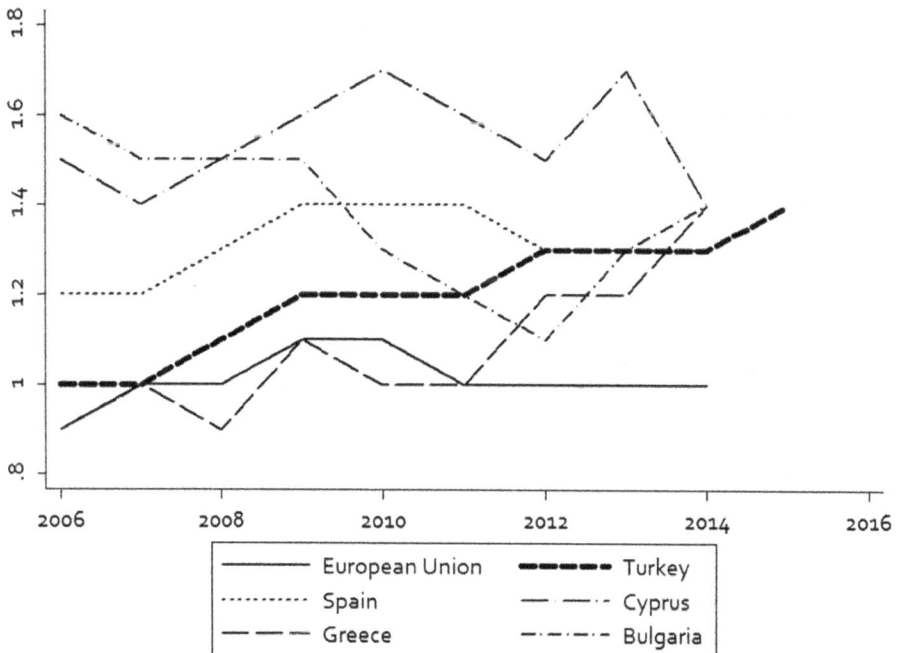

Figure 10.4 Share of resources allocated to police services as a percentage of GDP in selected countries. Source: Eurostat[37] & Ministry of Finance of Turkey.[38]

not count as an outright indicator of an authoritarian mentality, but it can surely be seen as a strong derivative of it.

Conclusion

Many countries run regular elections, have parliaments, and enjoy a more or less functioning civil society, but only a few are full democracies. One of the underlying reasons is that a great many of those political regimes exert severe restrictions on civil rights and liberties and systematically violate them. Some scholars even object to the identification of such regimes as kinds of democracy (however flawed) at all, and instead prefer to call them fractions of authoritarian regimes. In a way, these assertions can also be ascribed to Turkey. Often, we tend to talk about the history of Turkish "democracy" as one in which processes of democratization and de-democratization alternate. Under the successive single-party governments of the AKP, Turkey's political regime has also swung between these opposite paths. Lately, however, it has shown a persistent drift towards the latter direction in an accelerated fashion.

In this chapter, I have discussed the trajectory of the political regime in Turkey through the lens of the (less-than-respected) right to freedom of

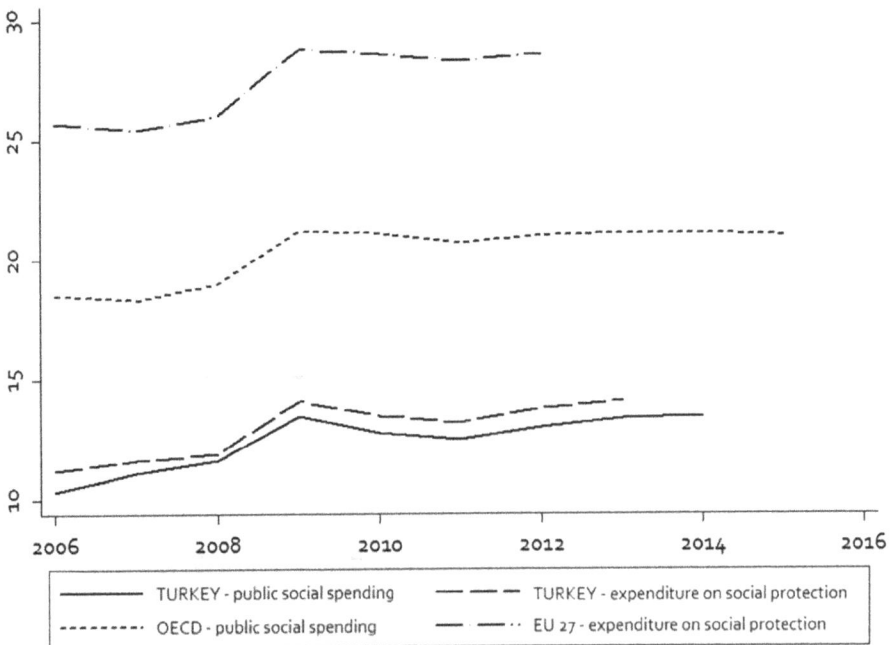

| ——————— TURKEY - public social spending | — — — TURKEY - expenditure on social protection |
| -------- OECD - public social spending | — —·· EU 27 - expenditure on social protection |

Figure 10.5 Selected government spending as a percentage of the GDP in Turkey, the EU, and the OECD. Source: OECD,[39] Eurostat.[40]

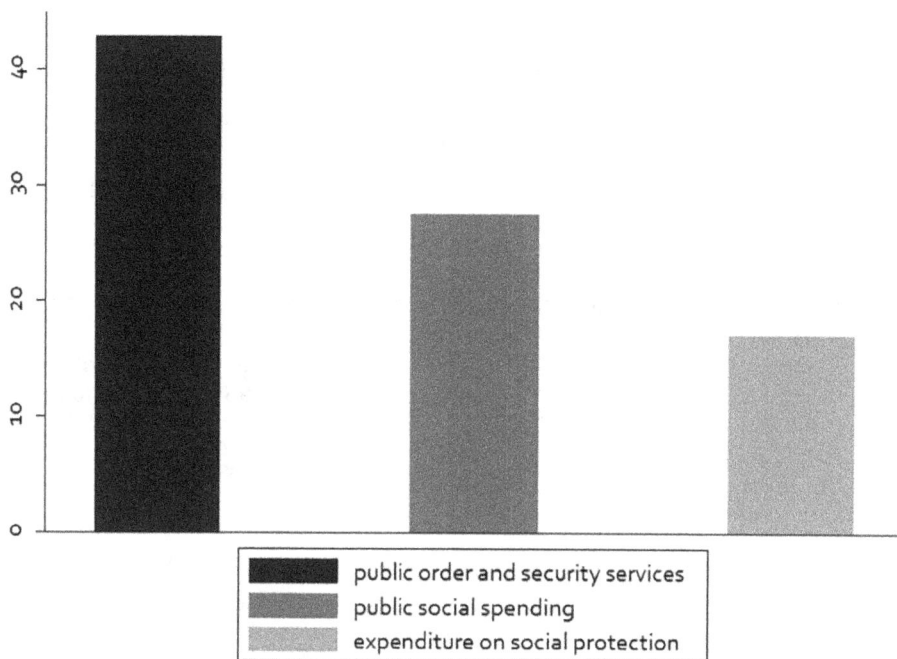

Figure 10.6 Percentage growth in selected government spending as a proportion of the GDP in Turkey, 2006–15. Source: OECD, Eurostat and Ministry of Finance of Turkey.

peaceful assembly. Turkey's extant failure to safeguard the exercise of this right is a salient and enduring problem, which I presented as an indicator of authoritarian practice. Such practice stands out in a comparative perspective and seems to be a product of a long-standing political process rather than a recent development. Indeed, recent minor revisions of the public assembly law kept the controversial clauses on unlawful assembly at the expense of the criterion of peacefulness. Not least, police powers to disperse essentially peaceful protests due to several unmet procedural requirements – above all, prior notification – set the stage for further violations of human rights in addition to the infringement of the freedom of assembly itself. Lack of institutional reform of the police complicates the situation and impedes the formation of means to prevent violations. Taken together, these practices reveal a particularly authoritarian "mentality", which treats the state as a vulnerable entity to be protected from the vocal, participant citizen, and civil rights and liberties as potential threats to the survival of the state. The comparatively high priority given to resourcing the police is, in a sense, self-evident as it contrasts with the relatively poor level of government spending on social services and protection, and therefore adds another piece to the puzzle. Thus, I conclude that an authoritarian equilibrium has been established in Turkey, one that seems, so far, likely to endure.

Notes

1. Juan J. Linz, *Totalitarian and Authoritarian Regimes* (Boulder, CO: Lynne Rienner, 2000).
2. Christian Davenport, "When Democracies Kill: Reflections from the US, India, and Northern Ireland", *International Area Studies Review* 15, no. 1 (2012): 4.
3. Sidney G. Tarrow, *War, States, and Contention: A Comparative Historical Study* (Ithaca; London: Cornell University Press, 2015).
4. Christian Davenport and David A. Armstrong, "Democracy and the Violation of Human Rights: A Statistical Analysis from 1976 to 1996", *American Journal of Political Science* 48, no. 3 (2004): 538–54; Christian Davenport, *State Repression and the Domestic Democratic Peace* (New York: Cambridge University Press, 2007).
5. Davenport, *State Repression and the Domestic Democratic Peace*.
6. Larry Jay Diamond, "Thinking about Hybrid Regimes", *Journal of Democracy* 13, no. 2 (2002): 21–35.
7. Fareed Zakaria, "The Rise of Illiberal Democracy", *Foreign Affairs* 76, no. 6 (1997): 22–43; Lucan Way and Steven Levitsky, "The Rise of Competitive Authoritarianism", *Journal of Democracy* 13, no. 2 (2002): 51–65; Andreas Schedler (ed.), *Electoral Authoritarianism: The Dynamics of Unfree Competition* (Boulder, CO: L. Rienner Publishers, Inc, 2006); Marina Ottaway, *Democracy Challenged: The Rise of Semi-Authoritarianism* (Washington, DC: Carnegie Endowment for International Peace, 2003).
8. Andreas Schedler, "The Menu of Manipulation," *Journal of Democracy* 13, no. 2 (2002): 36–50.
9. Metin Heper and E. Fuat Keyman, "Double-faced State: Political Patronage and the Consolidation of Democracy in Turkey", *Middle Eastern Studies* 34, no. 4 (1998): 259–77; Ergun Özbudun, "State Elites and Democratic Political Culture in Turkey", in *Political Culture and Democracy in Developing Countries*, ed. Larry Jay Diamond (Boulder, CO: Lynne Rienner, 1993).
10. Alfred C. Stepan (ed.), *Democracies in Danger*, Democratic Transition and Consolidation (Baltimore: Johns Hopkins University Press, 2009).
11. Ayça Çubukçu, "Turkey: The 'Progressive' Land of Repression", *Guardian*, 12 November 2011, http://www.guardian.co.uk/commentisfree/libertycentral/2011/dec/11/turkey-progressive-repression?INTCMP=SRCH.
12. Cihan Tuğal, "Democratic Janissaries? Turkey's Role in the Arab Spring", *New Left Review* 76, July/August (2012): 23.
13. Ibid.
14. John D. Inazu, *Liberty's Refuge: The Forgotten Freedom of Assembly* (New Haven, CT: Yale University Press, 2012).
15. Michael Lipsky, "Protest as a Political Resource", *American Political Science Review* 62, no. 04 (1968): 1144–58.
16. Paul Iganski, "Hate Crimes Hurt More", *American Behavioral Scientist* 45, no. 4 (2001): 626–38.
17. Orsolya Salát, *The Right to Freedom of Assembly: A Comparative Study*, Hart Studies in Comparative Public Law (Oxford: Hart Publishing, 2015).

18. Charles Tilly, "Major Forms of Collective Action in Western Europe 1500–1975", *Theory and Society* 3, no. 3 (1976): 365–75.

19. Charles Tilly, "Where Do Rights Come From?", in *Democracy, Revolution, and History*, ed. Theda Skocpol, Wilder House Series in Politics, History, and Culture (Ithaca: Cornell University Press, 1998), 57.

20. Akarsubaşı v. Turkey (European Court of Human Rights 2015).

21. "The instrument recognizing the compulsory jurisdiction of the European Court of Human Rights under Article 46 of the ECHR was deposited on 22 January 1990 for a period of three years. This also contained conditions which have been objected to on the grounds that they were in fact 'limitations' and 'reservations', and so were null and void. Turkey's acceptance of the Court's jurisdiction was prolonged for another three years on 22 January 1993 and consecutively on 22 January 1996." Semih Gemalmaz, "The CPT and Turkey", in *Protecting Prisoners: The Standards of the European Committee for the Prevention of Torture in Context* (New York: Oxford University Press, 1999), 238.

22. Ali Rıza Özer and Others, Murat Şen (Constitutional Court of the Republic of Turkey 2015).

23. TNP Department of Research, Planning and Coordination [EGM Araştırma Planlama Koordinasyon Daire Başkanlığı], "Polis 1993–1996, 2002–2003" (Ankara: Emniyet Genel Müdürlüğü, 1994–7); TNP Department of Strategy Development [EGM Strateji Geliştirme Daire Başkanlığı], "Faaliyet Raporu 2006–2013" (Ankara: Emniyet Genel Müdürlüğü, 2007–14).

24. Republic of Turkey, Ministry of Justice, General Directorate of Judicial Records and Statistics, "Number of Suspects in Trials according to the Turkish Criminal Law and Special Laws by Year", 2015, http://www.adlisicil.adalet.gov.tr/arsiv.html.

25. "HUDOC – European Court of Human Rights", accessed 8 December 2016, http://hudoc.echr.coe.int/eng.

26. For a comprehensive study, see Salát, *The Right to Freedom of Assembly*.

27. David L. Cingranelli, David L. Richards, and K. Chad Clay, "The CIRI Human Rights Dataset", 2014, http://www.humanrightsdata.com. Version 2014.04.14.

28. Ibid.

29. John D. McCarthy and Clark McPhail, "Places of Protest: The Public Forum in Principle and Practice", *Mobilization: An International Quarterly* 11, no. 2 (2006): 229–47; Don Mitchell and Lynn A. Staeheli, "Permitting Protest: Parsing the Fine Geography of Dissent in America", *International Journal of Urban and Regional Research* 29, no. 4 (1 December 2005): 796–813.

30. Another issue is related to the over-enforcement of the anti-terror law in the case of public demonstrations. Within the limits of this chapter, I set this question aside. For an informative discussion, please see Human Rights Watch, "Protesting as a Terrorist Offense: The Arbitrary Use of Terrorism Laws to Prosecute and Incarcerate Demonstrators in Turkey", 2010.

31. Linz, *Totalitarian and Authoritarian Regimes*, 162.

32. Ibrahim Cerrah, *Crowds and Public Order Policing: An Analysis of Crowds and Interpretations of Their Behaviour Based on Observational Studies in Turkey, England and Wales* (Aldershot; Brookfield, Vt: Ashgate, 1998); Kivanc Atak, "Encouraging Coercive Control: Classical Crowd Theory and Militarization in Turkish Protest Policing", *Policing and Society*, online first (2015), doi:10.1080/10439463.2015.1040796.

33. İsmail Boşnak et al., "Çevik Kuvvet Raporu' 2002 [Rapid Force Report 2002]" (Ankara: T.C. İçişleri Bakanlığı Emniyet Genel Müdürlüğü Asayiş Dairesi Bakanlığı, 2002).
34. "Toplumsal Olay Yönetiminde Özgürlük Güvenlik Dengesi [Liberty-Security Balance in the Management of Public Order Events]" (Ankara: Ministry of Interior Civil Inspection Committee, 2014).
35. Eurostat, "Government Expenditure on Public Order and Safety", 2016, http://ec. europa.eu/eurostat/statistics-explained/index.php/Government_expenditure_ on_public_order_and_safety.
36. Ministry of Finance, General Directorate of Budget and Fiscal Control, "Central Budget Expenditures [Merkezi Yönetim Bütçe Giderleri] 2006–2015", accessed 9 December 2016, http://www.bumko.gov.tr/TR,165/merkezi-yonetim-butce-giderleri-2006-2015.html.
37. Eurostat, "Government Expenditure on Public Order and Safety."
38. Ministry of Finance, General Directorate of Budget and Fiscal Control, "Central Budget Expenditures [Merkezi Yönetim Bütçe Giderleri] 2006–2015."
39. OECD, "Social Expenditure Database (SOCX)", 2016, https://www.oecd.org/ social/expenditure.htm.
40. Eurostat, "Social Protection Statistics", 2016, http://ec.europa.eu/eurostat/ statistics-explained/index.php/Social_protection_statistics.

CHAPTER 11

FREEDOM OF INFORMATION IN TURKEY: THE DEATH OF THE FREE PRESS AND THE CASE OF ACADEMICS FOR PEACE

Efe Kerem Sözeri

Introduction

From United Nations commissioners to human rights groups, there is a growing consensus among international observers that Turkey's human rights record is "alarming".[1] Yet, as detailed elsewhere in this book,[2] the Justice and Development Party (*Adalet ve Kalkınma Partisi*, AKP) has been winning elections and Erdoğan is still the most popular political leader in Turkey. Given that elections have provided cover for the rise of competitive authoritarianism in general[3] (and Turkey in particular)[4], the question of what happens between elections deserves our attention: Can we speak of "free and fair" elections if press freedoms and the freedom of expression are violated?

It is hardly surprising that the gradual decline of press freedoms in Turkey in recent years has occurred parallel to the breakdown of the country's human rights record,[5] since the right to information (be it to receive or to impart information and ideas) is not only a part of fundamental rights but also a guardian of the rights system itself against abuse,[6] including by the state.[7] Political science has long argued that a free press is essential for voters to make an informed choice[8] and necessary for the accountability of the executive.[9] There is substantial empirical evidence that a free press does indeed yield these outcomes.[10]

However, an unfree press environment – one that is shaped by powerful conglomerates owning much of the mainstream media and where the executive controls them via government contracts and media employees work under the risk of prosecution and practice wide (self-) censorship – can also be an apparatus for an autocratic regime to maintain a powerful image and silence the opposition. Turkey is one such case.

Turkey currently ranks 151 out of 180 countries in the World Press Freedom Index published by Reporters Without Borders.[11] While the country had never been a particularly safe place for journalists to work, three recent periods of difficulty stand out. First, from 2006 onwards journalists have been prosecuted in great numbers for "denigrating the Turkish nation" under provisions in the new Turkish penal code.[12] Second, from 2011 onwards an earlier amendment to the anti-terror law was put to use to prosecute journalists for "dissemination of terror propaganda" for merely reporting about the PKK conflict or criticizing security policy.[13] Finally, in the period since the 15 July 2016 coup attempt, journalists have been subject to widespread arbitrary imprisonment under the declared state of emergency.[14]

The judiciary is often accused of conflating political demands with terror propaganda, in compliance with changing government policies towards Kurdish matters. Right before the general elections of 2011, the number of Kurdish politicians, academics, and trade-unionists arrested for advocating confederalism and decentralization[15] reached "around 3,200" under the so-called Kurdistan Communities Union (in Kurdish: *Koma Civakên Kurdistan*, KCK) trials.[16] A separate trial of the members of press on "terror propaganda" charges included 44 reporters, columnists and editors, 36 of whom had been kept in pre-trial detention for more than nine months.[17] These setbacks made Turkey the worst jailer of journalists on the planet in 2012, according to the Prison Census of the Committee to Protect Journalists (CPJ).[18] The CPJ's special report, "Turkey's Press Freedom Crisis", noted that the majority of the 76 imprisoned journalists in mid-2012 were Kurdish.[19] While Turkey's Justice Ministry disputed that imprisoned journalists were investigated because of their journalistic activities,[20] a year later (2013), 24 out of 40 journalists in Turkish jails remained accused of being a member of the KCK, making Turkey the worst jailer in CPJ's census two years running.[21] Before the coup attempt, 46 members of the press were being tried for "being a member of a terror organisation", facing between seven and 25 years in jail.[22] Additionally, there were 35 journalists in Turkish jails, 17 of whom were in pre-trial detention, and 13 of whom were Kurdish reporters of the censored Dicle News Agency accused of "terrorism".[23] In the post-putsch period, these figures have quadrupled.[24]

Those who are not jailed are forced to work in a very insecure job environment. In addition to newspaper columnists and TV presenters losing their jobs due to government pressure[25]– sometimes because their bosses seek to censor all criticism of President Erdoğan[26] and sometimes at the president's direct request[27] – more than 2,000 workers in the media sector lost their jobs when the government seized and purged opposition media groups.[28] Those who were forced out of their jobs after government seizures also have to face daily harassment and intimidation.[29] In the post-putsch period, the government has abused the state of emergency powers to clampdown on oppositional media. In the first week after the coup, 131 media organizations, including TV and radio stations, newspapers, magazines, and publishing houses, were shut down purportedly for being linked to US-based cleric Fethullah Gülen's movement, which the government holds responsible for the coup attempt.[30] Two months later, 20 more TV and radio stations were shut down, this time for allegedly being linked to the PKK.[31] In the two months since the coup attempt, 620 press cards and an unknown number of passports have been revoked by the government.[32] Furthermore, a September decree cancels the passports of those people whose spouse's passport has been revoked.[33]

Even as communication technologies are increasingly able to cross porous "electronic borders", today the Turkish government's crackdown attempts to restrict the population's access to information via the internet. From corruption investigations to deadly blasts, Turkish courts and government bodies issued more than 150 gag orders.[34] As the intensity of the conflict has increased as both ISIS and PKK-affiliated groups claim responsibility for bomb attacks in Turkey, the government has developed a pattern of immediate response to gag news coverage[35] and throttle access to social media.[36]

Ordinary citizens' access to social media websites, which are recognized as an "unprecedented platform" for the freedom of expression,[37] is also under attack in Turkey. According to the 2015 Twitter Transparency Report,[38] Turkey's removal requests amounted to about 90 per cent of censored accounts and tweets worldwide. The upsurge in removal requests by Turkey in the last two years is remarkable.[39] The Turkish government is also among the top three governments in terms of content restriction requests to Facebook in the last three years.[40] Moreover, the number of censored websites has grown exponentially in the last three years. The 18,000 blocked in 2013, 25,000 in 2014, and 42,000 in 2015 make a total of over 110,000 according to figures from Engelli Web, a censorship monitor.[41] Such wide censorship of online content was made possible by two amendments to the internet law since 2011. After the December 2013 graft probe that involved Erdoğan's cabinet, fast-track censorship of online content on "personal rights" were made possible. An editor for the opposition daily *Cumhuriyet* newspaper reported that at least 150 news articles of the daily were censored on that basis in 2015.[42] In April 2015, months before the general elections, another amendment authorized cabinet members to ban online content directly. Within six months, access to websites of Kurdish news agencies, newspapers, and dozens of independent online news outlets were banned nationwide.[43]

Turkey's mainstream media has been conspicuously passive in response to these developments. The main reason for this is the media owners' fear of financial sanctions by the government, in addition to journalists' fear of persecution.[44] The majority of the national dailies and TV channels in Turkey have long been owned by a small group of conglomerates that also perform in other business sectors such as energy, finance, and construction.[45] In recent years, those groups that run favourable editorial policy towards the AKP and Erdoğan have been rewarded by government contracts and tenders, while critical ones have faced financial audits and heavy fines.[46] Starting from the 2007 sale of the Sabah-ATV media group to a company controlled by Erdoğan's son-in-law,[47] government control over media has increased. According to a pre-July putsch tally, 50 per cent of the newspapers in Turkey are "either created or transformed by" AKP governments, while 40 per cent "surrendered to the government as a result of economic and political pressures."[48] Agreeing with that figure, a veteran journalist has noted that "there are only three critical TV channels and no more than five small-scale independent newspapers left" in Turkey.[49] In the post-putsch period, two of these TV channels were among those closed, and two more pro-Kurdish newspapers, *Özgür Gündem*[50] and *Azadiya Welat*,[51] had their employees detained after police raids to their offices.

This restrictive environment and wide self-censorship was made manifest during the mainstream media's most recent election coverage. In the two months preceding the 1 November 2015 elections, the AKP's (now former) leader Davutoğlu was featured on 18 TV channels for more than 23 hours, while the co-chairs of the pro-Kurdish People's Democratic Party (*Halkların Demokratik Partisi*, HDP) were not invited to speak on any mainstream TV broadcast.[52] The public broadcaster, TRT, was criticized for its extremely biased pro-AKP election coverage, featuring the AKP leader for 30 hours while sparing only 18 minutes for HDP's co-chair Demirtaş.[53] TRT had actually been fined by the election board for very similar violations in 2014, broadcasting favourable coverage of Erdoğan many times more than other candidates before the presidential elections.[54] Even more concerning than its direct effect on election results, this lack of freedom of information has limited the scope of public debate. This has been particularly true for the most informed individuals in society who have taken risks in bringing their opinions to the public square – academics.

The case of Academics for Peace (AFP) sheds a great deal of light on the current state of press freedoms in Turkey. In the past, Turkish intellectuals who took a stand on political matters did not face such heavy repression and instead were at the heart of informed public debate in Turkey. Now, in the face of hundreds of civilians, security personnel, and militants being killed in the last year alone (making Turkey the least peaceful country in Europe)[55], academics face unrelenting accusations of "abetting terrorism" and the prospect of sacking, being prosecuted and even jailed for demanding peace. This fact unmasks the scope and reach of an authoritarian regime's power in controlling the public debate.

The Case of Academics for Peace[56]

On 11 January 2016, the Turkish civil society organization Academics for Peace released a petition signed by 1,128 academics that called on the Turkish government to end state violence and prepare the ground for meaningful negotiations to find a peace with the Kurdish political movement.[57]

Neither the claims nor the demands of the petition were particularly new. Two days before the petition, the *Human Rights Foundation of Turkey* had released a report on 162 civilian deaths that occurred during recent military operations. It reported that "at least 22 of these people were killed while they were within the boundaries of their homes, due to [live fire] or [being hit] by a missile or due to the direct stress effect of curfews on their health conditions".[58] At the same time, *Amnesty International* urged the Turkish interior minister to respect the basic human rights of civilians under curfew and ensure their access to food and healthcare.[59]

Members of the HDP, who receive most votes in Kurdish regions, were shot at while trying to rescue civilians in Cizre,[60] and went on hunger strikes at the Interior Ministry to demand officials allow ambulances to reach the wounded.[61] But it was the academics' letter that shifted the scales, both in terms of international support and domestic reactions. President Erdoğan's reaction towards the petition was less about the content and more directed at the academics who signed it. While ignoring their demands, Erdoğan called them "ignorant",[62] "so-called intellectuals",[63] and "lumpen circles" (by which he meant indolent and slothful),[64] and vowed that they would pay the price for their "treachery".[65] Indeed, a criminal investigation was opened immediately on the charges of "defamation of the state and of terrorist propaganda"[66] followed by house raids and a brief detention[67] of 33 academicians who signed the petition. Also within the first week, as many as 42 universities opened internal investigations to faculty members who signed the petition.[68] After receiving death threats, some of the academics ceased visiting their university offices or the campus, some applied for police protection and some even had to leave their cities after their pictures were published in local newspapers. One prominent threat came from a mafia leader who threatened to "spill the blood" of academics.[69]

Despite the repression and threats, the support from both domestic and international groups poured in. Over 2,000 academics from all around the world put their signatures to the AFP petition,[70] while others – including no fewer than 30 Nobel Laureates[71] – endorsed letters of support and called on the

Turkish government to "desist from threatening academics."[72] Inside Turkey, many NGOs, unions, chambers, and independent initiatives of various occupations declared support for the academics.[73]

Not everyone in Turkish academia was so supportive. Another group, Academics for Turkey (AFT), took a stand against the peace petition and released their own counter-petition with 2,071 signatures to "voice support to the [military] operations" in the East of Turkey.[74] Theirs was endorsed by the pro-government media outlets[75] and received no criticism from the government. These two samples of signatures reveal a lot about Turkish academia, pointing at significant differences in worldviews – a dichotomy that is also reflected in Turkey's geographic cleavages and goes well beyond the differences of opinion on the current government's military campaign.

Two Petitions, Two Academies

When both petitions were closed after a week, Academics for Peace had 2,212 signatories.[76] The second petition, however, decided to explicitly limit signatories to the apparently arbitrary figure of 2,071. Why, we might ask? The answer, as one organizer told the author via e-mail, was to send a signal. The figure referenced the battle of Manzikert in AD1071, the historical period after which the assimilation of indigenous populations in Anatolia at the hands of Turkish tribes began in earnest.[77] In the event, the symbolic force of this move was somewhat lost when the total number of signatories turned out to be 2,067 – an administrative error meant that four of the signatories had in fact been listed twice and duplicates had to be removed.[78]

In any event, the total data set was 4,279 academics and quite a few important basic variables within the sample were captured, including institutional affiliation, academic title, and location. For a subset of the sample, data on department and research field were also collected.[79] The sex of the signatories was unspecified on both petitions. However, based on given names, a dichotomous sex variable (woman or man) could be constructed. To distribute coding errors of unisex names evenly across the lists, half of the unisex names were coded women, and the other half were coded men on a list that is not pre-sorted by the petition type.

Of the 4,279 academics endorsing either of the two petitions, 33 per cent are women – ten percentage points lower than the national average in Turkish academia.[80] When grouped by petition, differences are wider: 54 per cent of the AFP petition signatories are women. The corresponding figure for the AFT petition is 10 per cent, and this ratio drops further to below 5 per cent among associate professors and full professors.

Men are known to have a higher tendency to have far right political views[81] but that does not explain the full story here. Signatories of the AFT petition

Academics For Peace   Academics For Turkey

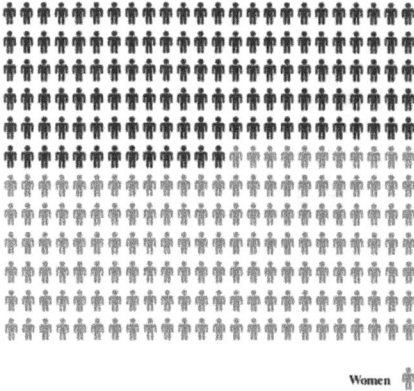

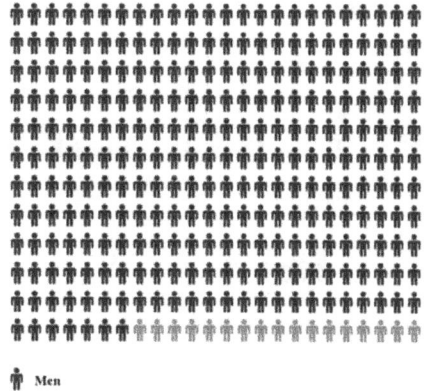

Women 👤   👤 Men

Figure 11.1   Distribution of women and men among Academics for Peace and Academics for Turkey petition signatories.

came mostly from smaller and more traditional cities, and the distribution of academic departments may have further facilitated the gap.

A subsample of 108 academics with at least a doctoral degree was randomly[82] chosen to compare the academic profiles and outputs of both groups on the following subject matter: human rights, law, national identity, military or security studies, or more particularly the Kurdish issue. Within the AFP subsample, there are scholars from political science, sociology and history who published extensively about recent Turkish political debates and the Kurdish issue.[83] However, there are not so many who did so in the AFT subsample.[84] Here, scholars of the hard sciences, such as mechanical engineers, biochemists, and medical doctors, predominate. The list also includes many theologists – in the Turkish case, researchers on Islam.

Broadly speaking, the AFP group is mainly composed of social scientists, while most AFT signatories were from hard sciences – with the significant exception of the high number of theologists among them.

A rather distinguishing character between these two lists of signatures is the network effect. Remarkably, the AFT signatures are in blocks, having quite concentrated endorsement by scholars from 168 different universities or institutions, most them being in Turkey. Just 21 of these institutions are outside Turkey and among the signatories, only 1 per cent of scholars work abroad. By contrast, the AFP petition has signatories from 433 different universities or institutions, of which 102 are in Turkey. Most of these scholars are still working at institutions located in Turkey, but a much more dispersed 33 per cent of scholars work at various institutions abroad.

Analysed at the university level, the geography of the petitions is in stark contrast (see Figure 11.4). There are some universities in Turkey with no AFP

Academics For Peace

Academics For Turkey

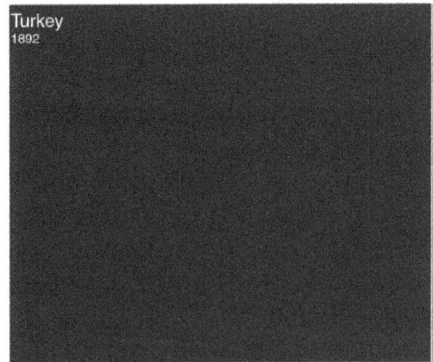

Figure 11.2 Word cloud of departments (font size by frequency) among Academics for Peace and Academics for Turkey petition signatories.

signatures at all, while majority of Peace scholars are from three big cities: Istanbul, Ankara, and Izmir. Outside Turkey, Academics for Turkey scholars are almost non-existent while AFP endorsements are very dominant in European and North American institutions.[85]

Only a handful of Turkish universities have reached the global top-500 rankings, including Istanbul University, the Middle East Technical University (METU), Boğaziçi University, Istanbul Technical University (ITU), and Bilkent University.[86] A sub-sample taken from these top five universities in Turkey shows that 85 per cent of signatures went for the AFP petition. The AFP petition also has signatories from the most prestigious institutions globally, including

Academics For Peace

Academics For Turkey

Figure 11.3 Distribution of Academics for Peace and Academics for Turkey signatures by institutional location (dichotomous: Turkey or Abroad).

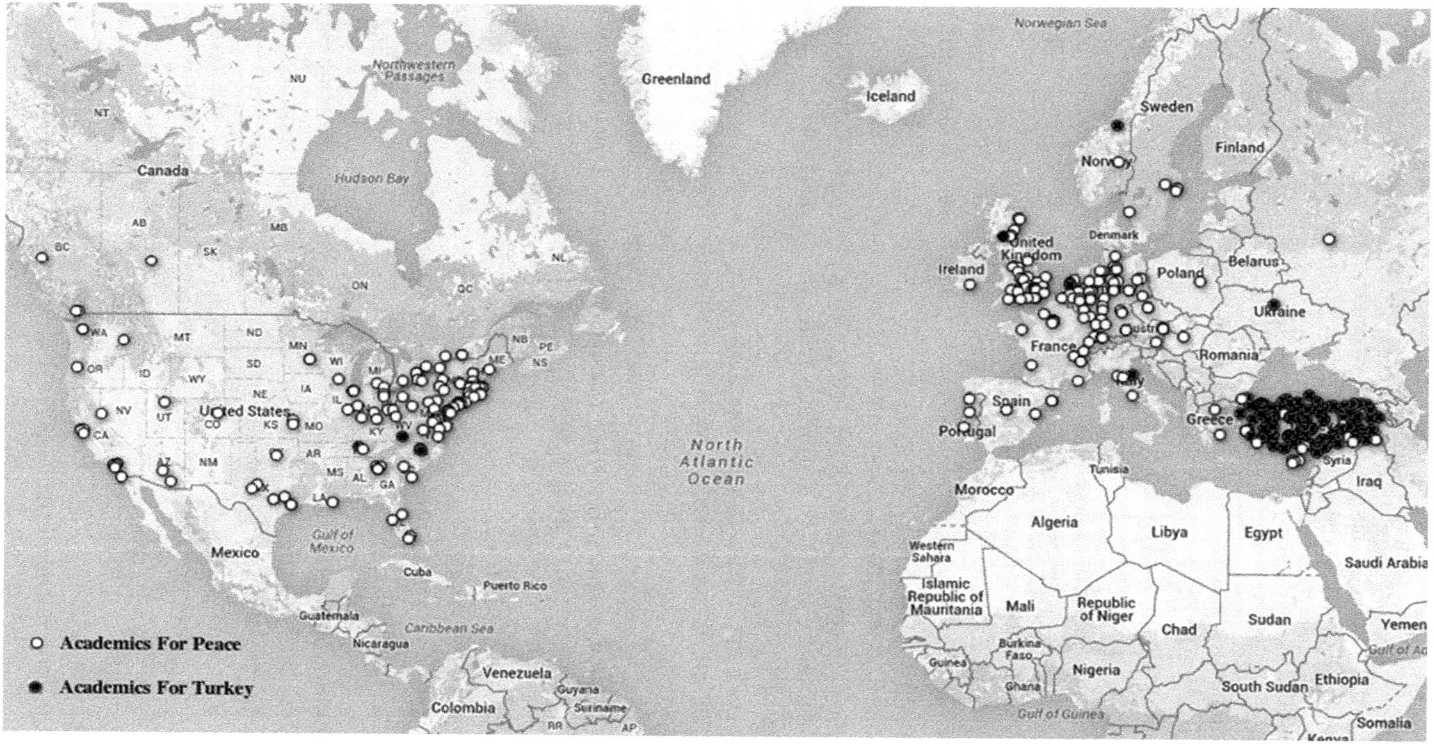

Figure 11.4 Distribution of signatories by institutional location (institutions in Europe and North America only). Credit: Google-Map data © 2017.

Harvard, Oxford, Cambridge, Princeton, Stanford, Yale, and MIT. Again, in a striking contrast, most of the universities where the AFT petition has a majority or an absolute majority are smaller-sized and recently founded institutions in the periphery.

Arguably, the quality of education and established academic tradition in an institution have much to do with critical thinking – which is the defining property of the AFP petition in the current Turkish political context. However, the institutional context is also critical for analysis of the distribution of Peace and Turkey petitions in other ways.

Most of the institution where the AFT petition signatures are dominant were founded after the AKP came to power in 2002. In fact, half of the state universities (56 of them) and two-thirds of the private universities (51 of them) in Turkey were founded under AKP single-party governments.[87] Some were converted from vocational school and others were founded following legislative amendments that lifted costly requirements for establishing private universities. This expansion, however, came at no expense to the taxpayer: public education spending flatlined during this period and Turkey remains at the bottom among the OECD countries in terms of education spending as a percentage of GDP.[88]

The underlying motivation for opening many low-quality institutions is political. Recent doctoral research looking at the minutes of the parliamentary sessions and commissions where MPs discussed the budget for new universities shows that since the 1970s, almost every Turkish MP has pushed for the construction of a university in his or her electoral district because universities are seen as boosting the local economy.[89] By 2008 (the sixth year of AKP government) all 81 provinces in Turkey had finally achieved at least one university. Most of these new universities, however, were focused on administrative sciences or theology, with little regard for local needs. Instead, as one researcher remarks, they were founded by governments motivated "to establish universities under the dominance of certain ideologies, and to consolidate political power via academic and administrative cadres".[90] A survey of academics working at these newer universities concluded that most are troubled by a lack of time and money for research, and many admit that they are publishing solely to gain a title.[91]

This institutional and political context helps to explain the overrepresentation of theologists among the AFT signatures and the less critical voice of its petition. As the name suggests, AFT is a patriotic exercise and oriented towards the political needs of today's Turkey. The persecution of Academics for Peace can therefore be read as the manifestation of a new "national" academy deployed in an ideological-political sense as a weapon of the state apparatus. While the Turkey vs abroad and top universities vs the recently founded dichotomies illustrated above help to profile their supporters and illustrate the nature and the purpose of these two petitions, the same dichotomies also determine the consequences of signing either of the petitions. While all AFP signatories are subject to political oppression, harassment, threats, and administrative and criminal investigations, it should be noted that these consequences occur differently among the provincial universities compared to the established universities in three big cities of Istanbul, Ankara, and Izmir.

Fully 90 per cent of those who work in an institution located in Istanbul, Ankara or Izmir signed the Peace petition. In the provinces, the percentage of support for the AFP petition drops to 40 per cent, while at some of universities where the AFT petition was very popular, only a handful of signatures dared to sign the Peace petition.[92] That minority was hit hardest. As the increasing political pressure on Academics for Peace turned into a nation-wide witch hunt, the first casualties were indeed from those smaller cities where the AFP academics were the minority (see Figure 11.5).[93]

A case in point illustrates the hardship and the actual risks of signing the AFP petition. Assistant Professor Latife Akyüz, the single signatory of the AFP petition at Düzce University, graduated from METU's academic training programme in 2002. After collecting data on ethnicity and gender dynamics in the rural town of Hopa in the Black Sea region of Turkey, she finished her dissertation as a visiting scholar in New York and Indiana.[94] After working on various projects on the education of displaced young female villagers in Turkey and abroad, she started at the sociology department at Düzce University, which had only recently been founded. However, immediately after her signature on the AFP petition was made public, the university board suspended her, police raided her house, and she had to flee the city and take refuge elsewhere due to death threats. Since the local court imposed a travel ban under the criminal investigation for "terror propaganda", she is not allowed to leave Turkey.[95]

In March, after two months of political pressure and criminal investigations, the AFP released a report on the systemic abuse that their members had been subjected to.[96] It found that 464 had been subject to administrative investigation, 30 had been fired, five had been forced to resign, and 27 had been suspended from their university positions. It also reported that 153 academics had been prosecuted in criminal investigations for "terror propaganda" or for "denigrating the Turkish nation", and 33 had been detained by authorities. Despite the political pressure, on 10 March 2016, four members of the AFP – Esra Mungan, Kıvanç Ersoy, Muzaffer Kaya, and Meral Camcı – held a press conference in Istanbul to share these widespread violations of rights with the public and repeat their demands.[97] The latter two, Kaya and Camcı, were among those fired for signing the petition.

On 13 March, TAK (a PKK-affiliated armed group)[98] executed a car-bomb attack in Ankara that resulted in the loss of 37 civilian lives.[99] During his remarks condemning the attack, President Erdoğan used the occasion to target

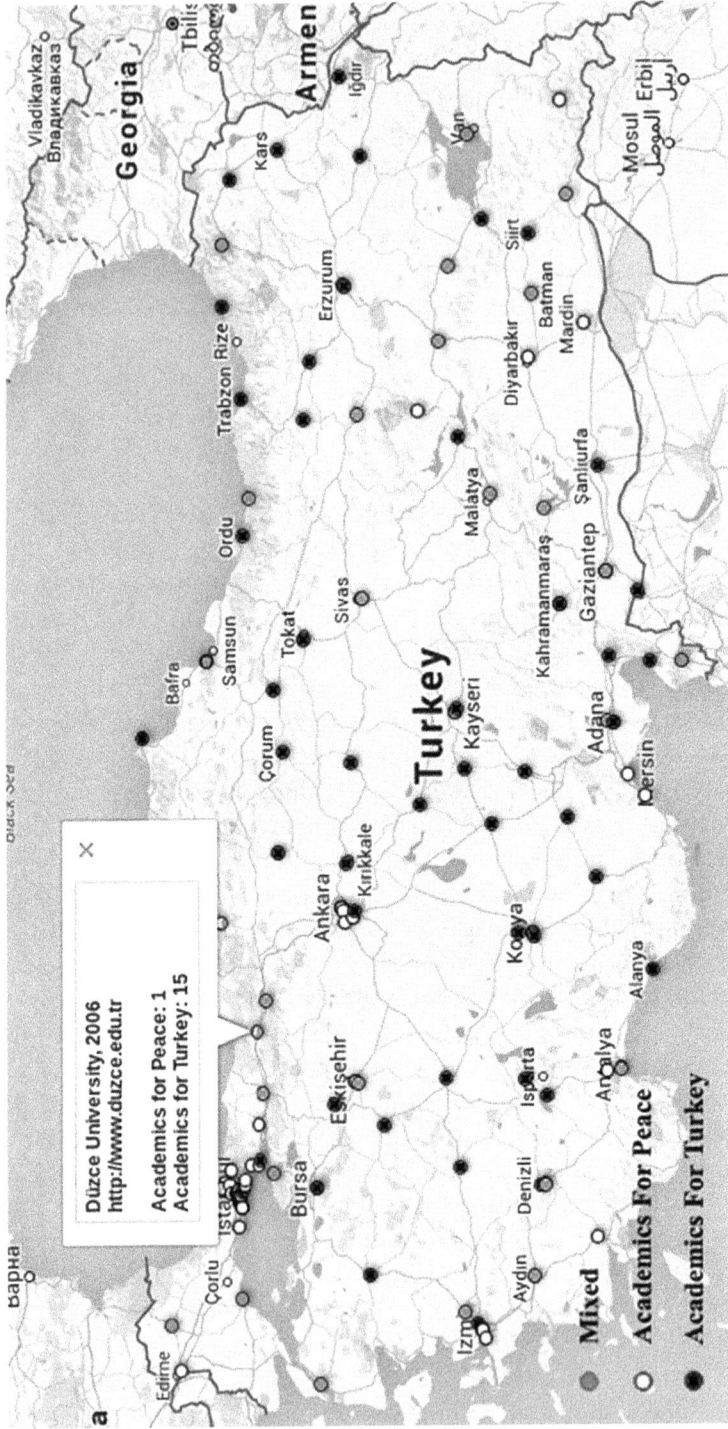

Figure 11.5 Map of academic institutions in Turkey by the majority of signatures. Credit: Google-Map data © 2017.

his critics, especially academics, and called for a widening of the definition of terrorism:

> There is no difference between a terrorist holding a weapon or a bomb and one who uses a pen or a title, nor with those giving orders to terrorists to reach their aims. It does not change the fact that they are terrorists, whether they are an academic, a journalist, or an NGO chair. One who explodes a bomb may be a terrorist, but those who allow the act to achieve this aim are his accomplices. We need to renew the definitions of terror and terrorist and amend the penal code accordingly. This is not a matter of press freedom, or freedom of association.[100]

Promptly, an Istanbul prosecutor, İrfan Fidan, issued arrest orders for the four academics of the press conference on charges of "making terrorist propaganda".[101] In the indictment bill, the prosecutor further claimed that the AFP petition was "in concert" with the demands of the PKK leadership.

Here it should be noted that prosecutor İrfan Fidan was appointed to his current position after the reshuffling of the police chiefs and prosecutors that occurred in the wake of the 2013–14 graft probe involving Erdoğan's son, Bilal.[102] His first act as the newly-appointed prosecutor of the investigation was to order the destruction of tapes of conversations from the register of official evidence. These tapes were leaked to the press but removal of them from the case was a sign that the charges of corruption would be dropped which in fact happened in October 2014.[103] Fidan was also the prosecutor who demanded arrest of journalists Can Dündar and Erdem Gül for reporting about Turkish intelligence agency trucks carrying arms to jihadists in Northern Syria.[104] An amendment that allowed greater government control over the judiciary, which was made possible after the graft probe, was strongly criticized by local and international groups alike[105] but Erdoğan's government went ahead regardless and weakened the separation of powers. Appointment of favourable prosecutors and judges to such critical cases was made possible by Erdoğan's appointment of AKP-linked names to the Supreme Council of Judges and Prosecutors (*Hâkimler ve Savcılar Yüksek Kurulu*, HSYK),[106] and the minister of justice's subsequent assumption of more control over the council's work.[107]

On 21 April 2016, at the first court hearing for the academics, prosecutor İrfan Fidan had a change of heart, demanded the release of the four, and dropped the charges of "terrorism propaganda". However he renewed accusations that the four had "denigrated the Turkish nation",[108] which remains subject to the justice minister's approval to open an investigation.

In the meantime, the scope of the administrative and criminal investigation for the remaining AFP members was widened further. Administrative investigations were opened on about 510 academics, leading to the dismissal of 43 and suspension of a further 85. Nine of those under investigation chose to resign. 412 academics came under criminal investigation, and besides the four academics who remained in pre-trial detention for a month, 41 more were detained for various periods of time.[109] During the post-putsch purges, the Turkish government dismissed 2,346 university staff under state of emergency powers,[110] 44 of whom were AFP scholars.[111]

Conclusion: Universal Values and Turkish Isolation

However irresponsible the government's reaction to the Academics for Peace petition may seem and however abrupt the discontinuation of "terror" related charges was, they still indicate the political nature of the judicial procedure from the very beginning. Moreover, the vilification of the academics, a typical AKP response to political opposition, may have served as signifiers of the "naming, blaming and framing"[112] phases of the fight against terror rhetoric. However, this would fall short of explaining why academics were chosen at this point, since this was not the first time that they were challenging government policies.

In 2008, during the debate for the lifting of headscarf ban in Turkey, more than 400 academics released a statement to extend the scope of freedoms even beyond the religious freedoms, and raised concern for the polarization in the country between the pious and the secularists.[113] Following the start of the Ergenekon trials in 2008, around 300 academics and artists signed a petition to demand that this investigation delve as possible into the true nature of this organization in Turkey.[114] At the start of the Gezi protests in May 2013, which challenged Erdoğan's power most significantly, both the Boğaziçi [115]and Bilkent[116] academics released petitions to support environmentalists' demands, and condemn police violence towards protesters. After the government reaction to the graft probe of December 2013, 100 academics and authors penned a letter to the government to stop covering up the corruption.[117] In March 2015, just three months before parliamentary elections, a group of law professors, including heads of faculty, higher bureaucrats and even a former Supreme Court judge released a statement raising concerns about the proposed shift to a presidential system in Turkey.[118] Moreover, only a few months before the AFP petition, a group of academics from Bilgi University released a statement condemning the suicide bomb attack at a peace march in Ankara, which criticized the government for failing to investigate previous attacks thus holding it responsible for events.[119]

The petition of 10 January 2016 was not even the first time that the AFP groups had released a statement critical of the government's security policy. As early as 2013, a smaller group that later formed the core of the AFP had issued a peace petition.[120] And right before the curfews began in August 2015, the AFP made an urgent call for peace.[121]

Addressing the question of why Erdoğan chose to threaten academic freedoms at the particular post-AFP juncture, one of the AFP signees wrote: "[In Turkey,] the value of an educated person is judged less by her inherent intellectual qualities and more by the ideological support she can offer for a political cause or the immediate material benefits her position accrues."[122]

The degradation of academic freedoms and the loss of value for intellectual production may lie in Turkey's isolation from the rest of world – not only in terms of losing credibility in international affairs, but as a value system. When Turkey's proposals for the Middle East were all but rejected by the global community, Erdoğan's foreign policy advisor İbrahim Kalın (himself a scholar of international relations) described Turkey's isolation as a "precious loneliness". In other words, Turkey's failures in foreign policy were a result of the rest of the world's moral weakness.[123]

While it is true that the AKP's pious voter base is easily sold on foreign policy failures, convincing the domestic audience that Turkey's loneliness is indeed valuable has concerning repercussions. In a society that has long been shaped by "internal and external enemies" (the Sykes-Picot and Sevrès treaties remain relevant subjects in daily conversation) and in which the Armenian, Assyrian, and Greek genocides remain hot-button issues, to propose to replace universal principles of rule of law and human rights with national standards sets a dangerous precedent.

The debate between the two academes that we have discussed in this chapter, therefore, plays out as Erdoğan's personal struggle for authority, and likely wins him support – but only within Turkey. Even though it consolidates power and wins elections, its influence ends at Turkey's borders as the moral high ground has been long lost abroad. The call made by the Academics for Peace, however, is without borders and is animated not by personality but by universal principles and ideas. In Erdoğan's Turkey, journalists and academics are under increasing pressure, losing their jobs, and jailed for merely voicing their criticism while a "nationalist" moment suppresses any discontent. But, we might ask, who really benefits from this, and for how long?

Appendices

Appendix A: Original English translation of the Academics for Peace petition released on 11 January 2016.[124]

As academics and researchers of this country, we will not be a party to this crime!

The Turkish state has effectively condemned its citizens in Sur, Silvan, Nusaybin, Cizre, Silopi, and many other towns and neighbourhoods in the Kurdish provinces to hunger through its use of curfews that have been ongoing for weeks. It has attacked these settlements with heavy weapons and equipment that would only be mobilized in wartime. As a result, the right to life, liberty, and security, and in particular the prohibition of torture and ill-treatment protected by the constitution and international conventions have been violated.

This deliberate and planned massacre is in serious violation of Turkey's own laws and international treaties to which Turkey is a party. These actions are in serious violation of international law.

We demand the state to abandon its deliberate massacre and deportation of Kurdish and other peoples in the region. We also demand the state to lift the curfew, punish those who are responsible for human rights violations, and compensate those citizens who have experienced material and psychological damage. For this purpose, we demand that independent national and international observers be given access to the region and that they be allowed to monitor and report on the incidents.

We demand the government to prepare the conditions for negotiations and create a road map that would lead to a lasting peace which includes the demands of the Kurdish political movement. We demand inclusion of independent observers from broad sections of society in these negotiations. We also declare our willingness to volunteer as observers. We oppose suppression of any kind of the opposition.

We, as academics and researchers working on and/or in Turkey, declare that we will not be a party to this massacre by remaining silent and demand an immediate end to the violence perpetrated by the state. We will continue advocacy with political parties, the parliament, and international public opinion until our demands are met.

Appendix B: Author's English translation of the Academics for Turkey petition of 12 January 2016.[125]

As academics of this country, we will stand with our state and our nation!

As everyone knows, the universities are leading institutions in societal change; they influence the society with their work on economics, technology and in social fields. Therefore, it is important that they are autonomous, independent, and impartial. However, when the subject matter is the survival of the Turkish state and Turkish nation, the academics who were raised by the opportunities provided by this country cannot be impartial. Under these circumstances, an academic can only take sides with the Turkish republic which is a democratic, secular, social state under the rule of law as defined in our Constitution.

Recently, a herd of so-called academics who use every chance to defame and shame the Turkish republic by libel and slander have accused our state of torture and massacre. However, the same herd never mentions the innocent babies massacred, the children orphaned, and the police officers and soldiers wounded or martyred by the PKK, a terrorist organization that uses rights and freedoms as an excuse. They never mention the national, religious and historical wealth destroyed by this group either. They keep harping on about democracy and peace, but they never name the terrorist organization that is responsible for these murders.

Unfortunately, our country has not only been subject to treacherous and despicable PKK terror, and to the bullets of this heinous organization, but has also been attacked by the so-called academics who were raised at the heart of this country to contribute to its scientific and technological development. Their stand and their words are more dangerous and heinous than the bullets of the bandits in the mountains. Like every other reasonable person, we all know that the so-called peace demanded by this herd from the Turkish republic is hiding the real purpose of their barricade politics. We believe that their petition which lacks every academic and moral sensitivity and reality has but one purpose – to hindering the struggle against terrorism and to demoralize our security forces.

Consequently, as a refusal of this malicious and ignorant petition disguised as an academic one, and in a desire to express and represent the real feelings and thoughts of the Turkish nation, we sign this petition to let everyone know that we support the operations being conducted in Sur, Silvan, Nusaybin, Cizre, Silopi, and in many other places. We openly express that we completely stand with our police officers and soldiers who carefully, sincerely and bravely fight there for the peace of the nation and for those orphaned children left behind.

Like those teachers and academics who went to the frontline with their students to fight against the enemy in Gallipoli, we promise and declare that we will stand against these heinous attacks with our pens and with our hearts, we will support the operations to the end, and at the same time, we will do our duty for establishing the peace as defined by the Turkish republic.

We expect the support of academics who think like us and are in love with Turkey.

Notes

1. See: Zeid Ra'ad Al Hussein, "Need for transparency, investigations, in light of 'alarming' reports of major violations in south-east Turkey", United Nations Office of The High Commissioner for Human Rights, 10 May 2016, ohchr.org/EN/NewsEvents/Pages/DisplayNews.aspx?NewsID=19937&LangID=E. Nils Muižnieks, "Respect for human rights has deteriorated at an alarming speed in recent months in the context of Turkey's fight against terrorism", Council of Europe Commissioner for Human Rights, 14 April 2016, https://www.coe.int/en/web/commissioner/-/turkey-security-trumping-human-rights-free-expression-under-threat. Dorian Jones, "Rights Group: Turkey on 'Trajectory Towards Authoritarianism'", *Voice of America*, 27 January 2016, www.voanews.com/content/turkey-human-rights-watch-report/3165445.html. See also: Human Rights Watch, Country Chapter: Turkey, *World Report 2016*, 27 January 2016, https://www.hrw.org/world-report/2016/country-chapters/turkey (all accessed 27 May 2016).
2. See: Karabekir Akkoyunlu, "Electoral Integrity in Turkey: From Tutelary Democracy to Competitive Authoritarianism", in this book.
3. Steven Levitsky and Lucan A. Way, *Competitive Authoritarianism: Hybrid Regimes after the Cold War* (Cambridge, 2010).
4. See: "Turkey's Gradual Shift to Authoritarianism", in this book.
5. For a detailed account of the latter, see "The state of democracy and human rights in Turkey (2002–15)" section of the "Turkey's Gradual Shift to Authoritarianism" chapter in this book.
6. Pippa Norris, "The Role of the Free Press in Promoting Democratization, Good Governance and Human Development", *matters*, 45.4–6 (2006), p. 66.
7. George A. Donohue, Philip Tichenor et al., "A Guard Dog Perspective on the Role of the Media", *Journal of Communication*, 45–2 (1995), pp. 115–28.
8. Arthur Lupia and Mathew D. McCubbins, *The Democratic Dilemma: Can Citizens Learn What They Need to Know?* (Cambridge, 1998).
9. See especially Amartya Sen, *Development as Freedom* (New York, 1999).
10. Aymo Brunetti and Beatrice Weder, "A free press is bad news for corruption", *Journal of Public Economics*, 87, 7–8, (2003), pp. 1801–24, doi:10.1016/S0047-2727(01)00186-4.
11. Reporters Without Borders, *2016 World Press Freedom Index: Turkey*, available at https://rsf.org/en/turkey (accessed 27 May 2016).
12. Freedom House, *Freedom of the Press 2007: Turkey*, available at https://freedomhouse.org/report/freedom-press/2007/turkey (accessed 27 May 2016).
13. Ibid., *Freedom of the Press 2012: Turkey*, available at https://freedomhouse.org/report/freedom-press/2012/turkey (accessed 27 May 2016).
14. P24, 'Journalists in State of Emergency – 19', 25 September 2016, available at www.platform24.org/en/articles/407/journalists-in-state-of-emergency---19 (accessed 1 October 2016).
15. Under the programme written by PKK's jailed leader Abdullah Öcalan, Koma Civakên Kurdistan, Union of Kurdistan Communities, known by its Kurdish acronym, KCK. See full Turkish text of the *KCK Charter* at https://tr.wikisource.org/wiki/KCK_Sözleşmesi (accessed 27 May 2016).
16. Cengiz Çandar, *'Leaving the mountain': How may the PKK lay down arms?*, (Istanbul, 2011), available at http://tesev.org.tr/wp-content/uploads/2015/11/

Leaving_The_Mountain_How_May_The_PKK_Lay_Down_Arms_Freeing_The_
Kurdish_Question_From_Violence.pdf (accessed 27 May 2016).
17. Constanze Letsch, "Turkey puts 44 journalists on trial for terrorism and
backing pro-Kurd group" *Guardian*, 11 September 2012, available at https://
www.theguardian.com/world/2012/sep/10/turkey-journalists-trial-terrorism-
kurd (accessed 27 May 2016).
18. Committee to Protect Journalists, *2012 prison census: 232 journalists jailed
worldwide* (1 December 2012), available at https://cpj.org/imprisoned/2012.
php (accessed 27 May 2016).
19. Ibid., *Turkey's Press Freedom Crisis* (October 2012), available at https://cpj.org/
reports/2012/10/turkeys-press-freedom-crisis.php (accessed 27 May 2016).
20. Ibid., "Appendix II: Government Responses, From Justice Minister Sadullah
Ergin", 10 July 2012, available at https://cpj.org/reports/2012/10/turkeys-
press-freedom-crisis-appendex-ii-government-responses.php (accessed 27 May
2016).
21. Committee to Protect Journalists, *2013 prison census: 211 journalists jailed
worldwide* (1 December 2013), available at https://cpj.org/imprisoned/2013.
php (accessed 27 May 2016).
22. Bianet, "KCK Basın Davasında Mahkeme AYM Kararını Beklemeyi Reddetti",
8 April 2016, available at http://bianet.org/bianet/medya/173747-kck-basin-
davasinda-mahkeme-aym-kararini-beklemeyi-reddetti (accessed 27 May 2016).
23. Journalists Union of Turkey, *Hapisteki gazeteciler* (10 June 2016), available at
http://tgs.org.tr/cezaevindeki-gazeteciler/ (accessed 10 June 2016).
24. P24, ibid.
25. Freedom House, *Freedom of the Press 2016: Turkey*, available at https://
freedomhouse.org/report/freedom-press/2016/turkey (accessed 27 May 2016).
26. Roy Greenslade, "Turkish newspaper columnist fired over tweet critical of
Erdoğan" *Guardian*, 27 July 2015, available at http://www.theguardian.com/
media/greenslade/2015/jul/27/turkish-newspaper-columnist-fired-over-tweet-
critical-of-erdogan (accessed 27 May 2016).
27. *Hurriyet Daily News*, "'Instructions rain down on Turkish media every day', says
prominent editor-in-chief", 11 February 2014, http://www.hurriyetdailynews.
com/instructions-rain-down-on-turkish-media-every-day-says-prominent-
editor-in-chief-.aspx?pageID=238&nID=62306&NewsCatID=338 (accessed
27 May 2016).
28. *Turkish Minute*, "More than 2,000 Turkish journalists lost their jobs in past 7
months, union says", 9 April 2016, available at https://www.turkishminute.
com/2016/04/09/2000-turkish-journalists-lost-jobs-past-7-months-union-
says/ (accessed 27 May 2016).
29. Nina Ognianova, "'Erdoğan is killing journalism', says *Today's Zaman* editor
forced out after takeover", *Committee to Protect Journalists*, April 2016, available
at https://cpj.org/blog/2016/04/erdogan-is-killing-journalism-says-todays-
zaman-ed.php (accessed 27 May 2016).
30. BBC, "Turkey coup attempt: More than 130 media outlets shut", 28 July 2016,
available at www.bbc.com/news/world-europe-36910556 (accessed 1 October
2016).
31. Committee to Protect Journalists, "Turkey closes at least 20 TV, radio stations",
29 September 2016. Available at https://cpj.org/2016/09/turkey-closes-at-least-
20-tv-radio-stations.php (accessed 1 October 2016).

32. Reporters Without Borders, "State of Emergency, State of Arbitrary", 19 September 2016, available at https://rsf.org/sites/default/files/turquie.etatdur-gence.eng_def_pdf (accessed 1 October 2016).
33. *Turkish Minute*, "Journalist Can Dündar's wife banned from travelling abroad", 3 September 2016, available at https://www.turkishminute.com/2016/09/03/journalist-can-dundars-wife-banned-travelling-abroad/ (accessed 1 October 2016).
34. *Hurriyet Daily News*, '10 issues Turkish media is banned from reporting on', 27 November 2014, available at http://www.hurriyetdailynews.com/10-issues-turkish-media-is-banned-from-reporting-on.aspx?pageID=238&nID=74904 &NewsCatID=339 (accessed 27 May 2016).
35. Efe Kerem Sözeri, "Turkey cracks down on Twitter and Facebook after deadly car bombing", *Daily Dot*, 18 February 2016, available at http://www.dailydot.com/politics/turkey-ankara-bombing-twitter-social-media/ (accessed 27 May 2016).
36. Internet censorship researcher group, Turkey Blocks, employed new techniques to monitor access to social media websites from Turkey in comparison to the access from the rest of the world. Results of this monitoring shows that Turkish ISPs no longer entirely block access to Twitter and Facebook after gag orders, but severely *throttle* the bandwidth to these sites, making access unusably slow for users from Turkey. See: D8 News, "Twitter and Facebook Restricted in Turkey following Ankara bombing", 17 February 2016, available at https://d8news.com/twitter-facebook-restricted-turkey-following-ankara-bombings-683 (accessed 27 May 2016). See a list of throttling response times in 2016: Efe Kerem Sözeri, "Social media throttling in Turkey points to wartime censorship efforts", 27 August 2016, *Daily Dot*, available at www.dailydot.com/layer8/turkey-wartime-censorship-syria/ (accessed 1 October 2016).
37. Yaman Akdeniz, *Media Freedom on the Internet: An OSCE Guidebook* (Vienna, 2016), available at http://www.osce.org/netfreedom-guidebook?download=true (accessed 27 May 2016).
38. Twitter, *Transparency Report 2015: Jul 1–Dec 31, Removal requests* (February 2016), available at https://transparency.twitter.com/removal-requests/2015/jul-dec (accessed 27 May 2016).
39. Twitter, *Transparency Report: Turkey* (February 2016), available at https://transparency.twitter.com/country/tr (accessed 27 May 2016).
40. Facebook provides number of "restricted content" at the request of governments since July–December 2013 period on "Government Requests Report" page, available at https://govtrequests.facebook.com/ (accessed 27 May 2016).
41. EngelliWeb, *İstatistikler* (27 May 2016), available at https://engelliweb.com/istatistikler/ (accessed 27 May 2016).
42. Efe Kerem Sözeri, "#Tekil11: Devlet Sansürüne Alternatif Çözümler", *Bianet*, 26 December 2015, available at http://bianet.org/biamag/ifade-ozgurlugu/170536-tekil11-devlet-sansurune-alternatif-cozumler (accessed 27 May 2016).
43. Kerem Altıparmak and Yaman Akdeniz, "5651, Madde 8/A: Büyük Sansür Donanmasının Amiral Gemisi", *Güncel Hukuk*, 11–143 (November 2015), pp. 38–42, available at http://cyber-rights.org.tr/docs/Guncel_Hukuk_8A.pdf (accessed 27 May 2016).
44. Ahmet Şık, *Journalism Under Siege* (March 2016), available at https://www.englishpen.org/wp-content/uploads/2016/03/JournalismUnderSiege_FINAL.pdf (accessed 27 May 2016).

45. Dilek Kurban and Ceren Sözeri, *Caught in the wheels of power*, "Annex 3. Which Media Group Owns which Companies", (Istanbul, 2012), pp. 77–81, available at http://tesev.org.tr/wp-content/uploads/2015/11/Caught_In_The_Wheels_Of_ Power_The_Political_Legal_And_Economic_Constraints_On_Independent_ Media_And_Freedom.pdf (accessed 27 May 2016).

46. Ceren Sözeri, "Hükümeti destekleyene bütün kapılar açılıyor", *P24*, 26 March 2016, available at http://platform24.org/medya-izleme/813/-hukumeti- destekleyene-butun-kapilar-aciliyor (accessed 27 May 2016). Also, Ahmet Şık, ibid., p. 13.

47. Mehul Srivastava, Benjamin Harvey and Ercan Ersoy, 'Erdogan's Media Grab Stymies Expansion by Murdoch, Time Warner', *Bloomberg*, 4 March 2014, available at http://www.bloomberg.com/news/articles/2014-03-03/erdogan- thwarts-murdoch-as-graft-probe-reveals-turkey-media-grab (accessed 27 May 2016).

48. Ahmet Şık, ibid, p. 11.

49. Yavuz Baydar, "Imminent collapse of journalism in Turkey", *Index on Censorship*, 3 May 2016, available at https://www.indexoncensorship. org/2016/05/yavuz-baydar-imminent-collapse-of-journalism-in-turkey/ (accessed 27 May 2016).

50. Committee to Protect Journalists, "Turkish police raid newspaper office, detain at least 23 employees", 29 August 2016, available at https://cpj.org/2016/08/ turkish-police-raid-newspaper-office-detain-at-lea.php (accessed 1 October 2016).

51. Al Jazeera, "Turkey: Pro-Kurdish newspaper Ozgur Gundem shut down", 28 August 2016, available at www.aljazeera.com/news/2016/08/turkey-pro- kurdish-newspaper-ozgur-gundem-shut-160817044530537.html (accessed 1 October 2016).

52. Ceren Sözeri, "Medyanın 1 Kasım seçim dönemi karnesi", *P24*, 4 November 2016, available at http://platform24.org/p24blog/yazi/1174/medyanin-1- kasim-secim-donemi-karnesi (accessed 27 May 2016).

53. Meltem Özgenç, "MHP leader pledges to bring public broadcaster to book for one-sided election coverage", *Hurriyet Daily News*, 27 October 2015, available at http://www.hurriyetdailynews.com/mhp-leader-pledges-to-bring-public- broadcaster-to-book-for-one-sided-election-coverage.aspx?pageID=449& nID=90414&NewsCatID=338 (accessed 27 May 2016).

54. Fırat Kozok, "!AKP döneminde 25'inci kez...TRT'ye tarihi ceza", *Cumhuriyet*, 12 November 2014, available at http://www.cumhuriyet.com.tr/haber/turkiye/ 139557/AKP_doneminde_25_inci_kez...TRT_ye_tarihi_ceza.html (accessed 27 May 2016).

55. Institute for Economics and Peace, *Global Peace Index 2016* (London, 8 June 2016), available at http://static.visionofhumanity.org/sites/default/files/GPI% 202016%20Report_2.pdf (accessed 27 May 2016).

56. An earlier version of this section was published online at the Platform for Independent Journalism (P24) website as "Two petitions, two academia: TR's loneliness & universal values", *P24*, 31 January 2016, available at platform24. org/en/articles/344/two-petitions--two-academia-trs-loneliness-ve-universal- values (accessed 27 May 2016). Author wishes to thank P24 for granting permission to republish sections, and to Translate For Justice editors for their suggestions on an earlier draft.

57. Academics for Peace, "We will not be a party to this crime! (in English, French, German, Spanish, Arabic, Russian, Greek)", 10 January 2016, available at https://barisicinakademisyenler.net/node/63 (accessed 27 May 2016).
58. Human Rights Foundation of Turkey, *Fact Sheet on Declared Curfews between 11 December 2015–8 January 2016 and Violations of Right to Life Against Civilians According to the Data of HRFT Documentation Centre* (9 January 2016), available at en.tihv.org.tr/fact-sheet-on-declared-curfews-in-turkey-between-11-december-2015-8-january-2016/ (accessed 27 May 2016).
59. Af Örgütü (Amnesty Turkey), Uluslararası Af Örgütü'nden Bakan Ala'ya Mektup (1 January 2016). https://www.amnesty.org.tr/icerik/2/1777/uluslararasi-af-orgutu (accessed 27 May 2016).
60. *Bianet*, "Demirtaş: Fire Opened on Group Coming to Retrieve Wounded in Cizre", 20 January 2016, available at bianet.org/english/politics/171326-demirtas-fire-opened-on-group-coming-to-retrieve-wounded-in-cizre (accessed 27 May 2016).
61. *Bianet*, "MPs on Hunger Strike: Don't Hinder Ambulances", 29 January 2016, available at bianet.org/english/human-rights/171626-mps-on-hunger-strike-don-t-hinder-ambulances (accessed 27 May 2016).
62. *Hurriyet Daily News*, "Erdoğan slams academics over petition, invites Chomsky to Turkey", 12 January 2016, www.hurriyetdailynews.com/erdogan-slams-academics-over-petition-invites-chomsky-to-turkey.aspx?PageID=238&NID=93760&NewsCatID=338 (accessed 27 May 2016).
63. *Today's Zaman*, "Erdoğan accuses academics of being fifth column", 12 January 2016. (*Today's Zaman* digital archive is deleted after *Zaman Daily* was seized by the government. Part of its digital archive can be reached via Internet Archive's Wayback Machine, available at https://web.archive.org/web/20160113163536/http://www.todayszaman.com/national_erdogan-accuses-academics-of-being-fifth-column_409479.html (accessed 27 May 2016).)
64. *Bianet*, "President Erdoğan: Lumpen, Half-Portion Intellectual", 20 January 2016, available at bianet.org/english/politics/171334-president-erdogan-lumpen-half-portion-intellectual (accessed 27 May 2016).
65. *Hurriyet Daily News*, "Turkish president vows 'treasonous' academics will pay the price", 20 January 2016, available at www.hurriyetdailynews.com/turkish-president-vows-treasonous-academics-will-pay-the-price.aspx?pageID=238&nID=94128&NewsCatID=339 (accessed 27 May 2016).
66. Quirin Schiermeier, "Turkish scientists rocked by accusations of supporting terrorism", *Nature*, 18 January 2016, doi:10.1038/nature.2016.19179. Available at http://www.nature.com/news/turkish-scientists-rocked-by-accusations-of-supporting-terrorism-1.19179 (accessed 27 May 2016).
67. Ece Toksabay, "Turkey detains 27 academics accused of signing 'peace declaration'", Reuters, 15 January 2016, available at www.reuters.com/article/us-turkey-kurds-idUSKCN0UT0RF (accessed 27 May 2016).
68. *Bianet*, "Investigations, Universities' Reactions against Academics", 15 January 2016, available at http://bianet.org/english/human-rights/171152-investigations-universities-reactions-against-academics (accessed 27 May 2016).
69. Gülten Üstündağ, "After Erdoğan, crime boss threatens academics who call for peace", *Today's Zaman*, 13 January 2016, available at https://web.archive.org/web/20160113180731/http://www.todayszaman.com/national_after-erdogan-

crime-boss-threatens-academics-who-call-for-peace_409569.html (accessed 27 May 2016).
70. Academics for Peace, "Bu suça ortak olmayacağız! – Yurtdışı akademisyenler ve entellektüeller desteği (International academics and intellectuals support to our petition)", 10 January 2016, available at https://barisicinakademisyenler. net/node/145 (accessed 27 May 2016).
71. International Human Rights Network of Academies and Scholarly Societies, "As of today, 30 Nobel Laureates have endorsed the attached 19 January 2016, H.R. Network's Statement to the Government of Turkey regarding the plight of hundreds of Turkish academic colleagues" (25 January 2016), available at http://www7.nationalacademies.org/humanrights/cs/groups/chrsite/docum ents/webpage/chr_170428.pdf (accessed 27 May 2016).
72. International Human Rights Network of Academies and Scholarly Societies, 25 January 2016, available at http://www7.nationalacademies.org/humanrights/ cs/groups/chrsite/documents/webpage/chr_170306.pdf (accessed 27 May 2016).
73. A collection of news articles and statements of support are listed under "Dayanışma" (Solidarity) section of the Academics for Peace website: https:// barisicinakademisyenler.net/Dayan%C4%B1%C5%9Fma (accessed 27 May 2016).
74. Türkiye için Akademisyenler ("Academics for Turkey"), "As academics of this country, we will stand with our state and our nation!", 12 January 2016 (see Appendix B for author's English translation), available at http://turkiyeici nakademisyenler.com/ (accessed 27 May 2016).
75. A collection of news articles are listed under "Us in the Media" section of the Academics For Turkey website: http://turkiyeicinakademisyenler.com/medya. htm (accessed 27 May 2016).
76. Barış için Akademisyenler ("Academics for Peace"), "Bu suça ortak olmayaca-ğız! Em ê nebin hevparên vî sûcî!", 20 January 2016, available at http://barisici nakademisyenler.net/node/62.html. Archived from the original on 21 January 2016: https://archive.is/7U5Gt (accessed 27 May 2016). The author of this chapter and one of the editors of this book are among the signees of the Academics For Peace petition.
77. John Julius Norwich, A Short History of Byzantium (New York, 1997), pp. 232–42.
78. Türkiye için Akademisyenler ("Academics for Turkey"), İmza Listesi, available at http://www.turkiyeicinakademisyenler.com/imza.htm. Archived from the original source on 21 January 2016. https://archive.is/Eyj6k (accessed 27 May 2016).
79. Efe Kerem Sözeri, Data set on the signees of Academics for Peace and Academics for Turkey petitions (2 February 2016), available at https://docs.google.com/ spreadsheets/d/1Ljf78XOe1q-MUB53H36VvRlXF-uxpAOShK6_9LLtow8/edit? usp=sharing (accessed 27 May 2016).
80. Higher Education Board of Turkey, Higher Education Management System, Öğretim Elemanı İstatistikleri ("Faculty Members Statistics"), available at https:// istatistik.yok.gov.tr (accessed 27 May 2016).
81. Marcel Lubbers, Mérove Gijsberts and Peer Scheepers, "Extreme right-wing voting in Western Europe", European Journal of Political Research, 41 (2002), pp. 345–78, available at doc.utwente.nl/61252/1/Lubbers02extreme.pdf (accessed 27 May 2016).

82. To ensure representation from both petitions and all academics titles, the following stratified random sampling rule was followed: After assigning a random number to each individual (between *1* and *subset size*) within each of the eight subsets (two petitions: *Peace* and *Turkey*; four titles: PhD, assistant professor, associate professor, and full professor), individuals with the number ten or smaller were chosen. Due to randomization, there were more than ten academics from each subset, taking the size of the sample to 108. Distribution of the sample by title is 25 PhDs, 31 assistant professors, 27 associate professors, and 25 full professors. Similar to the full data, overall percentage of women in the sample is 28, with 58 per cent within the Peace and 8 per cent within the Turkey sub-samples.

83. One prominent example is Prof. Kerem Öktem from Oxford University (currently at Graz University) who is a leading scholar on Turkish nationalism and recent history: https://scholar.google.com/citations?user=YUFIhzAAAAAJ (accessed 27 May 2016).

84. Even among the very few social scientists within the Academics for Turkey sub-sample, publications on the recent political debates are lacking, indicating more interest in Late Ottoman or Early Republican periods.

85. Using Google Fusion Tables, the institutional affiliations of the signatures (disregarding the independent scholars) are mapped to illustrate the geographical contrasts: Efe Kerem Sözeri, *Geographical distribution of Academics for Peace and Academics for Turkey signees by university affiliation* (27 January 2016), available at https://www.google.com/fusiontables/DataSource?docid=11-VfKbs3m8PLwS3HzWidIJVZCAZz5fc5QGiPOuz5E&pli=1map:id=3 (accessed 27 May 2016).

86. See *Shanghai Ranking*: http://www.shanghairanking.com/World-University-Rankings-2015/Turkey.html, *Webometrics*: http://www.webometrics.info/en/Asia/Turkey, or *US News*: http://www.usnews.com/education/best-global-universities/turkey (all accessed 27 May 2016).

87. Higher Education Board of Turkey, *Higher Education Management System, 'Birim İstatistikleri, Genel Bilgiler, Üniversitelerimiz' ('Unit Statistics, General Information, Our Universities')*, available at https://istatistik.yok.gov.tr (accessed 27 May 2016).

88. OECD, *Education spending (indicator)* (2016), doi: 10.1787/ca274bac-en. Available at https://data.oecd.org/eduresource/education-spending.htm (accessed on 27 May 2016).

89. Sultan Kavili Arap, "Türkiye yeni üniversitelere kavuşurken: Türkiye'de yeni üniversiteler ve kuruluş gerekçeleri" ("As Turkey welcomes new universities: The new universities in Turkey and their founding causes"), *Ankara Üniversitesi SBF Dergisi*, 65:1, (2010), available at dergiler.ankara.edu.tr/dergiler/42/1346/15599.pdf (accessed on 27 May 2016).

90. Ibid, p. 22.

91. Didem Doğan, "Yeni Kurulan Üniversitelerin Sorunları ve Çözüm Önerileri", ("Problems of recently found universities and solutions") *Bülent Ecevit Üniversitesi Journal of Higher Education and Science, 3(2)*, (2013), pp. 108–16, doi: 10.5961/jhes.2013.065, available at higheredu-sci.beun.edu.tr/text.php3?id=1610 (accessed on 27 May 2016).

92. The map can be reproduced by using predefined filters for majority/minority status along with other variables. On Figure 5, *Black*: Academics for Turkey absolute majority, *Gray*: Academics for Peace minority, *White*: Academics for Peace majority. Efe Kerem Sözeri, ibid.

93. *France 24*, "Turkey arrests academics over pro-Kurd petition", 15 January 2016, available at www.france24.com/en/20160115-turkey-arrests-academics-over-pro-kurd-petition-pkk-erdogan (accessed on 27 May 2016).
94. Latife Akyüz, *Ethnicity and gender dynamics of living in borderlands: The case of Hopa-Turkey*, (Thesis submitted to the Graduate School of Social Sciences of Middle East Technical University) (Ankara, June 2013), available at http://etd.lib.metu.edu.tr/upload/12615957/index.pdf (accessed on 27 May 2016).
95. Latife Akyüz, "35 günde hayatımın akışı değişti" ("My life has changed in 35 days"), *BBC Turkish*, 23 January 2016, available at http://www.bbc.com/turkce/haberler/2016/01/160123_akademisyen (accessed on 27 May 2016).
96. Academics for Peace, Report of the current situation (21 March 2016), available at https://barisicinakademisyenler.net/node/168 (accessed on 27 May 2016).
97. Beyza Kural, "İstanbul'daki Barış İçin Akademisyenler: Barış Talebinde Israrcıyız", *Bianet*, 10 March 2016, available at http://bianet.org/bianet/ifade-ozgurlugu/172877-istanbul-daki-baris-icin-akademisyenler-baris-talebinde-is rarciyiz (accessed on 27 May 2016).
98. Frederike Geerdink, "After Ankara bombing, questions over PKK-TAK ties resurface", *Middle East Eye*, 4 March 2016, available at www.middleeasteye.net/columns/after-ankara-bomning-questions-over-pkk-tak-ties-resurface-1097219220 (accessed 27 May 2016).
99. BBC, "Ankara bombing: Erdogan seeks to widen terrorism definition", 14 March 2016, available at http://www.bbc.com/news/world-europe-35807987 (accessed 27 May 2016).
100. Author's translation, BBC, "Erdoğan: Terörist tanımı yeniden yapılmalı" ("Erdoğan: Terrorist definition should be renewed"), 14 March 2016, available at http://www.bbc.com/turkce/haberler/2016/03/160314_erdogan_ankara (accessed 27 May 2016).
101. Alison Abbott, "Turkish academics jailed for 'making terrorism propaganda'", *Nature* (16 March 2016), doi:10.1038/nature.2016.19586, available at http://www.nature.com/news/turkish-academics-jailed-for-making-terrorism-propaganda-1.19586 (accessed 27 May 2016).
102. Canan Coşkun, "Savcı İrfan Fidan: 25 Aralık'la gelen şöhret Yargıç İsmail Yavuz: Saldırganları bırakmıştı", *Cumhuriyet*, 28 November 2015, available at http://www.cumhuriyet.com.tr/haber/turkiye/434805/Savci_irfan_Fidan__25_Aralik_la_gelen_sohret__Yargic_ismail_Yavuz__Saldirganlari_birakmisti.html (accessed 27 May 2016).
103. *Hurriyet Daily News*, "Turkey's massive corruption case dropped by prosecutor", 17 October 2014, available at http://www.hurriyetdailynews.com/turkeys-massive-corruption-case-dropped-by-prosecutor.aspx?PageID=238&NID=73149&NewsCatID=338 (accessed 27 May 2016).
104. Veysel Ok, "Dündar ve Gül hakkındaki iddianameye altı temel itiraz", P24, 31 January 2016, available at http://platform24.org/hukuk-birimi/1322/dundar-ve-gul-hakkindaki-iddianameye-alti-temel-itiraz (accessed on 27 May 2016).
105. Orhan Coskun, "Turkish graft scandal triggers feud over judicial independence", *Reuters*, 10 January 2014, available at http://www.reuters.com/article/us-turkey-corruption-idUSBREA090JR20140110 (accessed on 27 May 2016).
106. Mesut Hasan Benli, "Turkish president sends AKP-linked lawyers to key judges and prosecutors council", *Hurriyet Daily News*, 27 October 2014, available at

http://www.hurriyetdailynews.com/turkish-president-sends-akp-linked-lawyers-to-key-judges-and-prosecutors-council.aspx?pageID=238&nID = 73513&NewsCatID=338 (accessed on 27 May 2016).

107. Blaise Misztal and Jessica Michek, "HSYK Elections and the Future of Judicial Independence in Turkey", *Bipartisan Policy Centre*, 12 December 2014, available at http://bipartisanpolicy.org/blog/hsyk-elections-and-the-future-of-judicial-independence-in-turkey/ (accessed on 27 May 2016).

108. Margaret Owen, "'To demand peace is not a crime': Turkish academics on trial", *Open Democracy*, 29 April 2016, available at https://www.opendemocracy.net/5050/margaret-owen/to-demand-peace-is-not-crime-turkish-academics-on-trial (accessed on 27 May 2016).

109. Ebru Erdem Akçay, "Latest data on rights violations regarding #AcademicsFor-Peace. Opportunistically targeted in the post-coup chaos", Twitter, 5 August 2016, available at https://twitter.com/eerdem/status/761649066983976960 (accessed on 1 October 2016).

110. Alison Abbott, "Turkey sacks thousands of university staff", 6 September 2016, available at www.nature.com/news/turkey-sacks-thousands-of-university-staff-1.20550 (accessed 1 October 2016).

111. FIDH, "Turkey: 'Academics for Peace' suffer purge", 12 September 2016, available at https://www.fidh.org/en/region/europe-central-asia/turkey/turkey-academics-for-peace-suffer-purge (accessed 1 October 2016).

112. Lisel Hintz, "Adding Insult to Injury: Vilification as Counter-Mobilization in Turkey's Gezi Protests", *POMEPS*, 6 June 2016, available at http://pomeps.org/2016/06/06/adding-insult-to-injury-vilification-as-counter-mobilization-in-turkeys-gezi-protests/ (accessed on 27 May 2016).

113. *Bianet*, Akademisyenler, "Türban Üzerinden Kutuplaşmaya Karşı Özgürlükleri Genişletelim" Diyor, 11 February 2008, available at http://bianet.org/bianet/ifade-ozgurlugu/104802-akademisyenler-turban-uzerinden-kutuplasmaya-karsi-ozgurlukleri-genisletelim-diyor. Also see more concrete demands in a renewed petition text: Bianet, Akademisyenlerden Yeni Bildiri: Özgürlükten de Laiklikten de Vazgeçmeyiz, 11 February 2008, available at http://bianet.org/bianet/ifade-ozgurlugu/104805-akademisyenlerden-yeni-bildiri-ozgurlukten-de-laiklikten-de-vazgecmeyiz (both accessed on 27 May 2016).

114. *Haberturk*, '300 aydından bildiri', 14 August 2008, available at www.haberturk.com/gundem/haber/91132-300-aydindan-bildiri (accessed 27 May 2016).

115. Oda TV, Boğaziçi hocalarından Gezi bildirisi, 30 May 2013, available at http://odatv.com/bogazici-hocalarindan-gezi-bildirisi--3005131200.html (accessed 27 May 2016).

116. Akademisyenler.org, "Bilkent Üniversitesi öğretim üyeleri 'Gezi Parkı' olaylarına ilişkin bildiri yayınladı", 6 June 2013, available at http://akademisyenler.org/bilkent-universitesi-ogretim-uyeleri-gezi-parki-olaylarina-iliskin-bildiri-yayinladi/. Also see Bilkent Law Faculty call to all parties to over the law. Radikal, "Bilkent hukuk hocaları: Hukuk sınırlarında kalınmalı", 3 June 2013, available at http://www.radikal.com.tr/turkiye/bilkent-hukuk-hocalari-hukuk-sinirlarinda-kalinmali-1136117/ (both accessed 27 May 2016).

117. Gerçek Gündem, "100 aydından hükümete 'Yetti Artık' uyarısı", 24 January 2014, available at http://www.gercekgundem.com/guncel/20396/100-aydindan-hukumete-yetti-artik-uyarisi (accessed 27 May 2016).

118. *Hurriyet*, "Akademisyenlerden 'başkanlık' bildirisi: Kişiye özgü rejim Türkiye'yi dünya sisteminden koparır", 9 March 2015, available at http://www.hurriyet. com.tr/akademisyenlerden-baskanlik-bildirisi-kisiye-ozgu-rejim-turkiye-yi-dunya-sisteminden-koparir-28403823 (accessed 27 May 2016).
119. Birgün, "Bilgi Üniversitesi'nden Bir Grup Akademisyen Ankara Katliamı'na ilişkin bildiri yayınladı", 15 October 2015, available at http://www.birgun.net/ haber-detay/bilgi-universitesi-nden-bir-grup-akademisyen-ankara-katliami-na-iliskin-bildiri-yayinladi-92429.html (accessed 27 May 2016).
120. Taner Yener, "Akademisyenler barış için imza attı", *Milliyet*, 3 April 2014, available at http://www.milliyet.com.tr/akademisyenler-baris-icin-imza-atti/ gundem/gundemdetay/03.04.2013/1688681/default.htm (accessed 27 May 2016).
121. AGOS, "202 akademisyenden acil ateşkes çağrısı", 7 August 2015, available at www.agos.com.tr/tr/yazi/12411/202-akademisyenden-acil-ateskes-cagrisi (accessed 27 May 2016).
122. A. Kadir Yildirim, "Why Turkey's government is threatening academic freedom", *Washington Post*, 16 January 2016, available at https://www.washingtonpost. com/news/monkey-cage/wp/2016/01/16/why-turkeys-growing-anti-intellectu-alism-is-a-threat-to-academic-freedom/ (accessed on 27 May 2016).
123. Andranik Israyelyan, "Turkey: From 'zero problems' to 'precious loneliness'", *Foreign Policy Journal*, available at www.foreignpolicyjournal.com/2015/06/ 19/turkey-from-zero-problems-to-precious-loneliness/ (accessed 27 May 2016).
124. Academicians For Peace, "We will not be a party to this crime! (in English, French, German, Spanish, Arabic, Russian, Greek)", 10 January 2016, available at https://barisicinakademisyenler.net/node/63 (accessed 27 May 2016).
125. Türkiye için Akademisyenler ("Academics for Turkey"), "As academics of this country, we will stand with our state and our nation!" (author's own English translation), 12 January 2016, available at http://turkiyeicinakademisyenler. com/ (accessed 27 May 2016).

CHAPTER 12

DIGITAL CULTURAL CAPITAL AS A COUNTER-HEGEMONIC TOOL IN TURKEY

Dağhan Irak

Introduction

Turkey has been under the spotlight regarding its social media use since the 2010s. The country has 41 million Facebook users, which corresponds to a penetration rate of 52.8 per cent, 15 points higher than the European average[1]. According to a 2015 survey by the Reuters Institute for the Study of Journalism,[2] among 18 developed nations, urban Turkey ranks first in using social media as a news source (67 per cent), using Facebook as a news source (69 per cent), and using Twitter as a news source (33 per cent) while it ranks last in trust of the media. Meanwhile, the Turkish government led by Recep Tayyip Erdoğan, following the 2013 Gezi Park protests (where the number of retweeted messages skyrocketed over 15 million)[3], caught the eyes of the international community with its repeated ban attempts and content removal requests on Twitter and Facebook, as well as lawsuits against social media users.

A very lively debate has ensued over whether social media sites such as Facebook or Twitter play a role in the new wave of social movements that began with Occupy Wall Street in the United States and spread to Europe and the Middle East. The new dissidents' preoccupations are typically based on precarious economic, social, and political conditions in localized spaces. Nevertheless, this is a worldwide wave linked to the globalized digital realm, or in the words of Castells, the global "network society".[4] The general debate is mirrored among scholars too. Techno-optimists glorify the use of new media tools in social movements and emphasize their democratizing capacity, whereas techno-pessimists play down this role and even consider these tools as an extension of existing economically-driven class injustice.

The aim of this paper is not to pick sides in this debate. This is not because I do not have a point of view regarding the role of social media or new media tools in social movements. However, in the great scheme of things, the tools being overly discussed may be misleading in positioning the network society within social theory. The question that I feel compelled to ask is not *what* tools people use in social movements or *why*, but rather *how* they have made or failed to make these tools useful in their causes. In doing this, I introduce two important concepts to the discussion, one from media studies and one from sociology: the digital divide and (digital) cultural capital.

Digital divide used to be defined as "having access or not" to the new information technologies. Since the introduction of Web 2.0, which enabled users to become content creators, this definition has become obsolete. The digital divide, as I will elaborate a little later, may be now be defined as "being able or unable to create content and outreach". This requires a set of cultural and social capacities. To break them down, I will draw on Pierre Bourdieu, and his conception of different kinds of capital. Content creation is linked to cultural capital, as outreach is to social capital. The possession of these in different amounts results in different forms of new media use.

Turkey is an interesting case in this respect. The authoritarian shift, roughly between the modern secularists and the traditional Islamo-conservatives and outlined at length in other chapters of this book in a much more detailed way, has since 2010 become a matter of cultural hegemony. This hegemony has consolidated as the Islamo-conservative AKP, having recorded electoral victories thanks to its massive network of social relations, has started to impose its own codes to the cultural field (notably in media and education) and jettison those (such as alcohol consumption, abortion, LGBTQI rights and scientific secular education) that are incompatible with them. This has caused an expectable concern among the secular, modern, urban, middle classes of the country who are the principal beneficiaries of nation's cultural capital and who are already being excluded from social and economic networks dominated by the AKP. The June 2013 Gezi protests were, to a significant extent, a response by these formerly dominant classes to rising AKP hegemony in the streets and online. While the protest in the streets were dispersed by an unprecedented wave of police violence costing many lives, the online dissent has since become a constant nuisance which Erdoğan and his party-state have not been able to handle, despite bans, restrictions, lawsuits and threatening statements.

This chapter will therefore seek to explain how this situation emerged in the context of Turkey's digital divide and unevenly distributed cultural capital. In so doing, I hope to offer a new insight into why social media has appeared to be so crucial in the wake of the authoritarian shift in Turkey.

The Digital Divide in Turkey

As a result of Turkey's aggressive neo-liberal trade policies, access to Information and Communication Technology (ICT) has dramatically improved over the last decade, as imports from countries like China or Taiwan, marketed under Turkish brands, have become progressively more affordable. At the same time, internet access is still quite expensive in Turkey, since the partly state-run Türk Telekom still constitutes a *de facto* monopoly. Most ISPs use Türk Telekom's telephone infrastructure to provide service to their clients. An exception is the cable company, Türksat, which is also state-owned. Nevertheless, the internet penetration rate in Turkey has been rising steadily, reaching 59.6 per cent as of December 2014.[5] According to a survey by the Pew Research Centre,[6] the number of adults using the internet at least occasionally or reporting owning a smartphone in Turkey has increased by 31 points (from 41 to 72 per cent) in the last three years, making the country an exception even among other developing nations. The nation's overwhelming interest in ICTs can be explained by the culture of consumerism adopted by Turkey after the 1980 coup.

Until the 1980s, Turkish industrial policy privileged import substitution, leading to chronic current account deficits and unsustainable foreign debts, a condition exacerbated by the oil shocks and Turkey's isolation from the rest of the world following the invasion of Cyprus in 1974. Turkey's shift to neoliberalism commenced in early 1980 when then finance minister Turgut Özal announced a set of measures that opened the economy on a free-market model based. However, it was only after the 12 September 1980 coup that Özal was empowered to implement IMF and World Bank-backed reforms, under the sponsorship of the post-coup junta. The Turkish labour movement, which had been highly active through the 1970s, was immediately quashed in the wake of the military takeover, and the social movements of the 1970s were brought to heel, as were political parties, workers' political associations, the members of which were either murdered or ended up in torture chambers.

General Evren's junta appointed Özal as a super-minister to carry out the economic transformation plan. Özal later became the prime minister following semi-democratic elections in 1983, where only parties and candidates approved by the junta could run. Social movements and citizens' participation in politics were completely purged, replaced by a culture of consumerism in which the population was salved through the wholescale import of previously unavailable luxury products and entertainment such as television and football, both of which were actively financed by the government. Another objective of the Özal period was to restore national pride, wounded by Turkey's ostracism internationally after the illegal occupation Cyprus and the stain on the country's reputation in the wake of widespread human rights violations during the 1980–3 period of military rule.

Telecommunications somehow played a great part in doing that. Technologies like satellite television and telephony were introduced to restore Turkey's "connection to the wider world," in a context in which the United States had become the country's sole international backer. In the 1980s, VCRs and video rental joints were the pioneers of this technological proto-globalization. In the 1990s, this nascent culture blossomed when the first satellite dishes and mobile phones were introduced to Turkey. It was no surprise that the first private satellite TV channel, *Star1*, had been clandestinely founded by Turgut Özal's son, mostly using state equipment to broadcast football matches to millions in awe of this novel form of entertainment. Turkish viewers also followed the first Gulf War through satellite on *CNN International* and *Star1*'s rebroadcasts.

The internet was thus introduced to Turkish end-users in the mid 1990s, with the basic telecommunications and entertainment-friendly consumerist setting firmly in place. It is thus fair to argue that the recent sharp rise in access to ICTs is the result of an increase in service capacity, rather than demand, which as we have seen has been high for three decades. We may argue that availability is a bigger concern in Turkey than affordability; even expensive brands like Samsung and Apple, or the overpriced internet services, can easily find a consumer base in the country. In sum, since the 1980s, every available technology has been seized by Turkish consumers with relish, and increasing access to and demand for ICTs in Turkey witnessed over the last decade is mostly related to the widespread development of broadband internet infrastructure and 3G–4G mobile networks over that period.

All of this points to the conclusion that the digital divide problem, in its classic definition as an "access issue", seems to be more or less resolved in Turkey. Nevertheless, we have yet to explain precisely how the ICT take up has played such a major role in the "Kulturkampf" between Recep Tayyip Erdoğan's regime and its dissidents, to the extent that the regime systematically blocks access to the internet after any event that might generate a negative reaction against it. To answer this, we need to first redefine the digital divide and see how this applies directly within Turkey.

Digital Divide 1.0

The "digital divide", which can be roughly defined as the gap between "those who have" and "those who do not" have access to ICTs, was introduced in the mid 1990s to define the challenge (particularly of governments) of managing the distribution of access in the emerging fully-networked global society. Once exclusively a subject of governmental research, the "digital divide" has since become a powerful tool for applying social theory to the (new) media studies, as it indicates different dimenssions of inequality between different layers of society, and what consequences these might bring for the society we live in.

However, treating the "digital divide" as a mere problem of access is gradually becoming obsolete as ICTs now also play an important sociocultural role in society as well as an economic function. One of the main arguments this chapter defends is the inevitable necessity of redefining the "digital divide" to avoid a misleading over-optimism regarding the resolution of the access issue. However, before discussing that, we should first present the "digital divide" in its original form, and establish whether or not it still exists.

The "digital divide" is an issue with several dimensions. Since networked society is a global phenomenon, the divide shows up in the first instance geographically. Even this geographical digital divide has multiple facets, as it exists both *between* different countries across the globe and *within* them, manifesting as regional divides, often with a distinct urban–rural colouring. At the cross-national level, the global digital divide maps neatly onto the traditional North–South division. Both internet penetration and ICT owner-ship and use in North America and Europe surpass those in Africa in a very visible manner. And even within Africa, access to these technologies varies dramatically – rates are much higher in Egypt and South Africa, for example, than the poorest African states, who possess very few resources and are dealing with multiple additional developmental challenges, such access to clean water or electricity. Even in South Africa and Egypt, it would be very optimistic to claim that all habitants have equal access to ICTs. A recent Pew study documented that the geographical divide among continents, countries, and regions remains severe. For these reasons, it is fair to argue that the "access problem" as a whole remains a distinct problem, with many impoverished nations struggling to meet basic access standards. At the same time, the Pew study also shows that most developing and emerging countries, led by Turkey, have realized tremendous gains in ICT and internet access over the last decade and are in fact rapidly catching up with the Western world regarding the "access issue."

This particularity of developing nations – especially of Turkey – calls for an urgent rethink of the core assumptions of the digital divide. To think of this idea as merely an "access" issue is to miss very importance aspects of the role of the new digital platforms in explaining sociopolitical developments in many developing nations in the last half decade, such as the Gezi protests in Turkey and the "Arab Spring" in the Middle East. Just as modernization theory wrongly argued that brute concepts like "education" and "literacy" would act as "natural" harbingers of democratization, the scholarly work and media attention on digital technology has assumed that use of ICTs by social movements in these countries carries the likelihood of "natural", even inevitable, democratizing impacts. Further, the argument has been that ICTs and the internet lie at the core of recent popular mobilizations and democratic protests in the developing world. However, as we know, the two poster children of these developments, Turkey and Egypt, have in fact turned decidedly authoritarian after 2011, and we also know that large, often very digitally connected electorates, have been popular supporters of this authoritarian turn. Moreover, the aforementioned street movements have lost their impact on their countries' future. Much as modernization theory was beset by a profound "modernity-optimism", the recent scholarly and journalistic work on digital technology has suffered from a distinct "techno-optimism", deriving for the most part from an overly simplistic reading of the global digital divide as a basic issue of access. The Egyptian case is highly relevant in this regard and, while the scope of this book and this chapter are limited to the Turkish case, more comparative work on Turkey and Egypt regarding the use of ICTs in social movements would offer a major contribution to the literature in the field of media studies.

Digital Divide 2.0 and Digital Cultural Capital

After the introduction of the Web 2.0 technology in the late 1990s, which enabled regular users with little or no advanced technological knowledge to create content on the web, the aforementioned definition of the "digital divide" started to become insufficient. Users were no longer just people with access to content, but producers who would gradually drive content, thanks to end-user oriented content production tools such as blogs and micro-blogging sites. From then on, economic capacity was no longer exclusively essential to make use of the internet, as access alone was not necessarily equal to creating meaningful content that reach beyond the user's own personal network. To explain this transformation, we need to outline the different types of capital, a framework introduced by French sociologist Pierre Bourdieu to reinterpret the classical Marxist concept of capital.

According to Bourdieu,[7] "the universe of exchanges [cannot be reduced] to mercantile exchange", in realms called "fields" that consist "of a set of objective, historical relations between positions anchored in certain forms of power for capital".[8] Instead, Bourdieu's schema introduced a diverse set varieties of capital – economic, social, and cultural – that are convertible amongst each other. According to Bourdieu, social capital is "the aggregate of the actual or potential resources which are linked to possession of a durable network of more or less institutionalized relationships of mutual acquaintance and recognition".[9] Cultural capital is a more complex concept, as Bourdieu elaborates in the following passage:

> Cultural capital can exist in three forms: in the embodied state, i.e., in the form of long-lasting dispositions of the mind and body; in the objectified state, in the form of cultural goods (pictures, books,

dictionaries, instruments, machines, etc.), which are the trace or realization of theories or critiques of these theories, problematics, etc.; and in the institutionalized state, a form of objectification which must be set apart because, as will be seen in the case of educational qualifications, it confers entirely original properties on the cultural capital which it is presumed to guarantee.[10]

Cultural capital functions as a decoder of certain actions, appreciations, and tastes. Social and cultural capital are essential in a setting where users are content producers, because for a message to be successfully diffused, one needs to access to the necessary networks and the capacity to deploy the appropriate codes to pass messages through the public sphere.

Bourdieu's concept of different types of capital has found itself in the digital sociology literature. Bourdieu himself, even before the widespread use of the internet, made this distinction:

> To possess the machines, he [mankind] only needs economic capital; to appropriate them and use them in accordance with their specific purpose (defined by the cultural capital, of scientific or technical type, incorporated in them); he must have access to embodied cultural capital, either in person or by proxy.[11]

Indeed, Bourdieu's reference, albeit being very accurate, refers exclusively to embodied cultural capital, since the technological use of his time was limited to scientific and technical purposes. Meanwhile, the use of technology today is an inseparable part of the cultural field, and therefore requires a great deal of cultural capital in its objectified state. Selwyn summarizes the objectified cultural capital in ICTs as: "Socialization into technology use and 'techno-culture' via technocultural goods."[12] Again, this statement, ahead of its time, was made before Twitter and Facebook existed, so the relationship between the ICTs and social life is made through "socialization into technology use", rather than "socialization via technology use".

On the other hand, Van Dijk and Hacker underline that "information is a positional good", and claim that social and cultural capital owners use their capacity to "the benefit of [their] position [...] in the network society."[13] According to Zillien and Hargittai, "'capital-enhancing' user routines [render] digital inequality as a phenomenon of social inequality".[14] This statement may be connected to two concepts that define the distinction between internet users per their skill sets. The "digital natives versus digital immigrants" conception of Prensky[15] and the idea of "virtuosi" of Meyen et al.[16] both refer to a group of people who predominantly and consistently accumulate social and cultural capital through the internet.

While it is widely accepted that the use of technology is a form of cultural capital, generally this cultural capital is positioned by the scholar as of the "autonomous pole [within a restricted sub-field]".[17] Such positioning of cultural capital in the digital realm omits it from "the struggle among the holders of different forms of power".[18] In the networked society setting, such a restricted positioning would not suffice, as proven by the use of ICTs in social movements for political purposes. No matter whether the cultural and social capital originates online or not, they relate to an aggregate capital which goes beyond the digital realm. While, as in the Gezi example, digital cultural and social capital may be converted to online or offline political capital, elements of offline cultural capital (such as being able to read and write in foreign languages) also affect the cultural capital accumulated online. As in the Turkish example where all other democratic channels are blocked by a repressive regime, the owners of digital social and cultural capital may choose the online world as a "safe space" to debate or to organize as a counter-hegemonic entity.

The Use of Digital Cultural Capital as a Counter-Hegemonic Tool

One of the unique features of today's Turkey is that the social and cultural capital lie right at the core of the political crisis. As we mentioned, the Islamo-conservatives operate over a giant network of informal and semi-formal agencies which constitute the AKP's 8.5 million-strong membership base (more than 80 per cent of total party membership in Turkey), which has been gradually turning the country into a plebiscitary autocracy built around a party-state. The only counter power that holds this unrivaled social capital from becoming an utter hegemony is the cultural capital accumulated by the modern, secular, urban middle classes whose dissent became collectively visible in the Gezi protests. In the foundation of modern Turkey, the middle classes were deemed to be the archetype of the "society without classes and privileges", defending and serving the causes of the new republic. This layer of the society was, as Göle notes, the cradle of the "Republican elite endowed with cultural capital"[19] while economic capital was built upon a consensus between the state elite and the emerging Anatolian bourgeoisie, which later broke away from the single party and developed as a counter-hegemonic conservative movement that would ultimately create the predecessors of the AKP.

Until the AKP reign, the modern minority with cultural capital was protected against the conservative majority by the military and civil state elite. However, especially after the 2010 referendum these agencies either lost their power or were taken over by the government, which paved the way for the giant network of social capital capture the entire state apparatus and the lion's share of finance capital. While the causes and demands of the Gezi movement by no means represented a "reaction" of the old order against the new, but rather was a new, pluralist and democratic line of politics. Those who embraced the Republican "doxa" of the old regime gradually set the tone of the protests as the limited environmental campaign rapidly morphed into a massive protest movement of five million people. Even then, the Gezi movement preserved its plurality through park forums and Occupy Wall Street-style street gatherings in which various views could be freely expressed. The summer of 2013 for Turkey can be summarized as an avatar of two axes: "plurality versus majoritarianism" and "cultural capital versus social capital".

The Use of Social Media against the AKP Government Before, During, and After the Gezi Protests

In Turkey during the reign of the AKP, freedom of information has deteriorated dramatically. Since it came to power, the AKP in government has actively cultivated its own media to counter those channels that it has deemed harmful to its agenda. To reach this objective, the AKP has utilized a method that was introduced during the 2001 economic crisis to regulate the faltering banking system. The Savings Deposit Insurance Fund of Turkey (*Tasarruf Mevduatı Sigorta Fonu*, TMSF) was given the authority to seize the assets of holding companies that were dangerously exposed through their banking and finance arms. During the AKP period, this authority has been used as a method of hostile takeover, notably against media companies, which have traditionally been subsidiaries of major holding companies in Turkey.

This process began almost as soon as the AKP came to power. Cem Uzan, the owner of Rumeli Holdings, had campaigned in the 2002 elections as the chairman of populist right-wing Genç Party (competing for the same constituency as the AKP) and had won 7.5 per cent of the popular vote. After the elections, his newspaper *Star* (along with his other assets) were taken over by the TMSF and sold to a joint venture, which included Ethem Sancak, a businessman close to Erdoğan. Sancak later became an AKP official. In a similar vein, *Sabah*, one of the staples of the Turkish press, was seized in 2007 and sold in 2008 to Çalık Holdings, whose CEO at the time was Berat Albayrak, Tayyip Erdoğan's son-in-law. Albayrak is currently the minister for energy in the AKP government. *Akşam* newspaper was seized in 2013 and again sold to Ethem Sancak. In other cases, mainstream media was either punished heavily by tax penalties, as was Doğan Media Group, or were "encouraged" to take a pro-government editorial line. Given that most media owners have interests in other industries (such as energy and construction) that depend for their revenue on government concessions and contracts, there has been an intense pressure to do this. The cases of the Ciner, Doğuş, and Demirören groups, the owners of *Habertürk*, NTV, and *Milliyet*, respectively, are clear examples of corporate holding groups that have bent to the government's will in this way.

The pro-government media has also been fed by the state-run companies' advertising spending. Some 63 per cent of state advertising in 2014 was funneled towards pro-government media companies, while the anti-government media received just 2.2 per cent. Since 2015, there has also been a new trend of hostile media takeovers in Turkey. The government has started to appoint provisional boards to companies that it deems to be unstable. Unsurprisingly, these companies (mostly with media and banking activities) have often belonged to businesspeople close to Erdoğan's ally-turned-enemy Fethullah Gülen, a religious leader in self-exile in the United States. *Zaman*, *Today's Zaman*, Kanaltürk TV, *Bugün*, and *Samanyolu* media outlets were taken over by new boards through this method; most of the journalists working for them were subsequently sacked.[20]

Another new method of gagging the dissident media since 2015 has been to terminate their satellite contracts by Türksat, the state-run telecommunications company. Along with Gülenist Kanaltürk and Samanyolu TV channels, pro-Kurdish İMC TV was also ousted from the Türksat satellite. Another channel close to the Gülenist view, Can Erzincan TV was also given a notice of termination, while the socialist Hayat TV has had similar problems since 2013. These channels also receive heavy penalties from Higher Authority of Radio Television (RTÜK) for various reasons (mostly for not obeying the frequent gag orders imposed after important events that might generate anti-government feelings, such as bombings, police violence or mine accidents).[21]

Since 2014, the media in Turkey has been rated "not free" by Freedom House, a claim supported by other reports, like those of the US State Department, Human Rights Watch, the Committee for Protecting Journalists, Reporters without Borders, and the European Commission. In this context, the internet appears to be the only channel for the freedom of information and democratic debate in Turkey. Law No. 5651, known as the Internet Act, was enacted in May 2007 and gives permission to the government-controlled Telecommunication and Communication Directorate (TİB) to block access to websites without court warrant. Additionally, many courts release gag orders on political matters against websites at very short notice, often overnight.

Social media sites like Twitter – along with video sites such as YouTube and Vimeo, the blog sites Tumblr and Blogger, and even Google – have faced such bans since 2013. Additionally, unofficial throttling of these sites by TİB and the ISPs has become a routine practice after any event deemed likely to generate anti-government critique. However, many dissident internet users in Turkey have since discovered methods to surpass these restrictions, such as TOR or VPNs.[22] As the pro-government journalist Cemil Barlas lamented after the Atatürk Airport attack in June 2016: "When Twitter is throttled or blocked, it is only used by professional trolls, terrorists and insulters. Because they can all access it."[23] The AKP regime's frustration with social media, notably Twitter, continues.

Since it was introduced in 2007, Twitter has steadily become "the" anti-government debate platform in Turkey. This tool, unlike Facebook, has operated mostly through verbal communication (though it has switched to a more visual strategy in the recent years) but was slow in localization therefore mostly appealed to English-speaking users. It is, however, much more compatible with mobile communication and easy to use in smartphones. Also, again unlike Facebook (were users control the audience that can view their contents and mostly share with people they know), Twitter was built upon an "agora" setting that enables the formation of content-based networks, depending on retweets and hashtags, that can carry the message far beyond the user's own network. These features of Twitter make it popular among the new social movements, mostly formed by young, well-educated individuals placed in a precarious economic or sociopolitical position.

After the Occupy Wall Street movement, Twitter had its global breakthrough with the Iranian elections in 2009 and is now the tool of choice in many dissident movements. However, we should also note that the importance of Twitter in most cases are overemphasized, as in the Arab Spring case. In many countries where protests take place, the Twitter penetration rate is in fact strikingly low. The number of Twitter users in Turkey is also low compared to the number of Facebook users. Nevertheless, Twitter has produced enough volume in Turkey to be considered as a major communication channel, especially since 2013.

Recent research that I undertook with Onur Yazıcıoğlu[24] on over 250 political topics related to Turkey in 2011–12 shows that the overwhelming majority of Twitter users in the country are dissidents who need a channel to convey their criticism against the government. This may be because communication on Twitter is open to a vast public space. In Turkey, since the 1980 coup, which discouraged public participation to politics, engaging in political activities has been socially frowned upon. Right-wing politics has overcome this obstacle easily, since it has been built upon informal or semi-formal traditional networks, such as mosque congregations, village or town associations (hemşehrilik), craftsman guilds and the mobilization of conservative women isolated from social life in one way or another. The resilience of the AKP heavily depends on these, as it has succeeded in recruiting 8.5 million members from these traditional networks. However, this vast social capital is not coupled with sufficient cultural capital, leaving the AKP unable to produce a diverse discourse that could appeal to its critics, therefore constituting a cultural hegemony. Even the AKP's superior cadres lacked this capacity, so it had to form alliances with Gülenists and libertarian intellectuals whose anti-Kemalist views created a common ground with the Islamists.

These alliances collapsed gradually after the 2010 constitutional referendum, as the AKP no longer wished to share power with anyone and went on to establish its own regime. Consequently, the party was blindsided by the Gezi protests in 2013 which gathered masses with higher cultural capital together, based on a popular, humourous and democratic discourse in line with the global trends. The AKP's response to the Gezi movement's compatibility with similar waves of social movements in the world was borderline paranoid, and it went public with the accusation that the protesters were individually paid by "hostile" countries that would otherwise have counted as among Turkey's biggest allies and partners, such as Germany.[25] In other words, AKP cadres were so devoid of cultural capital that they were simply unable to even perceive the role that cultural capital was playing in these protests.

The "standing man" protest is a striking example of this. After the Gezi park occupation was violently dispersed, an artist started a protest in Taksim Square standing and doing nothing else. Hundreds of people later joined this artist, some reading a book while standing. As a response, dozens of pro-government people with t-shirts bearing "standing men against the standing man" arrived in Taksim Square by taxi, stood up facing the protesters for half an hour and left the square with the same taxis. After this attempt massively failed, pro-government media claimed that the "standing man" protesters were actually trained by US agencies who were trying to promote coups all over the world.[26]

In another example, the pro-government media claimed that a woman with a headscarf (daughter-in-law of an AKP-backed mayor) and her child were attacked by Gezi protesters wearing nothing but leather pants and that some of them had urinated on her. This scenario quickly proved to be an utter fabrication, as was Erdoğan's personal claim that protesters who took shelter in a mosque during the protests had been drinking alcohol on the premises. Meanwhile, the protesters organized Ramadan meals in Taksim Square to counter the Islamic Kulturkampf incited by Erdoğan, which was also attacked by the police.

In all these events, social media – notably Twitter – played an important role, as even the mainstream media abstained from reporting the events from an anti-government perspective or even a neutral one. Some channels, such as CNN Türk (which famously aired a documentary on penguins instead of the protests), completely disregarded events until government officials commented on them (a very common practice in the Turkish media). Other outlets, such as NTV and Habertürk, openly took a pro-government stance. On 16 June 2013, eight newspapers had all the same headline, quoting Erdoğan's statement "We're all for democratic demands." In this setting, Twitter became a major source of accurate information, which led to a massive increase in people using this site in a couple of days. It also functioned as a political "safe space" for dissidents as people with alike minds shared their critiques. As Erdoğan himself openly declared, the AKP's first response to Twitter was to "eradicate it all". After a series of bans failed to reach this objective, the party hired 3,000 social media users who were later labelled "AK trolls"[27] to promote the regime's causes against the protests. However, the AKP trolls and pro-government users encouraged to be active on Twitter against the protesters could not produce meaningful and diverse content. Their activities were mainly restricted to carrying the daily hashtag defined by the party to the trending topic list, which had practically no effect. Since these campaigns failed to counter the dissident content on Twitter, the AKP went back to blocking access and throttling, which has been very actively practised, as of the time this chapter was written.

Meanwhile, on the night of the 15 June coup attempt, President Recep Tayyip Erdoğan appeared on CNN Türk and NTV news channels via FaceTime, Apple's proprietary messaging application, to call his supporters to the streets against the putsch. This call was later rebroadcast by the vast majority of television channels in Turkey. This move was described in a hasty and sensationally farfetched manner by some scholars-cum-journalists as "the internet saved the President".[28] This claim does not reflect the facts in many ways. Firstly, while Erdoğan used FaceTime to address his supporters, it was the television channels, which retransmitted this message live on air, that allowed his call to reach the wider public. He probably opted for reaching his supporters via television; otherwise he could have used, for example, Periscope directly to broadcast his message on the internet. This is a very logical inference as television remains, by far, the most popular means of communication in Turkey.

Also, the heavy use of mosques to call people to the streets through *salah*s made a great impact on networking Erdoğan's mostly Islamist followers. Here, the role of Diyanet, the body regulating organized religion in Turkey, was critical. Diyanet has, during the AKP period, been frequently used as an ideological state apparatus.[29] It is also clear, as mentioned, that the private media is in the hands of the government. Therefore, it is highly unlikely that Erdoğan would choose such a problematic means as the internet, when Diyanet and the private media are so clearly under his control. Unver and Alasaad's diligent research also confirms, with online and offline data, that the anti-coup mobilization on June 15 was an offline-online hybrid in which mosques had a great effect on networking Erdoğan supporters.[30] Also, there are reports that the access to social media was throttled by the AKP government that night.[31] While we will not deny that the AKP camp may have improved their social media use since the Gezi events in 2013, where the online realm had been completely dominated by dissidents, it would be baseless and unscientific to claim that the coup was prevented by the use of social media and the internet.

Conclusion

The use of social media by dissidents in Turkey depends for the most part on both the lack of other democratic channels and sources of information and the fact that social media networks create a channel of organization for people who are otherwise inexperienced regarding political action. These two factors have similarities with other emerging social movements, although with different foci. In Iran, Egypt, and other Middle Eastern countries the lack of democratic channels is clear and social media acts to fill the gap. As far as the Occupy movements in the Western world are concerned, democratic channels are open, but social media use has been taken up predominantly as a particularly useful mobilizing mechanism for the previously politically inexperienced or unorganized. In the former case, urgency and necessity are the issue in a context where the need to overcome the information barrier is paramount, while in the other social media exerts its force as political strategy. As noted by Haciyakupoglu and Zhang,[32] while providing an alternative to the traditional media, less-regulated social media also contains the risk of false information which is compensated by social trust (social identification among protesters) and system trust (the technological ability to distinguish correct from incorrect). In the Occupy-style protests, "the embodied, territorialized political praxis associated [...] was indeed combined with the intensive and savvy use of social media."[33] In both cases, whether social media is used to overcome the information barrier or to develop strategies, digital cultural capital is needed to reach the sought objectives. What we can add to this debate is that the existence of this digital cultural capital *per se* may also be a reason why the social media, particularly Twitter, has become the centerpiece of all dissident activities in Turkey.

Notes

1. Internetworldstats.com (2016), "Europe Internet Stats – Population Statistics" [online], available at http://www.internetworldstats.com/europa2.htm#tr [accessed 8 July 2016].
2. Reuters Institute for the Study of Journalism (2015), "Reuters Institute Digital News Report 2015", pp. 13–17.
3. Insight Radar (2013), "Gezi Olayları. Sosyal Medya Yansımaları ve Analizi 29 Mayıs", 17 Haziran. 6.
4. For a detailed description of the "network society" concept, see Castells, M., (2011), *The Rise of the Network Society: The Information Age: Economy, Society, and Culture* (John Wiley & Sons).
5. Internetworldstats.com (2016), "Europe Internet Stats – Population Statistics" [online], available at http://www.internetworldstats.com/europa2.htm#tr [accessed 8 July 2016].
6. Pew Research Centre (2015), "Spring 2015 Global Attitudes Survey", Q70&Q72.
7. P. Bourdieu (1986), "The Forms of Capital", in Richardson, J., *Handbook of Theory and Research for the Sociology of Education* (Westport, CT: Greenwood), pp. 241–2.
8. P. Bourdieu, L.J. Wacquant (1992), *An invitation to reflexive sociology* (University of Chicago Press), p. 16.
9. P. Bourdieu, "The Forms of Capital" (1986), p. 247.

10. Bourdieu, Pierre, "The Forms of Capital", *Readings in Economic Sociology* 4 (2008): p. 296.
11. Ibid., p. 250.
12. N. Selwyn (2004), "Reconsidering Political and Popular Understandings of the Digital Divide", *New Media & Society* 6, p. 355.
13. J. van Dijk, K. Hacker, (2003), "The Digital Divide as a Complex and Dynamic Phenomenon", *The Information Society* 19, p. 324.
14. N. Zillien, E. Hargittai (2009), "Digital Distinction: Status-Specific Types of Internet Usage*", *Social Science Quarterly* 90, p. 279.
15. M. Prensky (2001), "Digital natives, digital immigrants part 1", *On the horizon* 9, pp. 1–6.
16. M. Meyen, S. Pfaff-Rüdiger, K. Dudenhöffer and J. Huss (2010), "The Internet in everyday life: A typology of Internet users", *Media, Culture & Society* 32, pp. 873–82.
17. P. Bourdieu and R. Johnson (1993), *The field of cultural production: essays on art and literature*, (Columbia University Press, New York), p. 187.
18. P. Bourdieu and L.J. Wacquant (1992), p. 76.
19. Göle, N. (1997), "Secularism and Islamism in Turkey: The making of elites and counter-elites", *The Middle East Journal*, p. 50.
20. Reuters (2016), "Turkey closes media outlets seized from Gulen-linked owner" [online], available at http://www.reuters.com/article/us-turkey-media-gulen-idUSKCN0W34ML [accessed 8 July 2016].
21. Rethink Institute (November 2014), *Diminishing Press Freedom in Turkey*, p. 11.
22. For a detailed account of Internet censorship in Turkey, see M. Akgül, M. Kırlıdoğ (2015), "Internet censorship in Turkey", *Internet Policy Review* 4, pp. 1–22.
23. C. Barlas [secondvirus] (29 June 2016), "twitter yavaşlatılıp veya engellenince tamamen profesyonel trollere, teröristlere ve küfürbazlara kalıyor. çünkü bunlardan giremeyen yok." [Tweet]. Retrieved from https://twitter.com/secondvirus/status/748140968059224064.
24. D. Irak, Yazıcıoğlu, Onur, (2012), *Türkiye ve sosyal medya*. Okuyan Us.
25. Hurriyetdailynews.com (2016), "POLITICS – A group in Germany conspiring against Turkey, says Erdoğan" [online], available at http://www.hurriyetdaily news.com/a-group-in-germany-conspiring-against-turkey-says-erdogan.aspx? PageID=238&NID=100071&NewsCatID=338 [accessed 8 July 2016].
26. Star.com.tr (2013), "Duran Adam Eylemi CIA Taktiği Çıktı! – Güncel" [online], available at http://haber.star.com.tr/guncel/duran-adam-eylemi-cia-taktigi-cikti/haber-763641 [accessed 8 July 2016].
27. "A troll is a person who interrupts communications on the Internet, and is often seen as problematic or even criminal." See Shin, J. (2008), "Morality and Internet Behavior: A study of the Internet Troll and its relation with morality on the Internet", *Technology and Teacher Education Annual* 19, p. 2834.
28. Z. Tufekci (2016), "How the Internet Saved Turkey's Internet-Hating President" [online], Nytimes.com, available at http://www.nytimes.com/2016/07/20/opinion/how-the-internet-saved-turkeys-internet-hating-president.html [accessed 27 September 2016].
29. For a recent account of the use of Diyanet under AKP rule, see A. Öztürk (2016), "Turkey's Diyanet under AKP rule: from protector to imposer of state ideology?" *Southeast European and Black Sea Studies*, pp. 1–17.

30. H. Ünver and H. Alasaad (2016), "How Turks Mobilized Against the Coup" [online], Foreign Affairs, available at https://www.foreignaffairs.com/articles/2016-09-14/how-turks-mobilized-against-coup [accessed 27 September 2016].
31. Motherboard (2016), "Turkey Throttled Social Media During Coup In 'Evolution' of Internet Censorship" [online], available at http://motherboard.vice.com/read/turkey-throttled-social-media-during-coup-in-evolution-of-internet-censorship-twitter-youtube-facebook [accessed 27 September 2016].
32. G. Haciyakupoglu and W. Zhang (2015), "Social Media and Trust during the Gezi Protests in Turkey", Journal of Computer-Mediated Communication.
33. B. Tejerina, I. Perugorria, T. Benski and L. Langman, (2013), "From indignation to occupation: A new wave of global mobilization", Current Sociology 61, p. 383.

EPILOGUE: THE DESIRE IS THERE

İştar Gözaydın

In his modernization theory, Seymour Martin Lipset formulated authoritarian-ism as merely a waystation on the road to democracy. Alas, this is not true, at least in some cases. Turkey has been struggling with processes and institutions to become modernized since the late eighteenth century. The Ottoman state was absolutist with the Sultan accountable to practically nobody and sharing power with no one, meaning that the inclusive institutions necessary to create a pluralistic and democratic system could never be developed.[1] Ottoman modernization was a period of transition towards modern supra-structures entirely for the sake of sustaining the state. The republican era that followed was a period of continuity and of change. Early republican decision-making elites sought transformation of the body politic into a modern one as their predecessors had done, but they also worked on the social corpus. To cite but one example, the adoption by republican elites of the civil code of the Swiss Neuchatel canton almost without any discussion (in contrast to the agonized debates in the nineteenth century that presaged the adoption of the Ottoman civil code, *the Mecelle*) was intended to bring about a radical transformation in the personal realm.

Enlightenment principles read through strictly positivist lenses meant that the period between the 1920s and the 1940s was one in which the "iron law of oligarchy" (in the sense of Robert Michels) reigned supreme.[2] Unfortunately, the Democrat Party, which emerged in the late 1940s as a source of hope for democratization through the 1950s, produced little more than bitter disappointment. The post-1960 regime brought forth a decade of relative liberalization but its birth from a military coup doomed it to fail. Thus, the 1970s and 1980s witnessed the suffocation of democratic institutions as well as basic rights and freedoms through military interventions and ongoing tutelage. Turkey fared no better in the 1990s, which were marked by ongoing atrocities:

the Kurdish war and state of emergency in the southeast, widespread torture and breaches of basic civil liberties, and a "code of silence" about all these issues among an overwhelming portion of the population. A severe intervention of military tutelage via the military-led National Security Council took place on 28 February 1997. The ensuing "February 28 process" was not only a military ultimatum given to the government of Necmettin Erbakan, Turkey's first overtly Islamist prime minister, but also the beginning of a dynamic that would lead to the banning of the Welfare Party (and its successors) and the trashing of freedoms and rights. The year 2001 witnessed an historic economic crisis but the crash was nevertheless emblematic of the political and economic problems that had been wearing on Turkey for years. Confidence in the government had been eroded by corruption and the inability to form stable governing coalitions.[3]

The impressive electoral victory of the Justice and Development Party (*Adalet ve Kalkınma Partisi*, AKP) in the parliamentary elections of 2002 was a profound change in Turkish politics. Initially, the AKP government sought to reduce the influence of the Turkish military establishment in politics. To do so, it introduced a series of legal and institutional reforms,[4] including the transformation of the National Security Council in 2003 into an advisory board on national security policy, which eventually brought the long period of military tutelage to an apparent close. Eliminating military tutelage and proposing significant initiatives to empower the citizenry and sustain civil liberties were important steps towards democratization. Additionally, there seemed to be a lot of achievements in the Turkish economy during the first decade of AKP rule. After Turkey's economic crisis in 2001, the country experienced an average annual growth rate of 6 per cent, and inflation rates fell from triple-digit to single-digit figures between 2002 and 2012. Positive steps taken towards solving the Kurdish problem and the democratization efforts taken to further European Union membership were remarkable indicators as well.

From 2007 signs of yet another fundamental transition emerged; as the emphasis on democracy appeared to fall away, the AKP's conservative Islamist discourse intensified, and attempts at constructing a hegemonic authoritarian regime appeared.[5] This shift may be read as a reaction by the AKP to the last-ditch efforts of the *ancien régime* in 2007 to rein it in. The April 2007 military "e-memorandum" may be considered a critical juncture in this process. On 27 April at 11.20 pm, a statement appeared on the official website of the Turkish armed forces referencing the approaching presidential elections.[6] Abdullah Gül, a co-founder of the party, was in line to be elected by a parliament dominated by the AKP. The fact that Gül's wife wore the Islamic headscarf, as well as his own history in political Islam, turned the elections into a political crisis in which the military felt compelled to issue a stern "warning" that it retained the power to "intervene" to protect the secular state. In response to these statements, Cemil Çiçek, a government spokesman, publicly protested and condemned the military's e-memorandum, reaffirming the AKP government's commitment to the secular, democratic, social, and lawful state. Çiçek added that the government took the military's statement as an affront to the democratically-elected government.[7] International reactions were negative as well. The European Union warned Turkey's military not to interfere in politics. EU Enlargement Commissioner Olli Rehn observed:

> This is a clear test case whether the Turkish armed forces respect democratic secularization and democratic values [...] The timing is rather surprising and strange. It's important that the military respects also the rules of the democratic game and its own role in that democratic game.[8]

The US also commented publicly. Dan Fried, assistant secretary of state for European and Eurasian affairs, said: "We don't take sides." Nevertheless, US Secretary of State Condoleezza Rice felt compelled to back the EU position, declaring: "The United States fully supports Turkish democracy and its constitutional processes, and that means that the election, the electoral system [...] have to be upheld. Yes. The answer is yes, the US would be in a similar position" to the EU on condemning military intervention.[9] In the event, Gül was elected president in later 2007 but in 2008 the old guard persisted, launching a prosecution to close the AKP and ban its 71 leading members from politics for five years, based on the charge that the party had violated the principle of separation of religion and state in Turkey. This was also a crucial turning point, especially in Erdoğan's public demeanor and approach. With only six members of the Constitutional Court voting for closure (a "super majority" of seven was needed), on 9 July 2009 the court rejected the demands of the prosecutor and did not ban the party, issuing instead a stern rebuke and a small fine.[10]

The Gezi protests of 2013 marked yet another milestone, the point at which Erdoğan finally took complete control of the AKP. A wave of demonstrations and civil unrest in Turkey began on 28 May, initially to contest the urban development plan for Istanbul's Gezi Park. On 1 June Erdoğan gave a televized speech condemning the protesters and vowing that "where they gather 20, I will get up and gather 200,000 people. Where they gather 100,000, I will bring together one million from my party."[11] On 2 June he used the inflammatory term *çapulcular* (marauders) to describe the protesters.[12] The government claimed that a wide variety of shadowy forces were behind the protests. In a conspiratorial speech on 18 June, Erdoğan accused "internal traitors and external collaborators" of fomenting unrest, declaring that: "It [the movement] was prepared very professionally [...] Social media was prepared for this, made equipped. The strongest advertising companies of our country, certain capital groups, the interest rate lobby, organizations on the inside and outside, hubs, they were ready, equipped for this."[13] Overall, the violent response of the Turkish authorities to the Gezi Park protests exposed the beginning of a striking intolerance of opposing voices that seems to be an indication of Erdoğan's belief that conspiratorial rhetoric is the best way to mobilize support.[14] It might be argued that he was anxious to avoid the fate of Adnan Menderes over five decades before,[15] and thus he undertook a radical lurch in the direction of authoritarianism as a self-preservation mechanism.

If the Gezi protests were a very significant milestone, the so-called "17–25 December process" was the penultimate stage of Turkey's clear path in the direction of authoritarianism. On 17 December 2013, a wave of arrests targeting businessmen, bankers, and most notably the sons of four serving cabinet ministers in Erdoğan's government, were made during an anti-corruption operation.[16] Following the operation, the government resorted again to its standard conspiratorial rhetoric, branding the investigation as a "planned psychological attack", "an illegal group within the state" and "dirty games being played within and outside the Turkish state."[17] Most media and political commentators claimed that the government's accusations were clearly directed at either the Gülen movement, or a segment within it.[18] Thus a crusade involving accusations of "terrorism", arrests, and imprisonments, and fatal attacks on media and financial institutions was initiated.[19]

On the night of 30 March 2014, as the results of local elections held that day showed a clear win for the government, then Prime Minister Erdoğan appeared on the balcony of the central office of his party before a vast crowd of cheering supporters. Appearing with him were not only his family members but several of the accused in the corruption allegations. The message was clear: this was now a "one-man regime" and one that would not be cowed by any attempt to hold it to account via the judicial organs.[20]

Turkey is currently part of a broader trend towards authoritarianism[21] observed in the weakening of political institutions and the erosion of rule of law by leaders across the globe who had initially come to power through the ballot box.[22] In the case of Turkey, this erosion is best termed as a process of "deconstitutionalization".[23] This had actually been foreshadowed by Ahmet İyimaya, AKP MP and chair of the Parliamentary Justice Commission and the Constitutional Consensus Commission on 2 April 2016.[24] A series of unconstitutional actions have made up the course of events. Curfews, for example, have been declared by governors in some east and south-east provinces of Turkey since the summer of 2015.[25] Then there is the apparent *de facto* amendment in Turkey's basic system of government to a "quasi presidential" regime.[26] Add to this the thousands of court cases opened for alleged defamation against Erdoğan;[27] reactions against the academics' "Petition for Peace",[28] crack downs on critical media and Twitter, several violations of judicial authority,[29] violation of the principle of impartiality of the President, and the stripping immunity for some members of the parliament.[30] These are just some, albeit extremely worrying, examples of the weakening of political institutions and the erosion of rule of law in Turkey. In sum, all four arenas of democratic contestation identified by Levitsky and Way[31] – the electoral arena, the legislature, the judiciary, and the media – have been seriously, even fatally, compromised in Turkey.

As I mentioned at the beginning, much of this is consistent with a long-standing majoritarian tendency in Turkish political culture: Turkey has long struggled with the concept of the "loyal opposition".[32] Whenever a ruling political actor (this may be a real person or a political party) reaches the realization that he has the support of the majority, that actor will start to act as if his approach exhibits the quality of "absolute truth" and the distribution of political power narrows dramatically. This malady is actually a legacy of the Ottoman period that reached its apogee between the 1920s and the 1960s. Yet, once again history is repeating itself and the AKP and Erdoğan claim to speak "absolute truth" in the name of the people in Turkey. I acknowledge that the long-standing posture of the secular establishment towards the religious-conservative periphery in Turkey has allowed the AKP and Erdoğan to manipulate this constituency by mobilizing its fears and the experience of past trauma at the hands of the republican elite. I have also realized that redistribution politics via neo-liberalization[33] have created benefits to various groups that were long ignored and marginalized.[34] Furthermore, I concede that economic progress helped by a favourable global liquidity environment in the early parts of the decade was a key contributor to the party's continued electoral success and the enlargement of its electoral coalition.[35] However, the other side of all this "progress" is that we are left with a fundamentally corrupt regime[36] that: (1) is based upon clientelistic policies sustained by mechanisms of economic and political dependency; (2) rules by repression and bribery, and; (3) has established hegemony through the control of a media sector that lacks either freedom or diversity and is concentrated in the absence of anti-trust legislation to prevent the formation of media conglomerates.[37] Erdoğan consolidates his power *per se* through polarization and populism. In this regime, *rule of law* has been replaced by *rule by law* where the concept of terror is used recklessly through securitization policies.

The rule of law is simply unimaginable within absolutist and autocratic political systems. The rule of law is a creation of pluralist political institutions and of the broad coalitions that support such pluralism. It is only when many individuals and groups have a say in decisions, and the political power to have a seat at the table with fair treatment, that rule of law can reach its full potential.[38] Sustainable democracy and welfare may only be achieved by exceeding the minimal requirements of democracy with proper checks and balances in the political system: secure property rights and freedom to contract and exchange. Erdoğan and the AKP's use of the law for repression of any opposition heralds a truly patrimonial regime in which formal democratic institutions exist on paper but are reduced to a façade in practice. It may still be a little early to use the word "fascist" for such a structure, but with everything discussed above, and with perverse institutions like *Osmanlı Ocakları*[39] and the like on the move, the desire is there. Actually (but still alarmingly), Turkey's politics since the 1930s have had more in common with the Italian form of "soft" fascism under Mussolini than the "hard" fascism of Nazi Germany. Corporatist ideology was an essential component in early republican policies,[40] and it seems history repeats itself in this sense in Erdoğan's era as well. Recent proposals to purge the judiciary and the fact that Turkey seems to be moving steadily in the direction of a command economy controlled by the president (where business can only be successfully done through the party in accordance with trustee legislation) are both indicators of a fascist state.

The totalitarian, if not fascist, tendencies of Erdoğan were evident to some observers from the very first days of his presidency onwards. He consistently chose to address the nation not through intermediaries like its elected representatives, the political parties, professional organizations, chambers of commerce or business, or even local governments, but as directly as possible through passionate speeches delivered in carefully orchestrated and choreographed mass demonstrations. He was the first political leader to make a habit of convening the "muhtars", the elected heads of rural villages and urban neighbourhoods, who are not allowed to represent any political party but are elected purely on their personal merits. Even before the 15 July coup attempt, the opposition parties, in a dramatic gesture of "national unity", voted in favour of suspending parliamentary immunities – a move that blatantly targeted the Kurdish opposition in the parliament. Since the putsch, all institutions ranging from the universities to the legal profession have been divested of whatever vestigial autonomy that had remained.

On the night of the putsch, Erdoğan personally asked people to take to the streets and, for about a month or so, he repeated his demand for all-male crowds to stay on the streets, responding to the emergency calls for action being broadcast throughout the night through all the minarets of the country. In a sense, before the proclamation of the official "state of emergency", a virtual state of emergency was in effect through a massive popular mobilization. The coup attempt seems to have given Erdoğan the ideal opportunity to achieve what he has been yearning for all along – allegiance not based on self-interest, conviction, or even admiration, but a purely passionate, instinctive devotion.

Erdoğan has already accumulated a trove of achievements; yet, on the other hand, there is much that he fears, so one can hardly call him a satisfied man. Much passion to refashion the minds and bodies of the nation according to his own ideals remains. Even at this (admittedly transitional) stage, we can probably say this much in relation to how things stand: something has permanently changed in Turkey, which will be extraordinarily difficult to reverse. Erdoğan's way of dealing with things and the style he has imposed – polarization, divisiveness, creation of new real or imaginary enemies at each significant juncture, the adoption of a personality cult to suppress a climate of negotiation – have been adopted to such an extent at all levels (from institutional down to an almost interpersonal level) that they are likely to outlive him. Sadly, were he to be toppled by an unforeseeable confluence of events, there remains little ground for hope that his replacement would embody a more democratic and peaceful understanding of governance, policy, or even of life.

Notes

1. In answering the question of why nations fail, I am very much inspired by a book with the same title, Daron Acemoglu and James A. Robinson, *The Origins of Power, Prosperity, and Poverty: Why Nations Fail* (New York: Crown Business, 2012).
2. "The iron law of oligarchy" is a political theory, first developed by the German sociologist Robert Michels in his 1911 book, *Political Parties: A Sociological Study of the Oligarchical Tendencies of Modern Democracy*. It claims that rule by an elite, or oligarchy, is an inevitable "iron law" within any democratic organization because of the "tactical and technical necessities" of organization itself.
3. For a thorough reading of the phenomena see, Erinç Yeldan, "Behind the 2000/2001 Turkish Crisis: Stability, Credibility, and Governance, for Whom?" (Unpublished manuscript), http://yeldane.bilkent.edu.tr/Chennai_Yeldan2002.pdf, accessed 12 June 2016.
4. For an evaluation see Müge Aknur, "Civil-Military Relations during the AK Party Era: Major Developments and Challenges", *Insight Turkey*, 15/4 (2013), pp. 131–50.
5. As Mühlenhoff states, this phenomenon displays a neo-Gramscian discursive approach to hegemony. See Hanna Mühlenhoff, "Funding Democracy, Funding Social Services? The European Instrument for Democracy and Human Rights in the Context of Competing Narratives in Turkey", *Journal of Balkan and Near Eastern Studies*, 16/1 (2014), pp. 102–18.
6. An excerpt from the army's statement published by the BBC reads: "The problem that emerged in the presidential election process is focused on arguments over secularism. Turkish Armed Forces are concerned about the recent situation [...] the Turkish Armed Forces are a party in those arguments, and absolute defender of secularism. Also, the Turkish Armed Forces is definitely opposed to those arguments and negative comments. It will display its attitude and action openly and clearly whenever it is necessary [...] Those who are opposed to Great Leader Mustafa Kemal Atatürk's understanding 'How happy is the one who says I am a Turk' are enemies of the Republic of Turkey and will remain so. The Turkish Armed Forces maintain their sound determination to

carry out their duties stemming from laws to protect the unchangeable characteristics of the Republic of Turkey. Their loyalty to this determination is absolute." See BBC News, "Excerpts of Turkish army statement" (28 April 2007), http://news.bbc.co.uk/2/hi/europe/6602775.stm, accessed 21 June 2016.

7. NTV-MSNBC, "Cemil Çiçek'in açıklamasının tam metni" (28 April 2007), http://arsiv.ntv.com.tr/news/406662.asp, accessed 21 June 2016.
8. BBC News, "EU warns Turkish army over vote" (28 April 2007), http://news.bbc.co.uk/2/hi/europe/6602661.stm, accessed 21 June 2016.
9. For a reading of these reactions, see Philip H. Gordon and Ömer Taşpınar, *Winning Turkey: How America, Europe and Turkey Can Revive a Fading Partnership*, (Washington, DC: Brookings Institution Press, 2008), pp. 68–9.
10. For a journalistic evaluation of the Court decision see Sabrina Tavernise and Şebnem Arsu, "Turkish Court Calls Turkish Party Constitutional", *The New York Times* (31 July 2008), http://www.nytimes.com/2008/07/31/world/europe/31turkey.html?fta=y.&_r=0, accessed 21 June 2016.
11. "Erdoğan: For Every 100,000 Protesters, I Will Bring Out a Million From My Party", *Haaretz* (1 June 2013), http://www.haaretz.com/middle-east-news/1.527188, accessed 21 June 2016.
12. For a journalistic evaluation see Şebnem Arsu, "Turkish Leader Says Protests Will Not Stop Plans for Park", *The New York Times* (3 June 2013), http://www.nytimes.com/2013/06/03/world/europe/turkey-premier-says-protests-will-not-stop-plans-to-demolish-park.html, accessed 21 June 2016.
13. "Turkish prime minister vows to increase police force", *Hürriyet Daily News* (18 June 2013), http://www.hurriyetdailynews.com/turkish-prime-minister-vows-to-increase-police-force.aspx?pageID=238&nID=49006&NewsCatID=338, accessed 21 June 2016.
14. For an evaluation of the Gezi process from a human rights perspective see the report by Amnesty International, *Gezi Park Protests: Brutal Denial of the Right to Peaceful Assembly in Turkey* https://www.amnestyusa.org/sites/default/files/eur440222013en.pdf, accessed 21 June 2016.
15. Adnan Menderes (1899 – 17 September 1961) was the Turkish Prime Minister from 1950 to 1960. He was one of the founders of the Democrat Party in 1946. He was hanged by the military junta after the 1960 coup d'état, along with two other cabinet members.
16. "İşte gözaltına alınan isimler" *Habertürk* (17 December 2013), http://www.haberturk.com/gundem/haber/904362-iste-gozaltina-alinan-isimler, accessed 21 June 2016.
17. "Psikolojik harp var", *Yeni Şafak* (19 December 2013), http://www.yenisafak.com/politika-haber/psikolojik-harp-var-19.12.2013-594913, accessed 21 June 2016.
18. Sedat Ergin, "Erdoğan'ın Fettullah Hoca Söyleminin Şifreleri", *Hürriyet*, 24 December 2013, http://www.hurriyet.com.tr/erdogan-in-fethullah-hoca-soyleminin-sifreleri-25437545 accessed 21 June 2016; Burhaneddin Duran, "Gülen Cemaati ve Sünni Kodların Kaybı", Star, 28 December 2013, http://haber.star.com.tr/acikgorus/gulen-cemaati-ve--7csunni-kodlarin-kaybi/haber-822278 accessed 21 June 2016; Arif Beki, "Bir Paralel Cemaat de mi Var?", Hürriyet, 6 January 2014, http://www.hurriyet.com.tr/bir-paralel-cemaat-de-mi-var-25513485 accessed 21 June 2016; Fehmi Koru, "Bir Kuşkumuz var ...", Star, 7 January 2014, http://haber.star.com.tr/yazar/bir-kuskumuz-var/yazi-825948 accessed 21 June 2016.

19. For an early evaluation see Mustafa Akyol, "What you should know about Turkey's AKP-Gulen conflict", *Al-Monitor*, 3 January 2014, http://www.al-monitor.com/pulse/originals/2014/01/akp-gulen-conflict-guide.html accessed 21 June 2016. See also later postings: BBC, 3 November 2015, http://www.bbc.com/news/world-europe-34709324 accessed 21 June 2016; Aljeazeera, 14 March 2016, http://www.aljazeera.com/programmes/listeningpost/2016/03/erdogan-gulen-turkey-media-crackdown-160313115624084.html, accessed 21 June 2016.

20. I totally share Prof. Tayfun Atay's evaluation of this particular instance as well as his inspiring statements on the AKP he expressed in an interview. See Selin Ongun Tuncer, "AKP Neydi, Ne Oldu, Ne Olacak?", *Cumhuriyet*, 20 May 2016, 15.

21. Immanuel Wallerstein has been predicting this phenomenon since the mid-1990s. See Immanuel Wallerstein, *After Liberalism, The New Press* (1995) and Immanuel Wallerstein *The End of the World As We Know It: Social Science for the Twenty-First Century* (University of Minnesota Press, 2001).

22. For a brilliant discussion on the reasons why "competitive authoritarianism" better captures Turkey's regime trajectory than types of defective democracy see Berk Esen and Sebnem Gumuscu, "Rising competitive authoritarianism in Turkey", *Third World Quarterly*, 37/9 (2016), pp. 1581–1606.

23. This term was coined by Kemal Gözler, a professor of constitutional law at Uludağ University Law Faculty in Bursa, Turkey. See Kemal Gözler, "1982 Anayasası Hala Yürürlükte mi? Anayasasızlaştırma Üzerine bir Deneme [Is the Constitution of 1982 Still in Force? An Essay on Deconstitutionalization]" (Unpublished manuscript), http://www.anayasa.gen.tr/anayasasizlastirma.htm, accessed 21 June 2016.

24. http://www.milliyet.com.tr/ak-partili-ahmet-iyimaya-5/siyaset/detay/2220197/default.htm, accessed 21 June 2016.

25. For a fact sheet by the Human Rights Foundation of Turkey on curfews in Turkey between the dates 16 August 2015 to 5 February 2016, see http://en.tihv.org.tr/recent-fact-sheet-on-curfews-in-turkey-between-the-dates-16-august-2015-5-february-2016/, accessed 21 June 2016.

26. "Erdoğan: Türkiye'nin Yönetim Sistemi Değişmiştir", *Milliyet* (14 August 2015), http://www.milliyet.com.tr/erdoganturkiye-nin-yonetim/siyaset/detay/2102172/default.htm, accessed 21 June 2016. For Erdoğan's video, see https://www.youtube.com/watch?v=YaECGxHgY0I, accessed 21 June 2016.

27. "Cumhurbaşkanına hakaretten 1845 dosya! (1845 court cases for Defamation Aginst the President!)", *Milliyet*, 2 March 2016, http://www.milliyet.com.tr/cumhurbaskanina-hakaretten-1845/siyaset/detay/2202727/default.htm, accessed 21 June 2016.

28. For a Human Rights Watch posting on 16 March 2016, see https://www.hrw.org/news/2016/03/16/turkey-academics-jailed-signing-petition, accessed 21 June 2016.

29. Ergun Özbudun, "Turkey's Judiciary and the Drift Toward Competitive Authoritarianism", *The International Spectator*, 50:2 (2015), pp. 42–55, DOI: 10.1080/03932729.2015.1020651.

30. Ahmed al-Burai, "What's behind Turkey's bill of immunity: Is it a democratic move or another step towards a one-man rule?", *Al Jazeera*, 29 May 2016, http://www.aljazeera.com/indepth/opinion/2016/05/turkey-bill-immunity-160529083635081.html, accessed 21 June 2016.

31. Steven Levitsky and Lucan A. Way, "Elections Without Democracy: The Rise of Competitive Authoritarianism", *Journal of Democracy*, 13/2 (April 2002), pp. 54–8.
32. For an excellent study on this tendency reaching back to Ottoman times, see Şerif Mardin, 'Opposition and Control in Turkey', Government and Opposition 1, no. 3 (April 1966), pp. 375–88, doi:10.1111/j.1477-7053.1966.tb00381.x.
33. For redistribution politics via neo-liberalization see Menderes Çınar, "Explaining the popular appeal and durability of the Justice and Development Party in Turkey", in Elise Massicard and Nicole F. Watts (eds), *Negotiating Political Power in Turkey: Breaking up the Party* (Abingdon: Routledge, 2013), pp. 49–51.
34. For production of a new middle class and its interaction with creating a competitive authoritarian regime, see Nikolaos Stelgias, "Turkey's Hybrid Competitive Authoritarian Regime: A Genuine Product of Anatolia's Middle Class", Hellenic Foundation for European and Foreign Policy, working paper no 60/2015.
35. Ziya Öniş, "The Triumph of Conservative Globalism: The Political Economy of the AKP Era" *Turkish Studies*, v. 13/no. 2 (2012), DOI: 10.1080/14683849.2012.685252.
36. I use the concept "corrupt regime" in the Kantian sense. Corruption, economic growth and the quality of political institutions are related through a complex web. It is also valid that corruption could increase economic development, mainly because illegal practices and payments as "speed money" could surpass bureaucratic delays; the acceptance of bribes in government employees could work as an incentive and increase their efficiency and because corruption is possibly the price people are forced to pay as a result of market failures. For a micro-level study that also conceptualizes interactions between these concepts, see Hasan Ayaydın and Pınar Hayaloglu, "The Effect of Corruption on Firm Growth: Evidence from Firms in Turkey", *Asian Economic and Financial Review*, 4(5) (2014), pp. 607–24.
37. Susan Corke, Andrew Finkel, David J. Kramer, Carla Anne Robbins, Nate Schenkkan, *Democracy in Crisis: Corruption, Media, and Power in Turkey, A Freedom House Special Report* (2014), https://freedomhouse.org/sites/default/files/Turkey%20Report%20-%202-3-14.pdf accessed 22 June 2016.
38. Acemoglu and Robinson, *Why Nations Fail*, p. 306.
39. *Osmanlı Ocakları* is an organization established after 2009. Publicly this organization became more visible by their alleged involvement in attacks some NGOs and opposition parties including the CHP and HDP in 2015. On their official website, the slogan "Recep Tayyip Erdoğan is our 'namus'" appears. This word does not have a direct translation in English; it is best understood as a combination of the ideas of honour, chastity, and virtue. This slogan recalls the Protective Squadron/SS of the Nazi Party. For further information see "Kim bu Osmanlı Ocakları? *Hürriyet*, 11 Eylül 2015 http://www.hurriyet.com.tr/kim-bu-osmanli-ocaklari-30039635. Osmanlı Ocaklarıkimdir, nasıl bir oluşumdur? *Sözcü*, 11 Eylül 2015, http://www.sozcu.com.tr/2015/gundem/osmanli-ocaklari-nedir-nasil-bir-olusumdur-932916, accessed 22 June 2016. For their official website, see http://osmanliocaklari.org.tr, accessed 22 June 2016.
40. Taha Parla and Andrew Davison, *Corporatist Ideology in Kemalist Turkey: Progress or Order?* (New York: Syracuse University Press, 2004).

INDEX

www.ingramcontent.com/pod-product-compliance
Lightning Source LLC
Chambersburg PA
CBHW060155280326
41932CB00012B/1764